[ROAD TO NOWHERE]

[ROAD TO NOWHERE]

The Early 1990s Collapse and
Rebuild of New York City Baseball

CHRIS DONNELLY

University of Nebraska Press | Lincoln

The University of Nebraska Press is part of a land-grant institution with campuses and programs on the past, present, and future homelands of the Pawnee, Ponca, Otoe-Missouria, Omaha, Dakota, Lakota, Kaw, Cheyenne, and Arapaho Peoples, as well as those of the relocated Ho-Chunk, Sac and Fox, and Iowa Peoples.

Library of Congress Cataloging-in-Publication Data
Names: Donnelly, Chris, author.
Title: Road to nowhere: the early 1990s collapse and rebuild of New York City baseball / Chris Donnelly.
Description: Lincoln: University of Nebraska Press, [2023] | Includes bibliographical references and index.
Identifiers: LCCN 2022034486
ISBN 9781496221421 (hardcover)
ISBN 9781496235978 (epub)
ISBN 9781496235985 (pdf)
Subjects: LCSH: New York Mets (Baseball team)—History—20th century. | New York Yankees (Baseball team)—History—20th century. | Baseball—New York (State)—New York—History—20th century.
Classification: LCC GV875.N45 D643 2023 |
DDC 796.357/64097471—dc23/eng/20220818
LC record available at https://lccn.loc.gov/2022034486

Set in Minion Pro by A. Shahan.

Contents

Acknowledgments   ix

1. Compound Interest   1

2. Out of Place   7

3. Borders on the Bizarre   11

4. Put Out of His Misery   37

5. Long Hair, Short Tempers   57

6. Now Trade the Rest of Them   97

7. Most Players Detest the Place   133

8. The Best Team I Ever Played On   189

9. The Once Unfathomable Notion   223

10. Full Circle   269

Notes   327

Bibliography   345

Index   347

Acknowledgments

In the summer of 2019, shortly after *Doc, Donnie, the Kid, and Billy Brawl* came out, I had an epiphany while listening to a YouTube clip of John Sterling announcing George Steinbrenner's banishment in July 1990. Doc/Donnie, I realized, was just the beginning of the story around the fight between the Yankees and Mets for New York City's baseball soul. I set out to write the next part of that story, which turned into this book.

Less than a year later, the pandemic began. While in theory that should have made writing easier, it made this process much harder. Then, just two weeks before this manuscript was due, my father died after battling cancer for four months.

This is all to say that, while I loved writing this book, it happened in an environment that was not easy. That makes me all the more thankful for everyone who helped me, not just literally with this book, but with getting through life as it kept tossing obstacles in the way. And so my sincere thanks to the following people:

My amazing wife, Jamie, and my two incredible daughters, Erin and Claire; my mother, Sandy; my brothers, Tim and Mike; my sister-in-law, Taylor; my brothers-in-law Glenn and Derek; my mother- and father-in-law, Karen and Roy; the Donnellys, Kassabs, Praschils, Leahys, Dudases, Salzanos, and Kennedys; my friends, from Lincoln to Lakeside to PLHS to TCNJ; my wonderful work friends at Kivvit; my editor, Rob Taylor.

[ROAD TO NOWHERE]

[1]

Compound Interest

David Mark Winfield strode to the plate in the Metrodome, unaware of what was unfolding 1,200 miles away. Fewer than twenty thousand fans had come to see this meaningless July 30, 1990, game between the hometown Twins and the visiting California Angels. It was just three weeks after the All-Star break, but both teams were more than a dozen games behind the juggernaut Oakland Athletics for the American League West Division lead.

His team trailing 1–0 in the top of the fifth inning, Winfield's enormous frame stepped into the batter's box with a runner on first base and no outs. It had been eleven weeks since the Angels had traded for the outfielder, a deal that ended his nine-plus years as a New York Yankee. He had battled through a bittersweet batting title fight with teammate Don Mattingly in 1984, only to lose out on the season's final day and watch as fans were happy he had done so. Winfield, a Black man, could not help but think race had been a factor in the fans' reaction. He had been arrested for hitting a seagull with a thrown baseball in Toronto in 1983. He had faltered in a 1981 World Series loss to the Dodgers, the Yankees' only playoff appearance during his time in New York. A herniated disc in his back had kept him out for the entire 1989 season. On and on it went. One on-the-field, one off-the-field distraction after another.

It wasn't all bad. Minus the injured '89 campaign, Winfield was an All-Star in each of his eight seasons with the Yankees. From 1982 through 1988 he had averaged 106 RBIs a year, becoming the first Yankee to drive in at least a hundred runs in five straight seasons since Joe DiMaggio. His

1982 home run total was the second highest in single season by a right-handed batter in team history. He won Gold Gloves and Silver Sluggers. Winfield had done just about everything that could have been expected of him when he signed that record-breaking contract with New York after the 1980 season.

That contract though. That was where it all started, the words on that piece of paper sentencing him to decade of hell in New York. He had outwitted the man on the other end of the negotiating table: a man who prided himself on being the smartest person in the room. Once Yankees owner George Steinbrenner found out he had been bested, he set out to have his revenge, nearly ten years' worth of it. Season after season Steinbrenner found ways to grind Winfield down: to insult and embarrass him whenever and wherever possible.

It had all started so beautifully. A courtship between the big-time major league star and the big-time major league owner, both only too eager to be wooed and sweet-talked. Winfield was coming off eight fantastic seasons in San Diego, but the Padres had never finished better than fourth place. Steinbrenner was coming off two consecutive seasons without a championship, a drought so long in Yankee years that he fired his manager despite notching 103 wins in 1980. Winfield would help end that drought for Steinbrenner. Steinbrenner would help Winfield get to the postseason and make him an incredibly rich man in the process.

There were flowers. Chauffeured limousines. Dinners and Broadway shows. There were even love notes in the middle of the night, including a telegram that read, "We want you in New York."[1] There was talk of Winfield in places Reggie Jackson was not welcome. And there was money . . . so much money.

Winfield could thank the New York Mets, in part, for that money. The struggling Queens franchise wanted to make a big splash in the off-season and give fans a reason to come to Shea Stadium in 1981 and beyond. They offered Winfield $7.5 million over five years. It was a substantial offer, one Steinbrenner could not let stand. He came to Winfield with something even better: a $1 million signing bonus and $1.4 million a year . . . for ten years! It was, by far, the largest proposed contract in sports history. There was even money for Winfield's charity, the David M. Winfield Foundation, which helped underprivileged children. Plus, there was a cost-of-living adjustment, something Winfield made clear to every interested team he would not sign a contract without. He took the Yankees' deal.

Steinbrenner was fine with the cost-of-living adjustment because he did not understand how it would work. Winfield was eligible to see his yearly salary match the rate of inflation up to ten percent. So far, so good. But Steinbrenner did not realize that the cost-of-living increases compounded annually. In theory, by the tenth year of the deal, Winfield could be making well over $3 million for the season. Winfield knew that. So did his representatives. And so, too, did Murray Chass of the *New York Times*.

"The total (of the contract) for 10 years would be $23,906,134," wrote Chass the next day, in an article announcing the deal.[2] Steinbrenner read the article and was livid. It wasn't about the money. It was about him looking foolish. Winfield was savvy enough to know that this was not the best way to start the longest contract in professional sports history. He agreed to renegotiate the deal. The money would stay the same, but cost-of-living increases would be deferred and calculated on interest rates of every two years, not one. Steinbrenner agreed and the deal was done.

There was an introductory press conference at Jimmy Weston's restaurant in Manhattan. Smiles and kind words were everywhere. George was never one to forget though. He had been embarrassed, bested at something he so prided himself on excelling in: deal-making. Winfield could make it up to him, perhaps, by bringing the Yankees a few championships and shining brightly in the process. But when New York made it to the 1981 World Series in Winfield's first season, he went 1-22 as the Dodgers overcame a 2-0 deficit to take the title. Now Winfield had bested George at the negotiating table and failed to come up big in October. The strikes were adding up.

The next year Winfield seemed to take delight in antagonizing his boss. Reggie Jackson, whom the Yankees made little effort to sign after 1981, returned to Yankee Stadium as a California Angel and homered in his first game back in the Bronx. Fans chanted, "Steinbrenner sucks!"—much to the humiliation of the owner. He took his anger out on manager Gene Michael and the coaching staff, then left New York, many assumed, to hide rather than face more humiliation from the fans. Winfield thought it was the act of a coward and said as much publicly. "I'll be here long after everybody else anyway," said Winfield. "I might as well take my swings."[3]

It went on like that, year after year. In September 1985 the Yankees were fighting to overtake the Blue Jays for the American League East lead. During the ninth inning of the third game of a critical four-game series at Yankee Stadium, Steinbrenner entered the press box and lambasted several players. "Mr. October came up big in these kinds of moments," he said of Jackson. "Winfield is Mr. May." Not long afterward the two had a confrontation in the Yankees' locker room over having players sign a pledge to undergo drug testing. Steinbrenner threatened that Winfield would not return to the Yankees in 1986.

"Well, I'm not worried about it," Winfield replied. "Because you know and I know where I'm going to be next year, and that's right here!"[4]

In 1986 Steinbrenner decided he would no longer make the annual $300,000 payments to Winfield's foundation. The money was contractually required under Winfield's deal, but George simply decided not to honor that part. He also accused the foundation of wrongdoing. Meanwhile, on the field, Steinbrenner asked Yankees manager Lou Piniella not to play Winfield, a move the manager would not consider, given the outfielder's obvious value to the team. Winfield refused to waive his no-trade clause, a decision that continually drove Steinbrenner insane. He then published an autobiography in 1988, which painted Steinbrenner in a less-than-flattering light.

Finally, in January 1989, Winfield sued Steinbrenner for back payments to his foundation. Steinbrenner countersued, going after the foundation's books, saying Winfield himself had failed to make payments and charging misappropriation of funds. Some of his accusations were highly specific, causing more than a few to wonder where and how exactly he was getting this information. In September the two sides settled through arbitration, with both men agreeing to make back payments. It all seemed to be over. It was just starting.

In March 1990 the *New York Daily News* printed an incredible story: Steinbrenner had paid a former employee of the Winfield Foundation $40,000 to provide damaging information about Winfield. They had copies of two checks made out by the law firm of Steinbrenner's personal attorney and transcripts of taped phone conversations with the Yankees owner. The former employee in question, Howard Spira, was "a freelance radio reporter who showed up frequently with his tape recorder at Yankees and Mets home games, always nattily dressed in sharkskin suits."[5] Many people around the Yankees knew him, or of him, and most considered him a nuisance, but nothing more. He had been peddling a story about Steinbrenner, payoffs, job promises, and damning information about a star baseball player. It seemed crazy, until the story hit.

It was a bombshell. Within a week the FBI indicted Spira for trying to extort Steinbrenner; baseball commissioner Fay Vincent announced he was looking into the matter. Winfield, meanwhile, was trying to get back to baseball after missing the entire '89 season. He had been telling people to expect a typical Dave Winfield kind of year. Instead, he struggled; Yankees manager Bucky Dent began platooning him, then pushing hard for the team to trade him. Recognizing Winfield had no place on the Yankees anymore, the team arranged a deal with the Angels. It did not go smoothly. Nothing with Winfield and the Yankees ever did. Winfield had been in the league ten years and with the Yankees at least five, giving him veto power over any trade. The Yankees attempted to make the deal anyway and announced it publicly before Winfield signed off. Winfield found out in just enough time to crash the team's press conference and say he wasn't going anywhere. When he later showed up in the Yankees' clubhouse, Dent, who had thought the trade was a done deal, was astonished.

A stalemate ensued. The Yankees were prepared to go to court to argue that, because Winfield had agreed to be traded to a select few teams—the Angels being one of them—his ten-and-five status was irrelevant. If nothing else, it was a bold attempt to defang the league's collective bargaining agreement. But it never got that far. Steinbrenner met with Winfield and apologized for the team's "poor handling of the trade."[6] The Angels also agreed to give Winfield a $9.1 million contract extension. Ever the shrewd businessman, that was good enough for him. On May 11, 1990, Winfield—hitting just .213 and showing no power—agreed to be traded to the Angels in exchange for pitcher Mike Witt.

"I'm happy," said Winfield, who evaded questions about his relationship with Steinbrenner at a news conference announcing the trade agreement. "This is good for Dave Winfield."[7] Asked what he would remember most about his Yankee years, Winfield responded with words mirroring what someone might say about serving time in prison. "Two things for sure," responded Winfield, "When I signed and when I'm leaving."[8]

The trade had the potential to revitalize the career of the thirty-eight-year-old. He had escaped an overbearing owner and a sinking franchise for the sunshine of the California coast. The initial results were mixed. He raised his average and showed occasional power. But heading into his fifth inning at bat on July 30, 1990, Winfield was just 3 for his last 26.

Winfield stepped into the batter's box. Years later a player of his size would barely garner any special notice. But now, even a few months short of his thirty-ninth birthday, Winfield's gigantic 6-foot-6 frame dwarfed most other players'. His was an intimidating presence at the plate. Tapping his cleats with the handle of his wooden bat, he had yet to hear the news coming out of New York that night. He was unaware of the shock waves being launched throughout the game for which he, through no direct fault of his own, was responsible. The man who had tormented Winfield for so long was getting his comeuppance—and he was getting it exactly because of how he had treated Winfield.

In his first at bat since the news broke out of New York, Winfield lined a 2-2 pitch into left field for a single. It was probably just a coincidence, or maybe poetic justice, but with his chief tormentor now on the road to banishment from the game, Winfield went 12 for his next 22.

2

Out of Place

Sixteen hundred miles from Minneapolis and the meaningless Angels-Twins game, Gary Carter sat in San Francisco's Candlestick Park. The Giants were preparing for a home game against the Astros that night. San Francisco lost after giving up five runs in the top of the ninth. Carter watched the entire game from the bench.

It had only been a few years, but it seemed like ages ago when "The Kid" was hitting extra-inning Opening Day home runs and driving in the winning runs in National League Championship Series games for the Mets. Acquired before the 1985 season, Carter produced and then some during his first three years with the team. Averaging 25 home runs and 96 RBIs a year, he was an All-Star in each season, finishing third in the 1986 National League MVP voting.

Then came 1988. After being named team co-captain with Keith Hernandez, Carter got off to a fast start, one of his best ever. On May 16, he hit a big three-run home run, the 299th of his career, late in a victory at San Diego. But Carter then went through an offensive slump, the likes of which he had never endured. Over the next three months his average dropped 30 points, his on-base percentage 60 points. He drove in only 16 runs and went the rest of May, June, and July without a home run. His 300th didn't come until August 11 in Chicago.

Some thought he was pressing too much to hit that milestone 300th home run. Maybe. But most certainly the years of foul tips, home-plate collisions, and all-out hustle had finally caught up to the thirty-four-year-old catcher. The sudden drop in production was startling. Carter managed one more heroic moment in New York when, in Game One of the '88 NLCS, his two-out, top-of-the-ninth double drove in the tying and eventual winning runs. His days as a starting catcher, however, were numbered. Moreover, rumors surfaced during the season that the Mets were looking to trade him, though the club denied it.

The year 1989 was the final one of his contract with the Mets. It was filled with heartbreak. Carter registered just nine hits in his first 79 at-bats, only three of them for extra bases. On May 9 he suffered a knee injury running on the turf of Riverfront Stadium. Carter needed surgery and missed more than two months. When he returned the Mets could no longer afford to play him on a regular basis. The front office was already looking to the future and telling Davey Johnson to play other, younger options at catcher. Before the season was even over, it became a poorly guarded secret that Carter would not be returning to New York in 1990. The Mets had an option on his contract, but Carter was an aging catcher with a bad knee. There were several players ready to take his place, including up-and-coming prospect Todd Hundley.

When Carter pinch-hit in the Mets' last home game of the season, he received a long, loud ovation. It was a show of gratitude for five gritty, heart-filled seasons at Shea that had led the Mets through their most successful stretch in team history. Carter, as he often did in big moments, came through one more time, lining a double deep to left field. A week later, knowing the Mets had no interest in exercising the option on his contract, he asked to be released. Had he instead opted to become a free agent while still remaining on the team's forty-man roster, the Mets would have to receive a compensation pick from whichever club picked him up. Carter knew that would make it that much harder for him to find a new team. The Mets granted him his request. It was a mutual decision, but still hard to believe. Five years after acquiring him in the biggest trade in team history, the Mets released Carter.

"I wanted to finish my career in New York. I would have played for a lot less money. I didn't want to move on. I really didn't," said Carter.[1] In January 1990 Carter signed with the reigning National League champion Giants.

Ten days before Winfield's fifth-inning Metrodome single, Keith Hernandez faced off against Bert Blyleven in the top of the fifth inning of an Indians-Angels match-up. Years earlier this would have been a battle to see. Hernandez, the line-drive, contact-hitter batting champion, versus Blyleven, the massive curveball–dropping, future Hall-of-Famer. Now? Blyleven still had a little left in the tank, but injuries would soon derail his career for good. And Hernandez? By his own admission, he'd tell you his career was winding down.

Like Carter, Hernandez had come to the New York Mets in a big trade that paid immediate dividends. Not only was he among the best hitters the Mets had ever had on their roster, but his leadership style brought a much-needed change to the clubhouse. "Mex" was unafraid to call people out or find ways to motivate them when needed. And his take-no-prisoners attitude on the field was adored by fans at Shea.

Hernandez finished in the top ten in MVP voting in all three of his first full seasons in New York. He hit for average, he walked, he drove in runs. And he played the most incredible first base you would ever want to see. He was named team captain in 1987, the first in the history of the franchise. But then came 1988 and Hernandez's playing career would never be the same. Like Carter, Hernandez had been on pace for a highly productive season. After a slow April, he boosted his average over .100 points by the end of May, playing his usual solid defense at first. In June he tore a hamstring and landed on the disabled list for the first time in his career. It cost him most of June and all of July. When he returned, Hernandez showed some flashes of the old Keith, but the injury clearly slowed him down. Like Carter, he had a single year left on his contract; like Carter, the Mets were making no commitment after 1989.

Hernandez faltered in '89, just like Carter. He started off slow before finding a little steam in May. On May 17, just a week after Carter went down with a knee injury, Hernandez fractured his kneecap in a painful collision with the Dodgers' Dave Anderson. He missed the rest of May and all of June. When he came back in July, he wasn't the same. Though never a power hitter, Hernandez managed just one more home run the rest of the season and was used as a pinch hitter nearly as much as he was a starter. The writing was on the wall and, like Carter, he received a warm ovation when he pinch-hit in the eighth inning of the Mets' final home game. A week later, an hour after the team informed Carter he was not coming back, they called Hernandez and told him the same. The organization was moving on. Younger, healthier, and less expensive players were making their way to Shea; there was no room for two thirty-five-year-old veterans who'd sustained crippling knee injuries.

That off-season, Hernandez signed a two-year, $3.5 million deal with the Cleveland Indians. Mex made his Indians' debut at Yankee Stadium, but just as Carter didn't look right in a Giants uniform, Hernandez seemed out of place in the powder-gray, mixed with pink and purple Cleveland uniform. In addition to a still aching knee, he also had a bad back. It limited his production to one home run in the first seven weeks of the season. After May 8 he drove in only one run until May 26, when he injured his left calf running the bases and had to go on the disabled list. He returned three weeks later and, in his first game back, sustained the same injury, going back on the disabled list almost immediately. Hernandez could still hit the ball, but he literally could not run to first base. He had played in only six games since the end of May. Batting in the fifth inning of this July 20 game against Blyleven, Hernandez managed a ground ball single, the 2,182nd, and last, hit of his career.

Cleveland management made no secret that they were running out of patience. "In the last two months, he's never been able to show us what he can do. The way he's been, he's been useless. That's been disappointing," said Indians president Hank Peters, feeling the pressure of a big contract that was not paying dividends for a team that had not seen the postseason in thirty-six years. "Hernandez is a gamble that has not paid off."[2]

Four days after his last hit, Hernandez reinjured his calf running out a ground ball in Chicago. Scratched the next day, his name never appeared in a major league lineup again. He spent the remaining year and a half of his contract on the disabled list, his career over at age thirty-seven.

It had been only five years since they'd won the hearts and minds of Mets fans, but here they were, Carter and Hernandez, no longer Mets on July 30, 1990, hampered by injuries, and riding into the sunset of their careers.

3

Borders on the Bizarre

Right around the time Dave Winfield lined his single into the Metrodome outfield, a wave of applause began rippling through Yankee Stadium. It was a rare sound that season. Going into that night's game, the Yankees were 38-61, fifteen games behind in the division. Only 24,037 fans had filed into the sixty-seven-year-old ballpark that night. In the top of the fourth inning, with one out, Alan Trammell came to the plate. Power-hitting sensation Cecil Fielder was on deck.

Behind home plate, and a short distance above the playing field, Yankees radio announcer John Sterling called the game. Sterling, a native New Yorker, had already made a name for himself in broadcasting. He had spent most the 1980s in Atlanta, calling games for the Braves and the Hawks. In 1989 he returned to call Yankee games for WABC radio.

Sterling was excited to head back to New York and watch a team loaded with offensive talent. But in just a few short months, the Yankees traded Jack Clark, who led the '88 team in home runs, then Rickey Henderson, who set a team single-season record for stolen bases in '88, and they had already lost Winfield to the back injury. "So from the team that I thought I was going to, they lost Henderson, Clark, and Winfield. All the sudden they didn't have a very good team," said Sterling.[1]

Now, Sterling shared with listening Yankee fans the most shocking news the team had endured in over a decade. "Today," Sterling stated, "baseball commissioner Fay Vincent announced that Yankee owner George Steinbrenner had agreed to resign on or before August 29 as managing general partner of the club for his dealings with gambler Howard Spira."

Trammell, facing lefty Dave LaPoint, lined a ground-rule double to right field as Sterling continued. "George Steinbrenner will remain as a limited partner with the Yankees, but he will give up as the managing general partner and that means that there will be someone new to run the Yankees."

Fourteen seconds after Sterling finished this announcement, cheers went up across Yankee Stadium. Fans inside the ballpark listening to Sterling on handheld radios were relaying the news, row by row, section by section. They stood. They applauded. And they didn't stop for over a minute. It was Christmas come early, some fans might have said. Even Fielder drilling a home run couldn't completely dampen the mood. Later, during the seventh-inning stretch, instead of singing "Take Me Out to the Ball Game," fans chanted, "No more George."[2]

For the first time in a long time, Yankee fans were happy with the direction their team was headed. Faster than you could say "Howard Spira," George Steinbrenner was being banished from his beloved Yankees.

Fay Vincent was no dummy. A law degree from Yale. Partner in a big Washington DC law firm. Top position with the Securities and Exchange Commission. Chairman of Columbia Pictures then executive vice president for Coca-Cola. In 1989 his business associate and good friend Bart Giamatti became baseball commissioner. Giamatti brought Vincent along as his deputy. Just five months into his term, Giamatti died suddenly of a heart attack, elevating Vincent to commissioner. Seven weeks into his tenure, an earthquake interrupted Game Three of the World Series and thrust Vincent into the spotlight, earning him high marks for his handling of the situation.

Not only was Vincent smart, but he hated bullshitters. The weekend after resolving that spring's lockout by the owners, he picked up the *Daily News* and saw their story about The Boss, gamblers, payoffs, and Dave Winfield. He could sense what was ahead. "I knew I was going from the labor problem to having to deal with Steinbrenner," he said. "And I knew that was going to get ugly and messy because I knew he was, in some respects, crazy—mentally ill—and I thought I couldn't imagine anything worse than having to take on an owner in baseball with his standing in New York City."[3]

Vincent began looking into the Spira affair immediately. He brought in John Dowd, the famous attorney whose investigation and report months earlier had led to Pete Rose's banishment from the game for gambling. Dowd began talking to various individuals who could provide information on the alleged payment of $40,000 from Steinbrenner to Spira. He eventually called Steinbrenner in for a deposition. George would later charge that Dowd had had his deposition altered and that he had removed passages unflattering to himself. Dowd denied this. A judge ultimately dismissed a lawsuit Steinbrenner brought against the stenographer and his employer. But George began telling reporters that Dowd's tactics were not on the level; most importantly, he began telling fellow owners the same thing. While many of the owners didn't particularly care for Steinbrenner, they certainly cared about their own best interests. If Dowd could do that to George, who among them was safe? Steinbrenner's accusations, while never proven, would have long-term implications for Vincent and Major League Baseball.

In late June 1990 Vincent received Dowd's report, which was damning for Steinbrenner. It showed Spira, whom Winfield referred to as a "go-fer" for the foundation, had been in touch with Steinbrenner for years.[4] Spira had, in fact, provided Steinbrenner with information about Winfield and the foundation that Steinbrenner had used in his countersuit. The report also connected Steinbrenner to the $40,000 that Spira received in two separate checks. There were, in addition, recorded conversations between the two. The evidence was overwhelming. Vincent made his next move. It was clear George had made the payment. But why? Was it for damaging information about one of his own players? Or was Steinbrenner the victim of a deeply-in-debt gambler looking to shake down a wealthy man?

On July 5, one day after Steinbrenner turned sixty, Vincent brought him in for a hearing in midtown Manhattan. Though it was not a formal court proceeding, Steinbrenner's lawyers had planned to call several witnesses. But Steinbrenner was the main event. Vincent went after him in a manner that would have made many fans, some owners, and a few former players and managers jealous. "He was an arrogant bastard," Vincent recalled. "At first, he tried to push me around and tell me that this was outrageous; that he was doing his duty. That Dave Winfield had been cheating on his taxes. He was ridiculous, although he wasn't stupid. He always blamed everything on somebody who was dead."[5]

Steinbrenner, meanwhile, did not know what was in Dowd's report. Vincent was not obligated to share it and didn't, so George's legal team could not adequately prepare him for Vincent's line of questioning.

It showed. Steinbrenner, who for years had generated a tough-guy image backed by immaculate business sense, looked weak and, at best, naive about his dealings with Spira. He made various claims about the $40,000 payment. That Spira scared him. That he took pity on a guy down on his luck. That he was protecting Winfield, not trying to damage him. He even managed to throw former Yankee player and manager Lou Piniella under the bus, saying Spira had threatened to expose information about Piniella's gambling habits. Piniella was less than thrilled that he was being dragged into George's mess. "George calls me his friend? With friends like that, who needs enemies?" said Lou, upon hearing the news.[6]

Vincent did not buy a word it. If he was being extorted, why didn't Steinbrenner, who had access to law enforcement, the commissioner's office, and some of the best lawyers in the country, take measures to protect himself? Did Steinbrenner not realize that if his payment was used to pay off Spira's gambling debts he would then be directly associated with gambling operations, one of baseball's biggest sins? Was Vincent really to believe that the owner of the New York Yankees would have cared at all about Howard Spira if he did not, in fact, provide him with information about the Winfield Foundation?

Steinbrenner's testimony all but buried him. Vincent then announced that Steinbrenner's lawyers would not be allowed to call any witnesses to defend him. This was not a trial; it was Vincent's hearing. Normal judicial rules did not apply. Steinbrenner's lawyers were stunned. Eventually this decision would also be used against Vincent by baseball's other owners.

It took several weeks, but finally the commissioner was ready to give his decision. On the morning of July 30, he called Steinbrenner to his Park Avenue office. When George walked in, Vincent was prepared to suspend him for two years for paying a known gambler to obtain damaging information about one of his players. "He hadn't done anything that was a capital crime, like betting on a game or doing something that I would throw him out for life," said Vincent. "I said I am going to suspend him for two years. Everybody agreed on my side."[7]

There was just one problem. Steinbrenner, already suspended once in the 1970s for illegal campaign contributions, did not want to be suspended again. He feared it would be an unalterable stain on his legacy. Moreover, as vice president of the United States Olympic Committee, Steinbrenner was afraid a suspension from baseball would mean he could not continue his role in the Olympics, which were less than two years away. Finally, Steinbrenner said he had simply grown tired of it all. He was done with baseball. He did not want a suspension. He wanted to be permanently banned from having anything to do with management of the Yankees.

Vincent had been given the heads-up that Steinbrenner would ask for this punishment. But he did not think George really understood what he was asking for. Banishment was not something to be taken lightly. Still, Vincent already had an agreement written up for Steinbrenner to sign. In it Steinbrenner would have to give up his position as general partner of the Yankees and reduce his financial interest in the team to below fifty percent. Outside of a few financial and business matters, George would have no role in the decision-making process of the team. No say on trades or signings. No say on managers or general managers. No contact with team personnel. He couldn't even attend games except as a paying customer and, even then, people would be watching him.

Vincent slid the agreement over to Steinbrenner and informed him it was nonnegotiable. He either accepted these terms or Vincent would suspend him for two years. The next few hours dragged on, with Steinbrenner wavering back and forth on what to do. Meanwhile the commissioner and Steinbrenner's own lawyers tried to talk him out of it. George was being offered house arrest and instead asked for a life sentence.

A press conference had been scheduled for the early evening so Vincent could announce his ruling. Now he was growing impatient with Steinbrenner's indecision. Finally, he got up to leave for the presser. He got into the elevator and, as if out of a movie, one of Steinbrenner's lawyers threw his arm between the doors just as they were closing.

"Fay, he is gonna sign," the lawyer told Vincent.

"Well, I am on my way over there, it's too late," replied the commissioner.

"No, no, get off and we will sign right here."[8]

Vincent got out and waited. Not much longer afterward, Steinbrenner signed the agreement that banished him for life. He left Vincent's office and as he got into his waiting car called fellow owner Jerry Reinsdorf of the Chicago White Sox. George bragged about how good the deal he just made was. What's the deal? Reinsdorf asked. Steinbrenner explained the terms. "George, let me be the first to tell you. You got fucked. You made a horrible deal."[9]

For years people have speculated that Steinbrenner signed the agreement thinking he could easily get around it. Others also felt that, like the Winfield contract, Steinbrenner did not truly understand what a lifetime ban meant. Or perhaps he really *was* tired of it all.

Whatever the reason, Vincent headed to his press conference to announce the news to the world. The commissioner had never had the kind of adversarial relationship with George that others developed. In fact, they had a connection, having both attended Williams College, though at different times, and having helped raise money for a former Williams' coach suffering from health issues. But Vincent was no George booster either. The commissioner had been temporarily paralyzed at a young age, the victim of a college prank gone wrong. He used a cane for his entire adult life. Vincent knew what it was like to have to overcome, to have to work hard in order to achieve your goals. The investigation and Steinbrenner's testimony further cemented the notion that Steinbrenner felt he would always get what he wanted: that whatever he said was truth, regardless of accuracy or evidence to the contrary. His methods, his style, and his overall manner of thinking did not sit well with the commissioner.

It showed in Vincent's comments. "I sat through the two days of Mr. Steinbrenner's testimony and I am able to judge the degree of candor and contrition present in this case. I am able to discern an attempt to force explanations in hindsight onto discomforting facts. And I am able to evaluate a pattern of behavior that borders on the bizarre," noted Vincent.[10]

He said that Steinbrenner's claims of extortion were "not credible" and that he did not "appreciate the gravity" of what he did: "In essence he heard no internal warnings because none went off."[11]

"I find the transaction that culminated in the payment to Mr. Spira to have been a serious error of judgment, and I must impose correspondingly serious sanctions as a consequence," said the commissioner.[12]

The agreement took effect on August 20. Steinbrenner had three weeks to get his affairs in order and find someone to replace him that would be acceptable to the Commissioner's Office. Once they learned the news, and unaware that Steinbrenner himself had asked for the punishment, players were shocked by the decision. "I was hoping it wouldn't be that severe," said second baseman Steve Sax. "He had been great to me and it started with my negotiations. When I hurt my leg he wouldn't let me drive my car. He sent a driver. Nobody did that, not the Dodgers. This is a drag."[13]

"I personally think it's quite a sad day," said LaPoint, the winning pitcher in that night's game.[14]

Fans, however, did not share the players' sense of sadness. "I think it was the best thing that could have happened to the Yankees and to baseball," said John Dell'Isola, the founder and head of an anti-Steinbrenner fan group called Fans Opposed to Useless Leadership (FOUL).[15]

"Yes!" said Mike Nisson, an out-of-town fan who happened to be in New York for a convention. "This is so sweet. Maybe it'll save the team. Now they can build a dynasty again."[16]

Such comments must have been heartbreaking for Steinbrenner, if he read them. He believed he had done everything he could to bring fans a winning team in New York, even if his decisions had resulted in just the opposite.

Members of the media could not help but rejoice. Though they had benefited immensely from the turmoil Steinbrenner caused, many were tired of his schtick, of the way he tried to play reporters off one another for scoops. "Will future generations of Yankee fans light the sky with fireworks on July 30, the anniversary of the night when George Steinbrenner was sentenced to life as a silent partner," wrote Newsday's Joe Gergen. "Or will they observe Aug. 20, when the decree of baseball commissioner Fay Vincent takes effect, as Liberation Day in the Bronx?"[17]

"Even among his fellow owners Steinbrenner's reputation has hit a greased ramp. Once regarded as a smart, if two-faced, wheeler-dealer, he is now considered no more than a buffoon," said C. W. Nevius of the San

Francisco Chronicle. "Worse yet for him, they [the Yankees] might turn things around. The farm system is not completely without talent and there is plenty of money for free agents. Wouldn't that be ironic, if the Yankees bounced back while Steinbrenner stood, disgraced, on the sidelines?"[18]

Under Steinbrenner's seventeen seasons of ownership, the Yankees had won two championships, four pennants, and made the postseason five times. No team won more games in the 1980s. It was a level of success no other baseball owner could claim during that time. So how could Yankee fans possibly rejoice over the news of his banishment?

The Yankee teams of the late 1970s were chaotic, as forever memorialized in Sparky Lyle and Pete Golenbock's *The Bronx Zoo*. But those teams were also champions and winning has a way of solving everything. The decay of the franchise and, in turn, the downfall of George Steinbrenner, began just hours after the Yankees lost the 1981 World Series to the Dodgers. Angered at his team's having blown a 2-0 games lead, Steinbrenner issued a public apology to Yankee fans.

Players were enraged. They had come within two games of winning the World Series: what did they have to apologize for? Still, they were the defending American League champions and there was hope for 1982. But Steinbrenner let outfielder, All-Star, and future Hall-of-Famer Reggie Jackson walk in free agency. Then he announced that the team would be moving away from relying on home runs and instead utilizing speed to score. He brought Harrison Dillard, an Olympic hurdler in the 1940s and '50s, to spring training that year to teach players how to run faster. It was an absurd premise; as a team, the Yankees averaged a stolen base every 2.3 games in 1982, marginally better than their 2.5 game average in 1981. While they did perform slightly better offensively in '82, their pitching—as it would be throughout the rest of the decade—was their undoing. Injuries and ineffectiveness saw the team ERA rise a full run from '81; they finished the year 79-83, their first losing season in nine years.

The 1983 team remained in competition until September, but ultimately fell short of first place. The first half of 1984 proved disastrous, as injuries and a historic start by the Detroit Tigers knocked the Yankees out of contention by May. Allowing some of their prospects to play and flourish in the majors in the second half of the year, there was renewed hope going into 1985. But a chaotic season filled with perhaps more off-the-field drama than any Yankee team had ever endured ended when the club was eliminated from playoff contention on the regular season's final Saturday.

Beginning in 1985 the team's record grew increasingly worse, year by year. From 97 wins to 90 in 1986, 89 in 1987, 85 in 1988, and 74 in 1989. The deterioration was due to a variety of factors, which all led back to Steinbrenner. His behavior had always been manic and, for those in his employ, generally brutal. But as the 1980s progressed and the team grew worse—and the Mets better—his mania grew to new heights. New York's heart now belonged to the Amazins, the first time it had ever truly been so for a prolonged period of time, and Steinbrenner became obsessed with the team in Flushing. His desperate need to eclipse the Mets, both in terms of record and in the back pages of New York's tabloid papers, seeped into every decision he made. The result was a vicious cycle of bad trades, bad signings, bad managerial decisions, and incredibly bad personal judgment.

It started after the 1985 season when, against the direct wishes of his top leadership, Steinbrenner approved a trade with the White Sox for pitcher Britt Burns. The lefty had been impressive in '85, winning eighteen games and finishing seventh in American League Cy Young voting. But the White Sox knew something about Burns no one else did: he had a degenerative hip condition that could end his career at any moment. "I think you better trade me because I'm not sure if I'm going to be able to pitch much longer," Burns told the White Sox team owner.[19]

Steinbrenner was infatuated with Burns. The two teams agreed to a trade pending Burns passing a physical. X-rays showed massive hip deterioration and the Yankees' team doctor recommended against the deal. Steinbrenner made it anyway. Burns lasted two starts into spring training in '86 before his hip prevented him from throwing anymore. He never pitched another game in the major leagues.

More lopsided trades followed. Doug Drabek, a future Cy Young Award winner who had put up respectable numbers for the Yankees as a rookie in '86, was shipped to Pittsburgh along with two other players that off-season. The deal was despised among Yankee brass. "We all hated trading

Drabek, but my dad wouldn't listen," said George's son Hank, who starting in the mid-1980s was brought on to learn the family baseball business. "That's when I realized no matter how many people had a vote on things there was really only one vote that counted."[20]

None of the three players they received in return was still with the Yankees when Drabek won his Cy Young in 1990. Bob Tewksbury, another rookie on that '86 team, was traded along with three rookies for reliever Steve Trout. Tewksbury averaged fourteen wins a season between 1990 and 1993, finishing third in the National League Cy Young Award voting in 1992. In sixteen appearances as a Yankee, Trout had a 6.60 ERA and a 1.89 WHIP. The Yankees traded him that off-season.

Jay Buhner, one of the team's top prospects who showed tremendous power, was sent to Seattle in perhaps the most infamous deal in team history, sending first baseman Ken Phelps to New York. Even Phelps said the trade made little sense, admitting that he wondered where exactly he was supposed to play when he got to the club. Jack Clark, the team leader in home runs in '88, was shipped off to San Diego just after the end of the '88 season. None of the three players the Yankees received in return lasted more than two years with the club.

Rickey Henderson, the future Hall of Famer who had already set the Yankees' all-time stolen base record in just four and a half seasons with the team, was sent back to the Oakland A's in the middle of the '89 season. The trade was not unjustified. Henderson had grown increasingly tired of the clubhouse drama that constantly played out in the newspapers. He had made comments that the team drank too much and that it cost them during the stretch run in '88. And his performance early in the '89 season left something to be desired, causing some to wonder if he was dogging it. But in return, the Yankees received three players—Luis Polonia, Greg Cadaret, and Eric Plunk—who, despite starting their careers several years after Henderson, were all retired by the time Rickey hung up his cleats in 2003. By then he was the all-time leader in runs scored and bases stolen.

Hal Morris, a left-handed first baseman, was traded after the '89 season to the Cincinnati Reds for former Mets top prospect Tim Leary. Morris played ten seasons in Cincinnati, hitting .305. Leary was out of baseball by 1995.

Drabek, Tewksbury, Buhner, Clark, Henderson, Morris . . . the Yankees had traded away some incredible talent. Except for Clark and Henderson, it all fit a theme: young players with whom Steinbrenner grew too impatient to see them reach their full potential, instead trading them for either marginal talent or players who, at best, had a few seasons left in their careers. It could in fact be argued that no trade made by the Yankees between 1985 and 1990 ultimately benefited them more than the team they traded with.

Moreover, as young talent was shipped off and older talent started to disintegrate, free agents became harder and harder for the Yankees to sign. Players became wise to what was happening in the Bronx; instead of running for Steinbrenner's money, as they had done in the past, they now shunned the Yankees. Joe Carter, an All-Star outfielder with the Cleveland Indians, was traded to the Padres after the 1989 season. As part of the deal, he signed a contract extension with San Diego that included a limited no-trade clause. Without provocation, Carter's agent, Jim Turner, noted the clause had been included because Carter refused to play in New York. "Joe wouldn't play for the Yankees if George Steinbrenner picked him up in a limousine," said Turner.[21]

Managers came and went, too. Lou Piniella, hired to take over in October 1985, lasted two seasons, the first time anyone had managed the Yankees for two consecutive seasons since 1976–77. But his time had been brutal. There were the constant phone calls, the bizarre requests, and the overruling on baseball matters. Piniella wanted to keep pitcher Phil Niekro, winner of sixteen games in 1985. George released him at the end of spring training in 1986. Piniella wanted to keep relief pitcher Pat Clements with the team during the division race in 1987. George sent him down to Columbus. When Piniella failed to get back to his hotel room for a 2:00 p.m. call from Steinbrenner, The Boss told Yankee executives they could not speak to the manager. It was a petty move, one that usually signaled the end was near for the one being frozen out. Moreover, George always had Billy Martin around to question and second-guess Piniella's decisions, despite Martin having been fired by George four times already.

After the '87 season, Piniella was moved up to general manager and Martin brought back a fifth time. The team was actually in first place into

June 1988 but then Martin was beaten up at a strip club in Arlington, Texas, and had the misfortune of getting back to the team hotel after the fire alarm went off. Everyone, including Steinbrenner, saw him sag out of his cab, his left ear nearly detached from his body. While the incident seemingly blew over, the usual warning signs from Martin appeared. His inability to work with Piniella caused Lou to resign as general manager near the end of May. Then Martin was suspended for throwing dirt on an umpire and he began openly clashing with Steinbrenner over personnel decisions. The hammer fell for a fifth and final time for Martin on June 23. Piniella replaced him, finished out the 1988 season, and never managed the Yankees again, escaping in 1990 to become manager for the Cincinnati Reds.

Steinbrenner, looking for someone who could instill discipline in his players, took the unusual step—for him—of hiring a manager outside the Yankees system for 1989: Dallas Green. A former pitcher who had managed the Philadelphia Phillies to a title in 1980, Green was known for his tough attitude. He signed on thinking he would have the power of Jack Clark and Winfield in his lineup. But Steinbrenner traded Clark, to Green's dismay, and Winfield suffered the back injury. Green thought he would have Claudell Washington, an outfielder who hit .308 for the team in '88. Steinbrenner did not re-sign him. Steinbrenner then traded pitcher Rick Rhoden, again to Green's dismay, while bringing aging pitchers Ron Guidry and Tommy John back. Guidry retired in 1989, having missed the entire season with an injury; John retired after posting a 2-7 record in ten starts. Green was not consulted or asked his opinion on any of these moves.

New York managed to hover around .500 heading into the second half, but Green's days were numbered. While some of the starting pitchers loved Dallas because he allowed them to go deep into games, many players were growing weary of his tough, blunt style. In early August when Steinbrenner criticized him in the papers, Green did what few had done before him: he went on the offensive. He began openly referring to Steinbrenner as "Manager George," mocking the man to reporters on a daily basis. In mid-August, Green was let go. He did not leave without a parting shot. "Let's face it, there is absolutely no hope that their organization will be a winning organization as long as Steinbrenner runs the show," Green told reporters before heading out.[22]

After Piniella refused to take the job a third time, Steinbrenner promoted Bucky Dent, the team's AAA manager, to the helm. Just thirty-seven years old, Dent was a hero to Yankee fans, forever loved for his home run at Fenway Park during the 1978 winner-take-all, one-game playoff against the Red Sox. But Dent's resume wasn't enough to spare the wrath of fans and reporters who had grown tired of all the changes. Different manager, same result, was what they thought. Dent might be a breath of fresh air, but he was taking over the same team, one that now stood at 56-65, second to last in the American League East. They ended up in fifth place, finishing under .500 for the first time in seven years.

By 1990 the misdeeds of the past had all caught up to the Yankees. The farm system was nearly empty of any high-quality prospects. The best ones were now playing for other teams. That year was an especially painful reminder of all the team had given up. Former Yankee prospect Doug Drabek won the National League Cy Young Award; former Yankee prospect José Rijo was named World Series MVP; former Yankee prospect Willie McGee won the National League batting title; former Yankee Rickey Henderson won the American League MVP. Former Yankee Hal Morris hit .340 for the Reds. Former Yankee Jack Clark hit 25 home runs and led the National League with 104 walks, nearly more than the entire Yankees' starting infield combined. Former Yankee manager Lou Piniella spent the entire season in first place with Cincinnati, ultimately winning the World Series.

The numerous trades the team had made over the previous five years had failed to pay any dividends. In fact, not a single player the Yankees had acquired for Drabek, Rijo, Tewksbury, or Buhner remained on the team by 1990.

The first three months of the seasons were rough. After starting 4-1, they lost 12 of their next 15 games, falling to sixth place. They never went higher than fifth the rest of the season. Pascual Pérez, an eccentric pitcher with some success in Montreal and Atlanta who had signed with the team in November 1989, made three starts in April, managed to lose two of them despite giving up only three runs total in those games, then suffered an injury that ended his season. Polonia, acquired in the Henderson deal, was already a marked man after having sex with an underage girl at a Milwaukee hotel the previous year. Before April was over he was traded to California for Claudell Washington and Rich Monteleone. Washington sustained an injury less than two months later, ending his career.

Meanwhile, Winfield's lack of production resulted in Dent platooning him; the drama over his trade just served as a further distraction. Once the Winfield deal was finalized, some players did not hide their disdain for the whole situation. "He never really had a chance to find his swing. He was certainly not going to find it as a platoon player," said Mattingly.[23]

As with so many before him, the clock on Dent was ticking. Steinbrenner had informed Billy Martin late in 1989 that he would eventually bring him back to manage a sixth time. But Martin died in a car accident on Christmas Day. Just before the start of spring training in 1990, Steinbrenner had Dent join him for a press conference at the 21 Club in midtown Manhattan.

"Bucky will be my manager all year," Steinbrenner told the gathered media.[24] No one there believed him. Steinbrenner had made this promise before but since 1978 there had been only five seasons in which a Yankee manager lasted the entire year. Rather than reassuring, Steinbrenner's claim was a kiss of death.

The Yankees fell into last place on May 26, then lost five in a row. After dropping two out of three to the Orioles, they headed for Boston and promptly lost the first game of the series. The next night, Tuesday, June 5, they lost in heartbreaking fashion when, after they scored four runs to tie the game in the top of the eighth inning, an error by Plunk led Boston to score the eventual winning run. The Yankees were now 18-31.

After the game, Dent called George Bradley, the Yankees' vice president for player personnel. He begged Bradley to acquire another starting pitcher. Someone. Anyone!

"Sure, Buck, we'll get back to you on that one," replied Bradley.[25] The terseness of the reply, which ended the conversation, raised Dent's suspicions. The next morning Bucky was in his room at the Boston Sheraton when he noticed a note slipped under his door. It told him not to leave, but to stay in his room for a call from Steinbrenner. Dent waited several hours until, at 12:20 p.m., the call finally came. Dent was out, the nineteenth managerial change in Steinbrenner's seventeen years of owning the club.

"Mr. Steinbrenner anguished long and hard about this decision," said Yankees general manager Harding Peterson in announcing the news. "We feel that the club is a better club than our win-loss record indicates."[26]

"I think it was the feelings of the players a change had to be made," said Steinbrenner that night. "In fact, I know it was."[27]

The comment was typical Steinbrenner. Rather than take responsibility for a decision he knew might be unpopular—no matter what the team's record—he made it sound as if the players were the ones who wanted a change. It was their fault Dent was gone, not Steinbrenner's. The players, however, did not support The Boss's statement.

"I don't think the players wanted Bucky fired," said Dave Righetti, the senior member of the club who had now played for over a dozen managers while with the Yankees. "Whatever reason George had, that's his reason."[28]

"He's been made the scapegoat," said catcher Rick Cerone. "We're the ones that got him fired. We're the ones with the worst record in baseball. This is no reflection on Bucky as a manager."[29]

Yankee fans, meanwhile, had long since had enough of the managerial firings.

"I've been a fan since 1963," said Ken Gray of Long Island, "and I've finally had it with them . . . And you fire the guy in Boston, where he had one of the greatest moments in team history."[30]

"I'm incensed because Steinbrenner has ruined the Yankees for those of us who have been fans for countless years," said Lillian Loeb of Yonkers.[31]

The press had also become tired of the whole thing, even reporters who did not have to cover the Yankees on a daily basis. "With each year that passes, the Yankees become more of a joke and these managerial changes become more hollow and less newsworthy," wrote *The Boston Globe*'s Dan Shaughnessy. "Outside of New York, the story of a new Yankee manager has been reduced to 'In other sports news . . .' Always, this message is delivered with a smile and a snicker."[32]

"The problem isn't the managers," said Marc Topkin of the *St. Petersburg Times* in Florida. "The Yankees are a collection mostly of players past their prime, or short of it. Don Mattingly is their only legitimate superstar. They have a collection of decent major-league pitchers, but no star, no one to set an example . . . . They're a short-sighted organization in a long-range game."[33]

For years the Yankees had hired a string of high-profile names to manage the team. Even those that had never managed before in the big leagues, like Dent, had established places in Yankee lore. But now, as the team struggled through one of its worst seasons in franchise history, Steinbrenner called on a man whom most fans probably had never heard of. The next manager of the Yankees would be Carl Merrill, known to his friends, colleagues, and players as "Stump."

Stump. The nickname just seemed right. All of 5-foot-8, with a paunch and a thick New England accent that was a walking contradiction in a Yankee uniform, Stump Merrill looked like a manager out of central casting. Hailing from Brunswick, Maine, Stump was a good enough catcher to be selected by the Phillies in the 1966 draft. While he never made it past AAA ball, he was a student of the game and had an eye for talent. Shortly after his playing career ended, an opportunity came his way. He took a job with the University of Maine baseball team under Jack Butterfield, who had coached Merrill as a student and given him his nickname. The two became close, so close that in a few years, when the Yankees hired Butterfield as director of player development and scouting, he brought Merrill along. Butterfield's death in a car accident two years later devastated Stump and at times made him feel like "an island by myself" within the organization.

It was hard to argue with Stump's track record, though. He began his time with the Yankees by managing a series of low-level teams. Wherever he managed, success followed. He became the Yankees' first base coach in 1985, only to be sent back to Columbus midseason to manage the team. Like many of the players he managed, Merrill went back to the Bigs in 1986 as a coach only to be returned to the minors in 1988.

Some might have viewed the transition down to the minors as a demotion, but Merrill dove into his managerial work. He took over the Yankees' Class AA Albany team in 1988 and led them to a championship. The next year he led Class A Prince William to a title. Now, as the manager of the team's AAA Columbus Clippers affiliate, Stump had them in first place on June 5. In five of seven seasons as a minor league manager, Merrill had led his team to a championship or postseason play.

Right around the time Dent was pleading with Bradley for another starting pitcher, Merrill was returning to his hotel room in Columbus, told to head there and wait for a call from Steinbrenner. At 1:00 a.m., The Boss called to let Stump know his time had come. He was the next manager of the Yankees.

A few hours later Merrill headed to the Columbus airport for his flight to Boston and an introductory press conference. He almost missed his flight. "I go by Stump and they weren't going to let me on the plane 'cause they thought it was an alias," he recalled, about how his nickname and the name on his identification did not match up. "So we had a little problem getting on the plane but we made it."[34]

"This has to be one of the happiest days of my life," Stump told the assembled press at the Boston Sheraton. "I can honestly tell you this has been a goal of mine for a long time." Merrill was smart enough to couch his glee in some reality. "I'm not going to tell you we're going to win a pennant, but I will tell you we'll put a product on the field that will perform."[35]

In many ways Stump was a gamble. He was an unknown and, in terms of the major leagues, untested manager. In other ways the move made sense. Merrill had been with the team for years. He knew the hierarchy, he knew the players who had come up through the system, he knew others from his time as a coach in the big leagues. He also had another quality that appealed to George Steinbrenner.

"He's cliché from the old school," said Randy Mobley, who knew Merrill from his days as a Clippers administrator. "He's a disciplinarian. That's one of the things he is noted for."[36]

Steinbrenner loved disciplinarians. It was usually when Steinbrenner thought a manager was not being enough of a disciplinarian that the manager got the ax. Now, with Merrill, he had a guy he had known for years, whom he respected, and who he felt would administer some tough love on a slumping ball club.

July 1990 had been an especially painful month, leading up to Steinbrenner's banishment. On July 1, the Yankees played their final game at the original Comiskey Park in Chicago. On the mound for New York stood Andy Hawkins, around whom much of the Yankees' notable July events would center. A Waco, Texas, native who'd signed with the Yankees after some successful years in San Diego, Hawkins led the team in wins—and losses—in 1989. He had been a steady workhorse, pitching deep into games and earning a decision in 30 of his 34 starts. Hawkins had especially liked pitching for Green, appreciating the way Dallas let starting pitchers work into and out of trouble.

The first few months of the 1990 season, however, had been rough. After his first seven starts, Hawkins's ERA stood at 6.69, his WHIP at 1.79. In his eighth start, at Kansas City, he surrendered five runs in fewer than two innings. On June 5, as Steinbrenner was planning to fire Dent, Hawkins surrendered five runs while getting only one out at Fenway Park. It was this performance that prompted Dent to call Bradley the night before he was fired, begging for another starting pitcher.

Like Dent after that night, Hawkins's time in New York was over. The team moved to release him days later. But then Mike Witt went down with an injury and missed the next two months of the season. Stuck without a starting pitcher, the Yankees, who had already told Hawkins he was being released from the team, decided to keep him on the roster. Andy turned things around immediately, putting in four solid appearances to finish June.

Now, on a bright, incredibly windy July 1 day on Chicago's South Side, Hawkins pitched the game of his life. Despite opponents hitting .300 against him coming into play, Hawkins headed into the bottom of the eighth inning without having given up a hit to the White Sox. On the flip side, the Yankees had barely been any better. Two singles in the sixth and seventh innings were the only base runners they had mustered, failing to score a run in either inning. The game remained scoreless as Hawkins worked on his no-hitter in the eighth.

Hawkins recorded the first two outs of the inning before Sammy Sosa hit a hard ground ball to third baseman Mike Blowers, who stabbed at the ball on his backhand, failing to field it cleanly. He recovered and fired to first, but Sosa slid in ahead of the throw. Immediately, everyone glanced up at the scoreboard to see if the no-hitter was still intact. The scoreboard operator had not heard from the official scorer, Bob Rosenberg, so he put a "1" in the hit column for Chicago.

The Yankees collectively lost their minds. Merrill and a few players stood outside the dugout and began shouting up in the direction of Rosenberg. Blowers threw his right hand up in disgust. He knew it was an error and did not want to be the guy who cost Hawkins his shot at history. Eventually, Rosenberg got word down to the scoreboard operator: the play was changed to an error. Hawkins then walked the next two hitters, bringing future Met and Yankee Robin Ventura to the plate with the bases loaded and two out. Ventura lifted a lazy fly ball to left field, where rookie Jim Leyritz was stationed.

Leyritz had been with the team a month, playing mostly at third base. He had started only two games in the outfield before this one. But the day before, Leyritz had hit his first two major league home runs. Overall, he was hitting .343. Merrill could not afford to keep him out of the lineup, especially with Chicago putting up lefty Greg Hibbard. So as Ventura's fly ball made its way to left field, Leyritz drifted back, looking uncomfortable as he tried to track its trajectory, shuffling his feet and squinting as he glanced up. As the ball came down, Leyritz stumbled and began to fall. "I came in on it because of the wind, but it couldn't get high enough for the wind to effect. So I had to run all the way back. Sure enough, it hit the back of my glove and it fell," recalled Leyritz.[37] The ball rolled all the way to the wall and all three runners scored. The Yankees were losing 3–0. When the next batter, Ivan Calderon, sent another fly ball to right, it looked like the inning was over. But Jesse Barfield lost the ball in the sun. He stayed with it as long as he could, but the ball hit and fell out of his glove. Ventura scored, and the Yankees had their third error of the inning.

Hawkins recorded the next out and walked off the mound having thrown eight no-hit innings, but still losing 4–0. The Yankees went down with ease in the top of the ninth, making Hawkins part of history: loser of a no-hit game by the largest margin ever. It was the first time in twenty-three years a pitcher had lost a no-hitter. "It's just the way our season has been going," said Hawkins afterward.[38]

Ultimately, baseball amended its rules and Hawkins's effort is not classified as a no-hitter because he did not pitch at least nine innings (a nonsensical distinction given that Hawkins is still credited with a complete game), but his place in baseball lore was forever cemented. "There it was," said Hawkins's teammate Chuck Cary, referring to that day. "There's the 1990 Yankees."[39]

Five days later, back at Yankee Stadium, Hawkins had, perhaps, an even more heartbreaking performance. Starting the first game of a doubleheader against the Twins, he threw eleven shutout innings. The Yankees, however, again failed to score a run for him. In the top of the twelfth, Hawkins got two outs before giving up two runs. The Yankees went down in bottom of the inning and Hawkins had now lost two consecutive starts in which he collectively gave up just two earned runs and only six hits in almost twenty innings pitched. "Those two starts right there are the two best starts of my life and I was 0-2 at the end of it. That's just the way it happens," said Hawkins.[40] The Yankees, meanwhile, fell to 28-49 and remained in last place.

In his next start, Hawkins gave up eight runs against the same White Sox he had no-hit two weeks earlier. Meanwhile, White Sox pitcher Mélido Pérez held New York hitless over six innings. In the seventh, the sky opened up and the game was called. Pérez's performance might have been even more remarkable than Hawkins's efforts two weeks earlier. Heading into this start, he was 1-3 with a 9.00 ERA in his career against the Yankees. In his previous start against New York, he had allowed seven runs in two innings. Like Hawkins, Pérez's six innings of no-hit ball did not count as an official no-hitter, but it was just one more indignity for the Yankees in 1990.

Less than a week later, on July 17, Hawkins faced the Royals at Yankee Stadium. By the bottom of the fifth inning, Kansas City led 8–1 thanks to three home runs and seven RBI from Bo Jackson, including one opposite field shot that went 464 feet. Jackson, the baseball and football star who had become a marketing sensation through his incredible athleticism and personality, seemed destined to hit a fourth home run. But in the bottom of the sixth, the Yankees' own baseball-football star, Deion Sanders, hit a line drive toward center field. Charging to his left, Jackson leapt, missed the ball, and landed hard on his side, dislocating his left shoulder. Sanders raced around the bases for an inside-the-park home run and Jackson missed the next month of the season. The Yankees lost, marking eleven consecutive starts in which Hawkins had failed to get a win.

Exactly one week later, on July 24, the Yankees lost 4–1 to the Rangers in Texas. Don Mattingly went hitless in that game, dropping his average to .245. Clearly something was wrong with the Yankees' first baseman.

Hailing from Evansville, Indiana, Mattingly had taken the league by storm, winning the American League batting title in 1984, his first full season. Even more surprising, after working with Yankee hitting coach Lou Piniella, Mattingly turned into a power hitter. In 1985 he produced the team's greatest offensive season since Roger Maris and Mickey Mantle in 1961. Leading the league in doubles, RBIs, and total bases, Mattingly took home the American League MVP. In 1986 he set a team single-season record with 238 hits and batted a career-high .352. He led the league in hits, doubles, slugging percentage, OPS, and total bases. Mattingly fell just short of the MVP that year, but he solidified himself as one of the game's best players. Moreover, as the Yankees kept falling short of the postseason and the clubhouse drama continued to ramp up, Yankee fans came to adore Mattingly. His gritty, hard-nosed style of play, matched by his overall production, made fans feel like his struggle to make the playoffs was their struggle. Kirby Puckett, the Twins' future Hall of Famer, gave him the nickname "Donnie Baseball."

Mattingly had another solid year in 1987, setting a single-season record for grand slams and tying a major league record for consecutive games hitting a home run. But during that year he first experienced the back pain that would come to define the latter part of his career. It began in June, when he injured two disks in the lower left side of his back, preventing him at first from even being able to bend over and touch his toes. He missed three weeks of action.

The next year, while taking extra batting practice at the Kingdome in late May, Mattingly reinjured his back. "I hit one right up the middle," said Mattingly, "then said 'Ow.' I felt a grab, like somebody was sticking a knife in my back."[41]

He landed on the disabled list again. Though he returned and put in a solid season, his power numbers dropped noticeably. Moreover, that August, Mattingly went off on an unexpected tirade against Steinbrenner, though he never mentioned him by name. "The players get no respect around here. They give you money, that's it," Mattingly told reporters after the Yankees had gone through a particularly rough stretch. "You can't get beaten over the head every day and want to play. I can't imagine a club being treated the way we have this season and playing as close to first place as we have most of the season. We get constantly dogged."[42]

Whether it was Mattingly's drop in production, his lashing out, or a combination of both, during the World Series that year, Steinbrenner attempted to trade him to the Giants in a multiplayer deal that would have brought first baseman Will Clark to New York. Ultimately, the Giants backed out of the deal.[43]

Mattingly rebounded for another All-Star season in 1989, hitting 23 home runs, driving in 113, and winning his fifth consecutive Gold Glove. It was a strong enough performance that rather than wait for him to become a free agent, the Yankees extended Mattingly's contract through the 1995 season. He rewarded that faith by starting off strong in '90, hitting .313 through April, providing one of the few sparks in the Yankees' lineup. But in late May, things began to slip away from the twenty-nine-year-old first baseman. He hit a game-tying bottom-of-the-ninth home run against the Royals on May 20, his fifth of the year. He wouldn't hit another until 1991.

In fifty-one games after that home run, Mattingly batted .208 with only six extra-base hits. Then came July 24 at Texas. In his last at bat of the night, Mattingly looked awkward and uncomfortable, hitting a soft line drive to the right for an easy out. For the first time he was feeling pain in his legs. The injured disks in his back were pinching against the nerves, causing an intense amount of pressure in the legs. It made driving the ball with any kind of power almost impossible.

Merrill could easily see from the dugout that something was wrong. "I knew . . . we were dealing with a hand grenade with a pin pulled," said Merrill.[44] He approached Mattingly before the next day's game. "I know you're hurt. Let's have a talk."

Mattingly said he was coming to see the manager anyway. Yes, he was in pain. But he thought he could play through it, especially that night. Nolan Ryan was going for his 300th win and Mattingly wanted a chance to deny Ryan his historic moment. But Merrill and the Yankees would not have it. Steinbrenner insisted he stop playing, return home, and start healing. Mattingly was placed on the disabled list with no indication of when he might come back. For fans who had already slogged through a horrid season, the news was heartbreaking. The one shining light, as Yankees future broadcaster Michael Kay called Mattingly, was now out of the lineup.

Even more shocking, a few days later Mattingly told the *New York Daily News* that "he would readily retire if his back pain persisted."[45] Ultimately, it did not come to that in 1990, but Mattingly would not appear in a game again until September 14, at which point the Yankees had already been mathematically eliminated from the postseason.

Perhaps the one positive outcome of all of it was the emergence of Kevin Maas. A tall lefty from Castor Valley, California, Maas was playing summer ball in Anchorage, Alaska, when the Yankees signed him to a deal in the parking lot of Maas's summer team's home field in 1986. Called up in late June to play backup first base, he began hitting home runs at literally a record pace. His first came on July 4. Just 20 games later, he had 10, setting the record for quickest hitter to reach his first 10 big league home runs. He subsequently set the record for quickest to 13 and 15 home runs. In the three game series in Texas where Merrill took Mattingly aside, Maas homered against Kevin Brown, Bobby Witt, and Nolan Ryan, a trio that eventually accumulated 677 career wins.

Still, while Maas was on a home run spree and Mattingly was making his way back to Indiana, the clubhouse festered with internal problems. Barfield, one of the team's few sources of power, was unhappy that his playing time had been diminished. Informed that he would be platooning with rookie Oscar Azocar, Barfield told the media, "I'm a proven big-league player. If I'm not going to play every day, the ballclub should trade me."[46] He made a formal request to be moved to another team; though the Yankees tried to honor it, he ultimately remained in New York.

Meanwhile, Deion Sanders, an eccentric personality whose perception of his baseball skills outweighed the reality, was disliked by nearly everyone. A standout cornerback for Florida State University, he also played for the baseball team and showed hitting ability and exceptional speed. Bo Jackson had already become a household name by the time the Yankees drafted Sanders in 1988. The following year the Atlanta Falcons selected him in the NFL draft. Though he had informed the Yankees that he would report to NFL training camp when it opened in July, a contract dispute with the Falcons led Sanders to use the Yankees as leverage to get a better deal. He made a handful of appearances with New York during that summer, accumulating more scorn from players for his antics than base hits. At times referring to himself in the third person, he gave himself a nickname that would stick: Prime Time.

Making the club out of spring training in 1990, Sanders continued to struggle at the major league level. But you would not know it by watching him play. His swagger gave off the appearance of a superstar; on May 22, someone decided they had had enough of the act. In a game against the White Sox at Yankee Stadium, Sanders came to the plate with a runner on third and one out in the bottom of the third inning. As he approached the plate, he drew a dollar sign in the dirt, as was his habit. White Sox catcher Carlton Fisk, the forty-two-year-old veteran whose career began when Sanders was still in diapers, was not pleased. He had been there before free agency, when owners controlled nearly every aspect of a player's career and could end it by simply refusing to give him a salary. He had been there for countless player strikes and lockouts, paving the way for players to earn large contracts. He did not begrudge anyone for wanting to make money, but for Fisk, it had to be earned, not simply awarded.

When Sanders popped up to short and proceeded to head directly back to the dugout instead of running the ball out, Fisk became irate.

"Run the fucking ball out you piece of shit," he yelled.

"What?" asked Sanders.

"Run the ball out," Fisk replied.

The lack of hustle offended Fisk as a baseball player, even if it was someone on the other team. He had an old-school, veteran's sense of pride about how to play the game. Sanders offended that pride in every way.

Sanders came up again in the fifth. As he strode to the plate, he told Fisk, "The days of slavery are over." Fisk had been mad before, but the implication that his comments had been race-driven made him apoplectic. He got in Sanders's face, screaming that it did not matter what color Sanders was, if he did not start playing the game right, Fisk was going to kick his ass right there.[47]

Acknowledging baseball etiquette, both teams emptied from the dugout, but no one actually knew what had happened between the two. No punches were thrown. There were not even any shoves. Order was restored and Sanders popped out to short again, leaving him with one hit in his first thirteen at bats of the year.

The next day Fisk was all too happy to share what had occurred. Already leery of Sanders, many in the clubhouse began simply ignoring him. On July 29, during the second game of a doubleheader in Cleveland, Deion hit his third home run of the year. His on-base percentage stood at .236. For weeks he had been telling anyone who would listen that he would leave the team when the Falcons' training camp opened in August. A free agent after the season, he was done with the Yankees. That is, of course, unless they were willing to meet his asking price. Both sides disputed what happened next.

The Yankees claimed Sanders asked for $1 million to play baseball in 1991. In the midst of dealing with his banishment, Steinbrenner managed to take the time to issue a clear and unequivocal statement: "George M. Steinbrenner today rejected Deion Sanders' request for a one-million dollar contract in 1991. Under no circumstances could we offer Deion that kind of salary for the 1991 season."[48]

Sanders denied ever asking for that kind of money, saying his advisers had been in talks with the Yankees for a week and he thought they were on the verge of a deal. "I don't want to call Mr. Steinbrenner a liar, but . . . I never asked for no money," said Sanders.[49]

Deion's teammates were incensed when they read in the papers that he, a .158 hitter, was looking at a contract totaling nearly $2.5 million with incentives. That was it for Prime Time. After Steinbrenner's statement came out, Sanders packed up his belongings in the clubhouse, gave his phone number to the few people on the team he considered friends, then stopped to offer parting shots on his way out the door.

"I'll say goodbye to . . . There are only about four or five I care about . . . The rest of them are happy to see me go," he told reporters. In a taped interview with Al Trautwig of MSG, Sanders summed up his feelings about the team: "We've got hitters talking about pitching and pitchers talking about hitting and people sitting on the bench who don't want the other guy to get a hit. A lot of guys here are always ripping the next guy."

With that, Sanders left New York, just around the time Fay Vincent was heading to his press conference to announce Steinbrenner's fate. In seventy-one games for the Yankees, Prime Time hit .178, accumulating more strikeouts than hits. Though he achieved measures of success later in his career with the Braves and Reds, he never played another baseball game at Yankee Stadium.

Lost no-hitters. Injured stars. Prima donnas. Last place. That was the Yankees 1990 season . . . and then came Vincent's July 30 decision.

[4]

Put Out of His Misery

At first glance, on July 30, 1990, the New York Mets were headed in the exact opposite direction of the Yankees. The Amazins had won eight of their last twelve, going from two games behind the Pittsburgh Pirates for the National League East Division lead to one game out in front. A total of 176,936 fans had just come out to Shea over four days to watch the Mets take three of five from their division rival St. Louis Cardinals. Now, on an off day as the team headed to Montreal, they learned the fate of their crosstown rival owner. The Mets were hot, exciting, and drawing fans out to Queens in numbers that were embarrassing George Steinbrenner to no end. They were on top of the New York baseball world with no sign of giving up the reins.

Or so it seemed. In reality, the team had been slowly coming apart at the seams almost the minute Jesse Orosco threw his glove in the air after getting the final out of the 1986 World Series. The tumult of a season filled with alcohol, drugs, and on-the-field/off-the-field fights had culminated in perhaps the most cathartic celebration a New York franchise had ever seen. But the very things that made the Mets so entertaining—so, not the Yankees—would be their undoing.

Overslept was how the Mets put it. That was why Dwight Gooden, less than twenty-four hours after winning the World Series, failed to show up at the Mets' championship parade. The twenty-one-year-old pitcher, now a superstar whose image graced the side of a nine-story building in midtown Manhattan, had simply partied a little too hard and slept through the festivities. He'd missed over two million fans cramming into the Canyon of Heroes in lower Manhattan to cheer on their championship team.

Gooden had not overslept of course. Instead, he was at the Long Island home of his drug dealer, getting high and watching the celebration on TV. The pitcher, who had electrified Mets fans and baseball fans alike for three thrilling seasons, had a serious drug problem. He had been able to hide it from most people after his cousin introduced him to cocaine in early 1986. But during spring training in 1987, Gooden failed a voluntary drug test, exposing his usage.

Faced with certain suspension from the major league baseball executive offices, Gooden instead opted to check into rehabilitation. On April 2, just five days before Doc was scheduled to start the season opener against the Pirates at Shea Stadium, the Mets announced all of this in a press statement. The next day, Gooden checked into Smithers Center for Alcoholism and Drug Treatment on Manhattan's East Side. He missed the first two months of the '87 season.

Six weeks after Gooden "overslept" the Mets traded Kevin Mitchell to the San Diego Padres in an eight-player deal. Nicknamed "World" for his ability to play almost every position, Mitchell finished third in the National League Rookie of the Year voting in '86. He played all outfield spots plus third base, first base, and shortstop. In the World Series Mitchell's two-out single in the tenth inning of Game Six kept the Mets alive when they trailed by two runs; he eventually scored the tying run on a wild pitch. Mitchell's most notable characteristic, however, was his physical presence. He was a big man who had run with gangs during his San Diego youth, while claiming never to have been a member. There were times during one of the many brawls the '86 team engaged in that some thought he might seriously hurt, if not outright murder, an opposing player.

Mets general manager Frank Cashen thought Mitchell was negatively influencing Gooden and Darryl Strawberry. That was not true. Gooden and Strawberry had set their own path, regardless of Mitchell. But the rookie was made the fall guy; despite how much his teammates loved him and his presence, World was shipped three thousand miles away. Mitchell was traded again in the middle of the '87 season to the Giants, whom he helped lead to the playoffs that year. In 1989 he won the National League Most Valuable Player award and led the Giants to the World Series.

In return for Mitchell, the Mets acquired outfielder Kevin McReynolds. The quiet country boy from Arkansas was a solid player, averaging 25 home runs and 90 RBIS over the next four seasons in New York. But he wasn't an '86 Met. He was not a partier nor in your face. He was not Kevin Mitchell.

Two months after Mitchell was traded away, third baseman and World Series MVP Ray Knight signed with the Baltimore Orioles. Knight had chosen to become a free agent after the World Series, thinking his MVP performance and his ability to stay healthy for all of 1986 was enough to earn a two-year contract. The Mets offered Knight a raise, but only a one-year deal. Knight refused it, dug in, and ended up with nothing. The Mets would not budge on another year. In the midst of collusion—where owners decided to limit the cost of player contracts by refusing to offer long-term, high-salary deals—Knight was left without a team until mid-February, when Baltimore agreed to give him a one-year contract with incentives to trigger a second year. The deal was $300,000 less than what the Mets offered.

"I still don't understand his thinking," said Frank Cashen.[1]

Knight, the Gold Glove boxer whose right hook of the Reds' Eric Davis had started a brawl in Cincinnati that was emblematic of the '86 team's swagger, was now another piece gone. While they were perhaps not among baseball's, or even the Mets', elite players, former teammates would later lament that when the Mets lost Mitchell and Knight, they lost a lot of their heart.

"I don't think the front office realized how important he was to us winning," said Lenny Dykstra of Knight. "We could have had another guy hit for the same average with the same homers and RBIS and make the same plays at third. It would have been different, though. The front office underestimated what he did for us."[2]

Regardless of the deals, the Mets still had to press on in 1987, this time with an enormous bull's-eye on their back. They were not just the defending champions, they were hated. The rest of the National League had grown tired of the Mets' cockiness and swagger. So the eleven other

National League teams must have been ecstatic when the Mets stumbled out of the gate in '87, a team riddled with injuries.

Gooden was out at least for the first two months of the year for rehab. Roger McDowell, the eccentric right-handed sinkerballer who logged over 142 innings in relief throughout the '86 regular and postseason, missed the first six weeks of the year after a hernia operation.

Bob Ojeda led the Mets in wins in '86 and pitched them to key victories in the NLCS and World Series. He replaced Gooden as the team's Opening Day starter but began feeling discomfort in his pitching elbow in late April. He skipped a start to be safe, made a May 3 against Montreal but then in a May 9 start in Atlanta, he lasted one inning before the pain become too much to endure. The ulnar nerve in his left elbow required surgery. Ojeda did not return until September.

Sid Fernandez, the kid from Hawaii who battled with self-confidence on the mound but emerged as an All-Star and World Series Game Seven hero in '86, suffered a knee injury on May 15. Five innings into a no-hitter against the Giants, El Sid, who had originally injured his knee sliding into third after a fourth-inning triple, felt the knee buckle as he threw the first pitch of the sixth inning. Though there was no permanent damage, he missed his next start.

On May 26, Rick Aguilera felt pain in his right elbow while warming up for his start in San Francisco. Scratched from the appearance, he had a sprain of the medial collateral ligament in his pitching elbow. He did not appear in a game again until August 24. The day after Aguilera was scratched from his start, starting pitcher David Cone, acquired from the Royals that off-season, was attempting to bunt when a pitch struck him on the pinkie finger of his right pitching hand, shattering it. Cone was lost until mid-August.

The injuries had come so quickly that Cashen did not immediately place Aguilera and Cone on the disabled list. "There's no point in disabling them right away," said Cashen. "I don't have 24 guys available to even fill the roster."[3]

Instead, Cashen was frantically trying to find pitching from other teams, willing to trade Mets prospects for quality pitchers who could fill the growing void in the rotation. No one would make a deal. "You tell them you need pitching, and they all say, 'So do I.' Every team I spoke to needs pitching," said Cashen.[4] Ultimately, the Mets used twelve different starting pitchers in '87, with only Ron Darling giving them more than thirty starts.

As May ended, the Mets had lost three of five of their starting rotation for nearly the entire season. Only Darling had avoided injury, and no one was willing to make a deal with them to plug the holes. The result was a 24-23 record, fourth place in the National East, and five and a half games back of first.

Gooden returned and, miraculously, the Mets managed to stay afloat despite all the injuries. Two of the biggest reasons were Darryl Strawberry and Howard Johnson. Strawberry, healthy and driven, was putting together his greatest season yet, eventually hitting 39 home runs, driving in 104 runs, and setting career highs in runs scored, hits, doubles, stolen bases, walks, on-base percentage, slugging percentage, OPS, and total bases. Johnson, who for years had struggled with questions about his ability and with being labeled as a platoon player, exploded that year, hitting 36 home runs, driving in 99 runs, and providing stability at third base, a position the Mets had struggled with throughout the entire existence of the franchise. Strawberry and Johnson both hit over 30 home runs and stole over 30 bases that year, the first teammates to accomplish that feat in an age when stolen bases were still considered important.

An 18-11 August moved the Mets up to second place; despite having been as far back as ten and a half games, they trailed the Cardinals by only a game and a half when St. Louis came to Shea on September 11 for a three-game series. Leading 4–1 in the top of the ninth inning of the first game, the Mets were one out away from moving within a half-game of first. With Ozzie Smith on second, McDowell gave up a run scoring single to Willie McGee. Terry Pendleton came up as the tying run. The Cardinals' third baseman was a great hitter, but not known for power. In a season where home run records were being obliterated, Pendleton had only ten on the year, and had not gone deep in a month. But McDowell's 0-1 sinker stayed over the plate and Pendleton drilled it to center field. The ball carried over the fence, tying the game and short-hopping into Darling's car, leaving a dent. St. Louis won in extra innings. The Mets continued to fight for first, but the Pendleton home run would long be remembered as the moment their dreams of repeating as champions were officially crushed. The Mets finished the year 92-70, three games out of first.

That off-season, another key component of the '86 team was sent packing. Orosco, who had been with the club as far back as the dreadful years of the late '70s, went to the Dodgers in a three-team trade. With young lefty Randy Myers in the bullpen, Orosco was expendable. Moreover, as one of the leaders of the team's infamous Scum Bunch, Orosco's after-hours activities did not thrill Cashen. Like with Mitchell before him, trading Orosco had, to Cashen, the added bonus of ridding the team of one more bad influence.

Still, when the Mets got off to a 15-6 start in 1988, it looked like the team was on the cusp of establishing their first dynasty. On May 3 Cone shut out the Braves, putting the team in first place by half a game. They stayed there the rest of the season. The injuries that had decimated the staff the year before all but disappeared. Gooden, Darling, Cone, Ojeda, and Fernandez started 156 of the team's 160 games. The staff ERA was 2.91, the lowest in the majors. Mets pitchers struck out the most batters, walked the fewest, gave up the fewest home runs, and had the majors' lowest WHIP. In his first full season Cone emerged as one of the game's top pitchers, going 20-3 and finishing third in Cy Young Award voting. Gooden, sober and healthy, won 18 games. Myers filled in for Orosco and pitched to a 1.72 ERA, leading the team in saves. Incredibly, Myers, McDowell, and Terry Leach accounted for nearly 70 percent of all innings pitched out of the bullpen.

Matching the pitching was the Mets' offense, which led the league in home runs, runs scored, on-base percentage, and slugging percentage. Strawberry and McReynolds finished second and third respectively in the National League MVP voting. The Mets would face the Los Angeles Dodgers in the National League Championship Series. Fate seemed to be on the Mets' side. They had beaten the Dodgers in ten of eleven games that year, their best record, by far, against any opponent.

A two-out, ninth-inning comeback in Los Angeles gave the Mets the win in Game One. In Game Two, the cockiness that characterized the team came back to bite them. Cone had always been fascinated by sports writing. Before the NLCS began, he decided to team up with *New York Daily News* reporter Bob Klapisch to write a column that would appear during the series. The idea was that Cone would provide his insights and thoughts in what essentially would be real time. In his first column, published the day after the team's comeback win, Cone made several disparaging remarks, dictated to Klapisch, about the Dodgers, including that Game One losing pitcher Jay Howell had a curveball equivalent to that of a high school pitcher. The Dodgers, who already hated the Mets and had for some time, were up in arms over the comments and used their anger to bash Cone for five runs in just two innings in Game Two. Cone apologized and stopped the column, but the damage was done.

The Mets rebounded with yet another late-inning comeback at Shea in Game Three, scoring five runs in the eighth to take a lead in the series. The next night, New York led 4–2 going into the top of the ninth. Gooden had not been his sharpest, but he had managed to strike out eight Dodgers and hold them to just those two runs over eight innings. Manager Davey Johnson had full faith in Gooden as Doc took the mound in the top of the ninth. Even a lead-off walk to John Shelby did not shake Johnson's confidence. The next batter was Dodger catcher Mike Scioscia, who in 37 career at bats against Gooden had mustered only 7 hits. In the Mets' dugout, even with the tying run at the plate, players felt this game was over. Scioscia had hit only 3 home runs all year and just 35 in his eight-plus seasons in the big leagues. He was not a threat to tie the game. The Mets were just three outs away from taking a 3-1 lead in the NLCS and all but assuring themselves a second World Series appearance in three years.

Gooden came to his set, briefly side-eyed Shelby at first, then wound up and delivered. Carter had set up on the outside of the plate, but Gooden's fastball missed its mark, staying right over the center. Scioscia swung hard and changed the course of Mets history.

The crowd knew it almost instantly. The ball had barely left Scioscia's bat when 54,000-plus people at Shea Stadium let out perhaps the loudest mass groan the stadium had ever known. They watched as Scioscia's shot disappeared into the Mets' bullpen in right field. It was one of the most unlikely home runs in postseason history, one even Scioscia himself could not believe. "I just closed my eyes and hoped, and then I ran for second base as quickly as I could. I didn't want to get thrown out at second. I would've been thrilled with just a double," said Scioscia.[5]

The game moved into extra innings. In the twelfth, Kirk Gibson homered to put Los Angeles on top. The Mets loaded the bases with one out in the bottom of the inning, but former Met Orosco got Strawberry to pop up and future Met Orel Hershiser got McReynolds to fly out to end the game. The Dodgers took Game Five; while the Mets forced a Game Seven, Hershiser shut them out, giving the series and the pennant to the Dodgers. Hopes of a Mets dynasty now faded away, thanks to two ninth-inning home runs from two guys who hardly ever hit home runs.

While the Mets licked their wounds in the off-season, more pieces of the '86 team disappeared. In December 1988 they traded Wally Backman to the Twins. Backman had been a sparkplug in the lineup, his uniform always dirty, his talk always blunt. He had publicly called out teammates who he felt failed to hustle or give their all. Fans loved him. But with an up-and-coming infield stud in Gregg Jefferies and a continuing desire to rid the team of the hard-core element of '86, Backman was expendable. Also, it had become increasingly apparent that Cashen was not solely calling the shots anymore. Instead, the Mets were now run by Cashen and team vice presidents Al Harazin and Joe McIlvaine. The more influence in the decision-making process Harazin and McIlvaine showed, the less satisfied players and fans seemed to become. In time all three would take the blame for the dismantling of the team during the late '80s.

There was hope that 1989 would see redemption for the NLCS loss the year before. Instead, the team fought and faltered. In spring training, with cameras rolling, Strawberry and Hernandez engaged in a fight. Strawberry was upset that Hernandez and Carter had been quoted talking about Strawberry's contract negotiations with the team. He was also upset over rumors Hernandez had told writers the previous season that McReynolds, not Strawberry, was the league MVP. When Hernandez and Strawberry were placed next to each other for a team picture, words were exchanged, punches thrown, and shoving ensued.

Jefferies, more a third baseman and shortstop by trade, was moved to second to replace Backman, but he had never played the position and needed more than spring training to adjust. Taking advantage of a weak division, the Mets were in first place in late May, despite hovering just above .500. But Hernandez and Carter went down to injuries that effectively ended their seasons. Gooden, on pace for his best year since 1985, suffered a shoulder injury in early July, sidelining him until mid-September.

In between the injuries, the Mets orchestrated one of the most lamented trades in team history. On June 18, they sent Dykstra and McDowell to the Phillies for Juan Samuel. The deal was crushing for fans, who had fallen in love with both players for their eccentricities and style of play, and for teammates, some of whom would later say that the trade represented the day the '86 Mets were officially no more.

"What was that," asked Carter, years after the trade. "For Juan Samuel? That did nothing for us."[6]

To make matters worse, both Dykstra and McDowell went on to have continued success in their post-Met careers. Meanwhile, Samuel, who had played all of three games in the outfield prior to 1989, was made the Mets' center fielder. He hit just .228 for the year, slugging only .300. Samuel was traded to the Dodgers after the '89 season.

One of the reasons Dykstra was traded was his constant complaining about having to platoon with Mookie Wilson. But the Mets had made Samuel their center fielder, negating part of the reason for the deal. Then a month later, they traded Wilson to the Blue Jays. One more connection to their championship past gone. They hung around in the division race until mid-September, but ultimately ended up in second place, six games below the Cubs. Their eighty-seven wins were the team's fewest since finishing last in 1983.

As their play on the field diminished, the Mets clubhouse became increasingly uncomfortable to be in. The wild, hard-partying group of the past was replaced with a mishmash of personalities that never seemed to gel. Strawberry continued to have run-ins with his teammates. In July 1987 Lee Mazzilli and Backman criticized him for loafing it on the field or making excuses not to play. "Nobody in the world that I know of gets sick 25 times a year," said Backman.[7]

Darryl threatened to "bust that little redneck" for his comments. In an *Esquire Magazine* interview that appeared just before the start of the

'88 season, Strawberry claimed Carter and Hernandez quit on the team during the pennant race and that Johnson's managing had cost the Mets victories. "Nobody could figure out some of the stuff he was doing all [1987] season," said Strawberry.[8]

Before their trades, Wilson—one of the nicest people to ever don a baseball uniform and considered the polar opposite of many of his hard-partying teammates—and Dykstra had both been complaining about their playing time. During the final weeks of the '89 season, Myers wrote "Are we trying" on the team's lineup card after Davey Johnson had Jefferies leading off. The comment was a shot at Johnson but an even bigger shot at Jefferies. The young infielder had earned a degree of animosity from his teammates that was, even for the Mets, staggering.

Jefferies, the Mets' first-round draft pick in 1985, had shot up quickly through the system, winning Minor League Player of the Year for two consecutive seasons. He debuted with the club in 1987, but a late-season call-up in '88, where he hit .321 with 6 home runs, brought Jefferies the kind of attention reserved for superstar players. Reporters and fans began talking about him as the next big player to come out of the Mets system, like Strawberry and Gooden.

The Mets' old guard did not appreciate all the newfound attention. Many viewed Jefferies as a threat to their own playing time. They saw a young up-and-comer whom the Mets were grooming to be the next face of the franchise, despite having no major league accolades to point to. When Davey Johnson started Jefferies at third base in the '88 NLCS, many thought it split the team between guys who were fine with any measure that would help the Mets win and those who didn't think Jefferies had done a thing to earn it.

Moreover, many just simply did not like the guy. Jefferies was young and intense about his performance. He had grown up laser-focused on baseball, one of the first in what would eventually become a long line of specialized sports kids who focused only on one sport in the hopes of making it big. His teammates came to see him as self-obsessed and oblivious to the team concept.

"In the minors Jefferies had been in the habit of cursing loudly, a trait that embarrassed manager Mike Cubbage," wrote Peter Golenbock in

Amazin', his exhaustive history of the Mets. "When Cubbage asked him to stop, he refused. When he came up to the Mets, Jefferies refused to take counsel from batting coach Bill Robinson. He said he would only listen to his father."[9]

Jefferies obsessed over the condition of his bats, to the point where he asked that his bats be packed and shipped separately from the rest of the team's. Though some of the '86 crowd was gone, there was still enough of the Scum Bunch mentality in the clubhouse to smell blood in the water. McDowell sawed some of Jefferies's bats in half. On another occasion Strawberry dumped all of them in the garbage, proclaiming, "Fuck these things. Fuck 'em."[10] The best thing to do would have been to ignore these incidents, but Jefferies made his anger clear. It only made things worse.

Jefferies struggled in '89, not living up to the hype that others had unfairly built for him. Some delighted in his misfortune. It was enough to embolden Myers to make his and his teammates' dislike for the young infielder clear by writing on the lineup card. Four weeks later Jefferies made the last out of the last home game of the year, grounding out to second base against Roger McDowell, now a Philadelphia Phillie. As Jefferies ran the ball out, he and McDowell began jawing at each other. Jefferies touched first and immediately turned and ran to confront, then tackle McDowell, starting a brawl. Some would later joke that most, if not all, of the Mets were rooting for their former teammate over Jefferies.

Three weeks after Myers scribbled on the lineup card, Strawberry and McReynolds were both absent from the dugout as the Mets attempted a ninth-inning rally against the Cubs at Wrigley. Upset that two of the team's key players were in the clubhouse instead of invested in the game, Davey Johnson fined and benched them. Strawberry and Johnson began screaming at one another, and players had to step between the two to prevent a fight. Then, with a week left in the season, Strawberry began opting out of the lineup, claiming various ailments.

"That ticked off a lot of guys," said Dave Magadan. "It got to the point where we were sick of Darryl always being injured or tired or whatever."[11]

Johnson, the manager who'd brought a championship to Shea and who had been the perfect fit for the Mets teams of the mid-'80s, grew increasingly unhappy in the dugout and increasingly distant from the front office. His management style had always irked Cashen. He thought Davey was too close to his players. Too willing to protect them at any cost and indulge their off-the-field shenanigans. For his part, Johnson had long had trouble stomaching how Cashen made moves without his input, about how he had to read things in the paper sometimes to know what was going on with the organization.

The two had been able to coexist when the Mets were champions. But after the parade up Broadway, the threads began to unravel. Johnson threatened to hold out over the 1987 season if he did not get a raise; specifically, if he did not get a salary equal to or better than that of Yankees manager Lou Piniella. Johnson got his way, but in some respects it was a Pyrrhic victory. Cashen was enraged that Johnson had taken the issue public. Then the Mitchell trade happened and Johnson was angered that he had not been consulted on the deal.

Johnson's frustration grew exponentially as Harazin and McIlvaine's influence became larger. He despised how decisions were made by a troika. Privately, he began referring to them as the "three-headed monster" and complaining that he never really knew who was in charge.[12]

"McIlvaine would become more involved in deals and Harazin would handle contracts," Johnson wrote in his autobiography. "So now not only did I have to deal with Frank, but also Joe and Al. I had nothing against those two guys personally . . . but it felt like I was working for three bosses now."[13]

During the '87 season Johnson, whose contract was up after 1988, had sought an extension. It became clear that management did not want to give him one. As the team was on the cusp of being eliminated from postseason contention, Johnson said he would quit as manager if he did not get the extension he wanted. "If they don't appreciate what I've done, then I'll go someplace else," he told reporters.[14]

The troika, however, was not going to be bullied. On the next-to-last day of the season, Cashen released a statement saying Johnson had voluntarily agreed to leave the team after the '88 season.

Johnson had not in fact agreed to do that. "It's the most vengeful thing anyone's ever done to me," Johnson said, two and a half years later, still clearly upset over what happened.[15]

In spring training of '88, Cashen warned Johnson to clean up his act, a not-so-veiled shot at both Johnson and the players' off-the-field habits that had come to grate on Cashen so much. After the Mets came within one win of going to the World Series, the two managed to put differences aside and Johnson signed a three-year extension. When the Mets slipped early in '89, Cashen asked Johnson to ban cards from the clubhouse and playing golf. Johnson obliged at first, but then told his players they could carry on, so long as they kept it out of sight. Then late in the '89 season, Johnson became angry with team psychiatrist Allan Lans, feeling Lans was exerting too much influence over the players and the clubhouse. Cashen supported Lans, which Johnson perceived as another slap in the face. When the season ended, most people in and around the Mets assumed Johnson would be gone. The troika wanted him out. But Mets owners Fred Wilpon and Nelson Doubleday supported keeping Davey at the helm.

The year 1990 had a lot riding on it for Davey Johnson. He had already been dangerously close to being fired; now, if the Mets got off to a slow start, it was all but assured he would be. Meanwhile, that off-season Strawberry created a string of distractions and turmoil. It began almost immediately after the '89 season ended. Darryl had hoped that the Mets would offer him a contract extension and that he could avoid his impending free agency after the '90 season. But when Strawberry, making $1.8 million a year and coming off his least productive season, asked for $3 million a year, the Mets balked and declared he was not worth it.

"Of all the players I've ever seen come into baseball," said Cashen that off-season, in comments expressing his frustration over the outfielder's on- and off-the-field actions, "Darryl Strawberry had the most potential . . . A couple of years ago, we got to the stage where we said we've got to stop thinking about his potential."[16]

On January 24, 1990, a blood test confirmed that Strawberry was the father of a child born in 1988 to a St. Louis woman who was now seeking child support payments. Strawberry did not dispute the results. Two days later Darryl was arrested in Los Angeles after a domestic dispute with his wife, Lisa. It began when Strawberry hit Lisa in the face. She then took a metal rod and hit him in the ribs and wrist. Strawberry pulled out a

.25-caliber pistol and pointed the gun at her. Strawberry was picked up and sent to jail before posting bond. The charges were eventually dropped.

Two weeks later Strawberry checked into the Smithers Center for Alcoholism and Drug Treatment in New York—the same place his teammate Dwight Gooden had gone to three years earlier—for alcoholism. "This is an alcohol and not a drug problem," Strawberry's agent noted, in words that were eventually found to be untrue.[17] In fact, Darryl had first done cocaine during his rookie season and used amphetamines throughout the 1980s.[18]

Strawberry's contract and state of mind would be a distraction all year long.

The 1990 season did not start off well. The team was crushed on Opening Day by the Pirates and lost their first three series. On the last day of April Cone pulled one of the game's most infamous blunders. With the Braves ahead 2–1 in the fourth inning and two out, Cone induced Mark Lemke to ground out to first with two runners on base. First baseman Mike Marshall tossed the ball to Cone, who appeared to touch the bag with his right foot. First base umpire Charlie Williams called Lemke safe. Cone began arguing with Williams but failed to call time-out. As Jefferies pleaded with Cone to pay attention and give him the ball, both runners circled the bases and scored. "I was yelling as loud as I could," said Jefferies. "I never felt so helpless. It was like slow motion."

"Call it vapor lock, no concentration [or] losing it. Whatever. He's not focused," said Davey Johnson of Cone. "His thought process was out of whack. It's not acceptable." Feeling the pressure of a season slipping away, Johnson berated Cone on the bench after the incident, then berated his team in the clubhouse after the Mets lost the game and fell below .500.

"It was appropriate and needed," said Cone of Johnson's comments to the team.[19] If it was supposed to incite the team to play better, it did not work. They lost the next night, dropping two games to an Atlanta team that had not won two games in a row all season. The Mets fell to fifth place.

Winning six of seven offered a minor reprieve, but the Mets then lost 8 of 12, leaving them at 20-22 on May 29. The team was in Cincinnati to play the Reds when Frank Cashen unexpectedly showed up at the team hotel. Davey Johnson ran into Harazin in the hallway. Harazin told Johnson to head up to his room. Cashen was waiting for him there.

Johnson was no fool. He knew he was walking into his own execution. The conversation was short. Cashen explained he was letting him go. "Frank, it's been a great run," Johnson replied.[20] He wanted to keep it civil. Cashen wanted Johnson out of sight as soon as possible and asked him to slip out the back door of the hotel. Johnson gathered his things and headed to the airport. "I would have liked to have met with the ballplayers to say goodbye but [management] didn't want me to stay around," he said.[21]

He left New York the winningest manager in Mets history, the only National League manager to win ninety or more games in each of his first five seasons, and one of only two managers in history to lead the Mets to a championship.

Many players did not know what had happened until they got to Riverfront Stadium and found Cashen waiting to address them in the clubhouse. He explained his decision, saying the team was underachieving and that he wanted them to refocus on winning.

How much impact his words had is unknown. Even though many had seen it coming, most players were still in shock. And, naturally, Johnson's firing could not help but cause more controversy.

"This pretty much finalizes my future. I can't see me coming back," said Strawberry.

"Davey was a friend, I like him a lot. I can't see my coming back here after my contract runs out," added McReynolds.[22]

And these comments were coming from the guys Johnson had fined just nine months before.

The media, much as they had with Bucky Dent, sympathized with Johnson and vilified the Mets' front office.

"Davey Johnson didn't get fired Tuesday," said the *St. Louis Post-Dispatch*'s Bernie Miklasz, "He was put out of his misery. How satisfying could it have been for Johnson to come to the ballpark each day, knowing that he was in charge of an enigmatic, selfish New York Mets team and would be held responsible for their actions . . . since winning it all in '86, Cashen and his baseball men started making the kind of panicky moves usually associated with New York's other overbearing boss, George Steinbrenner."[23]

Replacing Johnson was the team's third base coach, Bud Harrelson. The Mets had almost given Harrelson the reins in '89, before Wilpon and Doubleday gave Davey a temporary reprieve. But Harrelson's taking over was not guaranteed. In fact, the Mets, wanting someone who could whip their undisciplined and egotistical players into shape, had tried to lure former Yankee manager Dallas Green to Shea. But Green did not work out and Harrelson was given the job.

Outside of, perhaps, Ed Kranepool, no one could say they experienced the dizzying highs and embarrassing lows of the first two decades of the Mets franchise like Bud Harrelson did. Barely 145 pounds, Harrelson walked into a Mets instructional league camp in 1963 and earned a contract as a free agent. He was the epitome of a 1960s shortstop: small, skinny, all glove and no bat. In just over 5,500 career plate appearances, Harrelson managed only seven home runs and a .616 OPS. But Harrelson had that quality that New York fans always seem to love in small players: he was gritty and tough, at least on the field.

Harrelson was with the organization long enough to remember when, if guys dropped a pop-up in the infield, it was laughed off as just the ole' loveable, inept Mets. He hated that. Having grit his teeth and borne the ugly play of those early years, Harrelson earned his stripes as part of the Miracle Mets championship of 1969. Then, in 1973, he cemented his legacy in team history when he got into a scuffle with the Reds' Pete Rose after Rose slid hard into second base in Game Three of the 1973 NLCS.

History began repeating itself, though, after '73. The Mets did not make it back to the postseason again in the 1970s; by 1977, the team had fallen into disarray. Harrelson, like most Mets fans, was devastated when his teammate and friend Tom Seaver was sent to the Reds in the middle of the season. Buddy's turn out the door was not far behind. The Mets traded him to the Phillies just before the start of the '78 season and he finished out his career with two years in Philadelphia and one in Texas.

Shortly after his retirement, the Mets came calling. They asked Harrelson to manage in their minor league system; in 111 games at Class A, he was

67-44. Then, when third base coach Bobby Valentine took the manager's spot with Texas in 1985, Harrelson was called up to replace him. Buddy remained there right up until May 29, 1990, when Cashen informed him he would be taking over as club manager.

It was not an enviable position to be in. Harrelson inherited a clubhouse teeming with strife. Players were unhappy about contracts, about playing time, and, now, about their manager being fired. Many had come to distrust the front office. And while they liked Harrelson, there was an assumption that the front office had made him manager because he would be more inclined to enforce team rules that had gone by the wayside under Johnson.

Cashen had told the team he thought they were underperforming. He hoped a change in leadership would wake them up. But the team lost four of Harrelson's first five games as manager. The Mets were on the cusp of the longest summer the team had experienced since 1983. Then, on June 5, one day before Harrelson turned forty-six years old, the Mets showed some of that Amazin' magic.

Tom O'Malley was a journeyman infielder. In nine major league seasons, he played with six different teams. The last of them was the Mets. As he stepped to the plate in the bottom of the eleventh inning against the Expos' Dale Mohorcic, the Mets' season was on the brink. They were 21-26 and eight and a half games out of first. The team across town was playing some of its worst baseball in nearly eighty years. But it was the Mets' clubhouse that seemed to be a bigger mess. They needed a moment.

Up came O'Malley. As he dug into the box, O'Malley was just 2-22 on the season. He had appeared only as a pinch hitter or defensive replacement and had driven in just two runs. Before the first pitch Harrelson remarked that he would give back all his birthday presents the next day if O'Malley would hit a home run. O'Malley did just that, drilling the ball over the center-field fence for the win.

O'Malley's home run, the third to last of his career, propelled the Mets on a streak that overwhelmed their division. From June 5 to June 29, they won 20 out of 23 games, making up the entire deficit in the division and earning them a tie for first place. Gooden won four of those games. Strawberry, looking to show he was worth every penny he was asking for, went on a tear, raising his average from .256 to .300, hitting 9 home runs and driving in 25 runs.

The team stayed hot in July, going 17-11 and winning some memorable games in the process. On July 25, they led the Phillies 9–0 in the seventh inning and then 10–3 going into the bottom of the ninth. Philly started the inning with seven consecutive singles and a walk, making the score 10–8 and leaving the bases loaded with no outs for former Met Lenny Dykstra. Mets closer John Franco got Dykstra, who was leading the National League in batting average, to bounce into a double play, making the score 10–9 with a runner on third. Franco then gave up a line drive that seemed destined to tie the game. But shortstop Mario Diaz snared it, saving the game and the win. Bob Murphy, the Mets' legendary radio announcer, was so drained by the bottom of the ninth that he couldn't help but let out his exasperation. "And the Mets win the ballgame," said Murphy after Diaz caught the ball. "They win the damn thing by a score of 10–9!"

The next day the Mets were tied for first and the day after that they were up one game over the Pirates. In his first 56 games, Harrelson was 38-18 and now managing a first-place team. That is where they stood as news of George Steinbrenner's banishment broke out across baseball.

The Mets were still a competitive club on July 30, 1990. But as they had done multiple times over the past few seasons, they fell apart during the stretch run. A 16-14 August dropped them out of first. They were three and a half games out when the Pirates came to town for two games on September 12 and 13. Over 99,000 came out to watch the Mets win both, with Strawberry hitting a big three-run home run in the second game to give the Mets the lead for good. Two days later they were just a half-game out. It was the closest they would be to first place this late in the season for nearly the rest of the decade. Five straight losses all but ended the year. As they tried to claw their way back into first, Strawberry again came up with the usual assortment of injuries that kept him out of the lineup. In reality, the front office had made clear they were not going to bring him back in

1991. Seeing no reason to give his time and talent to an organization that did not appreciate it, Strawberry missed the last six games of the year.

The Mets were officially eliminated from playoff contention during their last home game of the season. Strawberry never showed his face to the crowd, even though he knew it was likely his last game as a Met at Shea. Franco, leading the league in saves, blew a ninth-inning lead. The fans, who had come to adore their Mets in the mid-'80s, had now grown tired of what they perceived as the underachieving, the turmoil, and the complaining. When Harrelson removed Franco in the middle of the inning, the fans booed him off the mound. Franco thought Harrelson had embarrassed him. On the last day of the 1990 season, many players openly discussed what they felt the Mets' shortcomings were.

"You have to have balance; this team is not balanced," said Ojeda. "When it goes into a power shortage, this team shuts down."[24]

"We played dispassionately in too many games," said Darling. "It's the nature of the ballclub. And we definitely didn't have a sheriff here. Certain things happened in the clubhouse and the dugout that should be policed by the team."[25]

It was no surprise that two of the most vocal critics were guys from the '86 championship team. But this was the Mets now. Boos. Embarrassment. Dispassion. Bitterness.

The Mets had taken over New York in part because they acquired stars like Hernandez and Carter. Even though both were no longer productive players, their banishment from New York signaled the beginning of the end of the city's being a Mets' town. Meanwhile, Dykstra and McDowell were in Philly. Mookie was in Toronto. Orosco was in Cleveland. Mitchell was in San Francisco. Backman was in Pittsburgh. Knight was retired.

The 1980s were over, literally and metaphorically.

5

Long Hair, Short Tempers

The Yankees' 1990 season got no better after Steinbrenner's banishment was announced. In September the A's swept them at home. Oakland took all twelve match-ups against the Yankees in 1990, becoming the first team in major league history to complete a season sweep of New York. In those twelve games, the A's outscored the Yankees 62–12. Throughout their entire history, the worst the Yankees had ever done in a season series against any team was two wins.

Then, on the final day of the regular season, Tigers first baseman Cecil Fielder was in town, sitting on 49 home runs for the year. To that point, only ten players had hit at least 50 in a single season and none had done it since George Foster in 1977. In the fourth, Fielder crushed a pitch from Yankees rookie Steve Adkins into the upper deck in left field, the final indignity of the Yankees' 1990 season. New York lost 10–3.

At 67-95, they were the worst team in the American League, finishing last for the first time since 1966. The team's offense was crippled by a lack of power and over-aggression at the plate. Outside of Jesse Barfield, no one walked more than 49 times during the entire season; the team's on-base percentage was an anemic .300, dead last in baseball. Their 603 runs scored were last in the American League and only slightly better than two other National League teams that had played without the benefit of a designated hitter.

"I think there are going to be major, major changes on this team," said Dave LaPoint, as he left the clubhouse that night.[1]

LaPoint was right. Change was coming to the Yankees. The biggest one had already occurred two months earlier. It was a parting gift from George Steinbrenner to the organization as his punishment took effect. That gift was Gene Michael. The Boss had installed Michael as general manager on August 20, his last day in charge. Michael, the former coach, team manager, and general manager, knew he was taking over a sinking ship. He also knew no quick fixes were going to save the Yankees. Instead, he had a plan for the long haul.

He had been moody, confrontational, and, when he had a few drinks in him, downright cruel to anyone in his line of sight. He was a less-than-stellar teammate. Many assumed he deliberately quit on them during the last week of the 1990 season. He had tried to fight Keith Hernandez. He threatened to fight Lee Mazzilli and Wally Backman. He yelled at Davey Johnson. He was fined multiple times for his seeming indifference to the rules. He was abusive toward his wife, even pulling a gun on her.

For all that, for everything Darryl Strawberry encompassed and for all the turmoil he had brought to the Mets over eight seasons, when he signed with the Dodgers on November 8, 1990, players and fans were crushed. The most talented player the Mets had ever put on the field—the franchise's all-time leader in home runs, RBIs, runs, walks, and slugging percentage—who had wanted nothing more than for ownership to simply show they appreciated him—jumped ship to a league rival that offered him the money he wanted, the appreciation he sought, and the love he craved.

"I kept saying, 'I'm having a great year. I am a valuable asset to this team. If you don't see that, other teams will. I'm walking.' And they kept replying, 'Well, okay, if that's how you feel. We're not really going to pursue you. If you want to go, go,'" wrote Strawberry of the Mets in his autobiography.[2]

The Amazins had grown tired of Strawberry and all that came with him. That was, in part, because they failed to understand the psychology of Darryl. They never grasped that Strawberry—like many children whose father or mother leaves—craved admiration and affection. That all he wanted to hear was that he had value. But Frank Cashen and upper management did not want to put up with the neediness anymore. And they likely had some inclination about where Strawberry's career was about to go.

Asked about Strawberry's signing with the Dodgers, Cashen made clear that he had no regrets about the decision. "I don't say that you can replace that kind of talent overnight, but I think that we have enough resources to win without Darryl and I think we have a chance to even be a better team and organization within a couple of years than if we were with him," said Cashen.[3]

"Oh my god," said Dave Magadan, when he heard the news.[4] Doc Gooden laid blame on the Mets for not being more willing to sign a deal with Strawberry during the season. Fans flooded sports talk radio to complain about the organization letting their premier player go.

Meanwhile, in Los Angeles, Strawberry was all smiles. He had signed the second-largest contract in baseball history and his new manager and teammates could not gush enough about how excited they were to have him. And, perhaps most importantly, he was going back home to LA. Surely, back in the comfort of his familiar surroundings, he would finally receive the love and adulation he never felt he got in eight seasons in New York. Instead, signing with the Dodgers turned into the worst decision of Strawberry's career and perhaps his life.

While players and fans were disconsolate over the departure of Strawberry, Mets brass was already looking ahead. They were happy to be rid of the moody, unpredictable outfielder. Still, they were fully aware that the lineup now had a huge hole in it. In terms of raw offensive production, there was no player on the market who could replace Strawberry's home runs or sheer intimidation factor. And the Mets no longer had the minor league talent to barter a deal for some other team's top offensive producer.

The organization's offensive mindset, for years, had been power-focused. Without Strawberry, that had to change. They were going to need a new way to score runs. That way was speed. The Mets were going to use the running game to boost their offensive production and, hopefully, fill the hole left by Darryl's departure. But who would provide that speed? Howard Johnson could steal a base or two, but not enough to be the deciding factor in the Mets' offense. Same for Gregg Jefferies. Keith Miller and Daryl Boston could swipe a bag when needed, but they were not full-time players. The Mets needed a new addition. Four weeks after losing Strawberry to the Dodgers, they got one.

Vince Coleman had taken the National League by storm as a rookie with the Cardinals in 1985. The left fielder easily won the league's Rookie of the Year Award after leading baseball with 110 steals, the third-highest single-season total of any player in the modern era. He stole 107 the next year and 109 the year after that, becoming the only player in baseball history to steal over 100 bases in three straight seasons. Moreover, Coleman had terrorized the Mets, successfully stealing his first 57 attempted bases against them until finally being thrown out in June 1990. Only Rickey Henderson brought more excitement to the game when he got on base than Coleman.

A free agent after six seasons in St. Louis, Coleman received an offer from the Cardinals, who wanted him back at the top of their lineup. But Coleman became hesitant to re-sign after St. Louis traded Willie McGee late in the 1990 season. When his friend Terry Pendleton ended up signing with the Braves, Coleman was all but certain he would not be heading back. The Mets swooped in, giving him a four-year deal worth $11.9 million. It was the largest contract the organization had ever given anyone in their history. It was also, somewhat shockingly, only the sixth time the Mets had ever signed a free agent and the first time they had signed one in nine years. Throughout the 1980s Cashen had built his team around early draft picks, shrewd trades, and maintaining key players through long-term deals. But with Al Harazin now sharing control of team operations and Joe McIlvaine having left to become general manager for the San Diego Padres the old ways of shunning the free agent market were done. The Mets were averaging nearly three million in attendance over the last four years; they had money to spend. Not the kind of money the Yankees had, but still enough to begin investing in free agents.

"The price was steep," said Harazin of the Coleman signing. "But we understand that we had to pay premium to get Vince. We certainly feel this player is worth it to us."[5]

It was an exciting moment for the club, but there were certainly risks. Coleman was not a prototypical lead-off hitter. He walked at a respectable rate, but not nearly the amount hoped for in a guy with his speed.

Coleman's career average the day he signed with the Mets was also just .265. He hit with almost no power and, while this was not really his role, drove in few runners. Moreover, while he led the league in steals for each of his first six seasons, his totals had dropped from 109 in 1987 to 77 in a 1990 season where he lost time to an injury. Still, the Mets were hopeful he could provide a spark in Queens come April 1991.

Now that Coleman was signed, Harazin made clear he had a few more pieces of unfinished business: further dismantling the remnants of the 1986 team. Bob Ojeda was next.

"A lot of clubs are interested [in Ojeda]," said Harazin, after the Coleman announcement. "Ron Darling and Kevin Elster, too. We'll see."[6] Ojeda had lost his spot with the club. Harrelson had moved him to the bullpen during the '90 season, mostly in mop-up duty. Angry over his situation, Ojeda requested a trade late in the year. With the rotation and bullpen remaining largely the same going into '91, there was no role on the team for the lefty, so the Mets were happy to oblige his request. A week and a half after signing Coleman, the team traded Ojeda to Los Angeles. In return they brought back an old fan favorite in Hubie Brooks, the right-handed outfielder who had been traded six years earlier as part of the Gary Carter deal. Brooks was coming off one of his best offensive seasons, having hit 20 home runs and driven in 91 for the Dodgers. Still, Brooks and Coleman's combined 1990 Wins above Replacement (WAR), a measure of how many wins a player contributes to his team versus a replacement-level player at that same position, was 4.2. Strawberry had a 6.5 WAR for 1990. The two combined would not replace Strawberry, but, the Mets hoped, they would certainly help.

The Mets then essentially ended their off-season. They signed catcher and former three-time Yankee Rick Cerone to serve as a backup to Charlie O'Brien and Mackey Sasser. But that was it. The 1991 Mets would largely resemble the 1990 Mets, but now with a focus on speed over power. That said, as they headed into spring training, they still had to resolve some internal contract issues that threatened to linger over the entire season.

Gooden had one year remaining on his contract and was facing, to him at least, a similar situation as his recently departed friend Darryl. Gooden wanted to be the highest-paid player in the game. Like Strawberry, he wanted money *and* respect. Gooden had put asses in the seats at Shea for seven years now. Yes, he had missed time to rehab from drugs and alcohol. Yes, he had missed time because of injuries. But Gooden was coming off a season in which he'd gone 19-7, finished fourth in the Cy Young Award voting, and put up his best numbers since his '85 performance. He was still among the most feared pitchers in baseball, even if his curve wasn't as crisp or his fastball as blazing.

Doc had the benefit of looking for a contract extension at the same time the game's most dominant pitcher was getting one. Boston's Roger Clemens signed a four-year extension that February worth $5.385 million a year. It could be argued who the better pitcher was and, in essence, who deserved a bigger contract, but as far as Gooden was concerned, he was that person.

The Mets brass did not necessarily agree. Though they did not treat Gooden in the same manner as Strawberry, whom they seemed relieved to be rid of despite his offensive prowess, early discussions about an extension went poorly. The numbers put forward by the Mets were not what Gooden wanted to hear, while the numbers put forward by Gooden were not something the Mets could accept, especially with Frank Viola also looking for an extension and David Cone just two seasons away from free agency. Things were so bad that, at the start of spring training, Gooden all but declared that he was done as a Met the second his contract was up.

Ultimately, with days to go before the season started, cooler heads prevailed and both sides were able to work out a deal. Gooden got a three-year extension, to begin after the '91 season, that paid $5.15 million a year. It was just below Clemens's deal, but an incentive in the contract would give Gooden an extra $750,000 if he pitched over five hundred innings during the entirety of the extension, and that would be enough to make Doc the highest-paid player in the game.

Despite the contention during negotiations, both sides were all smiles when the deal was announced. "He will be the best-paid player in the National League," said Harazin. "In general, it's a unique contract for a unique player. If there's one player who is the heart and soul of our ball-club, it's Doc Gooden."[7]

Gooden would be a Met for at least four more years. Fresh off his new extension, he would take the ball for Opening Day at Shea against the Phillies.

That left Frank Viola. The left-hander had been the team ace in 1990, leading the league in innings pitched, winning twenty games, and finishing third in Cy Young voting. A free agent after the '91 season, unlike Gooden, Viola was not asking for the richest contract in baseball. But he was pretty close. Around the same time they were finalizing their deal with Gooden, the Mets offered Viola an additional three years at $4.33 million a year. Viola wanted four years but was willing to drop that demand to three if the Mets would pay him $5 million a year. The Mets balked. There would be no $5 million a year for Viola, who at that point was thirty-one years old and coming off bone spurs in his left elbow. Two days before the season started, both sides announced there would be no further negotiations.

"We were not able to get a deal done and no new offer was put forward by the Mets," said Viola's agent. "Thus, Frank will play out the last year of his contract and file for free agency. He will go out this season and do what he's paid to do: he'll pitch."

Cashen, meanwhile, made clear that the Mets were not willing to spend the extra money on Viola if it meant not being able to hold on to Cone when his contract was up the next year. "You can't go out and sign everybody," Cashen said. "You have to pick and choose."[8]

Both sides acted like it was just business, but Viola was now another Strawberry: a top line player upset that management did not think enough of him to pay him his perceived value. Like Strawberry, he would play out the year in New York then take his talents elsewhere in 1992. Viola would not be the only unhappy player in the clubhouse in 1991. By season's end discontent would spread like a cancer to nearly everyone on the team. But that would come later. As the Mets took the field on Opening Day in 1991, there was hope, based on seven straight seasons of playoff chases, that there would be postseason baseball again in Queens that fall.

The Yankees were in shambles. Their owner had been banished for paying for damaging information about one of his star players. Their most beloved and most popular player was coming off the worst season of his career and dealing with a back injury that left his future in serious doubt. The clubhouse was filled with players angry about either their own personal situation or the state of the team. Meanwhile, the Blue Jays traded shortstop Tony Fernandez and first baseman Fred McGriff to the Padres for All-Star second baseman Roberto Alomar and outfielder Joe Carter. The Red Sox signed power-hitting Jack Clark. The Tigers signed slugger Rob Deer and traded for power-hitting catcher Mickey Tettleton.

Each of those moves bolstered the offense of teams that were already offensively strong. The Yankees, however, had one of the least offensively impressive teams in the league in 1990 and had made no moves to improve it going into 1991. That was, in part, because most free agents still wanted nothing to do with them, even if Steinbrenner had been banished. It was also because the Yankees had little left in their farm system to trade and the few pieces they did have Gene Michael refused to part ways with. He was not going to gamble away the team's future for the possibility—but no guarantee—of short-term team success. And so the Yankees headed into 1991 fielding nearly the exact same team offensively as they did in 1990. It was a team of little power, little patience, and little outcome.

The two biggest moves of the off-season were both pitchers. Scott Sanderson, a thirteen-year veteran who had won seventeen games for the AL champion A's in 1990, was purchased from Oakland. Steve Farr, a reliable reliever for years with the Royals, was signed to replace Dave Righetti as the team's closer. Righetti, the senior member of the club, had grown leery of the sideshow that was the Yankees and of his uncertain future with the club. Robert Nederlander, acting as general partner in Steinbrenner's absence, wanted to give Rags a four-year deal, fearing what would happen if a long-term, beloved Yankee left town. Michael did not let sentimentality cloud his judgment. He wasn't going to rule this club that way anymore, signing or bringing back players just because they were liked or had some sort of personal history with the Yankees. If he didn't think you were going to contribute to the team's future, you weren't going to be on the team.

Michael was willing to give Righetti a two-year deal at most, believing the pitcher had little left. Before the offer could be formally made, Righetti signed with the Giants, had one more year as an effective relief pitcher, and retired after the 1995 season. Farr filled Righetti's void, but his signing was more than just that. Farr, quiet but intense, had won a championship with the Royals in 1985 and knew what it was like to play for both quality teams and poor teams. He hated losing. If he failed to perform, his postgame anger was not about the impact to his personal stats, but to the team. It was a qualification that was lacking in many of the current Yankees. Farr was essentially the first, but not the last, of many signings and trades Michael engineered that were geared not just toward improving the quality of the team, but the character.

Michael made other modifications that, while providing little short-term benefit to the team, gave every indication of where he wanted the club to go in the years ahead. Left-hand-hitting outfielder Oscar Azocar, who hit .350 with 4 home runs and 11 RBIs in his first 20 major league games, had no plate discipline. It took 129 plate appearances before he drew his first big league walk; until that point, he actually had an on-base percentage lower than his batting average, a near impossibility after so many plate appearances. He drew only one more walk in 218 total plate appearances that year; not surprisingly, his offensive numbers sank as pitchers discovered they could get Azocar out by throwing anything even remotely close to the plate. Azocar was the epitome of a Yankee team that swung at nearly everything with no tangible results to show for it. In December 1990 Michael traded him to the Padres for a player to be named later.

In February Michael released Dave LaPoint. Just about everyone on the team loved LaPoint for his clubhouse antics and goofy nature. But since signing with the Yankees in December 1988 he had failed to materialize as the team hoped, yielding a 1.5 WHIP over two seasons and walking nearly as many hitters as he struck out. The Yankees tried to trade him, but "we couldn't get anyone to take him," Michael bluntly told *Newsday*.[9] Perhaps Steinbrenner would have kept LaPoint on the team, refusing to concede his signing wasn't working out. But Michael was willing to let LaPoint go and fill his spot with someone from the minor leagues if it came to that. The Yankees were no longer going to keep people around just because. Post-release, LaPoint started two more big league games before calling it a career.

These were small moves that ultimately had little discernible impact on the team in 1991 but gave every indication that Michael was set on taking the Yankees in a different direction. That became even clearer when, on the second day of workouts during spring training, Stump Merrill announced that Don Mattingly would serve as the Yankees' tenth team captain.

The announcement made perfect sense to those on the club. Mattingly wasn't boisterous. Despite some public spats with Steinbrenner, he generally refrained from adding to the craziness of the clubhouse. His teammates respected him for his quiet leadership and ability to wade through the daily bullshit that was now a staple of the team. Moreover, with The Boss out of the way, the team was going to leave a little more room for error with their younger players, giving them time to grow and, hopefully, flourish in the Bronx. They were going to need someone on the field to help them adjust to playing in New York.

"Who else could you name captain?" asked Randy Velarde, himself now a senior member of the team despite having been a Yankee only since 1987. "When you think of the Yankees, who do you think of? Don Mattingly."[10]

Mattingly was also in the first year of a five-year, $19.3 million contract extension. The deal had been made before Mattingly's back robbed him of two months of the 1990 season. But whether Steinbrenner was in the owner's box or not, a New York player making that kind of money was going to be expected to step up. Not only would Mattingly have to lead the team, but he would also have to show that the back injury wasn't going to keep him from being a productive player.

"This year is more challenging because a lot of things are up in the air, a lot of people are saying what I can and can't do," said Mattingly, at the announcement of his being named captain. "I've got a lot to prove—mainly that I can stay healthy—and the only way I can do it is out on the field."[11]

The new captain would do what he could to guide the team's younger players, but Merrill was still running the ship. Perhaps the biggest question—bigger than Mattingly's back or the team pitching or if the youth movement would bear any fruit—was whether Stump would last the entire season. No Yankees manager had done so since 1987 and, even without Steinbrenner in charge, the Yankees seemed destined for the kind of year that could put Merrill's job in jeopardy early.

On Opening Day Gooden held the Phillies to just one run in eight innings, thrilling the crowd of 49,276 with flashes of the old Doc. Coleman doubled in his first Met at bat and then scored the first run of the year when Jefferies doubled him home. In the fourth, Harrelson rolled the dice on a double steal that worked perfectly, with the newly acquired Brooks swiping home for the eventual winning run. Fate smiled again on the Mets the next day. After being held to just three hits over the first eight innings, Cerone took Roger McDowell deep in the bottom of the ninth inning for a game-tying home run, the first home run McDowell allowed to a right-handed batter since April 1988. Then in the bottom of the tenth, in a moment reminiscent of Gary Carter on Opening Day in 1985, Brooks hit a game-winning home run to left. In his first two games back in New York, Hubie was 3-7, had stolen home, and hit a walk-off home run.

"I'm not feeling the weight," said Brooks after the game, when asked about the pressure of replacing Strawberry.[12] Still, he was under no illusion that two games would seal his relationship with the fans. "Things will change on you. It's a long season."[13] That quote would sum up the '91 season like no other.

Questions about the potency of the Mets' offense, the worst of any team during spring training, were answered when the team scored 21 runs and took three out of four games from the Expos. Though they dropped four of six games to the Pirates, a team they were most likely going to be chasing again for first place, they ended April at 12-8, one game out of first. Gooden was making the Mets hopeful about his contract extension, posting a 3-1 record and 2.43 ERA for the month. Viola was even more impressive, going 3-0 with a .086 ERA and showing the Mets that he was worth every penny of the extension he wanted from them.

There were some warning signs, though. Jefferies, after a solid 1990 season, started the year hitting just .192 with only four extra-base hits. Coleman was stealing bases but hitting just .219 with an anemic .301 slugging. Kevin McReynolds, without whose offensive production the Mets could not ultimately succeed, hit .128 with just a single home run and only six runs driven in for the month. Still, the Mets were only a game out of first; even if pieces of the offense weren't moving at full speed, they were more exciting than their struggling crosstown rivals. And on May 7, the most anticipated moment of the season was coming to Shea. It would not disappoint.

The Yankees opened the season in Detroit. While some positions were determined with certainty, third base was a question mark among Mike Blowers, Randy Velarde, and Torey Lovullo. Left field was up for grabs between Hensley Meulens and Mel Hall. Three men—Matt Nokes, Bob Geren, and Jim Leyritz—were vying for playing time at catcher. And only the release of Steve Balboni, just before the start of the season, prevented the team from having three players for first base and DH. Even with the positions that were set, a bevy of questions remained. Would Mattingly's power return? Would it be the Steve Sax of 1989, who hit .315, or the Steve Sax of 1990, who hit .260? Would Kevin Maas continue his power streak or would the league's pitchers figure him out?

The starting rotation was an even bigger question. Would Tim Leary rebound from a nineteen-loss season? Which Andy Hawkins would show up, the one released with an 8.56 ERA the previous June, or the one who gave up just two earned runs in 19⅔ innings in his first two July starts? Would Dave Eiland and Chuck Cary become reliable starters? Could Pascual Pérez return and provide meaningful innings? And in the bullpen, could Farr fill the shoes of Righetti as the team closer?

If Opening Day could provide one encompassing answer to all those questions, then the answer appeared to have been no. Leary coughed up a 4–2 lead in the fifth inning. The Yankees squandered two late-game opportunities, the bullpen could not keep the Tigers in check, and the Yankees lost on Opening Day for the first time in six years.

There was a flash of mild hope the next afternoon, though. On a bitterly cold day at Tiger Stadium, Sanderson made his Yankee debut. The thirteen-year veteran starter had played nearly his entire career in the National League before jumping to the A's in 1990. In Oakland he enjoyed possibly his best season, becoming a core part of a pitching staff that brought the A's to the World Series. Armed with a slower-than-slow looping curve, the Yankees signed Sanderson to anchor a starting rotation whose five main pitchers—in a time when wins were still considered a top measure of a starting pitcher's value—won only 32 games in 127 starts in 1990.

Before he could throw a pitch, though, Sanderson stepped in controversy. For years, he had maintained a policy of not talking to female reporters in the clubhouse. Outside the clubhouse he had no problem giving an interview or responding to questions. But inside? That was a nonstarter. Sanderson felt, morally, that women should not be present where men were undressing and vice versa. While Sanderson claimed that many female reporters better understood his feelings after he explained them in person, the notion that a woman could not handle a guy being naked somewhere in her immediate vicinity did not sit well with some. Certainly Suzyn Waldman, the team clubhouse reporter for wfan, could handle it.

Sanderson had long maintained his policy but it drew renewed attention in New York, not least because Waldman was an established and respected presence in the clubhouse, having taken a considerable amount of sexist, macho nonsense along the way to get there. Confronted with pressure he had not faced in Oakland, Chicago, or Montreal, Sanderson had already agreed to modify his position slightly by talking inside the clubhouse but away from his teammates. The whole thing was an ominous sign for the distractions Merrill was going to deal with that year.

The focus shifted from off the field to on the field when Sanderson took the mound for the first time as a Yankee and proceeded to hold the Tigers hitless through eight innings. At 119 pitches and in frigid weather, Sanderson could barely feel the baseball, comparing it to "throwing ice cubes."[14]

Cold or not, Sanderson, who grew up just miles away from Tiger Stadium in Dearborn, knew he was flirting with history. Rather than observe baseball norms and not mention the active no-hitter, he openly talked about it on the bench with other pitchers. With winds now gusting at nearly thirty miles per hour, Sanderson's first pitch of the ninth was hit high in the air to right field by Tony Phillips. The wind pushed Phillips's drive farther and farther toward the wall. Jesse Barfield went to his right, then quickly pivoted back to his left and in that turn most likely lost sight of the ball. It struck the wall just out of the reach of Barfield's glove for a double.

"I was battling the wind and sun," said Barfield. "On a normal day, it's an easy out, but this isn't a normal day."[15] Sanderson came out of the game with an eight-inning one-hitter and the Yankees won, 4–0.

The next two weeks of the season, however, were void of additional highlights. The team lost their first three series of the year, split a series with the Royals, then dropped the first game of a two-game spot against the Tigers at home.

Meanwhile, Mattingly did not ease concerns about his back. Though he began the year with a seven-game hitting streak and was batting .294 going into their April 23 game against the Tigers, 14 of his 15 hits were singles. April had never been his strongest month, but there were doubts that Mattingly could regain the form that had made him baseball's best all-around hitter for six years.

A small measure of relief came in his first at bat of the April 23 game. Facing lefty Frank Tanana, Mattingly swatted a fastball down the line in right where it landed just over the wall. By no means a majestic shot—it probably would not have been a home run in any other ballpark—it got a huge monkey off Mattingly's back. It had been 312 at bats since his last home run. In a show of appreciation, the sparse crowd of under fifteen thousand gave the team captain a standing ovation.

The Yankees won that game but, on May 1, they suffered the indignity of being on the wrong end of history. It was the bottom of the fourth inning of their second of two games against the A's in Oakland. Standing on second base was former Yankee Rickey Henderson.

Rickey was two years removed from his time in New York and, by all accounts, better off for having been traded back to the A's. He captured the 1989 ALCS MVP on the way to winning his first World Series ring. Then in 1990 he took home the AL MVP, while leading the league for a tenth time in stolen bases. Now, as he took his lead off second base, Henderson was focused on an even bigger prize. He stood at 938 career stolen bases, tied for the most all-time with Lou Brock. Henderson had been promising that he would break the record against his old team and the fates—which included missing half of April with a calf injury—had lined up to allow him to keep that promise. Henderson took his lead off second and broke for third. Catcher Matt Nokes's throw bounced as Henderson slid head first into the bag and into history.

Luckily for the Yankees, and especially for Merrill and Michael, Steinbrenner was not around to witness the moment. The Boss despised it when his team was on the wrong end of history. And this moment, accomplished by a former Yankee, would no doubt have caused an epic outburst. Even more depressing for the Yankees, they lost, making it sixteen straight defeats to Oakland going back to 1989. They dropped four of the remaining six games on the West Coast and returned home 8-16, in dead last.

As soon as they got back to New York, the Yankees gave Hawkins his release. Just two years removed from being called the staff "anchor," Hawkins was 0-2 with a 9.95 ERA in four appearances, having allowed 29 runners in fewer than 13 innings. It was only May 10, but 8 of the 13 pitchers who started at least one game for New York in 1990 were now either no longer with the Yankees or out with an injury.

Replacing Hawkins on the roster was left-handed relief pitcher Steve Howe, who hadn't appeared in the majors since 1987 due to a series of suspensions for drug use. Howe, a chatterbox who to that point was also the last man to throw a pitch in a World Series game at Yankee Stadium, had thrown eighteen scoreless innings in the minors that year. He would bolster what was becoming the Yankees' only strength: their bullpen.

The clubhouse, meanwhile, continued to be a den of unhappiness. Looking like he was about to face another long, losing season, Mattingly made his despair clear before the first game of the next home stand. "We're on a road to nowhere," said Mattingly. "It's depressing."[16]

Things felt so bad that the captain, who had openly quarreled with Steinbrenner over the years, lamented his absence, saying The Boss would be doing something, anything, to change the team's course. Mattingly then noted that the team didn't just need to end its losing streak against the A's that night, but they had to make a statement in that series.

In a moment long since forgotten, Mattingly set the example. Down 3–2 in the seventh, he hit a two-run home run to give the Yankees the lead. When Maas followed with another home run, an exultant Mattingly could be seen with arms raised, shouting in the dugout. They beat the A's that night, ending the nightmarish losing streak, and took three of four from Oakland, with Mattingly going 5-14 with 5 RBIs in the series. After stumbling against the Angels and Mariners, the Yankees took four in a row and moved out of last place.

The boos started as soon as he walked out of the dugout, his first time ever on the field at Shea Stadium as a visiting player. He took his stance in the familiar left-handed batter's box and began swatting medium-speed fast-balls over the right field fence. The crowd had seen it hundreds, perhaps thousands, of times before, but never had they booed him when he was doing it. But now, as Darryl Strawberry returned to New York for the first time since signing with the Dodgers, he was Public Enemy Number One to Mets fans. They understood that ownership had not made a full-fledged effort to re-sign him. They understood that if he'd received the love he so desperately sought he would probably still be playing right field for the home team. But as is so often the case when a star player leaves the team he came up with, the fans turned on him mercilessly.

It had hardly been the Hollywood story Strawberry had hoped for in his first month with Los Angeles. The team was fighting to stay at .500 and his offensive struggles were partly to blame. In 24 games leading up to his first away game at Shea, Darryl had managed only a single home run with an OPS of just .665. Hubie Brooks's OPS, meanwhile, stood at .698. Strawberry was pressing. The question now was would the pressure of going back to New York make him press even harder or would it awaken the competitor and produce the kind of game-changing player the Dodgers thought they signed.

As double the normal Shea Stadium press contingent watched his every move, Strawberry's first two at bats proved inconclusive. Boos continued to rain down on him when he flied out to center in the first inning and then to the warning track in right center in the fourth. When he took the field in the bottom of the first, the chants of "Dar-ryl! Dar-ryl!" that Red Sox fans had popularized during the '86 World Series emerged from the stands with giddiness. When Straw, as he had done in Boston, gestured to the crowd to keep it coming, they gladly indulged him. The Mets built up a quick 6–0 lead, seemingly taking the drama out of the day's events.

But in the sixth, with one on and two out, when Viola tried to sneak a first-pitch fastball past Strawberry he drilled it over the wall in deep left center field. Almost immediately, most of the crowd of 47,744—the third-largest crowd at Shea that year—began cheering their former hero, as if the boos of the pregame and first five innings plus had all just been some standard ball busting among friends. As Strawberry stood at the top step of the dugout, receiving congratulations from his teammates, manager Tommy Lasorda, perhaps worried for his player's safety, grabbed hold of Darryl's elbow and began yanking him into the dugout.

Down 6–3 in the ninth, the Dodgers made it 6–4 when another old friend from the '86 team, Gary Carter, doubled in a run. Back-to-back singles brought Strawberry up with two runners on, two out, and the Dodgers now down just a run. The moment was set. The slugger, shunned by penny-pinching owners who never appreciated him, returns with his new team and delivers the home run that beats his adversaries.

But it didn't happen. Perhaps overanxious, Strawberry swung at the first pitch and grounded out softly to third base, ending the game and sending fans home both elated over the victory yet pondering how wonderful it could have been to see Darryl pull it off. For Strawberry, the game invigorated him.

"Coming here put an extra kick in me," he told reporters after the game. "When I was up at the plate, the crowd was really into it."[17]

Perhaps it was the rush of playing back in New York or maybe it was just the normal course of events for a notoriously slow starter, but Strawberry's offensive numbers began to climb after the Dodgers left New York. He missed some time in June with an injury but, by season's end, his numbers were typical Darryl Strawberry numbers as the Dodgers missed out on the postseason by a single game. It was the last full season Darryl Strawberry would ever play.

Mike Blowers, who had won the starting job at third base out of spring training and homered on Opening Day in Detroit, had yet to drive in a run since then. Gene Michael's patience was greater than Steinbrenner's, but he had seen enough and traded Blowers to the Mariners. That left a hole at third base that no one had stepped up to fill. Michael brought up

Pat Kelly, a slick-fielding second baseman with speed, perhaps the best bunting ability in the organization, when that was still considered an asset, and what many hoped would one day be an above average bat. But the Yankees already had a second baseman, and an All-Star one at that, in Steve Sax. Yes, Sax was struggling at the plate early in 1991, but he was still the team's lone All-Star the previous season and a respected veteran around the league.

Despite all that, the Yankees decided to move Sax to third base and put Kelly at second. Sax had played all of two games at that position in his entire career; his discomfort was evident in the three errors he made in just five games there after Kelly joined the team. Many felt the move was ridiculous. Mattingly publicly called out the organization in a scene that would become more common as the season progressed. After a week Sax moved back to second and Kelly shifted to third. But it was clear that Michael was pushing toward a youth movement. So long as Kelly was not a complete bust in his rookie season, Sax was on his way out.

Kelly was playing his second game at third base when the rival Red Sox came to town on Memorial Day for the start of a three-game series. Boston, the defending American League East champions, were again sitting at the top of the division and had a 5–0 lead after four and a half innings. What looked like a dreary holiday ballgame grew more interesting when Barfield homered in the fifth and then Mel Hall and Barfield both homered in the seventh. Boston was up 5–3 in the bottom of the ninth when Red Sox ace closer Jeff Reardon took the mound. Reardon, climbing his way up the all-time saves list and having converted 14 of his 15 save opportunities that season, gave up consecutive singles to start the inning. Hall stepped up as the winning run. In the dugout, Steve Howe sat next to a despondent Dave Eiland, who had given up all five runs to Boston, his head down. Don't worry, Howe told him, Hall was going to hit a three-run home run.

No sooner had Howe said it when Reardon hung a breaking ball and Hall crushed it into the right-field stands, the ball smashing off the facing of the mezzanine. Hall, immediately after contact, lifted his arms in triumph.

The Yankees' marketing department had come up with a slogan that season, one that graced the cover of the team's yearbook: "At any moment, a great moment." Meant to play off the team's decades of history, the notion seemed rather humorous given their recent downfall. But Hall's home run exemplified the idea the Yankees were hoping to convey. Despite their slide into irrelevance, which dampened the long-standing rivalry with Boston, the home run unleashed the Stadium's 32,369 fans, who reveled in defeating the Red Sox, and in such a crushing manner. In the clubhouse the team celebration resembled one that might be seen after clinching a postseason berth.

"Suddenly Yankee Stadium is loud and lively," wrote *Newsday*'s Jon Heyman. "Suddenly the Yankees are hitting and winning and fun to watch. And suddenly the prospect of a long and dreary Bronx summer isn't nearly so certain."[18]

The majesty of that moment would be ruined, however, by two things. The first was the ultimate performance of the Yankees over the course of the season. The second would not be known for some time, at least not publicly. In the same yearbook that touted the team's slogan there was a section showing the players with their families and, in some cases, their girlfriends. One such picture showed a smiling Hall, dressed in a black tux with a color-splashed bowtie, his arms around the waist of a clearly younger woman in a black dress, with white flowers scattered across the front. On her left arm sat a corsage. It looked like a picture you might see at a high school couple take at the prom. And that's what it was. The individual in the picture was a seventeen-year-old girl that Hall had been seeing for two years. In fact, Hall had moved into her family's home, crashing on a couch in the living room despite making over $1 million a year. Hall had overwhelmed the girl and her family with gifts and the allure of being around a New York Yankee. Who wouldn't want a New York Yankee living in their home?

The truth was that Hall was a sexual predator, preying on underage girls and using his fame and wealth to get close to them. He had always been deemed eccentric, brash, and outspoken. During the 1990 season, Hall loudly expressed his displeasure over not playing full time in a memorable tirade that ended with his slamming and breaking pieces of the door to Merrill's office. He was always fuel to the fire of an unhappy clubhouse, never the one trying to provide calm. Perhaps the only moment of levity he contributed that entire season was when he brought his two pet mountain lion cubs into the clubhouse one day. The animals were confiscated from Hall at the end of the season, and he was arrested and fined for possessing potentially dangerous animals and importing wildlife without a permit.

Many teammates felt Hall was weird, and not in a quirky way. They shook their heads at the tremendous amounts of money he spent, seemingly erasing his entire paycheck the moment he got it. And many looked askance at the yearbook prom photo but did not question it. Hall's criminal behavior continued for years after his career was over, until, finally, several women stepped forward and brought charges against him. He was convicted of aggravated sexual assault of a child and indecency with a child and sent to prison, where he will remain until at least 2031.

On May 27, 1991, none of that was yet known. Hall was a hero to Yankee fans and his teammates. He had seemingly overcome the ego trip that had made him nearly unbearable in 1990. Given a chance to play, he was letting his bat do the talking, leading the team in RBIs and keeping any displeasure about his playing time to himself.

Meanwhile, over a two-week stretch in June, the Yankees attempted something they had not done with any success for at least a decade: they turned their starting rotation over to the youth movement and tried to develop, rather than purchase, the future. Outside of Sanderson, Yankees starters had been abysmal. Leary was 3-5 with a 5.24 ERA. Chuck Cary, a lefty who had shown signs of hope in '90, was dealing with arm injuries that limited his effectiveness. At 1-6 with 5.85 ERA, he had only one more appearance left in his Yankee career. Eiland was 1-3 and landed on the disabled list after his May 27 start against Boston. Pascual Pérez, the flamboyant righty who once missed a major league start because he got lost heading to the stadium, returned on May 14 after a yearlong injury. He yielded only 9 hits in 17⅔ innings over three starts; in his fourth appearance, he threw five pitches and left with a shoulder injury. He did not appear in a game again until August 16.

The Yankees needed help, so they dipped into their minor league system and brought up three pitchers: Wade Taylor, Jeff Johnson, and Scott Kamieniecki. History was not on the Yankees' side. During the course of the 1980s, despite having a remarkable level of talent in their system, the team had promoted sixteen starting pitchers who made their first major league start for New York: none won more than sixteen career games for the team. That was due in large part to Steinbrenner's lack of patience. But now that he was out of the picture, Michael was going to be far more patient with prospective talent. The Yankees were hoping these three pitchers represented the future; they were going to give them as long as possible to find out.

When Taylor, the first to make his debut, started off with 5⅓ strong innings and a victory against the Brewers on June 2, the talk coming out of the stadium was more enthusiastic than it had been in years.

"Could he be a No.1?" asked pitching coach Mark Connor. "I don't like to put labels on guys, but he reminds me of [reigning NL Cy Young Award Winner Doug] Drabek, and Drabek is a No. 1 pitcher."[19]

Born in Mobile, Taylor spent his youth in Alabama, then in Houston, Texas, when his father was transferred for work, then he moved back to Mobile again when his dad was transferred back. After some junior college ball, during which he was twice drafted but never signed, he transferred to the University of Miami and played there a year before inking a deal with the Mariners. He played half a season of rookie ball with Ken Griffey Jr. in Bellingham, Washington, before a trade brought him to the Yankees. Now here was the righty with the thick Alabamian drawl walking off the mound at Yankee Stadium to "a joyous ovation, as if the crowd that came to the Stadium had found itself a new Yankees hero."[20]

Taylor's win brought the Yankees to within four games of first place, closer than their crosstown rivals were to the lead in the National League East. That fact did not go unnoticed.

"There was no sense looking at the standings a few weeks ago," said Roberto Kelly. "But now we're getting close."[21]

Three days later lefty Jeff Johnson made his debut against the Blue Jays. Though he took the loss, he retired 12 of the last 13 hitters he faced, providing a glimmer of hope for the future. Following Johnson's loss, they swept a three-game series against the Rangers, the last game featuring dramatic game-tying and game-winning home runs from Mattingly and Pat Kelly, respectively. The Yankees were now just three and a half games out of first and somehow, someway, playing more exciting baseball than the Mets.

On June 18 the last of the trio made his debut when Scott Kamieniecki took the mound at SkyDome in Toronto. The twenty-seven-year-old rookie—he was only one year younger than three-time Cy Young Award winner Roger Clemens—was a Michigan native with a degree from the University of Michigan. His path to the big leagues had been impeded due to shoulder tendinitis as well as an inability to control his emotions on the mound. But on June 8, in a start for Columbus, he struck out fourteen against only one walk, impressing Michael enough that he decided it was time for Kamieniecki to join the big leagues.

The Wolverine responded by going six innings, giving up only two runs and picking off two runners, earning a win in his debut. The impressive debuts of all three gave the Yankees reason to hope. On July 7 the youth movement continued, this time on offense, when the team called up promising young outfielder Bernie Williams.

Expectations for Bernie were high. A native of Vega Alta, Puerto Rico, Williams caught the attention of Yankee scouts at age fifteen, thanks to his speed and pleasant demeanor. Shy and reserved, Williams often seemed, even at a young age, as if he would rather be playing the guitar than baseball. This apparent aloofness masked a strong determination to succeed at the game. Bernie did not, and did not need to, think about baseball twenty-four hours a day. When the time came, he came to play. The Yankees were impressed. They were also fearful that they would lose Williams to another team if they waited until he was old enough to legally sign with them. So, in essence, they kidnapped him by sending him to a baseball academy in the months leading up to his seventeenth birthday. Bernie became a Yankee in September 1985.

Williams did not tear through the minor leagues. However, the team hierarchy was drawn to a few things. Bernie was using his speed to steal bases, 117 in his first four minor league seasons, and he was getting on base, a lot. His .409 OBP at AA Albany in 1990 was 50 points better than anyone on the major league club that year.

A Roberto Kelly sprained wrist gave the Yankees an opening to see if Williams could handle major league pitching. In his first game, Bernie singled and drove in two runs.

Meanwhile, the team continued to make news around its youth movement. With the first overall pick in the draft, the Yankees chose left-hand pitcher Brien Taylor out of Beaufort, North Carolina. Words cannot adequately describe just how impressive and dominating a pitcher Taylor was when Yankee scouts first laid eyes on him. Tall and somewhere between thin and husky, with a three-quarters delivery similar to that of Randy Johnson, Taylor posted numbers that, even for high school baseball, were so dominant as to border on unbelievable. In his senior year he struck out 213 hitters in 88 innings, doing it with a fastball that clocked anywhere from 95 to 100 miles per hour. In 1991, almost no one threw 100 miles per hour, much less a kid in high school.

But Taylor did. Yankees scouting director Bill Livesay called him the greatest amateur pitcher he had ever seen. "I don't know that there was anyone else who was even all that close to Brien," said Livesay. "Brien had size, strength, a live, loose arm, athleticism, and he had a pretty good curve ball, too."[22]

Taylor was also soft-spoken and humble. His family lived in a trailer lit by a single lightbulb. His mother, Bettie, picked the meat out of crabs for a living. Bettie had a number in her head for what she felt her son was worth to the Yankees and it was not the $300,000 they were offering him after he was drafted. To her, that figure was an insult, far less than the $1.2 million the Oakland A's had given pitcher Todd Van Poppel when he was selected fourteenth overall the year before. Bettie Taylor wanted her son to get Van Poppel money, or he would go to college in the fall and reenter the draft in 1992. The team went up to $600,000, which was still not good enough. Taylor was utilizing the services of mega-agent Scott Boras. Between Bettie and Boras, a stalemate occurred that remained in place the rest of the summer. When the Yankees would not budge, Bettie accused them of trying to put one over on her and her son because they were poor and black.

Pressure began to build. Then one day, a reporter decided to call Steinbrenner and ask what he thought of the whole situation. "If they let him go, they ought to be shot," replied The Boss, saying he thought Taylor had the potential of a Gooden or a Clemens. The comments gave Bettie and Boras leverage in the negotiations. A week later, just as Taylor was getting ready to head off to college, the two sides reached a deal for $1.5 million. Who was most upset that the Yankees had not, in fact, let Taylor go? George Steinbrenner.

"Never in my wildest dreams would I have paid that kid a million-and-a-half," he told the Associated Press, when asked about the signing. "I'm getting damned tired of people spending my money like this."[23] At the next quarterly ownership meeting, which Steinbrenner was allowed to attend, he lambasted Michael for spending that much money. "You're the one who jacked up the price by saying I should be shot if I didn't sign him," Michael yelled back.[24]

By the All-Star break, the Yankees were 38-40, nine games better than where they were at the break in 1990 and miles ahead of where anyone thought they would be. While the record may not have appeared impressive, the call-ups and injection of youth into the clubhouse had made the Yankees exciting . . . at least so far.

As the Yankees figured out what kind of team they really were, the Mets pressed on from the Strawberry drama with a solid May, followed by missteps in June. There were no long winning streaks nor any prolonged losing streaks; the team wavered back and forth between second and third place in the division. Cone, a workhorse who ate up innings while racking up high pitch counts, slowly emerged as the team ace, averaging 9 strikeouts per 9 innings over the two months, along with 5 wins. Viola did not duplicate his April performance, but still remained one the game's best lefties. Gooden, meanwhile, was going through his worst stretch ever. Over 8 starts, the last of which came on June 30, he allowed 36 runs and 69 hits in 52⅓ innings, numbers that would have been even worse if not for a shutout on June 15 against the Astros. Perhaps even more troublesome, Doctor K was not blowing hitters away, striking out only 31 over that time. The Mets were starting to wonder if the extension had been a mistake.

On June 14, while running out a ground ball, Coleman suffered a hamstring injury. Though Coleman had not been the offensive sparkplug the team had hoped for, he had stolen 33 bases, a pace more in keeping with his earlier Cardinal days. But when he grabbed the back of his leg after running through first base, his season was largely over. Coleman appeared in only 17 more games the rest of the year.

The Mets were looking for ways to improve the club offensively. Rumors flew throughout May that the team would move a package of players to the Pirates for outfielder Bobby Bonilla, an impending free agent. The trade, however, was always a long shot, as it was unlikely either team was going to try and improve a division rival. Instead, on May 31, the Mets removed yet another piece of the '86 championship team from the clubhouse. Tim Teufel, who for five seasons served as a key platoon player and pinch hitter, was sent to San Diego for veteran Garry Templeton. Teufel's role with the team had largely vanished in '91, as he appeared in just twenty games, nearly always as a pinch hitter.

"It's kind of sad. I've got a lump in my throat," said Teufel, who found out he was moving on just an hour before that night's game. "It's not the first thing I wanted to happen."[25] Teufel went on to have one of his best seasons with the Padres, while Templeton came to New York, hit .228 in limited playing time, and retired after the season.

As June moved into July, the Mets were still afloat in the National League East. But they weren't generating the same kind of excitement as seasons past. There seemed to be more a question of when this would fall apart instead of when they would make their move for first. Then the Metropolitans did not lose a game until July 14; suddenly, with the parallel emergence of the Yankees, the city was abuzz with talk of postseason baseball.

The Mets headed to Montreal on July 1 for a four-game series. They were six and a half games out of first; while that was not an insurmountable deficit, there were doubts that this particular team had the ability to make it up. The Mets, however, went on a streak of pitching and hitting that reminded fans of the glory days of the mid-'80s. It started with a sweep of the Expos. One of those victories came after eight shutout innings from Darling, his last win as a Met. In the process, the team shaved two games off their first-place deficit. They then went to Philadelphia, where Gooden, Viola, and Cone gave up only four runs over three games and the offense provided just enough to complete the three-game sweep.

New York was just two and a half games out of first at the All-Star break. When play resumed, they returned to Shea and won their first three games, extending their winning streak to ten and keeping pace with the Pirates. Gooden regained his dominant form. Franco, battling an injury, saved half of those ten games. Sid Fernandez, out since spring training after breaking his arm, was set to return in a week, bolstering an already strong rotation. Everything was working right.

"Three weeks ago, I didn't know whether we were capable of putting together a streak," said Cone, who tied a career high with thirteen strike-outs in winning the tenth consecutive game. "Now I'm convinced this is a contender. Do we have enough to win? Over this last stretch, it would be tough to argue against it."[26]

The next day, the Mets lost 2–1, ending their winning streak and costing them a game in the standings. Still, the Amazins' run had generated an enormous level of excitement in the city. Baseball was the talk of the town; the Mets, even with the Yankees exceeding expectations, were still the city's team. The winning streak reinforced that. The Mets, deemed boring in an unrealistic comparison to the '86 champions, had shown that they still had some thrills left in them. After losing to the Padres, they took two of three from the Giants and split four games with the Dodgers. On Sunday, July 21, after beating LA, they were fifteen games over .500 and trailing Pittsburgh by four games in the division. Up next was a nine-game West Coast trip to finish July.

The following two months, however, would be some of the worst, most internally chaotic in team history to that point. It would be nearly six years to the day before the Mets were ever fifteen games over .500 again.

As the Mets began their West Coast trip, another member of the '86 team was dropped. One day after taking the hard-luck loss that ended the team's ten-game winning streak, Darling was traded to the Expos for relief pitcher Tim Burke. The move was not unexpected. With Fernandez's imminent return, Darling was the odd man out in the starting rotation. The senior member of the team, Darling was largely stoic after hearing the news, recognizing that it was part of the business and would, perhaps, create new opportunities for him in a different atmosphere. Some of his teammates, however, were not so sanguine.

"It's been like seeing a friend die. You know it's coming. When it get[s] here it just [stinks]," said Kevin Elster. "We're supposed to say, 'I'm happy for Ronnie', right? That's a lot of crap."[27]

As more upset teammates began to gather around him, Darling asked them to break it up. They were depressing him. But the reaction was a revealing sign. Only four players remained from '86: Elster, Fernandez, Gooden, and Howard Johnson. They were upset to see the continuous *drip drip drip* dismantling of that championship roster. Even some of the guys who joined post '86 were unnerved by the trading off of guys with postseason experience and grit.

The road trip, meanwhile, started with three losses in San Francisco, each one costing the team a game in the standings. The Mets headed for San Diego. Disaster ensued. Coleman was back from the disabled list and ready to rejoin the starting lineup. Before the first game against the Padres, the Mets were taking batting practice at Jake Murphy Stadium when Coleman went up to take his swings. There was one problem, though: it was not his turn to hit. Mets third base coach Mike Cubbage told him as much, as did a few of Coleman's teammates. Coleman did not listen and instead turned on Cubbage, who Coleman felt had harangued him once too often about work ethic, in a fury. "No one's ever talked to me like that," said Cubbage.[28]

Coleman's tirade happened in full view of the media and his teammates. When he was done yelling at his coach, Coleman threw his helmet and bat against the back wall of the dugout, then disappeared into the clubhouse. Nearly everyone who witnessed the incident was stunned, but not nearly as stunned as when Harrelson said he was not going to do anything about it. "As far as I'm concerned, it's between them," Buddy told the media.[29]

Players were incredulous. When Harrelson then fined Mark Carreon for leaving the ballpark early the next night, they became incensed. Did Carreon deserve the fine? Sure he did. But Coleman's offense seemed so much worse, and yet it went unpunished.

For many, this incident was not the beginning but the closing argument in a long-held belief that Harrelson was not up for the challenge of managing in New York. It was not necessarily the decisions on the field—though, for some, that was a part of it—but the lack of communication and outright refusal to confront those who might deserve it off the field. To his detractors, Harrelson was simply unwilling to take any action that might place him in an awkward or uncomfortable situation. The evidence had been building up all season.

It started in April. Buddy had agreed to participate daily in a pregame show with WFAN, the city's main sports talk radio station and the broadcaster of Mets radio games. But after what he perceived to be criticism mixed with a negative tone from the show, on April 24 he decided not to take part. The next day, he quit the show for good, walking away from $30,000 in the process.[30]

The scorn that many teammates felt for Jefferies had not disappeared just because he had had a solid season in 1990. If anything, as the offense struggled in 1991 and Jefferies's defense continued to be a problem, it got worse. Anonymous quotes knocking him showed up in the papers; one quote in particular from Darling—where Darling seemed to be lobbying for Harrelson to play Tom Herr more and Jefferies less—especially riled him. In late May Jefferies reached his breaking point, penning a nine-paragraph letter to Mets fans that was faxed to and then read aloud on WFAN.

"Over the past three years, there has been an awful lot said and written about me," Jefferies wrote. "All too often, I have been criticized and blamed by some of my teammates. (I don't believe anyone can deny the fact that I have consistently taken it on the chin for the last three years.) In those three years, I have always accepted responsibility for my mistakes and errors. I have never made excuses or alibis, or blamed anyone or pointed fingers . . . When a pitcher is having trouble getting players out, when a hitter is having trouble hitting, or when a player makes an error, I try to support them in whatever way I can. I don't run to the media to belittle them or to draw more attention to their difficult times."[31]

The letter drew snickers from many and bewilderment that a player would air these grievances publicly and not within the clubhouse. Harrelson took blame for not shutting down the continued haranguing of Jefferies, then drew more blame when he said he was not going to deal with Jefferies's letter or the situation. He left it to the players, with veteran Cerone and emerging clubhouse leader Cone holding a team meeting to rein in on anonymous quotes.

Two weeks later Cone himself became part of a Harrelson-centered controversy. In the fourth inning of a game in Cincinnati, Cone refused to throw a pitchout called from the dugout by bench coach Doc Edwards. When the inning was over, Harrelson confronted Cone in the dugout. There was shouting and Harrelson poked and shoved Cone in the chest. Harrelson demanded Cone respect him. Cone told Harrelson to "keep his hand off" him and said he would respect Harrelson when his manager showed him respect.[32] Hubie Brooks had to get between and separate the two. All of it was caught on camera. But to Cone, what happened in the locker room afterward was the true problem.

Harrelson closed the clubhouse doors immediately after the game. Most thought it was for a team meeting. Instead, he was talking to Cone about getting their stories straight for the press. "Let's say there was a misunderstanding," the manager said to his pitcher.[33]

There was no misunderstanding, though. The truth was that Cone, like other Mets pitchers, resented how much control Edwards exerted over the course of any one game and that's why he ignored him. Harrelson did not want another fire in the clubhouse, so he asked Cone to lie about what had just happened. Cone refused and informed the press that night of how he really felt.

Confidence in Harrelson had been slowly eroding, but so long as the Mets were winning, the team could pull through it. Now, they weren't winning, so when Harrelson refused to take action against Coleman, players decided to step up in his place. Dave Magadan and Howard Johnson, two of the longest-tenured Mets, railed to the press that weekend about bad attitudes in the clubhouse, trying to set their teammates straight in a manner that Keith Hernandez would have been proud of. But the fact that they and not Harrelson were the ones laying down the discipline only made things worse.

"Bud Harrelson just doesn't get it," wrote *Newsday*'s Tom Verducci. "He can't seem to grasp that he is the manager, the boss, the man who is paid to make decisions, to control the clubhouse and to assert himself."[34]

Eventually, Harrelson called a meeting to try and smooth things over. It was far too late. The damage to his authority in the clubhouse was irreversible. The only thing that could be done to save his job was for the team to win. But after the Mets left San Diego, they stopped winning baseball games for nearly an entire month.

The Yankees opened the second half of the season by taking three out of four from the Angels in Anaheim. They lost two in Seattle, then went to Oakland and won the first three games of the series, with Kamieniecki, Johnson, and Taylor picking up the victories. It was the first time the Yankees had won a season series at Oakland since 1983.

"Win, win, win. Geez, it's boring," said Farr, after Taylor beat former Yankee Andy Hawkins, now with Oakland.[35]

At 44-43 the team had moved into third place. In his first ten career games, Williams was hitting .355 with a .475 OBP. The youth movement was carrying the Yankees upward in the standings and Merrill was being hailed for the work of this greatly overachieving team. There were even some whispers that Stump would be in contention for Manager of the Year when the season was over. Asked by a reporter to respond to that, Merrill said, "Fate and glory are as fleeting as the wind. Today you're a hero. Tomorrow you're a bum."[36]

Merrill was right to be cautious. That 44-43 record represented the high-water mark for the '91 Yankees. They managed to win only four more series the rest of the year. Meanwhile, the ugliness that permeated through the clubhouse in 1990 reemerged to pollute the entire atmosphere of the team. The tipping point, both for the club and for the managerial future of Merrill, came from an incident so bizarre it rivaled anything from the Bronx Zoo–era Yankees.

The Yankees dropped their final game in Oakland and returned to New York for a ten-game home stand. They lost seven out of ten. They went to Detroit and lost three of four, then got swept in Chicago. Since going one game over .500, the Yankees were 4-14. The losing began to fray the clubhouse and expose the worst of the team's problems. Upset over lost playing time, some of the veteran outfielders like Kelly and Hall began griping about Williams. They were unimpressed by the quiet, reserved outfielder with the big glasses and even more unimpressed when, after a hot start, Williams nosedived. The young outfielder went 16-74, with only four extra-base hits during the team's eighteen-game slide.

Williams began to experience rookie hazing that went beyond the standard ribbing. Hall was the worst offender. He referred to Bernie as "Mr. Zero," an elementary school–level taunt meant to convey Williams's worth to the team. If Williams made a mistake in the field or on the bases, which was not uncommon in his rookie year, Hall would mimic it the next day and not in the playful manner of a friend having some fun. Hall felt threatened by a younger, more capable player and was trying to establish dominance over him. Williams put up with it, never physically and rarely ever verbally fighting back. But, inside, he stewed.

During the team's eighteen-game slide, only a single game was won by any of the team's young-gun pitchers. Greg Cadaret won two of the other games, having moved from the bullpen to help support the starting rotation. But even that was not without problems.

"The thing that I knew when we were going to have problems is when we had to put Cadaret in the starting rotation and take him out of the bullpen," said Merrill. "We had three lefties and three righties in the bullpen and we could match up reasonably well against other teams. Then when we had to put him in the rotation, things fell apart because we weren't that strong in that area."[37]

Merrill's comments about the fleeting nature of fame and glory appeared prescient; with the team fading, the pressure began to build. Moreover, the Yankee brass felt the team was better than it was performing, even if that line of thinking was questionable. Now, in a move out of Steinbrenner's playbook, Gene Michael was about to meddle in clubhouse affairs, with disastrous results for Stump.

During the Yankees' late July home stand, Michael had sent a message to Merrill: Mattingly's hair was too long. The Yankees had long-standing player appearance standards, dating back to the beginnings of Stein-brenner's ownership. No long hair, though the definition of long was left to Steinbrenner's interpretation. No beards. No goatees. And mustaches had to be well groomed. Over the years, a few players had tested the lim-itations of these rules, but none had ever truly challenged them. Every spring players were required to sign an agreement saying they would adhere to these standards. If you didn't follow the rules, you didn't play.

Mattingly's hair wasn't long by most standards. Like many men in the early '90s, he sported a mullet: shorter hair on top, longer hair in the back, going down most of his neck. For Michael, though, the hairstyle violated the team's personal appearance policy and he wanted it cut. He informed his manager to tell the team's captain to chop off the hair, or else.

Stump did not treasure this assignment. It was the kind of inane task that had nothing to do with the team's performance on the field and everything to do with maintaining control of the talent. But Merrill was a company man, grateful to the Yankees for all they had done for him over the years and the opportunity to manage in the big leagues. So he went to Mattingly and relayed the order to cut his hair. Mattingly was not overly put off at first. He understood the team had a policy, though he thought it was ridiculous. He told his manager he did not want to get his hair cut, but he would think about it.

Two weeks passed. Two long weeks in which the team went 4-11. They had just played the first three games of a four-game home series against the Royals and lost them all by a combined score of 18-2. The team was spiraling, tensions were building internally, and, perhaps fed up with what he thought was the massive underperformance of his team, Michael phoned Stump and told him that Mattingly, along with Matt Nokes, Steve Farr, and Pascual Pérez, better cut their hair or they would be fined and benched.

The other three players were annoyed but followed the rules. When Mattingly walked into the clubhouse, he asked if he would be in the lineup that day. Merrill answered his question with a question.

"Are you going to get your hair cut?"

"No."

"Then you are not in the lineup."[38]

Now, the most popular player on the Yankees, perhaps in the entire history of the organization, the team's captain and leader, was benched for not cutting his hair. An enormous media firestorm ensued.

Mattingly was a mixture of livid and genuinely flummoxed. He took out his wrath and frustration on Michael. "We're not winning. This is [Michael's] club. He's setting the pace. Maybe he wants the organization to be a puppet for him and do exactly what he wants," Mattingly told reporters after the game, which the Yankees had won but no one really seemed to care about that.[39]

"I am overwhelmed by the pettiness," he continued. "It's embarrassing to me to get a rap as an attitude guy."

The situation was so ridiculous that, at first, some of Mattingly's teammates thought it was a prank. As many began to realize it wasn't, they let their feelings be known.

"I think it's so dumb, I'm not even going to talk about it," said Maas.[40]

"Where does it go from here?" asked Sax. "Pascual is pitching [tonight]. It's nickel-and-dime stuff. Somebody's hair is a ridiculous way to tear down a team."[41]

More began to express themselves when Mattingly called a team meeting and told his teammates not to get caught up in this mess. He would deal with it.

Then Mattingly let loose with a bombshell: in June he had asked for a trade and now, with this incident, perhaps he no longer belonged with this organization. He was only in the first year of a five-year deal, but it seemed clear that Donnie wanted out. He had seen the way the Twins— the eventual world champions—played the game, with joy and a carefree attitude. That's what he wanted.

Michael, for his part, refused to concede any wrongdoing. As far as he was concerned, the captain of the team should set the example. That example included getting a haircut when management asked you to get a haircut. He wasn't going to trade Mattingly, which outside of the impact to clubhouse morale would have most assuredly driven away the few fans still showing up to the ballpark every night. For many, Mattingly was the only reason to come. But the moment was an unnecessary distraction in Michael's effort to change the culture of the clubhouse.

Ultimately, the biggest victim of Haircutgate was Merrill, who was clearly embarrassed by the entire situation. Talking to reporters in the postgame, he looked uncomfortable trying to explain how this had all happened.

"I was ordered that if he didn't cut his hair, not to play him," Stump explained, nearly thirty years later. "I tried to explain it to him, that Donnie you're the Captain of this ballclub. Players look up to you. He chose not to do it. Hey, I'm the manager and I have given you an ultimatum and you don't want to do it, you're not gonna play. Simple as that.

"I did what I thought was right at the time. In the back of my mind, I am also saying, I don't know if anyone has had contact with George but this is a perfect place for him to say to me, 'Is the player gonna dictate you or are you gonna dictate that player?'"[42]

The incident was not Merrill's doing, but it became his undoing. There was anger at Michael for enforcing a policy many thought arbitrary and meaningless in a season where the team was fading fast. But the ridiculousness of the situation drained away any lingering sense of respect for the manager in the clubhouse. If something as trivial as hair length could sideline the team icon, what did it mean for every other player? Many were already on edge about playing time and the general state of the team. As the team's play grew worse, it was more likely that minor league players were going to be given a chance to perform at the big league level, greatly increasing the annoyance of many veteran players.

Mattingly returned to the lineup the day after being benched, having gotten a trim and auctioning off the shorn locks for charity. When he came to the plate for his first at bat, he received a standing ovation. The Yankees won that night and the next, eventually winning five out of six. But the season was over. The fans, so excited just two months earlier, stopped showing up. At the end of August, a four-game series against the Blue Jays, the division leader, drew a combined attendance of just 92,000.

September was merciless. Players lost interest as rosters expanded and more minor leaguers came up. The month turned out to be the worst of the season. Only a sweep of Baltimore in October prevented the team from finishing with nearly the same record as the year before. They went 83 straight games without a complete game from their starting pitcher, setting a since-broken major league record. In the end, for all the hope and excitement of that 44-43 record, the Yankees finished 71-91, 20 games out of first.

The last leg of the Mets' West Coast trip was Los Angeles. They watched Strawberry collect three hits and three RBIs as the Dodgers took the rubber match of the series. In nine games on the coast, the Amazins went 2-7. They were fortunate to lose only a game and a half in the standings. Returning to New York, they were swept in a four-game series by the Cubs. At two different points during the series, Harrelson refused to go to the mound to remove a pitcher from the game, not wanting to get booed by the crowd. He had pitching coach Mel Stottlemyre do it instead. Everyone noticed. Before the first game of the next series against the Pirates, Harrelson refused to meet with the media, upset over a column that criticized his handling of the Coleman incident. The Mets were able to pull off two wins in the series, keeping them just five and a half out of first. They did not win again for nearly two weeks.

The losing streak started with a four-game sweep by the Cubs at Wrigley, the last two losses both coming in extra innings. Then they were swept by the Cardinals. In less than a week, the Mets dropped five games in the standings and were struggling to stay above .500. A three-game series in Pittsburgh would determine if their season was salvageable. It wasn't. The Pirates swept the Mets, outscoring them 21–5 in the process, dropping them three games under .500 and thirteen and a half games out of first.

On Wednesday, August 21, the Mets returned to Shea without having won a game in thirteen days. The clubhouse was a mess. Team morale was nonexistent. And the fans had seen enough. The dynasty they had come unfairly to expect had not materialized; it was clear now that it never would. Throughout the first game of a doubleheader against the Cardinals that day, fans booed just about anyone in a Mets uniform. Harrelson got the worst of it. Any time fans got a glimpse of him, they booed loudly, even when the team held a 1–0 lead into the sixth inning. The lead did not hold. The Cardinals scored in each of the last four innings and won 7–3. In the process the Mets committed three errors and had only one hit from the second inning to the ninth. The losing streak went to eleven games.

"I hate using the word sickening but it's sickening to watch us play," said Harrelson, who seemed helpless to do anything about the state of his team.[43]

A victory in the second game ended the losing streak but provided no relief to players or fans. The Mets took the last game from St. Louis, then lost four of their next six. Between July 30 and August 29, they went 6-22, one of the worst stretches in the history of a franchise that had had many bad stretches in the early 1960s and '80s. The season and the Mets' firm hold on New York evaporated.

Meanwhile, the team's play, coupled with the constant criticism and attacks, took a considerable toll on Harrelson. "He didn't sleep well at night, and I saw him age considerably before my eyes," wrote Stottlemyre, in his autobiography. "Until then I had thought I might want to manage someday, but Buddy was a good friend, and I lost any taste for managing after I saw what it did to him."[44]

The only question left was when, not if, Buddy Harrelson would be fired.

The end came on September 28 after a 6–2 home loss to the Phillies. After the game was over, Cashen, himself about to officially turn over the GM reins to Harazin, met with Harrelson in the clubhouse. It was a difficult moment for Cashen. Theirs wasn't the adversarial relationship he had had with Davey Johnson, where things deteriorated progressively over the years. He truly liked Buddy. That's why he was firing him now. Cashen was going to wait until after the season, but then he saw Harrelson quoted as saying he thought he had a strong chance of returning as manager in 1992. That was not going to happen. The decision had already been made. Cashen did not want Buddy to have any false hope with a week remaining in the season. And so he made the move official. Cashen, unlike when he dismissed Johnson, gave Harrelson the chance to address the team before the next day's game, the last home game of the year. Harrelson declined. In two incomplete years as manager, he compiled a 145-129 record, better than history would remember. For the final week of the season, third base coach Mike Cubbage served as acting manager.

As news spread of his firing, players, reporters, and fans let out their frustration.

"You have to ask yourself if he was managerial material," said Viola. "I don't want to start any trouble, but you have to look at the results."[45]

"Buddy Harrelson is a nice guy. Everyone says so. But you don't hear many coming to his defense as a manager," wrote the *New York Times'* Ira Berkow.[46]

Only some sixteen thousand fans showed up at Shea to see the final home game of the year. Though the news of Harrelson's dismissal was announced just before the game, two fans in attendance were able to find a white sheet and spray-paint "Bye Buddy, don't stay in touch" on it.[47]

The Mets won that day but lost four of the last six games of the year, finishing 77-84. The only moments of joy in that final week were watching Howard Johnson—in the midst of the greatest year of his career—reach the 30/30 club for the third time. Ironically, despite the Mets' offensive struggles throughout the season, Johnson ended the year leading the National League in home runs and RBIs. On the season's last day, Cone tied a National League record when he struck out nineteen Phillies in a complete game shutout.

"He'd have actually struck out 20 guys if he'd listened to me," said catcher Charlie O'Brien with a laugh years later, referring to the final batter of the game, outfielder Dale Murphy, who grounded out. "I wanted to throw a fastball and he wanted to throw a slider. He [Murphy] was behind the fastball all day long."[48]

Though he fell short of the single-game strikeout record, it was a remarkable moment for the hard-nosed pitcher, but even the joy of watching Cone dominate Philadelphia was tempered by the mood of the clubhouse.

Earlier that morning, Cone had received a phone call from Cashen. A woman whom Cone had been with the night before was accusing him of rape. He had taken the mound that day thinking he might be going to jail; that a cop might even come arrest him in the middle of the game. Three days later the police said the allegations were unfounded and no charges were filed. Meanwhile, players could not wait to get out of the locker room. Viola, his contract about to expire, was in street clothes and out of the stadium within minutes of the game's end.

"Everyone just wants to get home and forget about the season and look forward to next year," said Franco.[49]

Perhaps Mets season ticket holder Frank Mediate summed it up best. When asked about the overall state of his favorite team, he remarked, "This is becoming just like the Yankees."

He was right. For the first time in a long time, the Mets were becoming just like the Yankees, for all the wrong reasons.

Stump Merrill's words earlier that summer about going from a hero to a bum were borne out. Less than twenty-four hours after the 1991 season ended, he was fired by Michael. In announcing Merrill's dismissal, Michael felt that the team had underachieved. Merrill, however, was not so sure.

"If this club underachieved, look at where we finished in pitching, defense and hitting. Tell me where we should have finished," said Stump shortly after being told the news.[50]

Merrill was not wrong, but it did not matter. He had lost control of the clubhouse as play deteriorated. The benching of Mattingly over his hair length was the final straw. By late August players began asking reporters to write more about Merrill's "inadequacies as a tactician," in an effort to get him fired.[51] With a few exceptions, many had expressed their displeasure over the firing of a manager in the recent years. No such displeasure was expressed this time.

"Stump's a nice man. But I felt he was overmatched on the field," said Cadaret, when hearing the news. "I felt many times that other managers were just toying with us."[52]

Hall, who had actually gotten along well with the manager throughout the course of the year, knew Merrill's time was up, referring to the Mattingly incident as "the final nail in the coffin."[53]

"It would have helped if he knew what he was doing," said one player anonymously.[54]

Along with Merrill went five of the team's six coaches, with only hitting coach Frank Howard surviving the purge. One of those losing his job was third base coach Buck Showalter, who had been a member of the organization since the late 1970s. For the first time in eight years, both the Yankees and the Mets would spend the first weeks of the off-season searching for new managers. Both teams were recovering from long regular seasons guided by managers who had been organizational men: managers who had both come in mid-season in 1990 and produced flashes of hope, only to eventually lose control of their clubhouses. Both would remain in baseball, but never manage at the big league level again.

This parallel experience pushed the Mets and Yankees to seek out new managers who were not only from outside the organizations, but who also had experience at the big league level. Managers who could handle the oil-and-water personality clashes within their respective clubhouses, while satisfying the press and the fans who were tiring of the lack of successful baseball in New York. Ultimately, one team followed through on this managerial path and the other did not.

As baseball came to an end in 1991 in New York, both teams were trying to move on from exhausting, controversy-filled seasons. And both teams were wondering if they were on the upswing or about to head into a deep valley of baseball irrelevance.

6

Now Trade the Rest of Them

Somewhere along the way, the relationship between White Sox manager Jeff Torborg and upper management fell apart. Torborg was not sure why, but he began noticing it after the 1990 season ended, a season in which he won the American League's Manager of the Year Award in a near unanimous vote after leading Chicago to a surprising second-place finish in the American League West. Torborg, a New Jersey native who grew up a Giants fan, served a stint as Indians manager in the late 1970s, then worked as a coach for the Yankees for almost the entire 1980s. He left to manage the White Sox in 1989 and quickly developed a sterling reputation with players and within the league. Torborg was sincere and direct, a deeply religious man who often attended services with his players. He had a "gift for working with pitchers, an understated toughness and a facility for relations with reporters."[1] This was someone who could instill values back into a club that had long ago lost its way, mentally and spiritually. Torborg was, by nearly every measure, the antithesis of Bud Harrelson.

When a report came out, just after Harrelson was relieved of duty, that Torborg was at odds with White Sox owner Jerry Reinsdorf and general manager Ron Schueler, the Mets pounced. The report was not necessarily true, but it acted as a form of self-fulfilling prophecy because it put all three on alert. Though Torborg was still under contract, the Mets wanted to talk to him anyway. Schueler told Torborg he had permission to talk to New York, possibly because he thought Torborg wanted out. Torborg took that approval as Schueler and Reinsdorf's way of saying they wanted him gone.

Two days after the regular season ended, Torborg sat down with the Mets' brass to talk about their vision for repairing the team and to hear Torborg's views on how to improve. It took less than forty-eight hours for both sides to agree on a deal: four years for $1.5 million total to manage the Mets, the largest contract the team had ever given a manager.

In what was hoped to be a good sign for the Mets, the news rattled White Sox players and coaches, who could not believe the team had allowed Torborg to leave. "I've been with Jeff the whole three years and every single sportswriter who covers the team loves him, every player loves him, every coach loves him," said Sox pitching coach Sammy Ellis.[2] Tim Raines and Scott Fletcher piled on, incredulous at how this happened.

"I don't know much about him but if he's someone who comes in and puts his foot down, that's what we need," said Dwight Gooden.[3] Torborg inherited a team about to be overwhelmed by scandal. Shortly after Cone finished striking out nineteen Phillies, it became public that he was under investigation for sexual assault. The day Torborg's hiring was announced, the police also announced that Cone was cleared of any wrongdoing. This was the first indication of things to come.

The Yankees also needed a new manager and, for the first time in nearly a generation, George Steinbrenner would not decide who it was. Gene Michael was going to make that call, with input from the higher-ups. Michael was sure of one thing: he was not going to hire someone without major league experience. The Yankees' two previous managers had both been first-timers, men who had only managed in the minors. Whether they were to blame or not, the results were not pretty: a 156-208 record over two-plus seasons.

This time the team would go with a manager who had been through the rigors of major league baseball before. Michael in particular wanted a known name. Not necessarily a flashy name, like Steinbrenner would have wanted, but someone who, by their body of work, would instantly create respect in the clubhouse.

On Friday, October 18, Michael sat down with the team's limited partners and laid out his top picks for manager: Hal Lanier, who had led the Astros to the postseason in 1986 but had not managed in the big leagues in three years, and Doug Rader, who had been let go midseason by the Angels. If those names were not enough, maybe even Davey Johnson, who had not managed since Frank Cashen dismissed him in Cincinnati a year and a half earlier.

The partners had other ideas. Lanier and Rader inspired no one. And Johnson, while certainly a headline grabber, would command the kind of money they just did not want to spend on a manager. They had another suggestion. Two weeks earlier, when he'd let Merrill and most of the coaching staff go, Michael said none of the coaches was under consideration to be manager. That included the third base coach, Buck Showalter. The partners wanted Stick to reconsider his edict: specifically, managing general partner Robert Nederlander directed Michael to take a stronger look at Buck. Stick had little choice. Buck was their guy.

Born William Nathaniel Showalter III in the Florida Panhandle, the Yankees' new manager had experienced much in his thirty-five years. Century, Florida, was like most southern towns of that era in terms of segregation. Showalter's father, a World War II veteran and hero, was principal of the local high school and led the charge for the Century school system to follow the law of the land and desegregate. It did not earn him many friends in town, but it taught his son lessons in courage and standing up for principles.

Nat, as he was known in youth, inherited his father's inquisitive nature and heightened sense of attention to detail. No amount of planning or preparation was too small, both in life and in sports. "Beware of coaches who do too much active coaching during games," the older Showalter told his son. "It means they didn't do their jobs before the game."[4]

Young Nat attended and played baseball at Mississippi State, where he set the single-season batting average record. It's also where he earned the nickname "Buck," for his habit of walking around the clubhouse naked. The Yankees drafted Buck in 1977 as a first baseman. While he had talent, he lacked power, an issue with a team that had Don Mattingly and Steve Balboni making their way through the system. His playing career never got past AAA Columbus. People in the Yankee system, however, noticed certain things about Buck. He tended to sit near the manager during games, something most players avoided. Buck was a sponge on the bench and in the field, soaking up whatever lessons he could learn and absorbing them for future reference. No detail was too small, no moment too inconsequential to be of later use. Not only he did remember events and moments, he processed them, analyzed them, and tried to determine where they could be of good use down the line. Showalter taped Yankee games, then came home after his own games and watched the tapes. Not only was it a way to keep him informed of what was going on in the Bronx, but it was one more way to learn about the game in general. That habit continued even after he became the team's manager. "He would literally watch the game again after the game," recalled Matt Nokes. "The coaches had to watch it with him and they would always complain because they had to stay and watch it."[5]

In 1983 the Yankees parted ways with Showalter as a player but kept him to assist in the instructional league and eventually made him manager of Class A Oneonta in New York. In five seasons as a minor league manager from 1985 to 1989, his teams finished in first four times, including twice with Oneonta, once with Single A Fort Lauderdale, and once with Double A Albany.

Showalter served as the eye-in-the-sky coach for the Yankees in the beginning of the 1990 season, a relatively short-lived concept that had him sitting in a mezzanine box, relaying information to the dugout. Following Dent's firing, he became Stump's third base coach. Buck had a great rapport with the players, even if the clubhouse was largely toxic. They respected his knowledge and passion for the game. Buck had never made it to the big leagues as a player, but that was largely irrelevant. He had seen, even managed, many of these guys in the minors and had learned enough from his time as a big league coach to see how things should— and should not—be run. Showalter had been fascinated with Billy Martin and come to know him during the team's spring training days. Martin could not help but see a kindred spirit who lived, ate, and slept baseball to a degree most would think crazy. Billy had told Steinbrenner to keep an eye on Buck, that one day he would be managing the team.

Now here was Showalter, less than a month after his firing, being named team manager. At thirty-five, he was the youngest manager in the game, the youngest Yankees manager in seventy-seven years, and younger, by nearly a decade, than still-active players Nolan Ryan and Carlton Fisk. Showalter set out with Michael to reshape the team, both physically and mentally. Changes were coming. They would not all happen before the start of the '92 season, as some problem players had contracts through the year. But the true rebuilding of the New York Yankees was about to begin.

Al Harazin had snagged his manager. Now he set about reshaping the team—and the way the Mets conducted off-season business—in his own image. The days of simply trading to improve the club were over. The Mets had fallen far in 1991, losing nearly 450,000 in attendance in the process. They could no longer rely on shrewd deals to plug holes in the roster. They had money to spend and were going to spend it.

The first signing came the day before Thanksgiving. Eddie Murray, the thirty-six-year-old switch-hitting first baseman, was headed to Queens. Murray, who was twenty-fifth all-time in home runs and second among active players when he signed, had been overwhelmed by the Mets' two-year, $7.5 million offer, all of which was guaranteed and far more than Murray was being offered by anyone else. The signing meant Dave Magadan, coming off surgery to both his shoulders, was no longer in the team's first base plans. In fact, once Murray inked the contract, Harazin told Magadan the team would make every effort to trade him. Meanwhile, though the Mets had never signed a free agent with such an extensive list of Hall of Fame credentials before, some worried how Murray would hold up under the glare of the New York media. He had never been cozy with the press, often simply refusing to interact with them; by his own admission, he had been uncomfortable playing in New York in the past.[6]

Murray was the biggest name the Mets had ever signed, bigger even than Coleman the year before. That lasted all of five days until they signed outfielder Bobby Bonilla to a five-year, $27.5 million deal that made him the highest-paid player in team sports. By guaranteeing Bonilla a fifth year, and a few more dollars to boot, the Mets were able to lure him away from offers by the White Sox and Angels. Though it was no secret that they were pursuing Bonilla, and in fact had wanted to trade for him a year earlier, the signing was still a coup. Bobby Bo, coming off two consecutive seasons of top MVP finishes, was an offensive force who could make fans forget about Strawberry. A South Bronx native, he was already familiar with New York and what fans expected. His personality could liven up a clubhouse, something the Mets desperately needed. By signing Bonilla and Murray in one week, "the Mets instantly became favorites to win the National League East in 1992," wrote the *Daily News's* Bob Klapisch.[7]

Harazin was not done. During the winter meetings, he sent Hubie Brooks to the Angels. Then, just before midnight on the day everyone departed for home, he made a blockbuster deal: Kevin McReynolds, Keith Miller, and Gregg Jefferies were traded to Kansas City in exchange for pitcher Bret Saberhagen and infielder Bill Pecota. Saberhagen, the two-time Cy Young Award winner with a career .585 winning percentage, was the key to the deal. The Mets had sought out an ace pitcher to replace Frank Viola. Now, they had one of the game's best. Though Saberhagen had suffered a bout of tendinitis in his pitching shoulder the previous year, the Mets' discussion with Kansas City's team doctor assuaged any concerns. With Saberhagen, Cone, and Gooden, the Mets had possibly the best top-three pitching rotation in baseball. Meanwhile, they had parted ways with Jefferies in a move that was beneficial for everyone. McReynolds, though a solid player for five years, was showing signs of slowing down; with Bonilla, Coleman, Daryl Boston, and Howard Johnson in the outfield, he was going to lose much of his playing time anyway.

The trade was a sensation in New York, perhaps the most well received deal since Gary Carter came over from Montreal. "The ugly summer seems so long ago this morning," wrote Tom Verducci, the day after the deal was announced. "Al Harazin took this tired fifth-place team, a club so bad that nearly three-quarters of a million people who bought tickets preferred not to use them and stayed home, and turned them inside out . . . This cannot be underestimated at a time when the Yankees have wasted one season and are working on giving away another with their failure to do anything."[8]

Speaking of the Yankees, for good measure, Harazin signed Willie Randolph to be the team's second baseman and number two hitter in the lineup. Randolph, the Yankees' second baseman for thirteen seasons and once a team captain, was coming off one of his best years, hitting a career-high .327 with the Brewers. Set to become the forty-fourth player to take the field for both the Yankees and Mets, Randolph admitted after the signing that, "deep in my heart, I'll always be a Yankee."[9] But he liked what he saw from the Mets that off-season and was eager to be a part of what looked like an amazing rebirth of the team.

A new manager with a sterling reputation. A future Hall of Famer. The off-season's top free agent. A two-time Cy Young Award winner. A solid number two hitter coming off the best season of his career. They traded away players who had no role or who had not reached the potential envisioned for them. And they had dominated the back-page headlines at a time when the Yankees were desperately trying to regain the heart of the city. It was the most active and, by all accounts, successful off-season in franchise history. The hopes going into the '92 season were sky high. What happened in 1991 was a mere blip on the screen. An anomaly during what would now be a prolonged run of success in the National League.

It had been a month since the Mets made their big splash signing Bonilla. New York was waiting to hear from the Yankees. So far, not a peep. Not a trade. Not a free agent signing. Not a release. Nothing. Rumor had it that Steinbrenner was not happy. Why wasn't anyone doing anything to make this team better? And, perhaps most importantly for The Boss, why were the people he left in charge of this team letting the Mets get away with signing the biggest free agent of the off-season? This could not stand.

What happened next could never be traced directly back to Steinbrenner, but it sure had the markings of a George decision. All the sudden, the Yankees showed interest in free agent outfielder Danny Tartabull. They already had Roberto Kelly, Bernie Williams, Jesse Barfield, and Mel Hall to play the outfield and Kevin Maas was at DH, with Don Mattingly occasionally filling in when he needed a day off in the field. Also, Tartabull missed 16 games in 1986 with anemia, 29 games in 1989 with knee and groin injuries, 72 games in 1990 with groin and plantaris muscle injuries, and 29 games in 1991 because of a variety of ailments. Some said of Tartabull at the time that "his work habits need work," that "he is preoccupied with money," and that "he expresses his opinion too often."[10]

The Yankees were now interested in "the Bull's" services. There was no question they could use the offense. With the Royals in '91, Tartabull hit 31 home runs, drove in 100 and led the American League in slugging. Still, their sudden interest was curious. Only four days after first reaching out to him, on January 6 they signed Tartabull to a five-year, $25.5 million contract, making him the highest-paid player on the team and the fifth-highest in baseball.

Tartabull's deal was significant, the biggest free agent the team had signed in years. "He wants to be the 'big guy' on the team" and carry "the burden of restoring the Yankees' glory," wrote the *New York Times*'s Dave Anderson.[11] That was the hope at least. And it might never have happened had the Mets not signed Bonilla. Meanwhile, for Maas, who had taken the city by storm in his rookie season just two years earlier, the signing meant the end of his full-time playing days in New York.

"Danny Tartabull came to the Yankees and frankly, instead of playing right field as much as I think they wanted him to, he ended up DH'ing a lot. So that hurt a lot of my playing time," recalled Maas.[12]

Still, the Bull, even if healthy, was only going to get them so far. "Unless Tartabull is worth 10 additional victories over last season, the 1992 Yankees won't make .500," noted the *Palm Beach Post* (Tartabull ended up being worth four additional victories in 1992).[13] And so, after months of inaction, the Tartabull deal spurred a series of moves. Three days later they signed utility infielder Mike Gallego to a three-year contract. Gallego had been part of the Oakland A's teams that went to three straight World Series from 1988–1990. He knew what it was like to win and what it took, outside of pure talent, to create a winning attitude in the clubhouse. His was a Steve Farr–type attitude, where winning was all that mattered.

The day after signing Gallego, they sent Steve Sax to the White Sox. Coming to the Yankees was starting pitcher Mélido Pérez and minor league pitchers Bob Wickman and Domingo Jean. On paper, it seemed like a steal for Chicago. Sax was a five-time All-Star coming off a season in which he set a career high in home runs and batted .330 over the last four months of the year. He was a proven hitter—the only Yankee regular to hit above .300 in 1991—in a lineup full of unproven hitters. But Sax was also heading into the first year of a contract extension that would pay him $2 million a year for four years. And while he was an excellent hitter, Sax was a free swinger who rarely looked for a walk, the kind of philosophy

Michael was trying to move away from. Also, the team was now all in on Pat Kelly as their second baseman. The deal freed up cash and gave the Yankees a solid starter in Pérez, who would be united with his brother Pascual in the team's rotation. Moreover, the two minor leaguers had real promise. Wickman was especially intriguing. A farming accident in childhood resulted in the loss of the tip of his right index finger. This gave his pitches movement that others could not replicate. Ultimately, Sax had a difficult year in Chicago in '92 and injuries forced him into retirement before his contract was up. This was the first of many trades Michael orchestrated that paid large dividends for the Yankees.

Two weeks after the Sax deal, the Yankees made a player signing that was so seemingly insignificant it garnered only four sentences in the *New York Times*:

> The Yankees signed Mike Stanley, a free-agent catcher, to a minor league contract yesterday, and he will attend spring training as a nonroster player. The 28-year-old Stanley hit .249 with 3 homers and 25 runs batted in last season for the Texas Rangers, but was sent outright to the minors after the season.
> In parts of six seasons with the Rangers, Stanley had a .251 average, 16 homers and drove in 120 runs. The right-handed-hitting Stanley will compete with John Ramos for the backup catcher's spot behind Matt Nokes.[14]

That was all the space dedicated to a player who eventually became so popular in New York that fans booed the mere mention of his replacement's name four years later.

In mid-February, the Yankees received third baseman Charlie Hayes from the Phillies. For months Michael had been after a third baseman, a position that had been a constant question mark for the team since trading away Mike Pagliarulo in 1989. Since then, Tom Brookens, Wayne Tolleson, Randy Velarde, Mike Blowers, Hensley Meulens, Steve Kiefer, Jim Leyritz, Jim Walewander, Álvaro Espinoza, Torey Lovullo, Steve Sax, Pat Kelly, and Mike Humphreys had all manned the hot corner for the Yankees, none with any degree of success. Michael had his eye on Steve

Buechele, the Pirates' power-hitting third baseman. When no deal worked out with Pittsburgh, Stick secured Hayes. A solid defensive third base-man, Hayes was not considered much of an offensive threat, but would be a pleasant surprise in '92.

This wheeling and dealing now done, the team reported to spring training with expectations low for '92. Their most consistent hitter had been traded. Tartabull was a force, but only if he could stay healthy. And, after Sanderson, the pitching staff was a series of question marks. Still, Showalter let it be known that the days of self-pity, of putting yourself over the team, and of insulting the proud history of this organization were over. "One of the things that was so great about Buck was he really stressed the importance of putting on a Yankee uniform," said Leyritz.[15] Buck was immensely proud of being a Yankee: if you weren't, your time in New York was ticking.

No sooner had Buck laid out what he expected when, as the Yankees were getting set to play their first spring training game, news came from the commissioner's office: Pascual Pérez was being suspended for one year after failing a drug test. The punishment came not from MLB official policy, but because, after having a failed a test three years earlier, Pérez agreed to this punishment should he fail one again. It was not a total surprise to Showalter. Pérez, already rail thin, had lost weight over the winter and shown up late to camp and to Picture Day.[16] Of course, there was also the $57,000 black Lincoln Town Car Pérez had bought, along with the services of a chauffeur.[17] It was uncertain just how much Pérez was going to contribute in '92, though there was hope that maybe with his brother Mélido on the team, his quirky behavior could be held in check. No such luck. Pascual's contract ended at the same time as his suspension, and no team would take the risk. He never pitched in major league baseball again. In 2012 Pérez was murdered at his home in his native Dominican Republic in a suspected attempted robbery.

The team did not make it through spring training unscathed by injury either. Wade Taylor reported to camp with a dead arm that turned into a shoulder injury that ended his career. Gallego suffered a heel injury, forcing him to start the season on the disabled list. Tartabull had a sore wrist. During the last spring training game, Velarde hurt his thumb and his knees. Maas made his displeasure at being relegated to the bench an open secret. Meanwhile, Showalter's three-and-a-half-month-old son had been rushed to the hospital with a high fever the Saturday before Opening Day. It was all making for a stressful start to his managerial career. Even after going 17-14 in spring training, *The San Francisco Chronicle* said the Yankees were missing two key things: "Pitching (top to bottom) and the old Yankees pride."[18] The *New York Times* noted that the Yankees were "not given much of a chance to carry their dreams of first place much past the shaking-out processes of early spring."[19]

Opening at home against the Red Sox, Sanderson became the eighth different Opening Day starter for the Yankees in eight seasons. Despite the chaos of the last few years, 56,572 came to Yankee Stadium, the largest regular-season crowd at the stadium since its refurbishing was completed in 1976. They did not leave disappointed. Down 2–1 in the sixth, Roberto Kelly doubled in two runs off Roger Clemens; Tartabull, playing through the wrist injury, muscled a pitch into short center field for another run. The Yankees never relinquished the lead, winning 4–3, but, almost as importantly, the atmosphere around the stadium was electric, giving the players a sense of what winning in New York could really be like.

"At one point, I turned to Melido Perez and said: 'What is this? We got a World Series going here,'" said Tartabull, who had signed with New York exactly for moments like this one.[20]

Meanwhile, Showalter spent his time studying something that was, to him, just as important as the win. "I sat in the dugout and watched how the guys reacted. It's interesting to see how differently people respond to a game like this," said Buck, after the game.[21] Showalter was doing his homework. He had not been kidding when he talked about the Yankee pride. He was going to reshape this clubhouse in the image of players who wanted nothing but to win and who would do whatever was called for to make it happen, including sitting on the bench and allowing others more playing time.

The Yankees beat the Red Sox again, then went to Detroit and ran over the Tigers in a three-game sweep, outscoring them 20–5. At 5-0 they headed to Toronto to face the reigning Eastern Division champs. The Blue Jays were also undefeated, making this the latest in a season two undefeated teams with this many wins faced each other in the twentieth century. Tied at 2–2 in the ninth inning of the first game, a Hall double and Tartabull's first Yankee home run gave them the win and a half-game lead in the division. At 6-0, they were one game away from tying the best start in team history. Not a bad way for Showalter to begin his managerial career.

"Break up the New York Yankees!" wrote USA Today, somewhat tongue-in-cheek but still conveying the excitement that fans were starting to feel.[22] The Yankees were thrilling, even more so because the other New York team was failing to meet expectations in the season's first week.

The clubhouse was abuzz, though players were keeping expectations in check. "I don't know what you want," said Greg Cadaret. "It's early. It's not like it's late in the season and we're in a pennant chase and doing some scoreboard-watching. Guys aren't going to jump up and down until we have a 20-game lead. It's nice winning. But it's only six ballgames."[23]

Showalter wasn't playing into it, either. Asked how many wins would reflect a successful 1992 season, he said he did not have a number in mind, just a position in the standings. What position? he was asked. "First," responded Buck.[24] It should not have been a shocking comment, but it was. No Yankees manager had spoken like this in years.

The remainder of the Toronto series brought the team back down to reality. The Blue Jays took all three remaining games, including the series finale in a tough, ninth-inning walk-off win. Still, the Yankees stayed afloat for the rest of the month, closing out April in second place. A six-game losing streak in the beginning of May was canceled out by then winning seven out of eight. Showalter endeared himself to fans when, on May 17 at home against the A's, he took exception to Tony La Russa and Willie Wilson's complaining about inside pitches from Pérez. As La Russa inched further up the A's dugout steps, Showalter walked out onto the field, screaming at La Russa to keep his mouth shut, then he charged the A's manager. Players broke it up before any punches were thrown, but Buck's refusal to back down was an immediate hit with fans and players. On Tuesday, May 26, they beat the Twins 5–4 in the Metrodome, their first win in Minnesota in two years. They stood at 25-19, just two games out of first. They had survived Tartabull's going on the DL, the worst start of Barfield's career, Mattingly's bat all but disappearing over the first seven weeks, and Gallego's missing the first thirty-five games of the year. But, perhaps most importantly, they had avoided the turmoil that was tearing the other New York team's clubhouse apart.

Bit players were stepping up in big ways. Andy Stankiewicz, the 5-foot-9 utility infielder who had not played a day in the majors prior to '92, earned his call up when Gallego went on the DL. He responded by hitting .348 and instantly winning fans over for his hard-nosed style of play. The comparisons to Phil Rizzuto were immediate. Charlie Hayes was off to a torrid start with the bat, but it was his defense that drew the most attention, providing stability at a position that had been unstable for years. Roberto Kelly, conscious of the team's desire to make Williams a star player, was on his way to his first All-Star team, hitting .331 with 28 RBIs. Pérez became the team ace, averaging just under 9 strikeouts per 9 innings and giving up more than three runs in a game only once.

That May 26 win against Minnesota, however, was as good as it got. The Yankees never reached six games above .500 again until 1993. Not only did the losing commence at 1989–1991 levels, but the distractions that plagued the team in the past would flare up again in spades, including news from the commissioner's office that would reshape the entire future of major league baseball. First, though, the Yankees had a decision of their own to make for that year's amateur draft.

The on-the-field results of the Mets' 1992 spring training were irrelevant, even more so than spring training statistics tend to be. By the end of March, nearly all attention on the club was off the field, going beyond the usual distractions of player unhappiness. Four Mets were being accused of rape or sexual misconduct. The first allegation, though from the previous spring, was revealed after the alleged victim pressed charges during the '92 spring training and the Florida state attorney released a 400-page police report on the incident. A woman accused Gooden, Boston, and Coleman of raping her at Gooden's home in March 1991. The woman had had a relationship with Cone, though how close a relationship was a matter of dispute between the two. She alleged that, one night after Cone had turned down her request for a date, she ran into the three at a Jupiter,

Florida, bar and, because of her relationship with Cone, she felt at ease giving Gooden a ride home after Coleman and Boston had left. When she got to Gooden's place, Boston and Coleman were there, to her surprise. She claimed Gooden pulled her into the bedroom and eventually forced himself on her while Coleman blocked the door. Then, eventually, Boston and Coleman coerced her into oral sex. She said the shock of it all prevented her from realizing what happened for a few days, but that she did call other players on the Mets and the police to tell them what had happened. Gooden, Boston, and Coleman did not deny that she had been at Gooden's home with them. But all three said the sex had been consensual. Eventually, authorities did not press charges, saying they did not have enough evidence to prosecute the case. They also didn't dispute the accuser's story either. It was hardly a declaration of the players' innocence.

"I'm just glad that the truth came out and people know we're not capable of such an act," said Boston.[25] All three moved on quickly, at least publicly, but the allegations left an indelible mark. And it wasn't the end.

In the last week of March, three women filed a lawsuit against Cone, alleging, among other things, that he had exposed himself to them in the Mets' bullpen three years earlier. "He uses that bullpen for his own sexual gratification. The Mets know about it," said the lawyer for one of the plaintiffs.[26] The women also alleged Cone had come into the stands in August 1991 and threatened them over comments he heard them make to Sid Fernandez's wife. The three sought $8.1 million in damages.

Cone denied the allegations without saying much further, leaving it to the legal process to sort everything out. From the other side of the country, Darryl Strawberry spoke up instead, saying the three women were well known to the players and that "they harassed everybody."[27] The allegations eventually came to nothing, with Cone admitting that he had yelled at them but never threatened them. Even though the lawsuit eventually petered out, it followed Cone throughout the season and his career. It also created a gigantic rift between the players and the media.

"The real problem started with Jeff Torborg," said Klapisch, "who decided the way to unify his team was to demonize the press, and basically created an us against them mentality, which made everything much, much worse."[28]

Cone was unhappy with his portrayal in the press, especially given how much time he spent with reporters. He could not understand why his private life had become front-page news. It had "no bearing on the way I pitch," he explained.[29] He wasn't the only one upset that private doings were now public record.

John Franco, who had emerged as the team's clubhouse leader after just two seasons, was not amused by the continued questions, allegations, and stories appearing in print. Looking and sounding like the stereotypical Italian New Yorker, Franco was small for a ballplayer but tough in stature. He was also a prolific ballbreaker in the mold of any number of '86 Mets. Few topics or moments were out of bounds for him, which only endeared him more to teammates. He was funny, vocal, and only too willing to helm the ship in a way Gooden never was. On March 27, when Franco gazed at page 6 of the *New York Post*, he knew he had had enough of the press. There he saw a cartoon featuring a pitching coach yelling from the mound to Cone, visible only from the waist up in the dugout. "Are you almost finished warming up yet?" the pitching coach asks.[30] The implication was clear and it set Franco off.

He had already discussed the idea with Bonilla, Cone, Murray, and Randolph. Now, Franco felt, it was time to implement a total press boycott. No comments, no insights, no anything to reporters. Their privacy had been invaded enough and they were going to put a stop to it. As a group, the five presented the idea to the rest of the team. Not everyone was thrilled. A few players were already tired of the constant non-baseball-related topics they had to discuss; it was not even April yet. This boycott would be exactly the kind of thing that just created more distractions.

Ultimately, however, no one wanted to be seen as going against their teammates. The vote was unanimous; afterward, a statement signed by everyone present at the meeting was handed to the press. Rather than take offense, reporters were thrilled. Ironically, the boycott gave them something to write about during the doldrums of spring training's final week. After a few days players began engaging reporters again but just in small talk. Nothing substantial or print-worthy. While several players were enjoying the boycott, Mets ownership and the league were highly worried about its impact to the team and the game. That worry grew to borderline panic when Bonilla began rallying the troops to keep the boycott going into the regular season.

Commissioner Vincent and the Players Association got involved. Along with team management, they called on Cone, the team's union representative, to convince the players to end the boycott. Another meeting took place; this time, the debate was lengthy. Bonilla wanted to keep going, believing the whole thing would be taken even more seriously if it bled into the regular season. Others also spoke up about how they enjoyed this newfound sense of privacy in the clubhouse. Randolph and Magadan, however, said enough was enough. The message had been sent. Also, there was a legitimate concern that some players might simply break the boycott on their own. If that happened, the boycott would serve only to tear the team further apart, not bring it together.

Another vote occurred and the boycott officially ended a little over a week after it started. There were just two days to go before Opening Day.

"Maybe it wasn't the most useful thing to do from a public-relations standpoint," said pitcher Jeff Innis, a senior member of the club. "But it was from a team standpoint. We feel this is the best chance we've had to win in years. But we didn't have that established cohesiveness. We were just starting to develop that when we began being torn apart."[31]

Unfortunately for the Mets, most of what Innis said would turn out not to be true.

All the noise seemed to disappear as the Mets battled the Cardinals in St. Louis on Opening Night. Much was expected of this team, perhaps more than any other Mets club since 1987. With baseball's largest payroll at $44.5 million, they had to produce and fast. Whatever his anger issues with the press, Cone showed no effects on the mound, striking out nine over eight innings and giving up only two runs. Down a run in the ninth, the Mets tied it up, thanks in part to a hit from their new first baseman Murray. Then, tied at 2–2 in the tenth, Bonilla, who had already homered in his second Met at bat, drilled a Lee Smith slider deep into the right-field seats for the eventual game-winning, two-run home run.

The era of good feelings did not last long. The Mets lost six of their next seven and ceded ground in the back pages to the suddenly hot and seemingly distraction-free Yankees. They did, however, rebound to take 11 of the final 14 games in April. Saberhagen, knocked around for 19 runs in his first three starts, closed out the month by pitching back-to-back games of nine-inning scoreless ball. Though not hitting for power, Murray still managed to drive in 19 runs for the month. Randolph wasn't exactly replicating his 1991 season, but his .390 OBP was welcome in the number two position, setting up Murray for many of those 19 RBIS. But there were indications of trouble to come. After a tough, late-inning loss to the Expos, Torborg noted, "Our pitchers always seem to be coming up." The comment seemed innocuous enough, but, for some, it was in indication that the manager was having trouble adjusting to the National League's style of play.

May brought trouble. Coleman, again dealing with hamstring injuries, missed most of April, attempted a comeback on May 1, reinjured himself, and missed the next four weeks. A shoulder injury to Elster ended his season. In the middle of the month, a right index finger injury sidelined Saberhagen and limited him to just nine more appearances the rest of the year. Franco began experiencing elbow issues that would limit him to just nine appearances in the second half of the season. Though he missed just a handful of games, Gooden was pitching through shoulder pain that limited his effectiveness. The offense, which was supposed to intimidate the rest of the National League, was shockingly flaccid. Howard Johnson could not replicate his numbers from the previous year. At the end of May he was hitting only .201 with just four home runs, three of which were hit before April 26. HoJo was known for his sensitivity to any criticism and, as his play worsened, he became even more surly and standoffish with the press.

From Opening Day until May 10, the Mets got only a single home run and just four RBIS from their shortstop position. Magadan, back in the starting lineup at third base, was hitting for average, but drove in only 12 runs with one home run for the first two months of the year. The only steady offensive production came from Murray, but he was causing problems of a different kind.

Murray was one of the most underrated players in baseball, known for his production but not truly appreciated for just how good he was. He never had over 200 hits in a season or hit more than 33 home runs. Yet, from 1981 to 1985, he finished fifth or higher in every MVP vote. Only the emergence of Mattingly in 1984 prevented Eddie from being the greatest first baseman in the game for the duration of the 1980s. As his career went along, he started racking up the kind of numbers that guarantee a spot in Cooperstown. With teammates, he was kind and outgoing, acting as a teacher when needed and a leader when called upon. The one thing he never did well, however, was deal with the media, especially print reporters. That was Murray's own choice. For reasons that were unclear to many, he was never comfortable around the clubhouse beat writers and took even the slightest perceived criticism as a personal affront. Sometimes his only interactions with reporters would be to confront them over some little thing they had said about him.

When playing with Baltimore, he just stopped talking to them, a practice he more or less maintained after going to Los Angeles. Even when he did talk, his quotes were often bland and so meaningless as not to warrant inclusion in a story. That was by decision. Murray seemed to delight in tormenting reporters whenever the opportunity arose. On May 3 he hit his 400th career home run in a 5–0 win over the Braves. It was a getaway day, meaning reporters had to try and file their game stories before getting on the plane to Houston for the next series. Almost certainly knowing that, Murray kept them waiting in the clubhouse while he sat and watched the NBA playoffs. When he finished watching the game, he meandered around to different areas, acting like he was finally going to speak before heading in another direction. Eventually, he addressed reporters, but gave them little to use.

"He's a bright man, but no matter how artfully we wanted to write about Murray's accomplishments, he wasn't going to talk to us," wrote reporters Bob Klapisch and John Harper. "So while the Mets were playing decent baseball at this point, having just won two of three in Atlanta to go five games over .500, we were starting to wonder if Murray could single-handedly make covering the Mets an act of misery."[32]

Murray kept hitting, though. On June 2 he hit his sixteenth career grand slam, the eighth-highest total in baseball history at that time, giving the team a 4–3 victory over the Giants. The win put the team just a half-game back of the Cardinals and Pirates for the division lead. It hardly seemed to matter. Another distraction emerged in the form of Bonilla. Perhaps no one was struggling more than the Bronx-born outfielder. After hitting two home runs on Opening Day, Bonilla did not hit another one until May 19, a span of thirty-nine games. He was getting on base and driving in runs when the opportunities came up, but the numbers were not what many thought they should be.

Worse for Bonilla, almost all his production came on the road. By May 30 he was hitting just .137 with no home runs and only four RBIs at Shea. The boos had begun raining down earlier in the year, but now they were heard with more frequency. You could not help but notice it every time he made an out. In general, he looked lost at the plate at Shea, so, that day, hitting coach Tom McGraw suggested Bonilla bat with ear plugs. They would drown out the noise of Shea and allow him to focus simply on hitting the ball. Bonilla went 0-4 and the boos cascaded through the ballpark. During the game TV cameras picked up on the plugs and a new story was born for the '92 Mets.

The assumption was that Bonilla wore the earplugs to drown out all the boos. Bonilla and the team denied it, saying he had tried them to help drown out the overall noise that permeated the stadium while playing. Few believed it, especially the fans. When Bonilla then made comments implying that he didn't care what the fans thought, it made the situation worse: fans were now going to ride him even more and Bonilla's patience with the media kept dwindling.

"I don't like fans? Where does that come from?" he asked a group of reporters, when trying to explain the whole situation. "Why wouldn't I like fans? Why wouldn't I want kids to come to a game?"[33]

In his next game he hit his first Shea home run as a Met, a grand slam, and the tide seemed to turn. A half-game out, the Mets went into Pittsburgh with high hopes, only to leave losing three of four games. At 28-27, it was the last time in 1992 the Mets were over .500. They lost two of three in Montreal, then were swept at home by the Pirates, losing every game by a single run. Montreal came in and won two of three; that's when the team's internal fractures really exploded publicly.

Torborg was already losing what little hold he had on the team. Before the first game against Montreal, he told WFAN that Franco was dealing with an injury, news he had not let the pitcher know he was going to divulge. An enraged Franco confronted his manager before the game, making a show of just how upset he was. Torborg's speaking to WFAN, the same managerial duty Harrelson had stopped doing, had become a sore spot in the clubhouse. As noted by Harper and Klapisch in their book chronicling the season, *The Worst Team Money Could Buy*, players began finding out whether they were in the lineup or not by listening to the radio. For many, it was unnerving, especially from a manager who had made a point of noting in spring training how he was going to keep family secrets within the family.

Meanwhile, the manager sat by helplessly as his players ignored or confronted the press and seemingly lacked any resolve to win ballgames. Players exited the clubhouse as quickly as possible after games, not seeing any reason to sit and rehash details about the latest loss. On the same day Franco confronted Torborg, Bonilla struck out to end the eighth inning as the tying run. Afterward, he refused to talk to the press. Torborg could do nothing about it.

When Murray refused to talk to the press, Torborg could do nothing about it. When Coleman sulked, Torborg could do nothing about it. When HoJo went off on a reporter for asking the wrong question, Torborg could do nothing about it. He was in an impossibly difficult situation. On June 25 it got worse. The Mets were already down 5–0 before they'd had a chance to bat when Cubs' pitcher Greg Maddux lined a double to right field. Bonilla misplayed the ball, allowing another run to score and Maddux to get to third. Afterward, Bonilla looked up as the Shea Stadium scoreboard flashed "E-9," which drew a round of boos from the crowd. Bonilla was not amused. When the inning was over, he beelined to the dugout phone and called Mets PR director Jay Horwitz to complain. Whether Bonilla was complaining about the play being scored an error or at the E-9 being flashed on the board is unclear. Either way, he was still complaining; Torborg was not amused. He screamed at Bobby to get his head in the game. Other Mets, who overheard Bonilla's side of the phone conversation, could not believe he was worried about an error while the team was losing 7–0. And SportsChannel, which covered Mets games for television, captured the whole thing, meaning reporters and fans knew what occurred before the game had even ended. Once it was over, the only question anyone wanted to know was what exactly happened. Instead of explaining the situation and asking forgiveness, Torborg and Bonilla lied. Bonilla said he was calling to check on Horwitz's health, while Torborg claimed to have not heard whatever it was that Bonilla had said on the phone. Neither was true and a few players had already told reporters what had happened, making the whole thing worse.

The furor did not die down. The next day callers flooded New York sports talk radio angrily denouncing Bonilla and the organization. The clubhouse beat reporters, not satisfied with the explanation given the night before, continued to press the issue. Torborg was forced to admit that his answers the night before had been "incorrect" and that it sounded like he "was lying." Not only did that further diminish Torborg in the eyes of reporters and fans who were already losing faith in him, but when Bonilla refused to concede what happened, it made Torborg look weak and not in control of his own clubhouse. Bobby said his comment about checking on Horwitz's health was meant as a joke and that he did not believe he had to explain his actions to anyone. In fact he thought it was "ludicrous that I would be asked why I was on the phone."[34]

In some ways Bonilla was not wrong. It was a single moment in a 162-game season that ultimately had no bearing on the outcome of the game. Had the call happened in just about any other year, it most likely would have been treated as a minor hiccup in a long season. This, however, was different. It was one more silly, unnecessary act in a season filled with silly, unnecessary acts. Moreover, this was the team that was supposed to dominate the weak National League East and return the Mets to the postseason. Instead, the season had now become all about the constant misery off the field and in the locker room. By the All-Star break, the Mets were four games under .500 and seven games back of first. It was by no means an insurmountable deficit. Plenty of teams had come back from that. There was no sentiment, however, that the Mets would be one of those teams. The only question was just how bad things would get before they found the bottom.

Derek Sanderson Jeter. That was a name you could remember. A four-syllable first and last name combo that was perfect for 57,000 fans at Yankee Stadium to chant. And his personal story was almost too corny-sounding to be real. Son of Dr. Charles Jeter, a black father who played college baseball, and Dorothy Jeter, a white mother who was an accountant and met her husband while both were stationed overseas in the U.S. military. Born in New Jersey but raised in Kalamazoo, Michigan, Derek Jeter knew from an early age exactly what he wanted to be: a New York Yankee. Again, almost too corny to be true, but it all was.

In high school it was clear that Jeter was far and away better than the other kids he played with. Even as a freshman, the only reason he was not put on the varsity baseball team was because they already had a senior at shortstop and there was little reason for Derek to just ride the bench. The traits that he would eventually be known for—the determination, the drive to win, not looking down on or criticizing teammates in public—were all present even in high school. So was the baseball intelligence. Pitchers learned that Jeter was a dead pull hitter and began throwing him outside. Derek simply adjusted and begin shooting the ball the other way, developing the Jeterian swing that would become famous.

His name began making the rounds; scouts started showing up in Kalamazoo. The Astros, the Reds, the Yankees, and more. He was wiry, but Jeter could hit. He made errors in the field, but he moved quick and had a laser arm. As the June 1992 draft approached, the Yankees had the sixth overall pick. Their scouts loved the young shortstop from Michigan. "Born to play ss. Quality defensive tools compare with Barry Larkin—Reds," wrote one.[35] He was who they wanted. But a lot of other teams loved Jeter, too, and the idea that five of them would pass on him seemed not just unlikely, but nearly impossible. And yet, in a twist of fate where every single decision made ultimately benefited the Yankees, five teams did in fact pass on Derek Jeter.

The reasons why are varied. Some were perhaps legitimate, others not. Jeter made no secret he wanted to be a Yankee, so one line of thinking was, why bother drafting him if he won't sign? Another was that, based on the $1.55 million bonus the Yankees had given Brien Taylor the year before, Jeter would ask for something similar. That was a price too steep for some. Another was that Jeter would rather commit to the University of Michigan than enter the majors. One more reason was simple enough: they thought other available players would develop faster and, ultimately, be better than Jeter.

Houston, which had the first pick, passed over him for that reason. They thought they would get a quicker, better return out of Phil Nevin. The move allegedly angered Astros scout Hal Newhouser, the former pitcher who loved watching Jeter play, so much that he resigned upon hearing the news and never took another job in baseball again. The Indians picked next and ignored Jeter because they wanted a pitcher, selecting Paul Shuey. The Expos did the same thing. Baltimore followed and had no reason to pick Jeter, not when Cal Ripken Jr. was already their shortstop. One more team and the Yankees could pull this off. That team, however, seemed almost certain to take Jeter. Reds scouts across the board had loved what they had seen of Derek. They already had Barry Larkin at short, but most of them did not care. This was just too good a prospect to turn down. "I thought I was going to Cincinnati and that I'd be stuck behind Larkin," Jeter said.[36]

Julian Mock, the Reds' scouting director, had different ideas. He did not see the need for another shortstop, one he did not even know for certain would get playing time in Cincinnati. He instead picked Chad Mottola, a hulking outfielder from Florida, in the hopes that Mottola would provide a more immediate and larger impact. Mottola played 35 games for Cincinnati and just 59 in his entire career.

When Mottola's name was announced, the Yankees' draft room erupted. "Derek Jeter of Kalamazoo Central," declared the team's director of minor league operations Kevin Elfering into the phone. Publicly, the team downplayed the selection. "Derek Jeter was the best athlete available when we had the opportunity to select," they said in a statement, making it almost sound as if they had gotten stuck with Jeter.[37] The coy attitude was strategic, as the Yankees still had to go about signing the seventeen-year-old; they did not want to give him leverage by publicly praising him too much.

In the meantime, the team on the field endured one problem after another. On June 17 Barfield returned after a monthlong stint on the disabled list due to an injured left wrist. He started in that day's game, got three plate appearances, and reinjured his wrist in the process. Barfield immediately went back on the DL and never appeared in another major league game. Meanwhile, to make room for Barfield initially, the team had sent Pat Kelly down to the minors, a decision that angered the young infielder. They called him right back up when Barfield reinjured his wrist, but the resentment had already been created.

Four days later the Yankees were in Baltimore on ESPN's Sunday Night Baseball broadcast for the rubber match of a three-game series. They had lost 12 of 18, falling below .500 and dropping to fifth place. On the mound for New York was Tim Leary, the nineteen-game loser of 1990 who had suffered through an even worse '91 season. Leary came into the game having pitched with mixed results that year. Sometimes he was lights out, like in his first start of the year when he held the Tigers to one run in eight innings. Sometimes he wasn't, like earlier in the month when he got hit for seven runs against the Rangers. His inability to remain consistent drove Showalter nuts, but the Yankees needed him in the rotation.

Now, in the fifth inning of a national televised game, Leary became the subject of controversy. Baltimore manager Johnny Oates came out of the dugout holding a baseball, one that had just been fouled off. He showed it to home plate umpire Terry Craft, explaining that Leary was doctoring the ball and showing him the scuff marks. Shortly after, television cameras caught Leary raising his glove to his mouth. While it was not totally clear, he appeared to remove something from the glove with his mouth. The umpiring crew checked Leary's mitt and found nothing, but they never checked his mouth, saying they did not have a right to. After the inning ended, cameras caught Leary heading down the dugout tunnel and seemingly removing something from his mouth.

"It was coarse sandpaper," claimed Oates. "I have five balls under lock and key and gave a sixth to [umpire crew chief Dave] Phillips that show a scuff mark in the same spot."[38]

Leary denied doing anything wrong. "I put my fingers in my mouth. I go to my fingers after almost every pitch. I have nothing to hide," he told reporters after the game.[39]

The Orioles played the rest of the game under protest, which was eventually denied. Leary continued to deny any wrongdoing, and nothing was ever proven. But the incident only further irked Showalter, who begged Michael to trade Leary, even offering to perform oral sex on him to make it happen. It took two months to fulfill that request, in part because Leary gave up eighteen runs over three appearances after the Baltimore game, but once Michael was able to trade him to Seattle, he showed up in Showalter's office and jokingly pulled his pants down.

Three days after Leary's Baltimore performance came more bad news. The previous winter, Yankees pitcher Steve Howe had attempted to buy a gram of cocaine in his home state of Montana. He was arrested and charged with attempted possession. Howe eventually entered a plea. But he had been suspended six times before for drug violations. His signing had been a gamble for the Yankees. It had paid off in 1991, as Howe was perhaps the most stable force out of the team's bullpen. Knowing that he was about to face punishment for his most recent arrest, Howe was still able to pitch in '92. He picked up where he left off, giving up just 9 hits in 22 innings and allowing a run in only 4 of his 20 appearances. But Fay Vincent, who some thought was growing more tyrannical by the second, decided Howe had been given enough chances. On June 24 he banished Howe from the game for life. Eventually, Howe was reinstated through an arbitrator, but his season was over.

It was during the initial phase of Howe's appeal process that trouble really began for the Yankees, while Vincent sealed his fate as commissioner. On June 30 Showalter, Michael, and the Yankees' vice president of baseball operations, Jack Lawn, all agreed to appear as character witnesses before the arbiter in Howe's appeal. Each said they did not agree that Howe should be given a lifetime ban from the sport. Vincent was apoplectic. "This is a kick in the balls to the commissioner's office," he was reported to have said, angry that three people he deemed employees of Major League Baseball—and thus, his employees—would undermine his authority in that manner.[40]

The next day Vincent hauled all three to his office and threatened them with suspension if they did not revoke their own testimony. Ultimately it came to nothing, but the threat was taken seriously enough by Showalter, Michael, and Lawn that they each hired lawyers. Word of the threats spread quickly, most likely from Showalter, Michael, or both. The Players Association was horrified that Vincent would try to influence the arbitration process in such a manner. The owners were horrified that he would take such seemingly baseless action against people who were merely trying to support their own player. This was on the heels of Vincent's letter to all owners just two weeks earlier, announcing that he was revoking baseball's rules of procedure, established by Vincent's predecessors to regulate procedures, investigations, and hearings. They were, in essence, baseball's Miranda rights, Bill of Rights, and Equal Protection Clause rolled into one. Now, because he felt they had "no practical benefit" and had been "intentionally misinterpreted," Vincent was revoking them and would simply announce the rules "on a case-by-case basis."[41] The baseball world was stunned. Owners had been leery of Vincent's methods since he had prevented Steinbrenner from calling witnesses in his own defense two years earlier. Now, the commissioner had officially decreed that the only rules that mattered were the ones he deemed to matter.

Vincent was not done with the Yankees. For well over a year, Steinbrenner had been waging a behind-the-scenes battle to return to baseball. He had immediately regretted asking for a lifetime ban and he wanted back in. The problem was, among other things, Steinbrenner had helped create a lawsuit against Vincent. In 1990, after finally realizing that the banishment he signed included a clause that forbid him from suing Vincent, attorney Robert Costello gave The Boss another idea. What if someone else sued Vincent? Costello had been hired by the Yankees to defend Chief Operating Officer Leonard Kleinman, who was alleged to have helped with the $40,000 payoff to Spira. Vincent had started looking into Kleinman immediately after George's banishment. That meant that Vincent, who had authority to approve or deny Steinbrenner's choice of the team's general partner, would never approve of Kleinman. With this in mind, Costello laid out the plan. Steinbrenner would put forth Kleinman as general partner, knowing he would be rejected. Once Vincent did that, Kleinman would have grounds to sue the commissioner. In the course of that lawsuit, Costello could then lay out how Vincent had denied Steinbrenner his due process rights, something The Boss was prohibited from doing himself in a court of law.

Steinbrenner put forward Kleinman, who was rejected. While Robert

Nederlander was named and approved as the next general partner, Kleinman filed a $22 million suit against Vincent and John Dowd. Two years later, that lawsuit was still in play, as were others that Vincent suspected George was behind. "They were all bullshit lawsuits," said Vincent. Still, combined with his perceived recent heavy-handedness, the commissioner began feeling pressure. Then one day he got a call.

"Fay, I want to come back," said Steinbrenner.

"George, there is no coming back," replied Vincent.

"Well, I want to talk to you about this."

"George, look, I am not even going to talk to you while those lawsuits are there. They are a pain in the ass and you started them all."

"Oh no, no, I didn't."

"That's fine if you say you didn't. We are gonna go through them and when those lawsuits are over and you want to talk to me I am willing to talk to you."[42]

Nothing had been resolved in the conversation, but Steinbrenner got the message: make the lawsuits disappear and I'll consider reinstating you. The Boss went to work. A few months later he called Vincent back. The lawsuits would soon be going away for good, though Steinbrenner could not help but point out how much money it cost him to do so. The commissioner did not care about any of that. After all, he reasoned, the lawsuits were George's fault anyway. Still, he was now willing to lift the ban, so long as Steinbrenner served the entirety of the two years' suspension Vincent was originally going to impose.

As early as June 15, Vincent was ready to announce he was allowing The Boss to return. But reports began coming to Vincent that Steinbrenner had been in direct contact with personnel about team decisions, against the terms of his banishment. Vincent had always suspected as much, as had many others in baseball and just about every member of the press. Yankee employees were required to sign statements every six months saying they, and no other employees they knew of, had not been in contact with Steinbrenner. An employee could refuse to sign, thus signaling that Steinbrenner had broken the terms of his deal. The problem was the statements were filed with David Sussman, the team's lawyer, not with the commissioner's office. Anyone who did not sign or who signaled a violation of the agreement would surely be ratted out to Steinbrenner and face severe consequences. So Vincent had to go on hearsay and rumors. It was enough for him to hold off on any announcement as he dragged several high-level employees and former manager Stump Merrill back to New York to interrogate them. Everyone swore that they had had no contact with Steinbrenner. Even if they had, they were not going to be the one to say anything: certainly not to Fay Vincent. The commissioner was absolutely positive that Steinbrenner had violated the terms of his banishment and that people within the organization had gone along with it. "Would I bet my soul on the fact that he was not cheating?" asked Vincent. "Of course not. I think he tried and I think there are probably instances where he put things over on me and was involved because he was fundamentally dishonest. He had some admirable traits but he would have cheated his mother."[43]

Left with no proof, nothing to go on, and with the promise that the lawsuits would disappear, on July 25, nearly two years to the day after banishing Steinbrenner, Vincent announced his reinstatement. George could return on March 1, 1993. Essentially, he was going to serve out the term of the suspension that Vincent had planned on giving him in the first place.

In Barcelona for the Summer Olympics, Steinbrenner received the news from Randy Levine, one of the many lawyers he had used to get himself reinstated.

"What the fuck do you want?" asked The Boss.

"Boss, I have great news," replied Levine. "You've been reinstated."

"Great. When?"

"You're back March 1."

"March 1! It should have been January 1. Terrible job."[44]

Steinbrenner called back the next day offering his appreciation. Vincent, meanwhile, received a vote of no confidence from the owners on September 3 and resigned as commissioner shortly thereafter. In his place, the owners appointed one of their own, Brewers owner Bud Selig, as acting commissioner.

"It's no problem with me," Michael stated calmly, after hearing the news of Steinbrenner's reinstatement. "I can handle all that. I've worked for him off and on for a long time. I have no problem at all."[45] Michael was probably being truthful. At the same time, he knew what George's return meant. He knew the craziness that would ensue. The pressures that would return to trade away young talent for aging has-beens. The calls for more discipline in the clubhouse. He would have to spend his days protecting Bernie Williams after a bad night or avoiding the demand to trade Scott Kamieniecki after a rough outing. It was inevitable.

The same went for Showalter. The season had not been perfect, but, by all accounts, Buck was a hit in the clubhouse. Players respected him, fans loved him, and, even if the record was not what many wanted, the desire to instill pride in the Yankees' clubhouse was clear. That was something Steinbrenner would eat up. Showalter, like Michael, said all the right things when hearing that The Boss would be back: "You don't spend 16 years in the organization without finding out how Mr. Steinbrenner wants things done. He doesn't want to see anything that reflects poorly on the Yankees. I feel the same way."[46] Still, Buck knew, just like Michael, that things were going to change on March 1.

"An end to an era, I think. The era of the arrogant Mets is gone."[47]

David Cone had just made the understatement of the year. It was August 27, an off day, but here he was in the Mets clubhouse, surrounded by reporters, explaining how he felt about having just been traded to the Toronto Blue Jays. The worst team in the league in dealing with reporters had dealt the player in baseball who best understood how to deal with the media. Showing just how good he was, Cone made a point of going to the ballpark after being informed of the deal so that he could provide a series of parting shots on his way out the door. Cone, like some of his teammates and most of the fans, had hated what he saw happening to the organization over the last few years. The Mets had deliberately scrubbed the team of any fun. Instead of curing the team's ills, it was more like when they tried to make Las Vegas a family-friendly city. It just wasn't in the makeup of Vegas, or the Mets, to be that way.

"The heart and soul of the club has been bred out of it," Cone continued. "The day it began was the day they traded Lenny Dykstra and Roger McDowell for Juan Samuel."

The trade was both surprising and not surprising at all. Surprising because, just weeks earlier, Harazin had stated that Cone would not be traded. "And I meant it," he explained after doing just that, adding, "I reached a position where developments force me to reassess my position."[48] Not surprising because the team was 56-67, sitting in second to last place. A moderately good July had provided the slightest glimmer of hope until August, when seven- and five-game losing streaks culminated in 14 losses over 16 games. The clubhouse continued to be a place of misery. Around this time Gary Carter, embarking on the final weeks of his playing career amid a playoff run with the Expos, asked a New York reporter, "What's it like covering a disaster?"[49]

The season was over and Cone was in the last year of his contract. In his remarks to the press, Harazin made clear why they were jettisoning their best pitcher.

"We were 14 games out. It was obvious, with about 40 games to go, that no one player was going to help us turn the season around." That was fair enough. What came next, however, was the true reason. "Secondly, our track record in terms of long-term contracts with pitchers is obviously checkered with respect to injuries . . . Not a very happy history. We knew, thirdly, we were not really looking to sign a pitcher to a five-year contract and might even struggle to guarantee four years at very large numbers."[50]

It was a statement remarkable for its sheer honesty. Not only was Harazin admitting that the team had a history of bad signings, despite how few they had made over the years, but he was also admitting that they did not think they could afford, and would therefore make no effort to sign, Cone.

The pitcher was gobsmacked. "How would they know they can't afford me. They never even asked me what it would take," Cone said, in response to Harazin's comments.[51]

Cone had been everything a team and teammates could ask for. He fielded media questions whenever and wherever, taking the pressure off guys who were never comfortable having their responses recorded or written down. He was the union rep. He was funny and intelligent. And then there was the pitching. Since returning from breaking his finger attempting to bunt in 1987, he had not missed a single start. There were the 20 wins in '88 and leading the league in strikeouts in '90 and '91. There was also the 20-strikeout game to end the '91 season. But there was more than that. Cone was a bulldog on the mound, incapable of giving in even if it meant pitch after pitch after pitch. Even by the standards of early 1990s baseball, David Cone threw a remarkably high number of pitches per start. In just his third appearance in 1992, he tossed 145 pitches in a complete game win. In the entire month of April, a time when pitchers are still trying to find their rhythm and work up their arm strength, he averaged 122 pitches per start. In six consecutive starts between June and July, he never threw fewer than 132 pitches in a game, including July 17, when he tossed an obscene 166 during a 1–0 victory.

Still, despite all of that, Cone was expendable. He made, or was about to make, too much money for the team. He was also a remnant of the '80s, an era the Mets were trying to get as far away from as possible. Moreover, Cone had never really trusted Torborg, just as he had never trusted Harrelson, which made team leadership uneasy. So he was dealt to the Blue Jays for infield prospect Jeff Kent and outfield prospect Ryan Thompson, who at that point was marked as a player to be named later because the team could not add him to the roster until September 1.

Cone's teammates were shocked and appalled. "I can't believe they didn't get one proven major league player for him," noted Magadan.[52] The beat writers were equally dumbfounded and made no secret of how little they thought of the deal. "The Dykstra deal told me this organization was confused," wrote the *New York Times*' George Vecsey. "They traded Lenny, who actually loves to play baseball, along with Roger McDowell, for a moper named Samuel, and things have not been the same. That was dumb. Letting Strawberry go after the 1990 season was more dumb than it was cheap. The Cone deal is cheap. Cheap is worse than dumb. Dumb is innocent. Cheap is calculated."[53]

"David Cone is gone. He was the best they had. They'll miss him. I'll miss him. Now trade the rest of them. Trade them all," said *Newsday*'s Steve Jacobson.[54]

Only the *Daily News*' Mike Lupica agreed with management's decision; his position may have been more about being a contrarian to sell papers than a principled stand.

The deal now done, the team still had a month's worth of games to play. It became their worst month of the year.

The low point of the team's on-field performance came at home on September 1. On their way to a 4–1 loss to the Braves, Coleman struck out to end the third inning on a check swing call by the third base umpire. Coleman turned to home plate umpire Gary Darling and began arguing with him, at which point Darling ejected him from the game. Things became heated between Coleman and Darling; Torborg quickly ran out of the dugout to protect his player. When he tried to put himself between the two, Coleman shoved him out of the way. Torborg tried again, this time pushing Coleman toward the Mets' dugout. "What the fuck are you pushing me for?" Coleman yelled, shouting in Torborg's face. Bonilla came to defuse the situation, but Coleman pushed him, too, before heading to the dugout and straight to the locker room. A clearly incensed Torborg followed him, confronting him in the clubhouse and demanding an apology. "Go fuck yourself," Coleman responded, before eventually apologizing.[55]

Coleman was suspended two games. Worse, for a second straight season he had challenged the authority of the team's manager, indirectly the previous year when Harrelson bungled the response to the Cubbage incident and directly now by pushing Torborg. The entire incident was a microcosm of the team: lawless, rudderless, and hopeless.

The Mets lost five in a row mid-month, then three in a row, then seven in the final week of September. A three-game series at home against Pittsburgh ended the year. Back in April, this was a mark-your-calendar series, one that could have meant deciding the division winner. Instead, the Pirates came in, having already clinched their third straight division title. Only 38,006 showed up for the entire three games, nearly ten thousand fewer fans than had attended the home opener. Perhaps the only noteworthy event occurred in the ninth inning of the last game, when Willie Randolph walked. Like so many, Randolph's year had not turned out as hoped. An injury had halted his season on August 12, but he got one more start in this final game. It was his last as a player. After walking, he came out for a pinch runner. As the six-time All-Star left the field, he received a warm ovation in recognition of what he had done for the city over fourteen seasons, even if almost all of it was as a Yankee.

Two batters later, Jeff McKnight flied out to end the game and the season. The Mets, seemingly destined to head to the playoffs when spring training had begun seven and a half months earlier, finished 72-90, twenty-four games out of first place. For all the trades and signings, they had actually performed five games worse than 1991. Collectively, the team hit .235, the Mets' lowest season batting average since 1974. Their on-base percentage was their lowest since 1983 and slugging the worst since 1974. They failed to hit at least a hundred home runs for the first time since 1982.

Though Saberhagen missed half the season, the starting rotation had mostly held in place. The trouble came largely out of the bullpen. Franco missed all of July and September due to injury. Anthony Young, a second-year pitcher, was moved from the rotation to the closer's role to replace him. In July Young was near flawless, recording seven saves and giving up just two runs in ten innings. In September Young blew five saves, all games the Mets lost. As a result Young ended the year 2-14. Meanwhile, a series of relievers failed to provide the team with any certainty in the games' middle innings. Paul Gibson, Lee Guetterman, Mark Dewey, Tim Burke, and Barry Jones appeared in a combined 138 games, pitching 169⅔ innings. Their collective ERA was 5.62, with 210 hits and 63 walks allowed.

The New York Mets were in deep trouble heading into that off-season. The question was, what could they do about it?

The Yankees were eleven games out on July 25. The magic of the first two months had disappeared. Offensively, the team was falling into old patterns: not enough walks, not enough power, not enough run generation. Except for Pérez, the starting pitching remained inconsistent. Sanderson was not repeating his All-Star performance of '91. Jeff Johnson was getting battered around in start after start of his sophomore season. Injuries mixed with failing performances robbed the team of a consistent fourth and fifth starter for most the season. The bullpen remained strong, but there were not many leads to protect.

On July 27 Tartabull injured himself again, suffering lower back spasms that landed him on the DL four days later. The Yankees called up Bernie Williams from Columbus. They had not had the room for Williams in the first few months of the '92 season. Now that they did, Showalter had no intention of sitting him on the bench. It was time for Bernie to show that he could play at the major league level. It also meant that the team was not going to experiment with moving Williams somewhere else. There would be no repeat of Pat Kelly at third base. Bernie was going to play center field, while Roberto Kelly was moving to left field. The team's lone All-Star that season was less than thrilled that he had to change positions for an unproven kid who had failed to impress in 1991. Moreover, Kelly made no secret of his unhappiness, criticizing the decision while escaping to the trainers' room to avoid elaborating further.[56]

Williams endured, though. He showed vast improvement at the plate, hitting .280, along with increased power, including a 440-foot blast in Detroit that was the longest home run hit in the American League in August. Though his base running never matched someone with Williams's speed, he also overcame the indecisiveness on the base paths that had driven teammates nuts in his rookie year. Williams was officially in New York to stay for the rest of his career.

Left with little to do but play out the string, the Yankees began calling up their minor league talent to see what they could accomplish at the big league level. In August and September, J. T. Snow, Gerald Williams, Sterling Hitchcock, and Bob Wickman all made their debuts. Wickman in particular created some highlights by going 6-1 in his eight starts despite not always pitching well, a pattern that would continue over the following years and create something of a good luck charm aura around him.

The most memorable debut took place on August 9 at Yankee Stadium. Twenty-two-year-old Sam Militello, owner of a 12-2 record at Columbus and a 34-8 career record in the minors, made his first start in a rubber match against the Red Sox. A Tampa native, it was his first time ever in a major league stadium. Utilizing a mix of off-speed pitches and never throwing a fastball more than 87 miles per hour, Militello flummoxed the Boston lineup. A seeing-eye single in the second inning by Tony Peña was the only hit he allowed over seven innings. After the hit, Militello retired the next 15 batters, going 7 innings and getting the win in a 6–0 victory. The 41,125 in attendance, who had not had much to cheer about in the last few months, loved what they saw. If this guy could shut down the Red Sox in his debut with a packed Yankee Stadium, who knew what the future would bring for him and the Yankees. Militello pitched eight strong innings in his next start, earning the victory, and finished the year with a string of impressive performances.

The Yankees played out the season merely going through the motions. The Blue Jays were on their way to a second straight division title and, eventually, their first world championship. New York ended the year in fifth place, 76-86. It was a modest five-game improvement from 1991, but they still seemed years away from being contenders. Yet Showalter had studied this team all year; he knew who he wanted to stay a Yankee and who he wanted gone. Coupled with Michael's awareness that some major moves were needed to make the team Boss-ready come March, the Yankees were on their way to one of their most transformative off-seasons ever.

7

Most Players Detest the Place

Gene Michael sank into his chair, his face noticeably red. Yankees general partner Joe Molloy put his hand over his mouth, looking like he had just seen some horrible traffic accident. It was only ten minutes into the November 17, 1992, MLB expansion draft—an event allowing the new National League expansion Colorado Rockies and Florida Marlins to select players from all twenty-six teams to fill up their roster—and the Yankees had just lost Charlie Hayes. Rules allowed each team to protect certain players while leaving others vulnerable to selection. New York had gambled, hoping that both teams would overlook a solid third baseman coming off a strong year in the American League East. It took all of three picks for the Rockies to gobble up Hayes. The Yankees' brass was stunned. After years of stopgap measures they had finally found a permanent third baseman in Hayes. Now he was gone. Even worse, the Yankees had no Plan B. The top free agents on the market were Kevin Seitzer and Wade Boggs, the latter coming off the worst season of his career. The Yankees were not interested in either. Dave Magadan made no secret that he would be happy to stay in New York as a Yankee. He even had dinner with a team rep, but nothing came of it. The Yankees had no one ready at the minor league level and no one capable of playing third on an everyday basis at the major league level. It got worse when they lost two of their best prospects, outfielder Carl Everett and catcher Brad Ausmus, to the Marlins and Rockies, respectively, in later rounds. No other team appeared to have been hit harder by the draft than the Yankees.

It could have been worse. The Yankees had also left unprotected a twenty-two-year-old, skinny starting pitcher that no fan had ever heard of. The pitcher, Mariano Rivera, was raised in Puerto Caimito, Panama, the son of a fisherman. By any measure, his surroundings were poor. He later recalled that, while they celebrated Christmas, Santa Claus did not visit that part of Panama. As a teenager, Mariano worked alongside his father on a shrimp boat. He hated it, recognizing early on that this was not where he wanted his life to go: "On the boat, I liked looking at all the different fish. But my father's life was not for me."[1]

Instead, sports offered a way out. The sport that appeared to give Mariano hope was the one he loved the most: soccer. He liked baseball, too, and he was good at it. But that was just to pass the time. Rivera was a remarkable athlete and gifted fielder. He could have been an outfielder, as he moved with a fluid grace that allowed him easily to track down fly balls. It was also the position he truly loved to play, "because," he said, "there's nothing better in baseball than running down a fly ball."[2] He played for a local amateur Oeste team, usually in the outfield but sometimes at shortstop. In 1989, during a national tournament game, Rivera was asked to replace a pitcher who had performed poorly. His performance was so impressive that a few of his teammates informed a scout for the Yankees about him. After a brief tryout, the Yankees liked what they saw. His fluid mechanics and the deceptive quickness of his pitches, plus his overall joyful demeanor while playing the game, led them to offer him a contract. Rivera signed in February 1990, joining the team for $2,000.

While he knew he would be playing baseball, Mariano had no true idea of what that meant. For him, the world outside of Panama did not exist. "Honest to goodness, I think that when the Yankees sign me I will continue to play my baseball in Panama," Rivera later wrote.[3] He had little to no idea what the major leagues were. He had never heard about Babe Ruth or Hank Aaron. Had no clue what or where Tampa, Florida, was.

But soon enough, Rivera was on his way. He pitched impressively from the start. In rookie ball, mostly as a reliever, he averaged 10 strikeouts per 9 innings with an 8:1 strikeout-to-walk ratio. "All around I see guys who are stronger than me and throw harder than me, and I am outperforming nearly all of them," recalled Mariano, in his autobiography. "It is almost an out-of-body experience."[4]

As he moved up the ranks of minor league ball, he became a starter and his numbers were no worse for wear. But then, trying to give his slider more movement, he adjusted his pitching mechanics. The result was nerve damage so severe that, in August 1992, Rivera had surgery on his elbow. Unsure how effective he would be post surgery, the Yankees left him unprotected for the entirety of the expansion draft. Perhaps equally leery of a pitcher whose fastball was only in the low nineties even before he had elbow surgery, neither the Marlins nor the Rockies selected him. It remains one of the luckiest breaks in the history of baseball, one of many that would benefit the Yankees throughout the decade.

The Yankees did not know that then; overall, it was shaping up to be a brutal off-season for Michael. Two weeks earlier Cincinnati Reds outfielder Paul O'Neill walked back into his house after mowing the lawn to find two messages on his answering machine. One was from Reds GM Jim Bowden informing him that he'd been traded to the Yankees. The other was from Michael, asking him to call back as soon as possible. O'Neill was shocked and less than excited about the deal. An Ohio native, he loved playing in his home state and had no desire to upend his midwestern life for the big city. In many ways, the feeling was mutual with Yankee fans. The deal involved Roberto Kelly, who was coming off an All-Star season and was one of the few Yankees who had turned in halfway decent seasons over the last three years. O'Neill, a big, tall lefty, had seemed to have a breakout year in 1991, when he hit 28 home runs and drove in 91. But in '92 he regressed badly, trying too much to appease his manager, Lou Piniella, by hitting home runs instead of just hitting the ball as hard as he could where he could. O'Neill also had trouble hitting left-handed pitching, which would do little to help the team overcome its league-high 29 losses against left-handed starters in '92. O'Neill was considered high-maintenance, unhappy that he did not get more opportunities to prove himself against lefties and unhappy that Piniella—who could not understand why a guy as big as O'Neill could not just hit the goddamn ball out of the park—kept pressuring him to hit more home runs.

But Michael was tired of waiting for Kelly to turn into the player the team thought he could be. He could not stand the way Kelly gave away at bats, refusing to make the pitcher work and swinging at anything. Stick was remolding the Yankees into a team that focused on a simple concept: getting on base more meant scoring more runs. Michael was looking for guys with high on-base percentages and a knack for grinding pitchers down. Kelly did not fit that mold. Plus, his response to being moved to left field during the season had put the team's brass on high alert. They were tired of guys complaining about their own lot instead of thinking about what was best for the team. That's why they made clear that Mel Hall, a free agent, was not coming back to the Bronx in 1993. Showalter could not stomach Hall's presence in the clubhouse anymore. His borderline abusive treatment of Williams was enough, but Showalter's feeling was cemented when, during Old-Timers' Day in 1992, Hall walked out onto the field and asked Buck, "Who are these old fucking guys?" Showalter, who lived and died by Yankee tradition and what it meant to wear the uniform, knew then and there the team had to rid itself of Hall.[5]

Hall was gone, but that created a left-handed power hole in the lineup. When Stick called his old friend and now former Reds manager Piniella to ask about O'Neill, Lou provided a glowing review and told Michael he'd be crazy not to get him if he could. Michael pulled the trigger. It was high risk. Most fans were not aware of Hall's deplorable behavior off the field and in the clubhouse. All they knew was that, in the last two seasons, he had driven in more runs while hitting for a higher average than the guy they'd just traded for. And that the team's lone All-Star from 1992, one of the few players who had actually driven in runs during the past three seasons, was now a Red.

Losing his only All-Star and his third baseman in a two-week span was certainly not what returning owner George Steinbrenner wanted, though he was still not allowed to be involved in team transactions. Michael needed to make some moves and fast. On December 4, he began an eleven-day stretch of trades and free agent signings that drastically changed the direction of the team.

The first move, while not splashy, was indicative of Michael and Show-alter's desire to keep changing the clubhouse atmosphere. Michael signed free agent shortstop Spike Owen to a three-year deal. Owen was not a household name, but he had been to the postseason twice with the Red Sox. He knew what it took to win and to win in cities that expected it. "There are certain things Spike can do," said Michael. "He's a switch hitter and a veteran guy. He's somebody who's been there."[6]

Two days later, just as team personnel from across the league were settling into Louisville, Kentucky, for the winter meetings, Michael traded for Angels' left-handed pitcher Jim Abbott. Born without a right hand, Abbott spent hours as a kid throwing a ball against a wall, as fast as he could, so that it would shoot back at him as quickly as possible. Then he would practice transitioning his glove, which during the delivery he placed on top of the stump of his right hand, to his left hand so he could field the ball. From there, he would quickly transition the glove back so that he could throw the ball again. Hour after hour, throw after throw, Abbott taught himself how to pitch, field, and throw with only one hand. When he played as a teenager, hitters would see a pitcher with one hand and figure they could gain an advantage by bunting. They didn't. Abbott would pounce off the mound and—so quick you could hardly notice—move glove, ball, and hand all at the same time.[7]

His athletic prowess created a stir; he made a name for himself as a star pitcher at the University of Michigan, then as the complete-game winning pitcher for the United States in the 1988 Olympics gold medal baseball game. The next year Abbott went straight to the major leagues with the Angels, finishing fifth in Rookie of the Year voting. Utilizing a good fastball and sharp slider, he finished third in the AL Cy Young Award voting in 1991 and possibly had an even better season in 1992, giving up the fewest home runs of any full-time AL starter, but he suffered from a devastating lack of run support. The Yankees loved everything about Abbott. The ability. The determination to succeed. The whole story.

The Angels loved it all, too. In fact, it was widely believed that Abbott was team owner Gene Autry's favorite player, which is why for weeks they refused to deal him to New York. But GM Whitey Herzog made clear that Abbott would be nearly impossible to re-sign when he became a free agent in two years. At that point Autry decided to get the best value he could from New York, which turned out to be first baseman J. T. Snow and pitchers Russ Springer and Jerry Nielsen. All three had spent limited time in New York in '92 and, for various reasons, did not have a future with the team.

"We're tickled to death to make this trade tonight," said a beaming Michael, when announcing the deal.[8] Pitching had been Stick's main priority going into the off-season; he had gotten the sign-off to spend the money to get it. But no one had taken those dollars yet, which made the ability to trade for a pitcher of Abbott's caliber all the more sweet.

Two days later Michael flew back to New York to give free agent pitcher and reigning National League Cy Young Award winner Greg Maddux and his wife a tour of northern New Jersey. The hope was that the couple would fall in love with the quaint atmosphere of the Garden State's suburbs and not be scared by the horror stories of New York. To sweeten the deal, the team had already made a five-year, $33.5 million offer to Maddux, the best offer any team had presented him. But, during the tour, Kathy Maddux noted more than once that the Jersey suburbs looked just like the Atlanta suburbs. "That kind of told us where they were going," said one Yankee official, who turned out to be correct.[9] Maddux took $6 million less to sign with the Braves. In 2021 Maddux contradicted that story by saying that he had been ready to sign with the team, but a formal offer never happened. "I went there to sign with the Yankees," said Maddux. "I didn't get offered a contract."[10] According to the pitcher, a prominent member of the Yankees' hierarchy had a heart attack, distracting the team and preventing them from finalizing the deal. Maddux's account is questionable, but, if true, speaks to the dysfunction permeating from the club that December.

The day before Maddux signed with the Braves, David Cone, possibly turned off by the horror stories he had heard from Blue Jays teammate Dave Winfield, accepted a personal plea from dying team owner Ewing Kauffman and returned to his hometown team, the Kansas City Royals. Doug Drabek went to Houston. José Guzmán went to the Cubs. Though he was not a pitcher, the Yankees had still made a huge offer to Pirates outfielder and reigning National League MVP Barry Bonds. He rejected it for San Francisco the same day Cone rejected the team's offer for Kansas City's. The joy of the Abbott trade was diminishing by the second, thanks to the brutal, but not wholly undeserved, reputation of both the Yankees and the city they played in.

"Most players detest the place," wrote the *Hartford Courant*'s Jack O'Connell, after Maddux, Cone, and Bonds had all rejected large offers from the Yankees. "To the majority, New York represents crime and grime, gridlock and 20 bucks for a plate of cold ham and eggs. The fans are demanding and coarse, the press corps enormous and intimidating. Just ask Bobby Bonilla."[11]

Michael desperately needed another pitcher to sign with the team. Though still not able to be involved in negotiations, Steinbrenner was sending messages through the press that the team better come up with someone. Just as the winter meetings ended, they did. While on a cruise with his wife, who also served as his agent, left-hander Jimmy Key agreed to a four-year deal. "The so-called bad guys were getting weeded out," said Key, of the team when signing. "I just felt like Buck had gotten the organization going in the right direction."[12]

Key was not Maddux or Cone, his former Blue Jay teammate, but he quietly had put together an impressive career. He was one of only two pitchers to have at least twelve wins each season from 1985 to 1992, winning an ERA title along the way while finishing second in Cy Young Award voting in 1987. Known as a "crafty" player, Key had a devastating changeup that he mixed with a fastball and slider, all while nibbling at the corners, to keep hitters off balance. He gave the team, along with Abbott, two strong, quality left-handed starters for the first time in years, another quality Michael was trying to reestablish. He did not understand why, for so many years, the starting rotation had been larded with right-handed pitching when the team played half of its games in the friendliest left-handed-hitting ballpark in the majors. Conversely, he did not understand why the lineup had been filled for years with right-handed hitters in perhaps the least friendly right-handed-hitting ballpark in the majors.

Key gave the Yankees the chance to breathe a sigh of relief. They were not done, though. While they had five guys—Owen, Randy Velarde, Mike Gallego, Andy Stankiewicz, and Pat Kelly—to play shortstop and second base, they still had no third baseman. On December 15 that changed in a way that almost no one who had lived through the 1980s could have imagined: the team signed former Red Sox Wade Boggs.

The Boggs signing was by no means a tranquil moment. It resulted from internal dissension, created uncertainty among standing members of the team, and could have hamstrung the Yankees like so many free agent signings of the 1980s did.

The Yankees, even in Steinbrenner's absence, had operated out of two locations. The first was New York, where Michael, Showalter, and other brass held court. The second was Tampa, Steinbrenner's base of operations and where, even under expulsion and then suspension, The Boss and his crew hung out. Some of these were lifelong baseball men who knew the game and were lucky enough to have a special place in Steinbrenner's heart. Some were merely yes-men. Others, like Joe Molloy, were family members who were part of the business. The Tampa crew held immense sway over decisions, which irked Michael to no end. It also irked free agents like Cone, who did not want to come to an organization where he wasn't sure where decisions were being made.

That the Tampa crew wanted Boggs was not shocking. "George Steinbrenner is going to love Wade," wrote the *Boston Globe*'s Dan Shaughnessy. "Both are Tampa guys. Both are sports fans. Both have been involved in weird fights that are hard to explain the next day. Both have been interviewed by Barbara Walters."[13] There was also a quirkiness to Boggs that, should he perform in the Big Apple, could become the stuff of legend. He ate chicken before every game, earning him the nickname "Chicken Man." He was obsessed with the number seven, which stemmed from his dream of going 7-7 in a single game; many of his pregame rituals revolved around the number. He also drew the Hebrew sign for life in the dirt as he came to bat.

The idea that a Red Sox could flourish in New York must have had some appeal, too. Molloy pursued Boggs and inked him to a three-year deal when few other teams in baseball, outside of the Dodgers, were interested.

The reasons other teams were not interested were the same reasons Michael did not want Boggs in New York. A left-handed batter who had made a living banging balls off Fenway Park's Green Monster, Boggs won five batting titles from 1983 to 1988. He had led the league in on-base percentage six times, showing a keen batting eye to match seven straight seasons of 200-plus hits. While not a power hitter, Boggs was still a threat, capable of setting the table for the home runs guys behind him. But, in 1992, he suffered the worst season of his career, batting just .259, 86 points below his career average. Wade thought the season was an anomaly, but the Red Sox did not. They figured that, at thirty-four, the eight-time All-Star had already reached the apex of his career and was now on the downslide. They were not alone.

"Boggs is a good player, but I don't know if that's the direction we should be headed," Michael told reporters, just a week before the signing.[14] Moreover, Boggs had a reputation for being stat-obsessed and selfish. These were exactly the kinds of traits Michael and Showalter were working so hard to get out of the clubhouse. There was also concern over how Boggs would get along with Mattingly, a player with whom he was not especially close and who, even if he was not the same player he was in the 1980s, was still a rival for attention and accolades. Then there was the matter of Margo Adams, with whom Boggs had had an affair in the late 1980s. The affair became public, with Adams exposing many embarrassing details of the relationship, ultimately leading Boggs to his Barbara Walters appearance. Would Boggs really fit into the team-centered, drama-free atmosphere Michael and Showalter were trying to create?

The signing exposed the rift between New York and Tampa. Almost no one was available for comment to discuss Boggs, including the team's general manager. Molloy made it clear that this was his baby, and he would stand by it. Still, the split in reaction did nothing but feed into the notion that there were two separate factions in charge of the Yankees. "What other team would issue "no comment" after signing a 10-time .300 hitter," asked *Newsday*'s Jon Heyman.[15]

The Boggs deal ended a week-and-a-half frenzy of signings and trades. The Yankees had added two formidable lefty starters, a five-time batting champion, and a veteran shortstop with postseason experience. They also acquired O'Neill from the Reds and parted ways with some staples of the lean years, including Hall, Jesse Barfield, and Greg Cadaret. Going into the '93 season, only three of the twenty pitchers who had made an appearance with the club in 1990 were still on the roster. Only five of the twenty-three position players who had made an appearance on the 1990 team remained in 1993. Michael and Showalter's plan to completely revamp the Yankees into a team that was fun, likeable and, most importantly, competitive, was set to get its first true test.

While the Yankees were wheeling, dealing, and doing everything they could to plug holes in the roster, the 72-90 Mets were doing . . . nothing. Or about as close to nothing as could be done. To Al Harazin, the team he had in front of him was already good enough to make the postseason. They had just been the victims of injuries, a relentless press corps that pursued every off-the-field angle possible, and some underachieving here and there. A wholesale makeover of the Mets was not necessary, especially after the Pirates saw their ace pitcher, Doug Drabek, sign with the Astros and then, a week later, watched reigning MVP Barry Bonds sign with the Giants. Meanwhile, the rest of the division was less than impressive. The Phillies were the only team to finish worse in the division than the Mets. No one considered them a threat. The Cardinals and Cubs? They were good teams, but not great. Certainly not intimidating. The Florida Marlins were entering their first season of existence. It was assumed they would finish last. The Expos were coming off a surprise season, competing for first until mid-September. They had some lineup and pitching deficiencies, but were poised to make another run. That left the Mets. Despite everything that happened in 1992, they still had Bonilla, Murray, Coleman, Saberhagen, and Gooden, five of the best players to put on a uniform in the late '80s and early '90s. Jeff Kent had potential written all over him and there were some young arms making their way through the farm system that could be the next generation of star pitchers. Unlike the Yankees, the Mets had lost no one of major consequence in the expansion draft. There was reason to believe the Mets could be the team to beat in the National League East in '93.

The few moves that Harazin did make were not back-page headline grabbers. Kevin Elster's Mets' career was over. Dick Schofield had been a fine enough placeholder in '92, but the team was not bringing him back. They were looking for an upgrade at shortstop, someone who could provide solid defense and the occasional spark. Harazin found that shortstop in a deal with his old coworker, Joe McIlvaine. Three players left New York for San Diego; Tony Fernandez landed with the Mets. Fernandez had made a name for himself with the Blue Jays in the 1980s, making three All-Star teams and piecing together several solid offensive seasons. His long, lanky body and somewhat herky-jerky motion in the field made him look like a wacky, waving inflatable tube guy. But his defense was solid, as evidenced by the four consecutive Gold Gloves he had won in Toronto. Fernandez had come over to the Padres in a blockbuster deal two years earlier. While the switch to the National League—as well as from a turf to grass home field—may have stunted his play a little, he was still the best all-around shortstop the Mets had ever had. HoJo at third, Fernandez at short, Kent at second, and Murray at first. That had potential.

Harazin then added one more arm to the starting rotation. For years, Frank Tanana had dominated the American League as a flame-throwing lefty. Injuries forced Tanana to ditch the blazing fastball and evolve into a junk baller who frustrated hitters with a mix of off-speed pitches. While the thirty-nine-year-old was not among the top-tier free agents available, Tanana could be counted on to eat up innings and keep his team in the game. The Mets signed him to support Gooden, Saberhagen, Sid Fernandez, and Pete Schourek in the rotation. It was by no means the most solid rotation in baseball. That prize belonged to the Atlanta Braves, who now sported 1991 NL Cy Young Award winner Tom Glavine, 1992 NL Cy Young Award winner Greg Maddux, and future NL Cy Young Award winner John Smoltz. But in the seemingly weak National League East, it might just be good enough to get the Mets to first place.

"I want to play on a championship team and I feel this ballclub has a chance to achieve the postseason as well as the World Series," said Saberhagen that spring, after signing a contract extension.[16] Hope was in the air for the Mets.

Around 10:15 a.m. on Monday, March 1, 1993, a small private plane landed at Fort Lauderdale Executive Airport. A sixty-two-year-old man emerged dressed in khakis, sporting a white dress shirt covered by a blue, bordering on purple, V-neck sweater. It had been a late night for George Steinbrenner. At exactly 12:01 a.m. he had joined Suzyn Waldman on WFAN radio to talk baseball until 1:30 a.m. A Mets fan had called in to tell him how happy he was that he was back in baseball: "I know how badly you'll screw up the Yankees. And that will make all Mets fans happy."[17] Despite all this, he gave no appearance of feeling weary. Instead, he looked around, trying to eye the car that was to take him to his next stop. After a few minutes, it became clear that no car was coming. That would be dealt with later. For now, this man had over two hundred guests waiting for him just a few hundred feet away. He began walking from the airport over to the Yankees' spring training complex. Instantly, everyone and everything about the Yankees changed.

The Boss was back. And with him came the circus. Reporters and media outlets from across the country were on hand to cover what was starting to feel like General MacArthur's return to the Philippines. Special press passes denoting "The BOSS is back!" were handed out to the assembled media throng. The walk from the airport to the field should have taken a minute. It took over an hour. Every few feet Steinbrenner stopped to talk to someone, shake hands, offer a compliment or joke, or just bask in all the attention. Halfway through his journey a reporter shouted, "Hey George, you fired anyone yet?" "No," responded Steinbrenner, "I can't get to them." The remark drew big laughs, no doubt making the moment even sweeter for The Boss.[18]

The scene was surreal, and yet it could have been a million times more over the top. Originally, the return was meant to be a theatrical performance. There was going to be a Marilyn Monroe look-alike and a former president George H. W. Bush look-alike. Steinbrenner himself was going to sport a fake beard and sit, incognito, in the stands while reporters looked around and waited for him to emerge. Finally, The Boss would rip off his disguise and reveal himself. The performance art had already started a week earlier, when Steinbrenner donned a Napoleon outfit and mounted a horse for the cover of *Sports Illustrated*, accompanied by the headline, "George II: George Steinbrenner Rides Back into Baseball."

Shortly after the photo shoot, however, terrorists exploded a bomb in the basement of the North Tower of the World Trade Center in New York City, killing six people. And just the day before, several people were killed in a Waco, Texas, shootout between federal agents and members of a religious sect known as the Branch Davidians. Given these events, Steinbrenner decided it would be inappropriate to make such a big show of everything and opted for the more subtle approach of just walking into the complex.

The media could not get enough. They peppered him with question after question. What was it like to be back? What did he think of Buck Showalter? Would Wade Boggs be allowed to have a beard? Were there any hard feelings with Fay Vincent? And, perhaps most importantly of all, just how involved did he plan to be now that he was back?

"I don't think you'll see me back in the swing of things like it used to be," said The Boss. "I'm not digging a hole and crawling into it, but I don't think I will put as big a stamp on it. Time will tell."[19] Players, fans, and reporters had heard this before. No one believed him.

Finally getting to the stadium, Steinbrenner got onto the field to greet Michael, Showalter, and Don Mattingly, smiling and taking pictures with each of them. While some fans booed him, he signed autographs for a few onlookers, interacted with babies, and said hi to some familiar faces from the area. Around 12:30 he left the field to do an interview with CNN, then headed for lunch with some friends before returning and, for the first time in years, sitting in his office. He did an interview with Michael Kay, the Yankees' radio announcer and correspondent for the MSG Network, before signing more autographs. Before the day was over, he did two more interviews for local New York stations, one radio and one television.

It was a whirlwind day. White Sox owner and Steinbrenner friend Jerry Reinsdorf compared it to the Resurrection. Meanwhile, 140 miles away in Fort Myers, Dave Winfield shook his head at all of it. Now playing for his hometown Twins, Winfield felt people were losing sight of just why it was that Steinbrenner had been banished in the first place. It was not because he had dealt with a known gambler: it was because of how he had treated Winfield. Now, people were tripping over themselves to get pictures of and comments from him, as if the entire 1980s had been some kind of dream instead of events that really happened. Winfield was fresh off winning a world championship the previous season with the Blue Jays, having driven in the series' winning runs in extra innings in Game Six. But that didn't negate what Steinbrenner had put him through. Now, all

Winfield could do was shake his head at the reception his old boss was receiving. If it was any consolation, Steinbrenner was no longer Winfield's problem. That part of his life was over. Instead, The Boss was now Michael, Showalter, and every single member of the Yankees organization's problem.

"The guys missed him," said coach Clete Boyer, "even though we'll all probably get fired."[20]

For years the Mets had annoyed George Steinbrenner by constantly stealing the city's back-page headlines. Even when the Mets were controversial, there was still an odd joy to the controversy, especially compared to the *As the World Turns* atmosphere of the Yankees. The attention became so bad, at least as far as The Boss was concerned, that he started lying about home attendance figures during the season (he would correct the numbers at season's end so as not to incur any serious penalties from the commissioner's office). But, progressively, the Mets began to catch up to the Yankees in on- and off-the-field headaches. Ironically, Steinbrenner's absence gave the Mets an even larger back-page presence for all the wrong reasons. Fights between players and coaches. Fights between players and managers. Stonewalling the press. The Mets were now New York's train wreck.

Which is why Steinbrenner's return from banishment must have felt like a gift to the Amazins. Let George have two hundred reporters follow him around. Let him harangue Showalter every day while complaining about Mattingly's contract. Anything that took the attention away from a team coming off one of the most underperforming seasons in major league history was just fine with the Mets. The hope was that they would perform better than the year before, better than the Yankees overall and with the fourth estate highlighting issues in the Bronx, not Flushing.

It all started hopeful enough. A crowd of 53,127, the largest ever for Opening Day at Shea, came out on April 5 to forget the misery of 1992. In what could have been interpreted as a nice little jab at their cross-town rival owner, the Mets invited former commissioner Fay Vincent to throw out the first pitch. It was also the first game ever in the history of the Colorado Rockies. Moreover, after a decade, gone from the Mets' jerseys were the blue and orange piping that had run down the sides of the sleeves and pant legs. "METS" was still scrawled out the jersey's front, but now a stylish slash extended from the S back below and across the team name. The road jerseys would feature similar changes. The '80s were dead at Shea, minus a few of the remaining '86 Mets, one of whom took the mound that day. Dwight Gooden was not the Gooden of old, but he was still a top-notch pitcher. On a better team in 1992, his 10-13 record would have most likely been flipped, at a minimum. The Rockies mustered just four hits off Doc, who went the distance for an Opening Day 3–0 win, his first shutout since the middle of the '91 season and the first time any Mets pitcher had thrown one in the first game of the season.

"The complete game is nice, the shutout is great, but after last year, I just want to win," said Gooden, most likely expressing what every single person in the clubhouse felt.[21]

Bobby Bonilla, eager to leave behind the previous season, homered for a second consecutive Opening Day. "The most important thing was the 'W.' Deep down, we're all really looking to prove something, to bring the fans back," said Bobby Bo after the game, smiles present everywhere in the locker room.[22] The Mets won the next game, too, thanks to eight strong innings from Saberhagen. It was only two games—and two games against an expansion team at that—but a 2-0 record was a 2-0 record. There could not have been a better way to wash away the stain of 1992. The excitement lasted as long as that two-game series with the Rockies. By the night of the season's fourth game, the first in a string of embarrassing and bizarre episodes that would plague the team took place. And it happened, not coincidentally, because of the 1992 season.

Just as the 1993 season was getting underway, a new book appeared on the shelves of bookstores across the country. Originally, it was meant as a season-long journal composed by two New York sports beat writers as they followed a team. John Harper of the *New York Post* and Bob Klapisch of the *Daily News* had conceived the idea based on the numerous times friends and associates would ask them about the ballplayers they covered.

"Nobody knew really what it was like to be in a clubhouse," said Klapisch. "Nobody really knew these players the way they do now. I mean, now, everyone has their own website, their own Instagram account. There's a million ways for fans to access players that don't require a newspaper subscription. But back then, I had all my friends ask me in the bar, 'What was Strawberry like? What was Hernandez like?'"

The book was not meant to expose a dysfunctional team. After all, the Mets were supposed to be competing for the championship from Opening Day to the season's final pitch. In the end, though, *The Worst Team Money Could Buy* could not help but show a ball club in despair, suffocating from a myriad of controversies and unhappy players. It talked about the rape allegations, the press boycott, Murray's surliness with the press, Torborg's losing the clubhouse, and Bonilla's handling of New York. Anyone watching the team in 1992 knew that it was encased in misery. But *The Worst Team Money Could Buy* spelled it out in fine detail.

Now that the book was out, players were angry. They felt Klapisch and Harper had betrayed them by printing things they should not have printed, made mountains out of molehills and, in some instances, just outright lied. The season had been a disappointment, but they didn't see why clubhouse talk or anything unrelated to play on the field should be fodder for a book. Even though he was not a specific target of the book and had not even read it yet, Bonilla was among the angriest of Mets. Not just about the book, but about how Klapisch seemed dead set on haranguing him over every little perceived misplay or slump. In spring training, Klapisch wrote a story critical of Bonilla's work habits, something Bobby Bo deeply resented and did not forget. Then came the book, in which no player was safe from the shrapnel of Klapisch and Harper's explosive work. After the press freeze-out of the previous year, a confrontation was inevitable.

Before the Mets lost to the Astros 6–3, Murray started things off by exchanging some angry words with Klapisch over the book's content. Then, Bonilla chimed in.

"Look who just walked in, motherfucker. Hey, Bobby, why don't you suck my dick? But don't take it personally."

The line about not taking things personally caught Klapisch's attention. He had heard it before. In fact, they were exactly the words he used when talking to Torborg before the book came out. He had explained to the Mets manager that the work was tough but fair and not to take anything personally. But that same book essentially called Torborg a coward for refusing to confront Murray or Bonilla during the year. Now, as those last five words rang in Klapisch's ears, he had a feeling something was about to go down: that Torborg had decided Klapisch should be taught a lesson and to let his much maligned, high-priced player be the one to teach it.[23]

After the game, the press, Klapisch among them, entered the clubhouse for postgame commentary. The *Daily News* reporter was talking to Gooden, that night's losing pitcher, when Bonilla caught wind of Klapisch's line of questioning. The Mets right fielder did not approve. He was tired of the constantly negative tone of the team's press corps, Klapisch in particular. Now, it was time for reporters to feel a little heat.

"Any time Bobby, I know you feelin' an itch," Bonilla said to Klapisch from a few lockers over. Other members of the press gaggle froze. They had heard his comments before the game and thought something might happen. Now, that something was happening. Bonilla wasn't yelling and, at first glance, did not even seem angry. But his tone was that of someone who, given just the slightest wrong word or glance, could cause serious physical harm.

"Make your move partner," Bonilla continued, shirtless with his uniform pants still on but zipped down as he fiddled with a red sweater. "Cause I'll hurt ya."

"Are you threatening me?" asked Klapisch, who was not dumb enough to challenge a man significantly larger than himself, but who also was not going to be made an example of or be embarrassed in front of his colleagues.

"Whatever, you can take it as you see it," Bonilla replied, never losing eye contact with Klapisch except for the two seconds it took him to pull the sweater over his head, "You know, it's just like the homeboys say back home, 'we just chillin.' Make your move."

Bonilla turned, then batted a reporter's radio mic away. The moment seemed over, until he turned around and addressed Klapisch again. "I'll hurt you. This isn't over."

"You want to fight me," asked Klapisch.

"I'll show you the fucking Bronx right here," replied Bonilla.

By this point, Mets public relations director Jay Horwitz, about six inches and sixty pounds smaller than Bonilla, stepped in front of the right fielder, who was inching closer to Klapisch. The reporter was getting closer to Bonilla as well, though his tone was not so much angry as incredulous that a player would threaten him in a room full of cameras and witnesses. After a few more words, Horwitz got Bonilla out of the clubhouse. He prevented a physical confrontation, but there was nothing Horwitz could do about the story. The whole incident had been caught on film; even if it hadn't been, every writer who covered the Mets was present to document the exchange. The season wasn't a week old and already the team had its first major headache.

The next day, Bonilla admitted he "said something I shouldn't have said," but made a point of emphasizing he and the team felt Klapisch had abused his clubhouse privilege to write a full-length gossip column that did nothing but embarrass them.[24] It took all of two weeks before the next embarrassing episode occurred.

Seventeen games into the season, the Mets stood at 8-9. They'd yet to string together more than two wins in a row and, during the last game of a three-game home set with the Padres, their record had fallen below .500, where it would remain until April 4, 1994. The Dodgers were now in town, with Gooden scheduled to take the mound. About forty minutes before the start of the game, Harazin got a call in his office. Gooden had gotten hurt in the clubhouse and would not be able to start. "Was it serious?" Harazin asked, of the injury. No, he was told. Since it was not serious, Harazin did not think a big deal needed to be made of it and the club did not willingly share with reporters what exactly had happened before the game. That made matters worse once people found out.

Coleman had recently gotten heavily into golf. He had been playing the game and losing bets over his performance, forcing him to take things more seriously.[25] Standing at his locker before the Dodgers game, Coleman had before him a brand new set of clubs. He grabbed a 9-iron and took a practice swing. Behind him as he swung was that night's starting pitcher for the Mets; Coleman's backstroke landed directly into Gooden's right shoulder. The pain was enough to keep Doc off the field. In the end the game was rained out anyway. Gooden took the mound the next night and the whole incident might have been written off as a silly misfortune. Instead, Harazin and Torborg decided not to divulge what happened, an ill-advised move that put players, including Gooden, in the awkward position of not being able to say why exactly he could not play. Naturally, word got out that night of what occurred; reporters began hounding the general manager and manager for why they had felt the need to hide something that would obviously be discovered.

"If it looks like we're paranoid, maybe it is," Torborg told reporters, making no attempt to hide his annoyance. "My job is to take care of this team like an extended family, and that means not telling something about a freak accident."[26] The rest of the team resented the attention, too. When an ESPN cameraman tried taking video of Coleman's locker for a story on the incident, several players, led by Murray, made Horwitz ask him to leave the locker room. Coleman, meanwhile, was already on thin ice. During spring training, he'd snapped at the first reporter to engage him. Just the day before plunking his teammate with a golf club, Coleman forgot to wear his sunglasses during an afternoon game and dropped a fly ball that allowed two runs to score.

The season was not yet a month old, and all the elements of 1992 had reemerged: upset players, constantly bad media attention, a manager and front office making all the wrong decisions. Only now, the team was playing even worse.

The strain was evident in abundance the next night. Down 1-0 in the eighth, Gooden managed to pitch through the pain and keep the Mets in the game. But a combination of walks, errors, and one single led to three runs. During the inning Doc felt home plate umpire Bill Hohn was pinching the strike zone. At one point he stepped off the mound and headed directly toward Hohn, screaming and gesticulating wildly. Few who had watched Gooden pitch could remember the mild-mannered hurler ever acting this angrily on the field before. The Mets lost the game. Then they lost the next one. And the next one. And the one after that. And the one after that. Seven in a row to close out April and start May. They were entrenched in last place, where they remained the rest of the season.

A win on May 2 ended the streak, but over the next fourteen games the team went 3-11. The Mets were 12-25 and, somehow, despite it being only May 18, already fifteen games out of first place. The season and the team were going nowhere. It was time for a change.

The mood inside Cleveland Municipal Stadium was a mix of anticipation and somberness. Located on the banks of Lake Erie, the sixty-two-year-old colossus had been built for another era: a time when Cleveland was twice as large and an industrial mecca for the rest of the country. But the rust-belt decline and inner-city riots of the 1950s and '60s hit the city hard, causing hundreds of thousands to flee. Meanwhile, the Indians suffered through perpetually meaningless baseball; the team was a constant afterthought in the American League that had not sniffed the postseason since 1954. On this day, over 73,000 crammed into the massive ballpark on a cold, dreary Ohio afternoon to watch Municipal Stadium's last Opening Day. The Indians were moving a few blocks south in 1994, to a new, modern ballpark that would play a key role in the Yankees' history throughout the rest of the decade. The Opening Day weather matched the mood of many in the crowd and of the Indians. Just two weeks earlier, Cleveland's closer Steve Olin and fellow relief pitcher Tim Crews were killed in a boat accident. Bob Ojeda, the former Met, was seriously injured as well and would not appear in a game that year until August.

Despite the somber mood, there was anticipation in the Yankees' clubhouse. A host of new faces dotted the landscape. Gone were many of the players whose attitudes Michael and Showalter abhorred. In their place were hard-nosed, win-at-all-costs gamers, all of whom carried a certain amount of risk for Michael now that Steinbrenner was back in charge. Would Paul O'Neill be as good as the All-Star Roberto Kelly? Could Jimmy Key possibly make up for the loss of Cone or Maddux? Was Wade Boggs done as a major league hitter?

Key took the mound for the start, the first player to make his team debut as the Yankees' Opening Day pitcher since Urban Shocker in 1925. Newbies Boggs, O'Neill (in left field), and Spike Owen also took their place in the starting lineup. If they felt any pressure, it did not show. With the score 2–1 in the sixth inning, Nokes hit a three-run home run to break the game open, leading the way to a 9–1 New York win. Key went eight innings, throwing only 71 pitches. Meanwhile, Boggs, O'Neill, and Owen combined to go 6-14 with two RBIs and four runs scored. Though the bullpen coughed up the lead the next day, Jim Abbott pitched a strong seven innings in his team debut. Still, the Yankees lost two of three to start the season, the last loss coming with the embarrassing historical footnote of the Indians' Carlos Baerga's becoming the first player to hit home runs from both sides of the plate in the same inning. But the Yankees went to Chicago, took two of three, and flew to New York at 3-3, setting them up for a home opener to remember in the Bronx.

A total of 56,704 fans, the largest crowd at Yankee Stadium since it was remodeled in 1976, came out on April 12 to watch the Yankees' first home game of the season. New York City mayor David Dinkins, about to embark on a brutal reelection campaign against former U.S. attorney Rudy Giuliani, was in attendance, as was NBC *Nightly News* anchor Tom Brokaw and well-known talk show host Regis Philbin. Reggie Jackson and college basketball coach Dean Smith, who threw out the first pitch, were there, too. Freddy Schuman, the diehard team supporter better known by many Yankee fans as "Freddy Sez," strode around the ballpark with his trademark pan, banging spoon, and a sign reading "93 is the year of the Yankees."[27]

The atmosphere within the stadium was the opposite of the overcast weather that hung over the game all day. There was true excitement that had not been felt in the Bronx for some time, not just the standard Opening Day hope. No one was certain if the Yankees could compete with the reigning world-champion Blue Jays, but everyone agreed that this was a totally different team from the one that had finished dead last three years earlier.

Enjoying it all was a man who had not been able to set foot inside the stadium since August 1990, at least not in an official capacity. George Steinbrenner was giddy to be back in the Bronx. Prior to the start of the game, he made a quick visit to the bleacher seats in right-center field then took his customary place in the owner's box. From there, he let the team's new acquisitions do the talking against the Royals. O'Neill went 4-4 with two RBIs, coming a home run short of the cycle. Boggs, the former Red Sox, heard some boos when he stepped to the plate for his first home at bat. But he quickly won over any doubters by driving in the game's first run in the third inning. Owen added a hit, too, as new acquisitions went a combined 6-11. Most of the damage came against Kansas City's starter, none other than David Cone. Meanwhile, Abbott shone, scattering eight hits and allowing just one run as he needed only 85 pitches to go all nine innings. As the last out was recorded, Abbott raised his hands in the air, a gesture of triumph rarely seen from a Yankees pitcher over the last decade or so. The day was especially memorable for the lefty, whose parents made the trip from Michigan. "There was something about New York, about wearing the uniform, about the fans and this team," said Abbott. "There was a playoff-type atmosphere."[28]

"This place is cool," said O'Neill, playing his first game ever at Yankee Stadium. "I was looking around during the game. The fans, the fights, the beer throwing."[29] Steinbrenner strode around the clubhouse after, congratulating O'Neill, Abbott, and Showalter. It was a day of pure joy; in many ways, the three-game opening series with the Royals was a portent of things to come in 1993. The first game saw O'Neill rise to the occasion. The second featured a four-hit performance by Boggs. Bob Wickman got the win despite giving up five runs (though only one was earned), continuing his pattern of picking up wins in the unlikeliest of circumstances. The third game saw Key throw eight scoreless innings and leave with a 4–0 lead, only to watch the bullpen give up five runs and the game in the top of the ninth. Still, they had taken two out of three and, after winning five of eight games on the West Coast, the Yankees ended April at 12-9, just two and a half games out of first place.

May brought more good news. A mid-month sweep of the Twins in Minnesota had them in second place as they headed into Boston for the first time that season. It was also the first time Boggs appeared as a visiting player at Fenway Park. His initial reception left something to be desired. Many former teammates had never been close to Boggs; others, like Roger Clemens, disliked him. The two had actually been together the night before the first game of the series, joining with many other celebrities to watch the final episode of the Boston-set NBC series *Cheers*. They talked in generalities but nothing in depth. Then, before batting practice the next day, few of Boggs's former teammates made an effort to say hi. The Boston faithful, however, had a different take. They knew Boggs had been driven out of Boston. It wasn't his fault the Yankees came knockin'. When their former third baseman came to bat in the first inning, he got an ovation long enough that Boggs stepped out of the box and doffed his helmet to the crowd. Then the Chicken Man singled to right field. In the third he singled to center. In the fifth he singled to center again. In the seventh he singled to center yet again. Four at bats, four singles in his return. He added a walk in the ninth for good measure. Even though the Yankees lost and Boggs called it "the most difficult game I've ever played," he made clear that by no means was he done as a major league ballplayer.[30]

The Yankees finished the month in second place. While they had yet to put together a long or even impressive streak of winning games, there were positive signs everywhere. Jim Leyritz, a rare holdover from the 1990 team who had shuttled back and forth between the minors and majors in '91 and '92, was finally making his mark. The Ohioan who had grown up cheering on Cincinnati's Big Red Machine was loud, cocky, and sure of his abilities. And if you didn't know about his abilities, don't worry. He would gladly tell you about them. "Jimmy would be hitting .180 and would say 'play me or trade me,'" recalled a former coach.

Leyritz had broken his leg in high school just before the draft, but refused to give up a chance to perform in front of scouts. In a batting practice session, with representatives from various teams looking on, he had to hit wearing a cast on his left leg, meaning it remained straight, at a forty-five-degree angle. The stance stuck after he was drafted; he matched it with a bat-twirling habit distinct in the game. It drove people nuts. They saw it as one more arrogant move by a guy who loved nothing more than to talk about how great he was. Soon, Leyritz earned the nickname "The King" and "Jumbo." They were meant derisively, but Jimmy didn't care at all. In fact, he loved it.

Now he was putting his money where his mouth was. After two months he was hitting .365 with a 1.075 OPS. His 7 home runs and 28 RBIS were among the most on the team, forcing Showalter to keep finding ways of getting The King into the lineup.

Mike Stanley, the backup catcher who for three consecutive seasons hit .249, became one of the biggest offensive threats of any American League catcher. Hitting .349 with a .948 OPS, it was now impossible for Showalter not to play him almost every day, which is why, one day in May, Buck called Stanley into his office and told him that his playing time was going to increase. "That was so liberating to me because he didn't put any parameters on it," remembered Stanley. "He didn't say you're going to be the everyday guy. He didn't say you are going to catch five days a week. He just said your playing time is going to increase. So I just came to the ballpark every day to see if my name was in the lineup."[31]

Key, the lefty consolation prize, was 5-2 with a 1.94 ERA. In 4 of his 11 starts in April and May, he had given up zero runs and pitched into at least the seventh inning in every start. There was talk of Key winning the Cy Young Award and starting the All-Star Game for the American League. Dion James, a bit player the year before, was hitting .358. O'Neill was hitting .325, thanks to an adjustment in his batting stance by hitting coach Rick Down that utilized a front foot–tapping timing measure. Pleasant surprises were everywhere, except in the bullpen, which kept disappointing. Still, the team was playing well and there was little discontent or the kinds of drama that had plagued the clubhouse in years past. Some players, like Maas and Nokes, were angry about their reduced playing time, but unlike previous clubhouse cancers, they didn't allow their anger to distract from the central goal: winning ball games.

The Yankees returned home from an early June road trip for three games against the Red Sox. At this point the team was still above .500 but had yet to truly break out in any sort of prolonged winning streak. They were staying competitive, but fans and the media could not help but wonder if, as had happened at this point the previous season, the club was about to begin its long fade into a summer of meaningless baseball. If the Yankees were to prove otherwise, now was the time to do it.

The road from Vince Coleman's golf swing to Jeff Torborg's firing was a brutal one. It was not just that the Mets went 5-15 during that time: it was the remarkable ways in which they lost, mixed with more tension between players and coaches. One day after Gooden pitched with a banged-up shoulder, the Mets headed to the West Coast for a seven-game road trip. In the first game in San Francisco, the bullpen blew a 2–0 lead in the eighth and, after the Mets managed to tie the game in the top of the ninth, proceeded to give up the winning run with two outs in the bottom of the inning. The next day Kent and Tony Fernandez committed two errors apiece and Saberhagen added one for good measure, as the Giants won

10–5. They then lost the first two games in San Diego, with both losses charged to the bullpen, now 0-10 in the first 23 games of the season. New York returned home having gone 1-6 on the trip. Two games into the home stand, Mike Cubbage and Bonilla got into a confrontation after Cubbage felt Bonilla had failed to run hard from first base on a Howard Johnson flyout. Not only did the incident create yet another soap operatic moment, but, because Cubbage had taken the lead in criticizing Bonilla, it reinforced the notion among players, reporters, and fans that Torborg was afraid to challenge his players.

A week later in Montreal, thanks to two errors, a walk, and a hit by pitch, Tanana managed to give up five runs in the first inning despite allowing only one hit. They returned to Shea on May 17 only to get smoked by the Pirates, 9–4. "Jeff Must Go" chants sprang up around the ballpark. Mike Lupica openly called for Torborg to be fired. Another columnist, tired of Torborg's failed efforts to control the narrative and conduct public relations, began referring to him as "Jeff from Flushing," a knock at Torborg's frequent call-ins to WFAN.[32]

On May 18 the team put together seventeen hits and still lost. Even if the Mets had somehow managed to win, it was too late. Torborg's fate was decided. Harazin made up his mind the night before that it was over. Just before the team's seventeen-hit performance, he secretly walked into a Philadelphia hotel and sealed the deal with the team's next manager. A half-hour before the final game against the Pirates series, Harazin told Torborg he was out. Torborg handled the news, which could not have been surprising, with the dignity that many had seen in him before this nightmarish run in New York. He thanked his coaches and brought out the lineup card that night, shaking hands with all the umpires. In Torborg's final game as manager, the Mets came back from a three-run deficit in the ninth and won the game in extra innings. Afterward, Torborg took no parting shots. He left with his head held high and an 85-115 record over two seasons at Shea.

"Everyone is to blame," Harazin told reporters, many of whom blamed him specifically for the team's current predicament. "The management, the coaches and the players. I had to do something to turn this franchise around. You win together and you lose together."[33]

It was the first time in franchise history the organization had had four different managers in four seasons (not including Mike Cubbage's seven-game interim stint in 1991). The Mets were now, officially, the Yankees, but not in any of the ways a team would want to be. The team's next manager knew all about that.

"Discipline" Dallas Green was, on paper anyway, just the right man to come in and begin the team's turnaround. Blunt and unafraid of conflict, Green would not hesitate where Torborg had refused to call out his players. Where Torborg spoke diplomatically and worked to protect his team from the New York glare at all costs, Green did not mince words and generally did not care what the media or fans thought of him or his team. This was a guy who would tell Bonilla to run, Murray to lead, and Franco to stop with the constant attitude. No one believed he could do much to salvage the team in its current form but at least he could get them focused on playing baseball the way it was meant to be played. That was the thinking at least. There was one more element, too: Green had already managed in New York. The Yankees had brought him in in 1989 to do many of the things the Mets were now calling for. It did not work. After his firing, his managing days appeared over and he went back to scouting, joining the Mets in 1991. He'd been mentioned as a possible Harrelson replacement late that season and, then, when it was clear Torborg would not last the entire '93 season, his name kept coming up again. Finally, Harazin made the decision.

Green knew what he had and did not have. This team was not going to contend but, at a minimum, he could improve the style of play and build some momentum heading into 1994 and beyond. Initially, the results were positive. The team went 5-7 in his first 12 games, a mark that was by no means impressive but certainly better than they had been playing under Torborg. But, after an 11–3 win in Chicago, the Mets went 3-20 over their next 23 games, a stretch of play that ranks among the worst in franchise history. The team fell another 12 games back of first, sitting a remarkable 29.5 games out on June 28. The stretch included two separate losing streaks of 6 games and another of 5, while being outscored 117-76. Tanana lost four times, Gooden three. Yet they were still the only two starting pitchers to win a game during that stretch.

On June 11 they traded Tony Fernandez. The shortstop was supposed to have been the key acquisition of the off-season, someone who could put a little jolt into the top of the Mets' lineup. Instead, Fernandez came down with kidney stones early in the year. Players were amazed at the four-time Gold Glover's inability to make the most routine of plays, while the extraordinary ones that had happened in abundance before disappeared completely. At the plate, he hit just .225, 60 points below his career average. Harazin had banked on Fernandez's help to put the Mets back on top. "We acquired Tony last fall with high hopes that with him we'd be a winner. Obviously that hasn't happened. I don't think we ever saw the real Tony Fernandez," said Harazin.[34]

Fernandez was shipped to the Blue Jays, where he regained his form, hitting .306, playing solid defense and, eventually winning his first and only big league championship. In exchange, the Mets received outfielder Darrin Jackson, who after a month on the team went down with an injury. All told he played thirty-one games for the Mets, hitting just one home run. By June 25, just two weeks after the deal, Fernandez already had more hits, home runs, and runs driven in for the Blue Jays than Jackson would get for the Mets during the entire '93 season. Not only was the deal a flop, but now the Mets had to rely on Tim Bogar to play short, a rookie who had never had an impressive offensive season above Class A ball.

By June 22 Mets owners Fred Wilpon and Nelson Doubleday had seen enough. They had paid a fortune to bring the Mets back to their 1980s heyday. What they got was a 21-48 team that more closely resembled the Mets of the early 1960s. Making matters worse, the Yankees were fun to watch. They were starting to draw fans to the Bronx again. And, perhaps most remarkable, they had remained nearly void of any off-the-field drama. The Boss was, to a degree, keeping to his word of not being as involved or as manic as he'd been before the suspension. Meanwhile, everything that could have gone wrong for the 1993 Mets was going wrong.

Harazin thought he'd made the right moves. He'd signed the big names. Traded away problem players and those who were probably never going to reach their true potential. He'd acquired standout players in return. Brought in a manager with a proven track record whose demeanor his former players praised. But in the end, it all failed. It was not enough for

Torborg to pay the price. He had not put this team together nor thrown Wilpon and Doubleday's money down the drain. Harazin had. The Mets were being mocked almost daily on *Late Night with David Letterman*; they were worse than the game's two expansion teams.

In mid-June the two owners approached Harazin with a proposal: remain as the team's chief operating officer but relinquish the title of general manager. Like Torborg, Harazin could not have been surprised. Still, he had always been sensitive to the idea that he was just a lawyer and not a true baseball man. That, in part, was why the team had gone after big-name free agents like never before. Harazin had wanted to make a splash, followed by a big impact, as soon as he inherited the title of general manager. It would prove all the doubters wrong. Now, here he stood, asked to give up the position. Harazin took a week to think about it, but his choice was clear. He could not be expected to relinquish that position and stay with the Mets. It would create an awkward situation for him, for management, and for whoever the next GM was. He decided to leave the organization he had been with for thirteen years and start anew somewhere else.

At a press conference announcing the decision, the New York press corps let the owners have it. They channeled the anger and frustration of millions of Mets fans who had expected a dynasty and instead watched their team be reduced to the laughingstock of baseball . . . and all while the Yankees were picking up steam. Reporters asked about the moves made over the past few years, almost none of which had worked out. "You want to tell me how many games Mr. Dykstra has played since he left; you want to tell me how many games Mr. Strawberry has played since he left. We go after talent. We don't go after citizens," said a defensive Doubleday.[35] He noted signs of instability in both Wally Backman and Dykstra, not realizing that one of the reasons fans loved them both was exactly because of their instability.

Reaction matched that when Steinbrenner was firing a manager every few months in the 1980s. "Harazin's departure was yet one more price to be exacted for the club's free fall from grace, a descent to comically incompetent baseball that has resulted in managerial firings, plummeting attendance and a virtual death struggle in 1993 to avoid being as bad as the club was in its inglorious inaugural season in 1962," wrote the *New York Times*'s Joe Sexton.[36]

The incoming GM was a familiar face. Perhaps that's why reporters were asking Doubleday and Wilpon about the trades of the past. Two weeks prior, Joe McIlvaine had left his job as general manager of the San Diego Padres. After walking away from the Mets after the 1990 season, McIlvaine had done yeoman's work making that team competitive in 1992, as the Padres surprised everyone with an 82-80 record. His biggest acquisition, Gary Sheffield, finished third in the National League MVP voting. It was the kind of performance Doubleday and Wilpon admired. But Padres ownership was putting the squeeze on McIlvaine, refusing to let him spend money on any upgrades. The team was falling apart, fast, and he simply could not work under those constraints. When McIlvaine announced his departure, Mets ownership contacted him almost immediately. Come back, they asked, and make this team a winner again.

"I think Joe McIlvaine is one of the best judges of talent—both young and at the major-league level—of anybody in baseball," said Wilpon at the press conference, in a statement that could be taken as a parting shot at Harazin.[37] At that point McIlvaine was not officially Harazin's replacement yet. That came a few days later. But it was inevitable. McIlvaine missed New York, but, perhaps most importantly, he wanted the challenge of building this franchise back up from the ashes and fulfilling the destiny that had eluded it in the late '80s. McIlvaine wanted to make this team *the* team in New York again. But he had a long way to go to make that happen.

The Atlanta Braves can trace their lineage back to 1870s Boston. They were there when organized baseball first took form in ways that would seem remarkably unfamiliar to fans a century and a half later. From the Red Stockings to the Red Caps to the Beaneaters, the franchise changed names yet again in the latter half of the twentieth century's first decade. Now known as the Doves, the most remarkable thing about them was how unremarkable they were. The Doves were perennial doormats in the National League, finishing 47 games out of first in 1907, 36 out in 1908, and 65 out in 1909. The new decade brought the same result: a 53-100, last-place finish in 1910. All that losing in the early stages of organized baseball was bound to create records that no one wanted.

Enter Clifton Garfield Curtis. Born in Ohio the day after native Ohioan and twentieth president James A. Garfield was shot—he died two months later—it is likely that Curtis was bestowed his middle name as a tribute to the slain president. Given that Garfield served the second-shortest term of any president in U.S. history, it might also have been a portent of how Curtis's major league career was to play out. Starting out in independent leagues throughout the Midwest, Curtis was a solid enough pitcher to join the Doves in 1909. The righty posted impressive numbers, holding a WHIP of exactly 1.0 and compiling a 1.41 ERA.

In 1910 Curtis pitched well again over the first month of the season, making the best of a team destined to be out of the race by midseason, if not sooner. On June 8 he threw a two-hit shutout over Honus Wagner and the Pirates, bringing his record to 6-6 for the year. He did not win again for another 352 days; when he did, it would set him on a path to being mentioned by fans and beat writers of a team Curtis would never know existed.

It began with his next start, a 4–2 loss to Cincinnati. Curtis then lost his next start, and the next, and the next, and the next. After a few no-decisions, Curtis lost five consecutive appearances, earned a save, lost five more, earned another save, then lost his last three decisions of the year. In his final start he held a 3–2 lead against the Phillies in the sixth before allowing the tying run to score. An inning later, the game was called on account of darkness, resulting in a 3–3 tie. Curtis's season was over after having lost his last 18 decisions in a row. For the year he finished 6-24, having allowed a remarkable 386 base runners in 250 innings pitched. The Doves changed their name to the Rustlers in 1911, but it was the same terrible team. Curtis, considered one of the their best pitchers despite his run of bad luck, opened the season by losing his first five decisions. On May 26 against the Dodgers, the impossible happened: Curtis got the win in a 7–2 victory. It mercifully ended a string of 23 consecutive losing decisions without a win for the righty, a record-setting run that, surprisingly, yielded little discussion at the time. Curtis appeared in four more games for the Rustlers, losing three of them, before being traded to the Cubs.

He pitched two more years in the big leagues, moving among the Cubs, Phillies, and Dodgers/Superbas, ending his career with a 28-61 record. Curtis returned home to Ohio and spent his post-baseball years running a car dealership. He died of a heart attack on April 23, 1943, with no idea that his name would be plastered all over the sports pages of just about every major American newspaper fifty years later.

Curtis's newfound notoriety came courtesy of Anthony Young. A Texan who played both baseball and football growing up, Young became a star at Furr High School in Houston, where he was drafted by the Expos but instead opted to attend the University of Houston. During that time, despite his residence in the Lone Star State, Young became a fan of the Mets, thanks to the dominating performances of Dwight Gooden. Though not large by baseball or even football standards, Young's 6-foot-2, 200-pound physique was strongly built and his numbers at Houston were good enough for his favorite team to draft him in 1987. Using a slider and sinking fastball with good movement, Young worked his way up the Mets' minor league system, not quite dominating but not falling apart either. His work earned him a call up to the big leagues in August 1991, where he made two relief appearances before returning to triple A. Brought back up in September, he made seven starts, pitching well but largely betrayed by a Mets offense that scored just seven runs in the four games he lost. Still, the Mets thought that he might have something and inserted Young into the rotation to start the 1992 season.

The move paid dividends in the early going. Young threw a complete-game six-hitter in his first start of the year. In four appearances in April, he was 2-0 with a 2.96 ERA. He'd walked just 4 hitters in a little over 24 innings and failed to yield a single home run. On May 6, in a start at Cincinnati, Young gave up all five runs in a 5–3 loss, his first of the season. Over the remaining 165 games of his career, Young never again sported a win-loss record above .500. The next loss came five days later, the third six days after that. In June he lost four straight starts, at which point the Mets converted him to the team's closer, when Franco went down with an injury. Young lost an appearance on July 4, his ninth consecutive losing decision. But then, as the team's closer, he excelled. From July 7 to September 2, he made 23 appearances, saving 11 games and losing none.

He allowed only one run in just over 29 innings, lowering his ERA a full run. It was one bright spot—perhaps the only bright spot—emerging from the Mets' disappointing season. But, after that, he blew four saves in a two-week period, taking the loss in all four appearances. He was now at 13 losing decisions in a row. In his final appearance of the year, he got the loss in another blown save. Fourteen in a row. Despite the strong April and nearly two months in which he allowed only a single run to score, Young ended the season 2-14. At that point, however, most people just considered it a run of bad luck that was bound to end sooner rather than later: a by-product of a team that had grossly underperformed in all aspects. Young was still 10 more losses away from matching Curtis's record, just barely halfway to the inglorious mark.

The paradox is that you can't be a bad pitcher to achieve a record as demeaning as losing the most consecutive decisions. Someone performing that poorly would not be allowed that many opportunities to keep losing games. No, the only person who could achieve such a record is someone just good enough to keep putting on the mound, but just unlucky enough to keep losing and losing and losing. That was Cliff Curtis. And, in 1993, that was Anthony Young.

Kept in the bullpen, but not in the closer's role, Young made his first appearance in the season's third game and got the loss in extra innings. In seven more April appearances, Young, betrayed by his team's defense, gave up seven unearned runs versus one earned. He lost two more games without winning any. The record was now just seven losses away. May brought two more losses. Misfortune then struck Young through no fault of his own. Injuries forced the team to put him into the starting rotation for the first time in over a year. On June 1 in Chicago, he held the Cubs to no runs over six innings and left the game with a 1–0 lead. The bullpen proceeded to give up eight runs, costing Young the win but, perhaps worst of all, failing to relieve the psychological pressure he was under. The streak was now getting national attention. It was all anyone wanted to talk to Young about, especially as the Mets sank further and further into the abyss, leaving the press with little else to discuss. The scenario was a nightmare for the right-handed Texan, who tired of having to constantly answer question after question about the streak. "What are your thoughts on it?" "When do you think it will end?" "What's going wrong?" Young wanted no part of any of it. He just wanted to pitch. Players also wanted the press to stop asking Young the same questions; perhaps feeling guilt over their own inability to get Young just that one win, they did not want to talk about it anymore themselves.

Meanwhile, the fans, who blamed a bad team more than Young himself for the streak, started doing whatever they could to try and stop it before history was made. They began sending "Anthony Young all sorts of good-luck talismans while he was enduring his infamous losing streak—four-leaf clovers, horseshoes, rabbit's feet. One woman gave him her treasured $2 bill. Psychics called the Met offices offering aid. Letters of encouragement poured in from folks who sat in the bleachers as well as Hall of Famer Bob Feller."[38]

Nothing worked. June 8 at home against the Cubs: 5–1 loss. June 13 at home against the Phillies: 5–3 loss. June 18 in Pittsburgh: 5–2 loss. Twenty-two losing decisions in a row. It just would not end. On June 22 Young took the mound at home against the Expos with just about everyone in attendance hoping they would not see history that night. In the second inning the Mets committed two errors, leading to three unearned runs. By the sixth inning they were down 6–0, eventually losing 6–3. Late in the game Green was ejected for arguing a third strike call with home plate umpire Charlie Williams. Perhaps exhibiting the frustration of everyone on the team, Green threw one of the ballboy stools at Williams. After the game, Young sported a T shirt reading, "IF I HAD ANY LUCK IT'D ALL BE BAD."

Cliff Curtis now had company, and Young wasn't going anywhere. The Mets needed him in the rotation and he wasn't pitching poorly enough to warrant a demotion. So out Young went on June 27, a Sunday day game at Shea against the Cardinals. The streak had gotten so bad that Cardinals starting pitcher Joe Magrane admitted that he would have preferred to face Gooden or Saberhagen that day instead of Young. "I've never been more nervous before a start," said Magrane. "I didn't want to be the answer to a trivia question: Who lost to Anthony Young?"[39]

When Murray hit a home run in the first inning, it looked like the trivia answer might be Magrane. But in the fourth, with runners on first and second, Todd Zeile hit a ground ball to Bonilla, playing third for the first time in his Mets career. Bobby stepped on third for one out and threw to second for the second out, but Zeile just narrowly beat the throw to first, avoiding a triple play. Two singles and a double followed, giving St. Louis the lead. They tacked on two more runs, winning the game 5–3. The Mets filed into the clubhouse emitting an overwhelming aura of helplessness and misery. Young was now the major league record holder for most consecutive losing decisions: 24 and counting.

Resigned to having to talk to the press afterward, Young made clear he no longer wanted to. "I have the record now. Hopefully, now y'all can leave me alone."[40]

"He was tough," recalled teammate Charlie O'Brien, about Young. "Just one of the kindest human beings I played with. Anthony's attitude never changed when he was going through that time. He just pitched and did his thing. He didn't really let it affect him. But in the end, you could tell he'd gotten frustrated a little bit."[41]

The numbers from the streak were amazing for all the wrong reasons. Since losing the first game to Cincinnati thirteen months earlier, Young had appeared in 48 games where he had received a no-decision. His ERA in those games was 1.44. In 1993 alone, to that point, he had appeared in 23 games. The Mets lost 22 of those 23 games. And as bad as setting the record was, the fact that it was still going was even worse. The questions would never end until that elusive *W* appeared next to Young's name in the box score. Moreover, the loss punctuated a series of bad news surrounding the team that day.

The Mets as a team had created a record of their own, having gone 63 games without consecutive wins. It was the longest streak in National League history and approached the all-time record of 80 that had stood for seventy-eight years (the Mets won their next two games, avoiding at least that record). They were 21-52 on the season, just a single game better than the worst team in baseball history, the 1962 Mets, after the first 73 games of the season. It was, to that time, the worst June, and one of the worst months, in team history, with only 6 wins in 27 games. Worse yet, the general manager position was still vacant. While McIlvaine was going to take the job, he had not started yet. The uncertainty of who, exactly, was in charge of the front office meant the Mets missed an opportunity to barter with the cash-strapped Padres for reigning National League batting champion Gary Sheffield. Instead of heading to New York, Sheffield ended up with the Marlins that same weekend. As the weekend ended, Bonilla was asked by a reporter what it would take to turn the Mets around. "Don't ask me," he replied. "I just work here. Ask Dallas, ask Fred Wilpon, or ask whoever's going to be the general manager."[42]

Meanwhile, Young's nightmare continued. In his next start, with the Mets down 3–1, the game was called after five innings due to weather. But it was his start on July 7 that, of all his appearances during the streak, was the most heartbreaking. Young allowed a lead-off single to the Padres' Jeff Gardner and then did not allow another hit through seven innings. His control was pinpoint, walking no one, while getting the Padres to hit into a series of weak ground ball outs. Matching Young zero for zero was the Padres' starter Andy Benes, himself having allowed only a second-inning single to Kent. With two outs in the eighth, Young gave up a single and then Archi Cianfrocco, owner of a .203 average and just eight career home runs, hit one over the wall in right field. Young's streak went to 26. Shortly thereafter, with Green saying he was not sure how many of his players "give a damn whether we win or lose," Young returned to the bullpen.[43] On July 24, he pitched 2⅔ scoreless innings of relief against the Dodgers, before walking in the winning run in the tenth inning. Twenty-seven in a row.

Four days later, it looked certain that Young's streak would go to 28. Entering a tie game against the Marlins in the top of the ninth, he pitched into a bases-loaded, no-out jam before inducing a 5-2-3 double play to maintain the tie. The next batter, however, dropped a bunt single, giving Florida the lead. The Marlins' ace closer Bryan Harvey, in the midst of one of the best seasons a reliever would have in the early '90s, entered the game. Young sat on the bench, staring blankly ahead, wondering when this was all going to end. Then luck went his way. A lead-off single and sac bunt put the tying run at third, which Ryan Thompson promptly singled in. Young was off the hook for the loss. After a second out, it came down to Murray. Harvey tried to get a forkball past him, but Murray drilled it down the right field line. Thompson sprinted around the bases and, when the ball was bobbled in right field, easily scored, giving the Mets a 5–4 win. The players and the crowd reacted as if the team had just won the pennant. Everyone had their eyes on Young, who sprinted across the field to greet Murray, a smile beaming from his face. Players surrounded him to offer hugs and a pat on the head. As they left the field, fans remained standing and applauding Young as if he were a team icon wearing the uniform for the last time. At 27, the streak was, mercifully, over.

"That wasn't a monkey off my back, that was a zoo," said Young, after the game.[44] It was his last win as a Met. He blew two more saves, one in which in all four runs allowed were unearned, losing both games. Shortly after, he was sent down to Norfolk after Green became frustrated with his pitch selection. Young demanded a trade. He returned to the majors in September, making two more starts. In the last one he allowed four runs, only one of which was earned, in a loss to the Cubs. Young ended the '93 season 1-16 with a 3.77 ERA. The Mets traded him to Chicago the following spring, ending a Mets career in which he was 5-35, with 18 saves. He played three more seasons in the majors, tried to make a comeback after a series of injuries, then called it quits in the late '90s. He returned home, managing a chemical company warehouse while offering pitching lessons to local youth. In 2017 Young died of brain cancer at fifty-one. He never, at least publicly, let the losing streak sour his outlook on life or baseball after retiring; the streak is viewed by many as the unfortunate result of a tremendous amount of bad luck, rather than a result of Young's pitching abilities.

The signs were white with "O'NEILL" on them in blue lettering. The O was in the shape of a bull's-eye. On this night, June 29, there were 125 of them in the lower right-field stands at Yankee Stadium. The signs had been brought to the ballpark all the way from Cincinnati by Joe Sweeney, a friend of the guy currently hitting .329 with ten home runs and who was now, officially, a fan favorite in New York. There was a carnival-like atmosphere in the ballpark that night, which made the signs even more perfect. The Yankees had disposed of the Red Sox two weeks earlier in most exciting fashion, with a shutout performance from Kamieniecki; a grand slam from Bernie Williams; and, in the second game, down five runs, a massive two-out, seven-run inning to send more than thirty thousand fans home exhilarated.

Now, the Yankees were in the middle of what the media dubbed simply as "The Series." The Detroit Tigers had come in a half-game ahead of the Yankees for second place, but both teams were just a few games behind the Blue Jays. In previous years such a match-up was more likely to break the Yankees' season. Not this time. In the first game a Mattingly home run and hits from every starter moved Key to 10-2 on the year. During the second game, the team was trailing 2–1 in the first inning when O'Neill came up to the plate. Those 125 signs, and the fans carrying them, rose in unison out in right field. As if in a scene out of *The Natural*, O'Neill drilled a home run into the middle of the signs. All 37,692 fans, the largest crowd for a night game at Yankee Stadium since 1989, went berserk. In the tenth, Boggs hit his first home run as a Yankee, a moonshot into the upper deck in right field, for the win. The victory moved the Yankees into sole possession of second place. More than that, something was happening in the Bronx that had not happened in a long time. Not only were the Yankees winning but they were exciting. And they were almost entirely drama-free. While, privately, Steinbrenner was making Showalter squirm over every decision and, publicly, he was constantly griping about the need for a new stadium (along with empty threats of moving the team to New Jersey), there was little public criticism of the team. All the drama was unfolding across town; the roles of the two teams over the past eight years had now been reversed. The Mets were brutal to watch and read about. The Yankees were, after all this time, now fun.

As if to prove that point even further, they finished off a sweep of the Tigers the next day, thanks largely to a grand slam by Stanley. It was July 1 and the Yankees were 46-33, just two games out of first place.

Jim Leyritz scrambled to the right-field wall at Yankee Stadium, trying in vain to scale it. Instead, he watched as Tim Salmon's three-run home run landed a few rows deep into the stands. The shot gave the Angels a 6–0 lead in the second inning that grew to 8–0 before the inning was over. The game looked hopeless for the Yankees. They had ended the first half of the season with a miserable West Coast road trip, losing eight of ten games, with six of those losses coming by one run. Still, they had actually ended up closer to first place after the trip than when it started. The Blue

Jays were enduring a string even worse than the Yankees'. On July 9 New York was within one game of first.

The second half started with a loss to the A's at The Stadium. But the Yankees took the next two games, propelling them into a tie for first place. From that date, July 17, to September 15, only once did the Yankees fall more than three games out of the top spot in the American League East. During that nearly nine-week run, they would be tied for first eighteen times without ever holding the division lead by themselves, setting a major league record. In the national televised Sunday night game against Oakland, a go-ahead home run by Mattingly and a grand slam by Stanley sent the crowd into a frenzy. Against the Angels, they took the first three games leading into this Sunday afternoon match-up. The 8–0 score was shocking to the more than fifty thousand fans in attendance, the largest crowd since the home opener. While attendance did not quite match what Steinbrenner wanted, fans were coming back to Yankee Stadium in droves. Gone were the summer weekend games when the wings of the upper deck were devoid of a single fan.

It would be tough to blame any fans who, after that second inning, wrote the Yankees off for the day. But this team was different. It was playing unlike any other club New York had assembled in years. On that Sunday afternoon, five of the nine starters were hitting above .300 and two of them had an OBP above .400, numbers unheard of in a Yankee lineup as little as a year ago. Stanley was putting together the greatest offensive season by a Yankees catcher since Thurman Munson. Boggs was back to hitting .300. O'Neill had yet to endure any kind of slump in the American League, remaining one of its top hitters. And then there was Mattingly. The team captain had slumped through most of the year, fueling the concerns of those who believed his days as a true threat at the plate were over. But, during this home stand, Mattingly showed shades of the guy who set the league on fire in the 1980s. In the first ten games of the second half, he went 18-41, a .439 pace, with four doubles and 13 RBIs. He had raised his average 20 points while hitting two home runs, including the 200th of his career. The fans ate it up, giving Mattingly ovations whenever he came to the plate, whenever he got a hit, and, especially, after his home runs.

This revamped team, down 8–0, slowly began chipping away. A run in the second. Two in the third. One more in the fourth. Then three in the seventh. Suddenly, it was an 8–7 game going into the bottom of the ninth. After a lead-off walk, Stanley hit what looked like a tailor-made, rally-killing double play to shortstop. But, in what fans took to be a sign of this team's destiny, shortstop Gary DiSarcina booted the ball, leaving everyone safe. A walk, a sac fly, and a one-out hit by Pat Kelly followed, giving New York the improbable 9–8 win and keeping them tied for first.

A week later the team was back home for the biggest regular-season series at Yankee Stadium since 1985. Toronto, a game up in first, came to New York for four critical games. It started out horribly for New York. They put eleven runners on base in the first game but were shut out. In Game Two, they blew a 3–0 lead as the bullpen gave up six runs over the final four innings. The frustration of the loss boiled over. O'Neill, in one of the first of what would become a series of legendary explosions after an on-the-field failure, bashed in the clubhouse door after ending the game with the tying runs on base. Toronto moved to three games up. Having taken 17 of their last 21 games against New York, they showed a total dominance over the Yankees that made dreams of a first-place run seem futile. Showalter called a clubhouse meeting: keep your head up, he told his players, almost all of whom held their manager in a regard that had eluded Merrill and Dent. Even though he was barely older than his first and third basemen, Buck had won these guys over with his demeanor, his resolve, and his ability to handle The Boss's meddling.

Unlike calls from managers past, the Yankees responded to Buck's positivity. For Game Three, they pushed Dave Stewart around for six runs, including a home run by Gallego that was called in the MSG broadcast booth by none other than Mets superfan Jerry Seinfeld. In the Game Four matinee, a Mattingly home run—which tipped off the glove of right-fielder Joe Carter and deflected directly into the beer belly of a fan wearing a Mattingly T-shirt—and an O'Neill home run gave the Yankees the game, a split of the series, and brought them back to within a game of first. The two wins, which improved the team's league-best home record, created a playoff atmosphere at Yankee Stadium. It also came at just the right time, as the Mets season continued with one miserable moment after another. "The Bronx had the feel of the consolation round the last four summers, and now Queens is the place for the leftovers," wrote the *New York Times*'s George Vecsey.[45]

A total of 192,078 attended the four-game series, a number that ruined Steinbrenner's narrative that fans were not willing to come to the Bronx. Fans were coming now, in numbers big enough to make a noticeable difference to the guys who had spent years playing in front of half-empty ballparks in the middle of summer.

"I used to have to create a reason to go to the park—like hurt someone else's pennant chances," said Mattingly, relishing the chance to play in meaningful baseball games again. "It's easy to come to the park now."[46]

"Every pitch, every at-bat. You can feel the intensity flow through the stadium. You can see it. You can feel it. You can hear it, from the fans," said Gallego, in the midst of the run.[47]

A week later the Yankees swept Baltimore in three thrilling games, the last a 1–0 decision won on a Mattingly eighth-inning home run. It was Mattingly's fifth home run and twenty-second RBI in his last nineteen games. A total of 136,194 came for the three games, more than had attended the Mets' entire most recent home stand. The sweep, however, only accomplished a tie for first place. On August 21 the Yankees tied for first again, fell out the next day, jumped back into a tie the day after that, then fell out the day after that. On August 26 they tied for first again, but were unable to jump ahead of Toronto when the Blue Jays lost their next two games, staying tied on August 30. Going into their Saturday, September 4, match-up at home against the Indians, they were two games out of first with Abbott on the mound.

Anthony Young's victory, which should have been the one shining moment of the season, was ultimately overshadowed by some of the most bizarre off-the-field incidents in team history. The first had taken place three weeks earlier, after Young's gut-wrenching loss to San Diego. While reporters were in the clubhouse for postgame questions, Saberhagen lit a firecracker and tossed it under a table near where the fourth estate had congregated. It went off, failing to amuse the beat writers who had grown tired of the players growing tired of their questions and acting, in their minds, like spoiled toddlers. Despite its happening in the confines of the clubhouse, there was some initial confusion over who, exactly, lit the fuse. The day before the come-from-behind win against the Marlins, Saberhagen fessed up, admitting to throwing the firecracker but taking exception to stories that claimed it was thrown into the middle of a group of writers.

"I didn't throw it in the middle of them," Saberhagen contended. "I wanted to get people's attention. There are always tons of reporters here when something bad is happening. I don't like a lot of them."[48]

If nothing else, the confession was brutally honest. Saberhagen *did* dislike most of the reporters covering the team. That dislike was even more evident in the same postgame in which he admitted to throwing a lit explosive device to get their attention. As reporters stood around Gooden asking him about his win that night, a stream of Clorox bleach, loaded into a Super Soaker, shot out from behind them, hitting *Bergen Record* reporter Dave D'Alessandro in the back and side of the face. Despite a carpet-stained trail of bleach leading back to Saberhagen's locker, he denied having done it: a denial he maintained in the face of abundant evidence of his guilt.

"This is no single-bullet theory. There's a clear trajectory and it leads to only one area," said D'Alessandro.[49]

The bleach incident remained publicly unsolved for the time being; that, matched with Saberhagen's firecracker confession, would have been more than enough for the Mets to deal with. But Saberhagen's confession occurred, in part, because of another, far more serious firecracker-related incident that had taken place the weekend before Young's streak came to an end.

An M80 is a small firecracker, about the length of an average thumb, with a short fuse. Its explosion is small, but compact, capable of removing fingers if not let go quickly enough. Like just about every firecracker, the sound of it going off is enough to put a jump in any unsuspecting person. On July 24, the day on which Young lost the last of his twenty-seven consecutive decisions, Coleman was leaving the players' parking lot at Dodger Stadium with teammate Bonilla and friend and Dodger Eric Davis. As they exited the lot, Coleman lit the fuse of an M80 and tossed it out of Davis's jeep toward a group of fans. It did what firecrackers do:

it exploded. Coleman, Bonilla, and Davis all laughed and drove away, believing they had pulled a harmless practical joke on some unsuspecting fans. But the explosion caused injuries to three people, including two-year-old Amanda Santos. The toddler sustained second-degree burns, cuts under her right eye, and a lacerated right cornea.

Multiple fans had seen the outfielder toss the м80. "It was Coleman," said eyewitness Salvado Hernandez. "I saw him and Davis get into the car; that's how I knew it was him. Right after they threw it, they drove off real fast, laughing. He definitely meant to throw it at the fans."[50]

The Los Angeles Fire Department began investigating the incident. Then the Los Angeles district attorney got involved. Coleman was widely identified as the person who threw the м80. It was impossible for him not to be. Too many people had witnessed him do it. Despite this fact, Coleman remained silent for days. Meanwhile, Davis spoke up on his behalf. It didn't help.

"Everybody throws firecrackers," Davis told a reporter. "The guy [Coleman] had a firecracker, and he threw it six feet from my car. We were laughing about it as we drove off . . . It's not like it was something out of the ordinary. Every time someone lights a firecracker, you laugh. At least I do."[51]

That might have been good enough if Coleman had merely injured himself. But he hadn't. Three people were hurt, a small child among them. Neither Davis nor Coleman seemed to understand just how seriously people were taking this attempt at a practical joke. But as the pressure mounted and the investigation continued, Coleman knew it would not be written off and forgotten about. Five days after the incident and the day after Young's streak ended, Vince finally addressed the media.

"Since the incident occurred, I haven't slept, nor have been able to concentrate on anything else. I want everyone to know that I now realize that my actions on July 24th were very inappropriate," he told the throng of media, while surrounded by his wife and two young sons.[52] He blamed the media for making him out to be a monster over the past week. While Coleman seemed genuinely disturbed by what had occurred, the press noted that his words fell short of an actual mea culpa; at no point did he say he was sorry for what happened. The lack of those two words—I'm sorry—was all that seemed to ring out to many who watched. It did little to save Coleman from the press, which had grown tired of his antics and attitude and now let loose on him.

"(I)f gunpower were brains, (Coleman) would have trouble blowing his nose," wrote Dave Lagarde of the *Times-Picayune*. "He's an obstacle to fun, a breath of foul air on the first day of spring training. He doesn't steal bases as well as he steals the joy from the people around him."

"He's as sour as grapefruit juice after maple syrup," wrote *Newsday*'s Marty Noble.[53] "No more evidence needs to be brought," wrote the *Seattle Post-Intelligencer*'s Art Thiel, about the pending charges against Coleman. "I'm not a law judge. I'm convicting in the court of public opinion, of jerkism of the worst kind."[54]

The *St. Louis Post-Dispatch*, Coleman's former paper of record with the Cardinals, even brought back stories of how Coleman used to light firecrackers while players were stretching in spring training, until Whitey Herzog put a stop to it.

Coleman had been out of the lineup as the controversy swirled. A day after his media statement, with the team now in St. Louis, he appeared as a late game pinch runner. The next day, he pinch-hit late in the game, getting two at bats in a 4–3 loss. It was his last game as a Met. Recognizing they could no longer put him in the lineup, especially after felony charges were officially filed against him on August 3, the Mets suspended Coleman, at first indefinitely, then for the remainder of the season. In late August team management announced that, even with a year remaining on his contract, Coleman would not return to Queens. His Mets career was over. He eventually pleaded guilty to a misdemeanor charge, was given a one-year suspended sentence, three years' probation, fined, and made to provide two hundred hours of community service.

In the days after Coleman's suspension, the cacophony of headlines and talk-radio chatter about firecrackers, injured children, and bleach-sprayed reporters forced Green to address the media. It did not go well. As Green began his remarks, which occurred on the field and not in the press room or manager's office, a team promotional video playing on the scoreboard screeched out the familiar "Yabba dabba doooooo!!!" of Fred Flintstone. The timing was coincidental, and Jay Horwitz immediately motioned for the control room to silence the noise. Reporters in attendance couldn't help but snicker over the symbolism of a children's cartoon interrupting a press conference meant to explain the behavior of a team they thought was filled with petulant children. When Green began speaking without interruption, he embodied the anger of his players, stating they cared about New York but perhaps didn't always show it; neither, he claimed, did members of the media. As his statement went on, Green said he didn't know who among the media was worse, the print or broadcast reporters. The press conference did little to stem the nonstop conflict; it was made worse by the Yankees' recent hot streak.

Meanwhile, Saberhagen kept denying he was the bleach shooter as the team kept losing. An internal investigation conducted by the Mets' legal counsel concluded otherwise. The Mets announced their review was complete without publicly announcing their conclusions. Saberhagen responded by ripping apart his locker that evening. It was clear that he would have to come clean. Two full weeks after the incident, he finally admitted he was the one who had shot the bleach into the crowd of reporters; it had been the worst-kept secret in New York.

"After the Mets-Marlins game of July 27, I tried, unsuccessfully, to return a practical joke played on me by a Mets employee," said a carefully worded, six-paragraph statement issued by Saberhagen. "My intention was simply to paint the employee's jeans with bleach."[55]

He had simply shot the bleach too far, hitting unintended targets, he explained. If that was in fact true, some wondered, why he did not just say so in the first place? Regardless, the cat was out of the bag. Saberhagen agreed to donate one day's pay to a charity chosen by the Baseball Writers Association of America and to sit out a number of games, to be determined, after his current stint on the disabled list was over. The association issued a statement saying they hoped to put this incident, as well as others involving the Mets, behind them. One person for whom this was difficult was Green. Saberhagen had lied to him when Green asked directly if he did it; Dallas took it personally. His reaction to his pitcher's confession was a mix of anger and incredulity.

"When I ask a direct question, I expect an answer that gives the respect we deserve . . . It will take [him] some time to win [my trust] back," he told reporters. "I was told, just as you were, that he didn't do it. That's the part that upsets me. He failed to take responsibility for a childish and dangerous act." Green added that, given what had just occurred with Coleman days earlier, the timing of the incident was "mind-boggling."[56]

Saberhagen, meanwhile, was done for 1993, having undergone surgery on his left knee shortly before his public admission. The off-the-field distractions were now, after three truly bizarre weeks, largely done for the Mets. All that was left was to play the game, which was perhaps worse than having to answer reporters' questions about firecrackers and bleach. On the day of Saberhagen's admission, the Mets were 39-73, in the midst of yet another losing streak. Green was not expected to work miracles, but he was having little impact on the club.

"I remember when he took over and we'd lose maybe two or three in a row and Dallas would come in and you'd hear this booming voice lift off and everyone would listen," recalled a former player. "But collectively, as a team, if you're playing poorly, after the fourth or fifth time that a manager has to come in and address you, it really has little effect."

"They thought everything he did and said was performative," said Klapisch. "Dallas was a nice man. But he was just putting on the act of the big tough guy. He turned over the food table on the team one day and nobody believed it was not an act. People were laughing behind his back. As soon as he walked out of the room, guys just ate the food off the floor."[57]

The remaining fifty games of the season could not pass fast enough. There was still one indignity left, though.

The Yankee Stadium crowd went silent when Félix Fermín crushed Jim Abbott's 2-2 breaking ball. There was one out in the ninth and the Yankees were securely ahead 4-0. No one was on base when Fermín sent the ball sailing into deep left center field. Still, the crowd held its collective breath as Bernie Williams raced into Death Valley and, striding onto the front lip of the warning track, snared the ball for the second out of the inning. It had been exactly ten years and two months since a Yankee pitcher had thrown a no-hitter, Andy Hawkins's losing effort in 1990 notwithstanding. On this overcast Saturday afternoon, however, Abbott was one out away from history.

In some ways, the moment could not be more poetic. In others, it could not be more unlikely. Abbott's first year in New York had been a mix of great, good, and sometimes awful. In each month of the season leading to September 4, he had given up at least five runs in a game. But those outings were often sandwiched between shutdown performances where he limited the opposition to a run or two. After his 83-pitch home opener performance against the Royals, he gave up 6 runs in his next start against Texas. On May 24 the Orioles crushed him for 12 hits and 6 runs. Five days later he held the White Sox hitless into the eighth inning. Abbott didn't win a game again for another month. The idea that he would be this close to history seemed impossible, given that, just six days earlier, Abbott had started against the Indians in Cleveland and given up 7 runs in the first 4 innings, a performance that made him so frustrated he left the stadium without talking to reporters. Coming into this Saturday game, Abbott was 9-11 with a 4.31 ERA and uncertain about whether this start would be one where he could command his breaking ball or leave it up for hitters to demolish.

"He'd been throwing a lot of cutters," said Matt Nokes, who was behind the plate that day. "We said let's change this up and pitch it backwards. Get ahead of 'em with off speed pitches."[58]

So far, it had worked, even with Fermín's drive. All that stood between Abbott and the no-hitter was one of the game's best hitters, Carlos Baerga. Batting .318 on the season, the switch-hitting Baerga opted to hit from the left side against the lefty Abbott. He wanted to avoid Abbott's cut fastball jamming him from the right side. After a first-pitch strike, Baerga lunged at an outside slider, meekly hitting the ball to Velarde at shortstop. Velarde easily tossed to Mattingly for the final out and a celebration ensued that engulfed Abbott near the mound. The first player to hug him was Nokes, the catcher whose playing time had been dramatically reduced because Stanley refused to stop hitting. Moreover, Nokes, one of the few players still on the team who had endured the dark years, had to hear how players, coaches, and writers talked behind his back about his weaknesses as a catcher. Nokes could now tell his grandkids he'd caught a no-hitter. "I was really happy it happened with him," said Abbott.[59]

Michael, who had attempted for so long to acquire Abbott only to see him struggle for consistency in pinstripes, could not stop smiling from his spot in a box above the field. Next to him, assistant general manager Brian Cashman pumped his fist. Not only were they thrilled over the outcome, but, like many, they were truly glad for Abbott the man, one of the friendliest, kindest players in baseball. He was an inspiration to countless kids and adults with physical disabilities, just by being a major leaguer. He entered another level of heroism through the no-hitter. But the kudos did not do anything to change Abbott's personality. As he left the stadium that day, accompanied by his wife, Dana, and two bottles of champagne, courtesy of Steinbrenner, he stopped outside the stadium to sign autographs for a handful of kids.

The Blue Jays lost that day, meaning the Yankees were now within a game of first. The next day Toronto lost again. The Yankees jumped out to a 4–0 first-inning lead over the Indians and never looked back. The win again tied New York with the Blue Jays for first place. It was the nineteenth time the Yankees were in first, but also the nineteenth time they failed to hold it by themselves. It was also the last time in 1993 they held first place at all. The team embarked on a nine-game Midwest trip, stopping in Texas, Kansas City, and Milwaukee. It killed their season.

Arlington Stadium in Texas had been a nightmare for the Yankees for some time. No matter how good or bad they were and no matter how good or bad the Rangers were, they never seemed to find a way to win there. A critical three-game September series proved it. Kamieniecki was knocked out early in the first game. In the second, clinging to a 3–2 lead in the seventh, Bernie Williams misplayed a Julio Franco line drive into a triple, allowing two runs to score. Texas won 5–4. In the final game, they fell behind in the first inning and never recovered. Three games. Three losses. At the same time, the Blue Jays were swept by the A's. Just one win against Texas would have given the Yankees sole possession of first place. How both teams responded to being swept determined the American League East. The Blue Jays won nine in a row and finished the year taking seventeen of their final twenty-one games. The Yankees went to Kansas City and immediately watched Steve Howe and Steve Farr give back a 5–4 lead in the eighth inning of the first game. They lost two of three to the Royals.

"I've got nothing to say," Steinbrenner told reporters, after the team lost the final game of the series to Kansas City. Then he said plenty. "I've said in the past they remind me of the 1977 Yankees. Now I would have to step back and pause to assess the club . . . I'm getting to the point where I'm going to be a little disappointed in some people."[60] In Milwaukee, with Steinbrenner sitting front now, they took two of three but returned to New York two and a half games out.

Michael knew the Yankees were not going to make it; they were simply not as good as the defending world champions. He sensed it all the way back in July, which is why he'd refused to make any major trades that would sacrifice prospects or young players like Bernie Williams. For Stick, the days of mortgaging the team's future on questionable, past-their-prime stars in exchange for the Yankees' top talent were over. He made a minor deal for reliever Paul Assenmacher to sure up the bullpen, but nothing more. In late August, recognizing the team had no closer because of the bullpen's ineffectiveness, he made another minor deal to acquire future Hall of Famer Lee Smith from the Cardinals. Again, minor changes with no major prospects changing hands. When the team limped back from their Midwest swing, he made one final move, with none other than the Mets. He traded for Tanana. Winner of 240 games, Tanana was weeks away from the end of his major league career. After twenty seasons in the American League, he had joined the Mets in 1993 with high hopes and, like almost everyone else in the organization, endured a miserable experience instead. Despite pitching moderately well, especially in the second half, his record stood at 7-15, which made him the second-most reliable starter on the team. "It has definitely been a tough year," Tanana told reporters, after hearing news of the deal. "Nothing else needs to be said about how tough a year it has been for the Mets."[61]

It still did not look good for New York, even after the Tanana deal. A moment against the Red Sox, however, gave them hope. Down 3–1 to Boston in the bottom of the ninth inning of a nationally televised game, the Yankees had quickly made two outs before Gallego was hit by a pitch. Stanley came to the plate as the tying run. He immediately flew out to left field and the game was over. Or so it seemed. Before Red Sox pitcher Greg Harris delivered the pitch, a fan had leapt out of the third base box seats and sprinted across the field. A second fan followed. Umpires immediately called time-out, but Harris never heard them.

"Out of the corner of my eye I noticed the [first] guy coming onto the field, onto the third base side," said Stanley. "If you go back and look at the film, as soon as I pop up to left field my first reaction is looking back like, 'What was that?'"[62]

The two fans, teenagers that were part of a church group attending the game, were nabbed by security and escorted off the field. The umpires declared the pitch null and void, meaning the game wasn't over yet. Red Sox manager Butch Hobson was livid, even though some of his own players tried telling him that time had been called before the pitch was thrown. Hobson's anger might have been more related to the fact that, the day before, nine fans had run onto the field; Yankee Stadium security seemed nonexistent. Order was restored, with the Yankees still losing 3–1, still down to their last out. Then Stanley singled. Boggs followed with an infield single that plated a run, making it 3–2. A walk loaded the bases for Mattingly. September had been a harsh month for the captain, his midsummer power surge having long since ended. A slump dropped his average down to .290 and he'd driven in only four runs the entire month. But Mattingly lined a single into right field, scoring the tying and winning runs. The Yankees poured out of the dugout, incredulous over what just happened. Mattingly and O'Neill were so excited over the win "they head-butted one another near the Yankee dugout, and O'Neill wound up with a bloody nose on his happy face."[63] Stanley joked about wanting to bring the guy who first charged onto the field into the clubhouse to congratulate him and said that they'd all probably see him on *Late Night with David Letterman*. There was a jovial mood in the clubhouse that had been missing since the day after Abbott's no-hitter.

"If the Yankees manage to rise from their precarious position and somehow win the American League East, they will remember yesterday's wacky game and smile," wrote the *New York Times*'s Jack Curry.[64]

The win kept the Yankees three games out of first, with twelve to play; it was wacky enough to make people think that perhaps a Blue Jays collapse was in the offing. Instead, the team lost its next five games as Toronto just kept winning. On the final Monday of the regular season, New York was eliminated from playoff contention. They returned home for the last three games of the year and provided the fans one last thrill when, in the final game of the season, Stanley singled home Owen in the ninth to win the game. The crowd, thankful for a season of meaningful baseball in the Bronx after so many years of playing second fiddle to the Mets, stood and gave the Yankees a prolonged ovation. The players returned the affection by leaving the dugout, waving and tossing caps and batting gloves into the crowd.

The season, which had started with Michael sinking in his chair during the expansion draft, ended with a standing ovation from the fans. And why not? "For what they did, these resilient and persistent Yankees deserve one final curtain call in a season full of them . . . second place was quite an accomplishment for a team with this many holes, without a real leadoff hitter or any speed, with one dependable, injury-free starting pitcher and a kerosene-carrying bullpen," wrote *Newsday*'s Jon Heyman.

At 88-74, the Yankees finished seven games out, but the final standings did not accurately reflect how close the race for first place had been. It was their best regular-season record in six years and their highest finish in the standings in seven. A deeper look at the numbers showed just how remarkable the Yankees' turnaround was. In 1990 they'd finished last in the American League in batting average, on-base percentage, and slugging percentage. In 1993 they led the league with a .279 average, were second in on-base percentage, finished a point behind the Blue Jays for highest slugging percentage, and were second in the American League in home runs. Six players with at least 250 at bats hit over .300, the most by any team since the 1950 Red Sox and the most for a Yankees team since 1937. Leyritz, Stanley, and O'Neill had breakout seasons. Boggs returned to form, hitting .302. Bernie Williams took a huge leap forward in his development, cementing his place as the everyday center fielder. Tartabull produced the kinds of numbers Michael had hoped for when signing him, hitting 31 home runs and driving in 102 runs. Despite his late-season slump, Mattingly had his best year since 1989, hitting 17 home runs and driving in 86 runs, despite missing nearly a month of the season to injury. More importantly, perhaps, Mattingly showed an excitement and enthusiasm for coming to the ballpark—as a New York Yankee—that had been missing for some time. While the rest of the rotation had faltered at times, Key finished 18-6 with a 3.00 ERA, good enough for fourth in the Cy Young Award voting.

More than numbers, however, the '93 Yankees brought excitement back to the ballpark. Outside of some gripes about playing time, the club had remained largely controversy-free; what controversy there was usually only endeared them to fans even more. It was the magic of the 1980s Mets, but in pinstripe form and without the hard drugs. When Showalter earned the ire of Tigers' manager Sparky Anderson for stealing a base with the Yankees leading a game 6–0 (the Yankees would lose the game), fans supported Buck and reveled in his willingness to break one of the so-called unwritten rules of baseball. They loved how Buck toyed and tinkered, worked and reworked, to put together the perfect lineup and take advantage of the perfect opportunities. All of it added up to the beginnings of a renewed love affair between the Bronx Bombers and their fans.

"There was an electricity we brought to the Stadium," said Stanley. "I got the feeling from fans that we had brought back the excitement of the Yankees. When it's something you've never been through, you sit back and enjoy it."[65]

A total of 2.416 million fans came out to Yankee Stadium in 1993, the largest yearly attendance for the team in five years. More importantly, for Steinbrenner at least, was that for the first time in ten years more fans came out to see the Yankees than the Mets. While the numbers didn't help George in his case for a new ballpark, outdrawing his crosstown rivals had to give even The Boss a modicum of satisfaction.

It was inevitable. A team this dysfunctional—riddled with injuries, under-achievement, and controversy—was bound to get no-hit. It nearly happened on September 5 in Chicago. The Cubs' Mike Morgan held the Mets hitless until the sixth inning when, with one out, Todd Hundley reached on an infield single. They managed only two more hits in the game, losing on a home run in the ninth. Three days later at the Astrodome, Houston's Darryl Kile did what Morgan could not. It was clear from the early going that Kile was on his game. His fastball was sharp. His curveball was breaking in a manner reminiscent of Gooden's heyday. The Mets could not touch him. Thanks to a walk, a wild pitch, and an errant throw, they managed to score a run in the fourth, but by the seventh inning they had not come remotely close to a base hit. Murray lined an outside fastball down the third base line, but third baseman Ken Caminiti snared it with a diving play. Joe Orsulak then sent a ground ball deep in the hole at short. Shortstop Andújar Cedeño grabbed it and, in one motion, slingshotted the ball across the diamond, beating Orsulak by a whisker. Orsulak maintained he was safe, arguing enough to get ejected from the game. Afterward, he indicated that the first base umpire had made the call knowing Orsulak was safe but to help preserve the no-no.

Kyle struck out four of the last six Mets he faced, including Chico Walker on a wicked curveball to end the game. Just four days after Abbott's no-hitter created the feel-good story of the year, the Mets were no-hit, creating the most predictable story of the year.

"The Mets had not been no-hit in 18 years," wrote the *New York Times*'s Tom Friend, "but if it was ever going to take place again, this was the season for it."[66]

In the clubhouse afterward, the mood went beyond the typical embarrassment a team usually feels after being no-hit. For most, it felt like another in a long list of forgettable moments from 1993, "just typical of what went on the whole season," said Walker.[67]

By winning that game, the Astros had taken 11 of 12 from the Mets that year, the worst New York had performed against any one team in a single season since losing 11 of 12 to the Padres in 1980. The day before Kile's no-hitter, Bonilla had slipped and fallen rounding second base, causing a partial dislocation of his left shoulder and ending his season. Despite everything that had happened that year, Bonilla had been having one of his best seasons, setting a career high in home runs with 34. He joined Gooden, who had made his last start of the year on August 31 and then went on the disabled list with pain in his right shoulder.

There was no reason to press on anyway. The team had been eliminated from postseason contention in the last week of August. Oddly enough, with nothing left to achieve, the Mets played their best ball of the season, going 10-5 in their last 15 games, including a six-game winning streak to close it all out. It was the only time all year they managed to win more than three games in a row. But even the last game of the year, the one moment that could not come fast enough for players, team personnel, and fans, was not without more headaches. Before the game, Green informed pitching coach Mel Stottlemyre that he would not return in 1994. Green told him it was McIlvaine's decision. Hours later, McIlvaine told him it was Green's decision. Stottlemyre had come with Davey Johnson in 1984, helping to usher in a new era of successful baseball, one the Mets had never experienced over a prolonged period of time before. The former Yankee star pitcher was as much a face of the Mets as any player, the third-longest-serving coach for the franchise to that time. He was the only pitching coach Gooden knew in the majors and while some would blame Gooden's arm issues and diminished statistics on Stottlemyre pushing him to throw a changeup, Gooden himself loved the man.

"He's been like a second father to me," said Doc, upon hearing the news. "I'll miss him more than Strawberry . . . No, I don't understand it. Maybe it's not for me to understand."[68] Gooden had hinted all year that when his contract was up after the '94 season, he was leaving. The decision to let Stottlemyre go presumably assured he would now do just that. With the Stottlemyre news hanging over everyone, the season's final game was delayed seventy five minutes because of rain. In what felt like the perfect ending to the season, in the top of the ninth, Walker, who had already been told by the team he was being released after the game, hit a home run. It turned out to be the last at bat of his career. In the bottom of the ninth, the rain returned, ending the game and the season.

There was no mincing words. The 1993 season was a disaster for the Mets. The manager was fired. The pitching coach was let go. The general manager left. There was no progress to point to in any capacity, even for individual players. The bullpen nearly blew as many saves (21) as they converted (22). They almost lost more games after scoring first (38) than they won (40). Franco, Gooden, Saberhagen, Sid Fernandez, Tony Fernandez, Bonilla, and Johnson all lost significant time due to injuries. The Marlins were the only team they had a winning record against. There were only eleven separate times all season where they had won at least two consecutive games. Only three times were they able to extend it past those two wins. They swept the season-opening series against the Rockies and the season-ending series with the Marlins, but only one other series in between. At 59-103 theirs was the worst single-season record in the expansion era by a non-expansion team. It was the fourth-worst record in franchise history.

In typically blunt fashion, *Newsday*'s Marty Noble summed up the season succinctly: "The chemistry was bad; the performance was worse. The record is wretched. With all that, a compelling case can be made that the Mets just have completed the worst season in the history of major-league baseball, victories in their last six games notwithstanding."[69]

"To make matters worse, the Mets lost the interest of their fans and Shea Stadium became a ghost town," noted the Associated Press's Jim Donaghy.[70] The assessment was spot on. The Mets had drawn over 2.7 million fans to Shea in 1990. Three years later, that number was down to 1.8 million, fourth-lowest in the National League. It was the first time in ten years the Mets had failed to be in the top ten in attendance in the National League. Their 29 fewer wins than the Yankees' was the largest win differential between the two teams since the Yankees had won 103 games to the Mets' 67 games in 1980. New York City, after eight years, was no longer a Mets town.

The Mets now had to look ahead to 1994. While there was little reason to believe they would be contenders, at a minimum they could take comfort in this thought: it would be almost impossible for the '94 Mets to be worse than the '93 Mets.

A day after the Mets suffered the indignity of being no-hit and the Yankees the indignity of being swept in Texas, Major League Baseball owners made a decision that would change the course of both teams for the rest of the decade. By a 27-1 vote, one that would later be affirmed by the players' union, they agreed to move from two divisions in each league to three and add an additional best-of-five series to the postseason. The top teams in each division would make the postseason; the team in each league with the best record that was not also at the top of their division at season's end would be a wild-card participant in the playoffs. First round match-ups would be decided on a rotating basis but the wild card team could not play a team from the same division in the first round. Whichever team played the wild card would have home-field advantage in the first round. Home-field advantage between the other two teams would be decided on a rotating basis, with individual team records playing no role. The team with home-field advantage in the first round would play the first two games on the road and, if necessary, the final three games of the series at home. Winners of the four first-round series would move on to the respective league championship series.

Perhaps even bigger than the playoff expansion was the creation of three divisions—East, Central, and West. Initially, the owners wanted to maintain the two-division system and have the second-place team in each division make the playoffs as a wild card. But the players' union made clear they would not support such a system, leading to the birth of realignment. This change would impact both New York teams dramatically. The Atlanta Braves, the two-time defending National League champs who were on their way to a third-straight division title that year, were moving from the West to the East, the Mets' division. The Cleveland Indians, about to become an American League juggernaut, were departing the Yankees' division and heading to the Central. This new setup also all but guaranteed that, since the National and American League West divisions would have only four teams compared to every other division's five teams, there would be the addition of two new franchises in the near future.

Had such a three-division, wild-card system been in place in 1990, the Mets would have won the National League East. In 1993 the Yankees would have taken the wild card.

What-if scenarios aside, the landscape had changed substantially in baseball. Through smaller divisions and a wild-card format, there were now more chances to make the postseason. While baseball purists might scoff at the thought, owners and players recognized it for what it was. "Our surveys have shown that this will enhance fan interest in the waning months of the season," said Boston Red Sox president John Harrington, who chaired the owners' schedule format commission.[71]

Time would prove Harrington right.

8

The Best Team I Ever Played On

Expectations could not have been further apart for New York's two baseball teams heading into the 1994 season. The Mets were coming off arguably their worst season ever, a year filled with losses but without the "lovable loser" label that had made 103 defeats bearable in the 1960s. Instead, the players, the fans, and the media were bitter, resentful, and all-around miserable to be in the presence of one another. The Yankees, meanwhile, were coming off a surprisingly good season, one where they contended for first place until mid-September. They'd weathered the return of Stein brenner, remained largely free of clubhouse strife, and won back a city desperate for competitive baseball after two consecutive years of subpar performances out of the Bronx and Queens. The Yankees were expected to take the next step in 1994 and get back to the postseason. The Mets? Well, the Mets could not possibly go further back, so 1994 was all about simply not being as bad as a fifty-nine-win team again.

Oddly, for all the shortcomings of the '93 team, the Mets did almost nothing in the off-season to improve the club. In some instances, they had little choice. Some players were under long-term deals for big money, making trades hard to finagle. The free agent market, filled with some of the game's biggest players the year before, had few marquee names this time. Even if it did, how much longer could the team rely on free agent spending to fix their problems? Moreover, the possibility of a work stoppage during or after the regular season hung in the air, creating an uncertain future and making teams resistant to pursuing big contracts. Instead, the Mets were hoping that some of their young talent would finally prove big league–ready. Jeff Kent, acquired from the Blue Jays in the David Cone trade, was a potential All-Star at second base. Todd Hundley had shown promise for years as a catcher but had yet to fully explode in the manner team officials thought possible. Outfielder Ryan Thompson had shown flashes of power but had yet to play a full season. Perhaps 1994 would be the year all three made a huge impact with the club. Meanwhile, down on the farm there were three arms that made the Mets' brass think they had the next generation of Dwight Goodens. They were not going to be ready for 1994, but they would be ready soon, meaning long-term deals for starting pitchers would only clog up the roster and keep them down on the farm.

Perhaps with all of this in mind, the Mets entered and exited that off-season without making a single trade or signing that would have much of an impact on the team. This occurred despite losing Eddie Murray, and his 27 home runs and 100 RBIS, to free agency. It occurred despite losing Sid Fernandez to free agency as well. It occurred despite the Mets having baseball's worst bullpen and no clear shortstop, third baseman, or first baseman heading into spring training.

The most noteworthy move was the most predictable one. Vince Coleman was never going to play another game for the Mets. After months of looking for a willing trade partner, on January 5, 1994, they found the Kansas City Royals, who were also trying to rid themselves of an outfielder that had not panned out. Kevin McReynolds had played through two injury-filled seasons in the Midwest since the Mets traded him in 1992. His power numbers sank and he bickered with Royals manager Hal McRae. Kansas City was eager to see him go.

McReynolds had been a solid player in Queens, but his relationship with the media and the fans had been strained at best. He didn't particularly care for the way the press and New Yorkers took joy in berating struggling players. His calm demeanor was also in stark contrast to just about every member of the '86 championship team. Fans took it to mean he was apathetic about the team and the game itself. When McReynolds left Shea Stadium early during a September 1989 game in which the Mets were still batting, fans were irate. His wife didn't make things any better when she told WFAN that he had left "to beat the traffic."[1]

But that was in the past. Now McReynolds and Coleman both looked to start over in familiar places: Coleman in Missouri, McReynolds in New York. In three years with the Mets, Coleman never played more than ninety-two games in a season; his legacy was that of firecrackers and errant golf swings. In time, for Mets fans, Coleman's name became synonymous with poor play and off-the-field controversy: he represented an era they would roll their eyes at the mere mention of.

Once the Coleman deal was complete, the Mets did almost nothing else. When spring training got underway, though, it was clear that the team, as it existed, could not go into the regular season in this form. They were not comfortable with Tim Bogar at short and could not find anyone to replace Murray at first. With a week to go before the start of the season, they acquired David Segui from the Orioles. The big switch hitter was coming off his first full season and had the potential to become one of the best offensive first basemen in the game. Three days later, Anthony Young bid farewell to New York in a trade that brought shortstop José Vizcaíno from the Cubs. While no one would confuse Vizcaíno with Ernie Banks, he was a reliable slap hitter coming off the best year of his career and could provide stability at short. The next day the Mets dealt for touted Tigers prospect Rico Brogna, a first baseman whose path in Detroit was blocked by Cecil Fielder.

Rather than work out another deal, the team decided the solution at third base was Bonilla. It wasn't as outrageous as it sounded. Bonilla had played third base for most of his first few seasons in Pittsburgh and, when Howard Johnson failed to produce in 1993, had shifted to the hot corner for fifty-two games. He'd had one of his best offensive seasons, so the Mets would not be hurting in that sense at third. But, on defense, Bonilla was at best average; while he had played there before, most of his time as a Met had been in the outfield.

None of the late spring training deals were blockbusters; ultimately, they would not have a substantial impact on the franchise. They did, however, make the Mets a better team going into 1994. That much became clear when the season started.

The Yankees headed into the off-season deficient in two key areas: speed and relief pitching. Their 39 stolen bases were the fewest in the league, nearly half as many as the next team ahead of them. Moreover, their abysmal 53 percent rate of success in stolen bases was, by far, the worst in the league. It meant that, even though the Yankees attempted to steal bases far less than any other team, they were more likely to cost themselves runs by trying to steal than create them. In the bullpen, their .677 save percentage was eighth in the league. While that was middle of the pack, it was hard not to look at the number and think of all the West Coast and Midwest games where leads were lost in late innings. The Yankees were also second to last in holds, with nearly half as many as the league leader. While not necessarily a stinging indictment, it did show a need to strengthen the mushy middle of the bullpen. Steve Farr, who had saved 78 games over three seasons with the team, was leaving via free agency; Lee Smith, a Yankee for all of one month, was doing the same. The team had no closer.

With those two objectives in mind, Gene Michael and the brass set to work. First up was the bullpen. In late November Stick sent pitcher Domingo Jean and Andy Stankiewicz to the Astros for righty Xavier Hernandez. The Yankees had high hopes for Jean but questioned whether he would work out long term in the big leagues, a feeling justified when Jean never appeared in the majors again after the deal. His biggest mark on the Yankees was being the last player to wear number 42 before a future Hall of Famer made his debut in 1995. Stankiewicz, the gutsy, gritty infielder loved by the fans, had been a victim of the numbers game. With Velarde, Kelly, Gallego, and Owen available to play the middle infield, that left Andy the odd man out (though Owen was traded to the Angels two weeks later). In Hernandez, New York acquired a solid reliever who had averaged 8.1 strikeouts per 9 innings over the last two seasons. Though he had not played the role in Houston, he was a prime candidate to take over as team closer. The team also signed Donn Pall, a reliever coming off a strong season for the White Sox and Phillies, to bolster their middle relief efforts.

With the Hernandez deal done, they looked for speed in a familiar place. Two weeks before his thirty-fifth birthday, the Yankees offered free agent Rickey Henderson a contract. Though his performance for them had been subpar, Henderson had just helped the Blue Jays repeat as world champions; even at thirty-four, he had stolen more bases in 1993 than the entire Yankees team. The idea of him at the top of the lineup, followed by Wade Boggs and Don Mattingly, left the team salivating. But Rickey chose to head back to Oakland for a third time, leaving the Yankees searching for another speedy outfielder. They looked in yet another familiar place.

Three years after being traded from the team following a conviction for having sex with an underage girl, Luis Polonia was heading back to New York. Polonia, who had served nearly a month in prison for the crime, seemed remorseful for what happened and was anxious to start over again with the Yankees. While not Rickey, his fifty-five stolen bases were second in the American League. Polonia was also determined to regain the hitting form that saw him bat .335 just three years earlier.

"Right now, if you compare all the leadoff hitters in the American League, I believe that Rickey is the only one above me," Polonia told reporters, no doubt aware that he was a consolation prize for not landing the all-time leader in stolen bases. "If you go after someone other than Rickey, there is no one better than me."[2]

The Yankees had their speed. Polonia was the last major free agent signing the team made that winter. What would ultimately be the most impactful event of that Yankees' off-season was not a signing or a trade. It did not occur at the winter meetings or in Tampa or at Yankee Stadium, but in Carteret County, North Carolina.

Brien Taylor had been living up to expectations after his first overall selection in 1991. In his first year in the minors, he averaged over 10 strike-outs per 9 innings and yielded only three home runs. His control was off but that could be figured out, just as Randy Johnson had. In 1993, in AA Albany, he progressed further, with over 8 strikeouts and just 7 hits per 9 innings and a 3.48 ERA. Again, the walks were astronomical but could be considered part of the learning process.

On Saturday, December 18, 1993, Taylor was at home when he received a call that his brother had been in a fight with a family friend. Taylor took off for the friend's home. When he got there, a scuffle ensued between Brien and others. Perhaps he did it while throwing a punch, but more likely, while falling to the ground, Taylor hit his left shoulder hard. It dislocated and his labrum was torn in the process. The Yankees found out

about the incident from an Associated Press reporter. Taylor was sent to
Dr. Frank Jobe, the famed pioneer of Tommy John surgery.

"I can remember Frank Jobe sitting me down," said Scott Boras, Taylor's
agent. "He said, 'This is one of the worst shoulder injuries I've ever seen,'
and I believed it. The way he tore it was unnatural."[3]

There was no way Taylor could pitch in 1994, a year in which he was
going to begin at AAA Columbus and possibly make his Yankees debut
later in the season. Brien returned in 1995; it was immediately clear that
the injury had created permanent damage. "He was a shell of what he had
been," said Michael. "His entire pitching motion was different."[4] Taylor
could not throw the same way due to the shoulder injury and his fastball
never reached the nineties again. From 1995 to 1998, he made 41 appearances in Rookie and A ball. He was 3-15 with a 10.85 ERA. In 108⅔ innings
he walked 175 batters. The Yankees released him after 1998.

While the Yankees' biggest off-season moves were behind them, on
January 13 they signed free agent outfielder Daryl Boston to a one-year
deal. Boston would serve as a backup outfielder, replacing Dion James,
who, after a career year, headed to Japan. The signing began what over
the next two years became a string of acquisitions and personnel changes
by the Yankees involving former Mets, many of whom would play their
last major league game in the interlocking NY navy-blue cap instead of
the blue and orange. Two weeks after Boston, it was Bob Ojeda. Having
failed to bolster the starting rotation after offers for pitchers Pete Harnisch
and Andy Benes were rejected, Michael took a minimal risk by inking
the former Met to a minor league deal and inviting him to spring training. Ojeda had recovered from the boat crash that had taken the lives of
two of his Indians teammates the year before and had made a handful
of appearances for Cleveland toward the end of '93. Offered a chance to
win the fifth spot in the Yankees rotation, he was eager to show there was
still something in the tank.

Nearly three weeks after Ojeda, the Yankees took a chance on another
former Met. Jeff Reardon, second all-time in saves, signed a minor league
deal and was invited to camp. It was another low-risk deal, with Michael
excited over a knuckleball the thirty-eight-year-old Reardon had devel-

oped to help him stay in the majors. Three former Mets in just under a month. There would be more.

Right before the start of spring training, Michael made one last deal to bolster the rotation, acquiring Terry Mulholland from the Phillies. It would now be Key, Abbott, Mulholland, and some combination of Kamieniecki, Sterling Hitchcock, Sam Militello, and Ojeda for the fourth and fifth spots. The deal created what would be the only controversy of the spring. Hitchcock, unhappy that he now had to compete with two new left-handed starters and with all of nine career starts to his name, publicly vented: "As far as I can remember, it's been give a guy six, seven starts, and if he doesn't do anything, then get him out of there and bring in Dave LaPoint."[5] The higher-ups were not amused. Hitchcock apologized to the organization and LaPoint.

The lineup was more certain, though it was dependent on several ifs. If Paul O'Neill continued hitting American League pitching, if Jim Leyritz kept hitting for power, if Mike Stanley had another season like the one he'd just had, if Tartabull stayed healthy, and if Bernie Williams progressed even further from his '93 form, they would be in good shape.

As the spring moved closer to Opening Day at Yankee Stadium, it became clear to many that the Yankees were for real. "Our first meeting in spring training that year Buck said this team can win. It was really the first time that we had heard somebody putting that out there," said Leyritz.[6] It was not just that this team thought it was good: last year's team had thought it was good in spring training, too. This was more an '86 Mets kind of feel. Not the in-your-face swagger, but the idea that they were going to dominate. The new divisional setup gave them two fewer teams to compete with in the American League East, making the division, in theory at least, easier to win. But as they left for New York after exhibition games at the Superdome in New Orleans, the Yankees were thinking beyond merely ending their thirteen-year playoff drought. They were thinking about going all the way to the World Series.

On Opening Day 1994, a brisk, windy day at Wrigley Field, Dwight Gooden, sporting a commemorative patch celebrating the 125th anniversary of Major League Baseball on his right sleeve, took the mound for his eighth career Opening Day start. The first batter Gooden faced was center fielder Karl "Tuffy" Rhodes, he of five career home runs in 280 at bats.

Rhodes ran the count full when Gooden hung a curve. The left-handed Rhodes, slipping off his back leg as he swung, drove the ball into the left-center-field bleachers for a lead-off home run. In the third, now staked to a 2–1 lead, Gooden tried sneaking a two-strike fastball past Rhodes, who again drove the ball into the left-field bleachers. In the fifth, the Mets now leading 9–5, Gooden again tried to get a fastball past Rhodes, who again drove the ball into the left-field bleachers. Three at bats, three home runs. It was the first time in the history of the game that a player began the season with three consecutive home runs; it was also the first time Gooden had given up three to the same player in a game. The three ultimately accounted for 23 percent of Rhodes's career home run total. He was out of major league baseball by 1996, eventually moving on to play in Japan.

Gooden left the game in the sixth inning after giving up 11 hits and 7 runs, 5 of them earned. His curve had looked flat and his fastball lacked any semblance of zip. The hope was that he just needed to work out some early-season mechanics. But the Mets' brass was leery of Doc's gradually wilting performances over the years, especially with Gooden set to become a free agent at season's end. Already there was talk about how much Gooden would want, a deal somewhere around $17–18 million. That was going to force the Mets to make a tough decision: re-sign an aging pitcher whose performances were declining by the year or let go a franchise player who was the only remaining link to their last championship. Preemptively, the team was trying to make the decision easier, at least in the minds of fans.

"He went from the greatest pitcher in the National League to one of the better pitchers in the National League," said McIlvaine, on the day Gooden was about to get shelled by the Cubs.[7] Still, despite the performance, Doc came away with the win, his sixth on Opening Day and his twenty-seventh against the Cubs. Gooden won, in part, because of the kind of offensive explosion that had largely been absent from the team the year before: 16 hits, 12 runs. Jeff Kent had four of those hits, with five other players contributing multi-hit games. The Mets were now 22-2 in the first game of the year dating back to 1970. But that did not mean much, as they'd ended up under .500 for many of those seasons. Dallas Green, for one, knew not to get too giddy.

"You've got to be pleased with the win," Green noted. "I am. But some of the things we did getting there didn't please me."[8]

He was referring to a slew of '93-esque incidents during the game. A throwing error by Vizcaíno. A missed fly ball by McReynolds. Two runners getting thrown out on the base paths. One failing to score from second on a double. Green had been around the game long enough to sense trouble, even if the result was still a win.

Green must have felt some relief, however, when the team returned to Shea 4-2 and then took three of the five games on their first home stand of the year. The season was only two weeks old, but the Mets were sitting in second place, a position made even more important by the new wild-card system. Carrying the team in those first two weeks was Kent. The pressure on him to perform was no small matter. Cone had gone on to help the Blue Jays win the championship in 1992 and was on his way to winning the Cy Young Award in 1994 with the Royals. In '93, however, Kent had struggled through much of the early portion of the season. His performance after the first third of the year was enough to earn him a three-game benching from Green. Though Kent's numbers picked up after that, overall, fans started to wonder when, or even if, the trade would pay off. Kent's first two weeks in '94 showed promise. Through 11 games, he was leading the National League with 7 home runs, 19 RBIs, and an astounding 1.424 OPS. He already had multiple games with two home runs and was among the league leaders in nine offensive categories, giving the Mets all the offense they needed as they awaited Bobby Bonilla's return from injury.

Kent did not desire any of the attention this success brought: "I don't like to be the focus. I don't like to be in the limelight."[9] It was a far cry from the days of '86, when you could hardly find a Met who didn't love the attention that playing in the Big Apple bestowed on them. Not Kent. He was more McReynolds than Carter, at least when it came to seeing his name in print. While Kent could not possibly keep up that pace for the rest of the season, his first two weeks were an enormous bright spot for a team that was playing pretty good baseball.

"I don't think there were a lot of people that gave us a chance to do what we've done so far," said Green, who wasn't letting the early-season success get to his head. "It's early and I've seen a lot of things that go in spurts. It still boils down to everybody contributing."[10]

The contributions kept coming, as the Mets finished April at .500. For many teams, a .500 month would be no cause for celebration. For the Mets it was a borderline miracle, considering where they had been just eight months earlier. At no point in the previous season did the Mets play .500 ball during a full calendar month. In May they continued their surprising run. During the first road trip of the month, they took three out of four in St. Louis, missing out on a four-game sweep only when Franco issued two two-out, base-loaded walks in the second game of the series. They then took two out of three from the Expos in Montreal. It was enough to put the Mets back into second place in what was turning out to be the highly competitive National League East. Meanwhile, Kent was still hitting the cover off the ball and others were also stepping up. Hundley had 8 home runs, nearly more than he'd hit in all of 1993, and a 1.004 OPS, tops on the team. Bonilla, back to playing every day, hit .350 with 4 home runs and 10 RBIs in the first two weeks of May.

While the team slumped in mid-May, they recovered to take two of three from the Pirates in Pittsburgh, then returned home to sweep the Central Division–leading Reds. On the morning of May 30, Memorial Day, the Mets stood at 25-23. Two teams were ahead of them in the division, but they were just four and a half games out of first and three behind the Expos for the wild card. Their unexpected performance was swept up in a series of incredible moments that made the Big Apple the most exciting and enthusiastic sports city in the country heading into summer. The New York Rangers and New Jersey Devils had just completed an epic seven-game playoff series the previous Friday to determine who would go to the Stanley Cup Finals. The Rangers, fifty-four years without a championship, won the series in double overtime at Madison Square Garden in a moment that rocked the entire city. On Memorial Day, the Indiana Pacers tied their best-of-seven Eastern Conference finals against the Knicks at two games apiece and then took Game Five, only to see the Knicks come back and win Games Six and Seven to advance to their first NBA finals in twenty-one years. Add to this the Mets, seemingly out of nowhere, playing competitive, exciting ball. Fans took notice.

During the ninth inning of the last game of the Reds series, with Cincinnati threatening to take the lead, the hometown crowd of nearly 25,000 stood and began a loud, reverberating "Let's Go Mets" chant, the kind that had not been heard since the last fading days of the dynasty that never was.

"I've never heard that chant that way since I've been here," said Bonilla, enjoying his first easygoing season in New York.[11] Bobby Bo was a big part of the enthusiasm now felt at Shea. He was in the midst of an eleven-game hitting streak, one where he broke the club record for most consecutive games driving in a run. Hitting .331 with 30 RBIs despite missing a week of the season, fans were warming up to Bonilla and he to New York.

Another reason for the turnaround was the bullpen. While there was still room for improvement, the seemingly endless string of blown games had slowed down. Franco led the National League with 12 saves, remarkable considering the entire Mets bullpen had saved only 22 games in 1993. Franco, who had suffered through a difficult '93 season due to injuries, and who had constantly bickered with the media over the last few years, would eventually end up as the league leader in saves and, for the only time in his entire twenty-one-season career, receive votes for the Cy Young Award.

The Mets won fourteen games in May, more than they had won in any single month the year before. The baseball world was talking about them, for all the right reasons now. June, however, would bring flashes of the previous year's team; in the process, a one-time legend would throw his final pitch for the only team he had ever known in the big leagues.

The sun was out. The stands were full. Excitement permeated through Yankee Stadium. There were expectations for this Yankee team beyond simply winning the season's first game. With 56,706 in attendance, the Bronx Bombers did not disappoint, racking up eleven hits in a 5–3 win over the Rangers. Boggs had four hits. Polonia stole a base as part of a double steal, giving the Yankees five percent of their entire previous season's stolen base total in just the first game of the year. For the second straight Opening Day, Tartabull homered. Stanley added a shot as well. Key pitched into the eighth and, in his team debut after having won the role of closer during spring training, Hernandez struck out two to earn the save. It was a banner day all around in the Bronx.

Two days later they scored in every inning but the eighth in an 18–6 blowout of Texas. Every starter had at least one hit and one run scored, with Mattingly knocking in the thousandth run of his career. It was a great start to the year, though Mulholland's giving up six runs was a precursor of things to come. After another win, they lost 6 of their next 9 games, bringing them to 6-6 on the year. Then the Yankees did something they had not done in a long, long time: they beat the hell out of the West Coast teams. It began by winning two of three against Seattle at home, with Reardon picking up his first win of the year in relief, and ultimately the last of his career. Oakland came next. In the first game Ojeda made his second start of the year, his first as a home starter in New York in four years. Ojeda's season debut had not gone well. In Detroit he'd yielded a home run to the first batter he faced, then gave up three more hits and three walks before leaving the mound without making it out of the first inning. The Yankees eventually came back to tie the game before losing in extra innings. Ojeda now sought redemption. After a scoreless first, he allowed four singles, two walks, and three runs in the second. The Yankees came back and staked him to a lead going into the third, but he allowed three more hits, loading the bases with one out. Showalter removed him from the game, his last as a major leaguer. In two starts with the Yankees, Ojeda pitched three-plus innings, allowing 17 base runners and 8 runs. Because the Yankees eventually came back against Oakland that night, he ended up with two no-decisions. Three days later he was designated for assignment and eventually released. Let go with Ojeda on the same day was Reardon. Though he enjoyed a small stretch of success that even saw him become the team's closer for a week, it became clear that Reardon's newly developed knuckleball was not enough to fool hitters. He made his last big league appearance, coughing up a three-run lead, in Anaheim. The first of Steinbrenner's former Mets rehabilitation projects had come up short.

The Yankees took the next two games against the A's, with Mattingly hitting his first two home runs of the season, sweeping Oakland. After splitting two games with the Angels, they headed west and took three of the first four games to end the month at 15-8, just a game and a half out of first. They looked sharper, crisper, and more determined than in 1993. But what happened in May, both on and off the field, represented transitional moments in the performance and image of the team. And it started with three games at home against Boston.

The Yankees began May 6, 1994, three and a half games out of first place, with the team they were trailing now in their home ballpark. In the first game, the Yankees scratched together three runs while Key went the distance for the win. The next day, trailing by one in the ninth, they staged a dramatic come-from-behind win. Mother's Day Sunday brought more excitement. In the sixth inning, with the score tied at 3–3, Tartabull sent a ball into the center-field bleachers known as "The Black," only the tenth player to have done so since Yankee Stadium was remodeled in 1976. Next up, Stanley reached out and hit one to right field, a ball that would probably have left no other park than the one in the Bronx. Gerald Williams then reached out and, with a one-handed swing, hit a shot that landed in almost the same spot as Stanley's. It was the first time in almost ten years that a Yankees team hit back-to-back-to-back home runs.

The Yankees took the game 8–4, sweeping Boston at home for the first time since August 1985. More importantly, they were just a half-game out of first, with the Boston series serving as a statement to the rest of the league: this is not some fluke team playing surprisingly well. This was a team using power, speed, and strong pitching to beat you. The Red Sox, who had gotten off to a fast start, never recovered. "This was our first test, and we didn't pass it," said Boston first baseman Mo Vaughn.[12]

Out went Boston, in came Cleveland, their lineup stacked with powerhouses like Albert Belle, Jim Thome, Eddie Murray, Manny Ramirez, Carlos Baerga, and Kenny Lofton. Armed with this abundance of offense, the Indians went into the Bronx hoping to make a statement of their own as they chased the American League Central lead. Instead, the Yankees buried them.

New York rode the strong pitching of Abbott to a 4–3 win in the first game. Combined with another Red Sox loss, the Yankees now had sole possession of first place, something that had eluded them throughout the previous season despite being so close, so many times. They had not had sole possession of first place this late in the year since May 16, 1989. An eternity had seemingly passed between then and now, with Mattingly being the only link between those two teams.

The New York Yankees were back in first, exhibiting signs of a team destined to win. "Maybe this is getting serious," noted the *New York Times*'s Jack Curry, about the now seemingly unstoppable Bronx Bombers.[13] Their 20-10 record was the club's best thirty-game start since 1953. Those were Yankee dynasty years, the mere mention of which was bound to create excitement, even in someone as generally poker-faced as Showalter. "I am tired of seeing anybody but us there first," said Showalter, referring to the pennants that flew atop the stadium and were arranged in order of standings in each division. "It will be nice to see us there first."[14] Showalter would look up and see the Yankees there in first for the remainder of the season, because after winning the first game against Cleveland, they did not let up. They beat Charles Nagy and then Dennis Martínez. A tenth-inning walk-off win completed the four-game sweep. Combined with the sweep of the Red Sox, it was the first time New York had swept a seven-game home stand since 1987. It also marked the team's first seven-game win streak of the decade.

They then went to Milwaukee and swept three games by a collective score of 28–7. They finished out the month winning seven of ten, standing three and a half games up in first place. Perhaps most remarkable about the team's success was that most of the off-season moves Michael had made were not paying off. Mulholland had given up at least 5 runs in 6 of his first 11 starts. Hernandez lost his spot as the team's closer after pitching to a 5.50 ERA. Ojeda and Reardon had already been released. Boston, in limited duty, was batting just .179, though he had hit a big ninth-inning home run to tie a game in Kansas City before the end of the month. Like Ojeda and Reardon before him, Boston, the former Met, would end his career that season as a Yankee.

Polonia was the only new player making much of a difference, providing stability at the lead-off spot and stealing ten bases. Largely, however, the Yankees rose to the top of the division thanks to contributions from the core of the '93 team. Key was surpassing his performance from the previous year, jumping out to a 7-1 record and failing to go at least six innings in only one start. Abbott, with a 2.99 ERA, was outperforming Key. Kamieniecki, annoyed with having to compete for a starting role despite his years with the club, earned his way back into the rotation after Ojeda faltered; he was 4-0 with a 2.53 ERA. Steve Howe, after a miserable '93 season, quietly emerged as the most reliable pitcher out of the bullpen and, by mid-June, solidified himself as the team's closer.

Offensively, the draw-out-at-bats, wear-pitchers-down approach of Michael had filtered through the entire lineup, meaning even hitters like Tartabull and Stanley, who struggled to find their groove in the early months, were still drawing countless walks. Leyritz, out to prove his long-held belief that he should play every game, was among the team leaders with nine home runs. Mattingly overcame a rough start to hit .363 in May. Boggs ended May with a .342 average and a .428 OBP. Toward the end of the month, he underwent a power surge, hitting six home runs over ten games.

No one, however, came close to matching the season that O'Neill was having. There was curiosity over whether O'Neill would continue to play at a level similar to his '93 performance. After all, despite his numbers, he was still being sat against left handed pitching. Or did the batting stance adjustment he'd made with Rick Down mean several more seasons of solid hitting?

The answer came quickly. It started with two hits on Opening Day. There were two more in O'Neill's next game. A few days later, against reigning Cy Young Award winner Jack McDowell, there were three more hits, including two home runs. He started the season with an eight-game hitting streak. He followed his first hitless game with three consecutive multiple-hit games. On April 25 against the Angels, O'Neill went 5-5. He began May with a thirteen-game hitting streak; despite ending the month 0-10, the Yankees' right fielder led the American League with a .428 average, a .534 on-base percentage, and a .731 slugging percentage. His

21 multi-hit games led the league as well. The numbers were remarkable, unlike any put up by a Yankees player in decades. He'd been held hitless in only 8 of the 42 games he played. When he wasn't getting hits, he was walking. O'Neill was not only proving that 1993 was no accident, he was establishing himself as one of the game's best outfielders.

O'Neill was pleased with the result, but hated how his hitting created more focus on him instead of the team. Unlike half the clubhouse across town, he wasn't confrontational with the press. He just despised having to talk about himself. It was a refreshing change from just years earlier, when players on the team made clear they cared more about individual statistics than team outcomes. If O'Neill hated talking about himself, he especially detested having to talk about how well he was hitting. That was just inviting a prolonged slump, which, when it came, he inevitably blamed on the media. And the idea that he might hit .400 over the course of the entire season? No way, thought O'Neill, so stop asking about it.

"He was the most negative person I have ever been around that used that energy to be as great as he was," Stanley said, years later, with a laugh. "Most people that talk the way he did wouldn't last two weeks in the big leagues. He just had a way of using negative energy because he always talked about how much he stunk. 'Stano, I stink,' he would say. I was thinking, *look at your average and look at mine, okay*?"[15]

Ironically, despite having the best all-around year of any player in the season's first two months, O'Neill wasn't even on the All-Star ballot. The team could only submit the names of three outfielders, so during spring training Williams, Tartabull, Polonia, and O'Neill drew straws to see whose name would be left off. O'Neill drew short straw. That was fine. Just meant more attention on others and less on him.

It had been a remarkable first two months for the Yankees on the field. Even more remarkable was something that occurred off the field the night of May 19. It was just forty seconds of television, but it helped change the image of the team for years to come and its owner forever.

Of his eventual sixteen seasons in the big leagues, 1994 was Dwight Gooden's toughest and worst. After his Opening Day clunker against the Cubs, he missed his next start, but took the mound again on April 16 and kept the Astros scoreless over six innings. In his next appearance, the Dodgers clobbered him for 10 hits and 7 runs. A few days later, an MRI exam found an injury to Gooden's big right toe. It was keeping him from fully pushing off the mound and generating the kind of power he needed to retire hitters. Doc landed on the disabled list for six weeks. The Mets were surprising everyone by their performance without their presumed ace pitcher on the mound. It certainly could not have been easy on the twenty-nine-year-old who once ruled New York City. Gooden now looked around and saw a clubhouse full of guys he hardly knew. Two of the club's other black players, Coleman and Young, had been traded in the off-season, further isolating Doc from the locker room. Who were these guys? How could they relate to Gooden's experiences of the '80s?

"It's different," Gooden had remarked earlier in the year, on a road trip. "I don't even listen to the same music as these guys."[16]

Not even thirty yet, Doc was somehow the old man of the club. His father was dealing with severe health issues that further took Gooden's mind away from the game. With few people to spend time with or confide in, he soon began searching out other ways to escape the loneliness and the longing for better days.

On June 9, Gooden came off the DL and was promptly smacked around for six runs by the Expos. A glimmer of hope appeared when he held the Phillies in check over seven innings in his next start. On June 19 he gave up just three hits and a run to the Marlins in a 6–1 win. It was Gooden's 157th and last win for the New York Mets, the second-most of any pitcher in franchise history. Five days later, at home against the Pirates, Doc had the worst outing of his career: seven hits, four walks, nine runs in five and a third innings. The sixth inning proved ominous. After a lead-off home run, Gooden walked the bases loaded. A black cat then appeared out of nowhere and walked past the Mets dugout. On the proceeding play, a ground ball to second, Kent threw wild to home, allowing two runs to score. Gooden struck out the pitcher, his 1,875th and last as a Met, also good enough for second all-time on the franchise list, then gave up a triple to Gary Varsho, previously 0-3 with three strikeouts in the game. Green mercifully removed Doc, who did not appear at Shea Stadium again for six years; when he did, it would be in a different New York uniform, for a team and a game that was substantially different from those on that June 1994 night.

Making matters worse, Gooden made the start that night because of clubhouse issues. It was Saberhagen's turn in the rotation, but the Mets pushed him back a day out of caution over a possible injury. Saberhagen expressed his anger internally over being skipped, but it inevitably got out in the media. He increased the tension by claiming the higher-ups were making no effort to improve the team's shortcomings; rather, they were merely filling holes to get by. The outburst came amidst a growing dissension within the clubhouse, thanks in part to a June that had gone brutally bad so far. Starting the month in third place and seven and a half games out of first, they lost 13 of 21, including Gooden's clunker against Pittsburgh. The team fell to last in the division, 14 games out of first and 10.5 games out of the wild card. The anger that had permeated the clubhouse over the last three seasons festered again.

The Pirates swept the Mets, who then lost both games of a short series at home to St. Louis. On June 28 news broke that, for all the Mets had been through during the 1990s, may have been the most shocking yet. Gooden had failed not one, but two drug tests and had been placed on a sixty-day suspension. Given his impending free agency and the now real possibility of a players' strike coming that summer, many who followed the game realized that Gooden's Mets career was probably over.

Looking back decades later, Gooden's positive tests do not appear as shocking. That April Darryl Strawberry, his former teammate and the man who would forever be linked with him around drugs, admitted to having a substance abuse problem and checked into Betty Ford. Things had gone downhill for Strawberry since leaving New York. Back in his hometown of LA, he was surrounded by old acquaintances who acted as enablers for drinking and cocaine use. His marriage, long troubled, officially fell apart. He was convicted of tax evasion for failing to pay taxes on income received from autographs. Strawberry was ordered to pay $350,000 in back taxes. The Dodgers even put him on waivers in 1993, but no team would take a chance on signing him. "That hurt a lot," said Strawberry. "I didn't even want to go back to the Dodgers after that, having them think I was just taking their money. So, yeah, I thought about what it would be like if I wasn't around anymore."[17] After a month of rehab, he left the facility, only to be released by LA. He signed with the Giants.

Given the link between the two, it is easy to think in hindsight that Gooden's lapse was obvious. But, at the time, Doc was undergoing a series of random drug tests as part of the aftercare program from his 1987 suspension. He had not failed a single one in seven years, at least not that the public knew of. Moreover, those around him, including his teammates, club personnel, and even his own father, had not detected any signs that he was using again.

Or maybe they had but, like the man himself, were just in denial. After word got out about the suspension, Gooden began informing friends and teammates that, despite the failed tests, he was not using drugs again. It was an implausible excuse that was easily disprovable by the tests themselves. In reality, after pitching for the Mets Double-A affiliate in Binghamton in June as part of his toe injury rehab, Gooden took drugs under the mistaken belief that, because he was outside of New York City, he would not have to take his usual drug test. Wanting to believe their teammate would not lie to them or do drugs again, many bought Gooden's story.

"I still don't believe he has a problem . . . Doc's Doc, he hasn't changed. From what I got from Doc, this is not for anything he's been doing," said Saberhagen, upon hearing the news.[18]

"I don't think there was a problem," said Bonilla. "If Doc says everything's cool, that's fine with me."[19]

One person who was not surprised by the news was perhaps the only other New York athlete who truly understood what Gooden was going through. "Why should I be shocked?" asked Steve Howe, playing baseball after seven drug-related suspensions. "An addict is an addict. Give an addict an inch, and he'll take it."[20]

Gooden checked into Betty Ford the next month, spending the summer there. In September he failed another test; cocaine again. Gooden was still under the terms of his sixty-day suspension because the season was on hold during the players' strike. League officials held off on further punishment, hoping there would be no need to extend the suspension longer if Gooden could stay clean over the course of several more weeks of testing. Instead, Gooden failed one test after another. In November the commissioner's office announced the failed tests and a suspension for the entire 1995 season. The announcement brought additional details. Doc had failed at least ten drug tests since his late-June suspension. It was also learned that he had failed a test in late 1993, but the league had not taken action because they believed it was an isolated incident.

"All of us who love this man urge him to get the help he needs, put God into his life and exhibit the same tenacity he showed on the mound," said McIlvaine, after hearing of the yearlong suspension.[21]

A day after the one-year suspension was announced, Gooden sat in the bedroom of his home and pointed a loaded handgun at his head. While he internally debated whether to end it all or to "be a man" and deal with his issues and be responsible to his family, Gooden's wife walked in. She took the gun from him and ran to call his mother and have her come over immediately.[22] Gooden did not take his life that night, but he had a long road ahead of him. His baseball career appeared over and he had to get his downward-spiraling life and addiction under control. Meanwhile, for the first time since October 27, 1986, the Mets played without a single representative from their last championship team on the club. The final link to that magical season was gone.

On Thursday, May 19, 1994, over thirty million people gathered in front of their televisions to watch the Season Five finale of *Seinfeld*. The NBC sitcom, which had begun in relative obscurity five years earlier, was now the third-highest-rated show on TV, trailing only *60 Minutes* and *Home Improvement*. While labeled as a show about nothing, *Seinfeld* had in fact become about many things previously unspoken about on television. Episodes about sex in the office, masturbation, exposed nipples, "shrinkage," and cursing in front of children had catapulted the show and its stars to the height of fame. Moreover, while filmed in Los Angeles, the show used the foibles of New York City in the early '90s to its advantage, even featuring recently elected mayor Rudy Giuliani in an episode about whether yogurt billed as nonfat actually contained fat. Two years earlier Keith Hernandez had appeared in two episodes as himself, becoming friends with (real-life Mets fan) Jerry Seinfeld while courting his ex-girlfriend Elaine.

Season Five was perhaps the best, most inventive season yet, eventually earning the show a dozen Emmy nominations. At the start of the season's final episode, titled "The Opposite," George Costanza, a neurotic, short, stocky, slow-witted bald man who constantly lies or exaggerates in interactions with women and coworkers, realizes that every decision he has made in his life has been wrong. Recognizing that if his instincts are always wrong, then the opposite of them would have to be right, he decides to do the opposite of what his gut tells him. So, instead of ignoring a woman staring in his direction, he begins by approaching her and being brutally honest: "My name is George. I'm unemployed and I live with my parents."

The approach works and the two start dating. George's new girlfriend, enamored by his approach to life, sets him up with a job interview through a relative. The job? Assistant to the traveling secretary for the New York Yankees. During the interview, George is again brutally honest. He talks about being fired for having sex in the office and for quitting a job because he could not use his boss's private bathroom. The interviewer, played by legendary character actor Paul Gleason, is so impressed with George's direct, honest approach that when George Steinbrenner comes walking past, he asks The Boss to step in and meet Costanza. All the audience sees is a silhouette bearing Steinbrenner's resemblance, and the voiceover is done by *Seinfeld* cocreator and writer Larry David. The exchange became an instant classic.

Steinbrenner: Nice to meet you.
Costanza: Well, I wish I could say the same, but I must say, with all due respect, I find it very hard to see the logic behind some of the moves you have made with this fine organization. In the past twenty years you have caused myself, and the city of New York, a good deal of distress, as we have watched you take our beloved Yankees and reduced them to a laughing stock, all for the glorification of your massive ego!

As the interviewer grimaces, expecting an outburst from the Yankees' owner, Steinbrenner replies, "Hire this man!"

With that, George Costanza becomes an employee of the New York Yankees. Costanza's outburst was no doubt an expression of David's true feelings. As a lifelong Yankee fan, he, too, had suffered through the '80s and early '90s. The Mets had already been featured on the show but, now, David had his turn to incorporate his favorite team into scripts. In "The Opposite," he paved the way for the soon-to-be biggest show on television to provide tens of millions of people a reminder every Thursday night for nearly three years about the existence of the Bronx Bombers. Several players, including O'Neill, Tartabull, Williams, Derek Jeter, and manager Buck Showalter, would appear on the show in hilarious cameos. But it wasn't just that the Yankees were mentioned or had guest spots. Steinbrenner himself, or at least the David-voiced version of him shown only in profile, became one of the show's many important secondary characters. He appeared in numerous episodes, interacting with Costanza in comical ways that at times also incorporated current or past Yankee events. Meanwhile, David continued to use the show to express the rage and headshaking many fans still felt about the pre-banishment Steinbrenner. In one episode Steinbrenner mistakenly believes Costanza has died and visits his parents to offer condolences. He instead gets confronted by Costanza's father, who berates him for trading Jay Buhner for Ken Phelps. It was a moment that Phelps himself credited and praised for helping maintain his notoriety years after he'd retired from the game.

The inclusion of the Steinbrenner caricature became so successful that people began to view the *Seinfeld* version as akin to the real-life version, even though The Boss himself never actually appeared on screen (a taped cameo was cut at Steinbrenner's request). Millions of people saw this wacky, comical, make-fun-of-himself character on TV, making it inevitable that the image of Steinbrenner, so bruised and tarnished through his years of mistakes and brutish behavior, began to change. Even for those who didn't equate the TV image with the real thing, if Steinbrenner was allowing himself to be lampooned like this, how bad could he really be? While the winning that came later in the decade surely played a large part in it, no off-the-field activity did more to rehabilitate the image of George Steinbrenner with the public than his run on the show. In turn, it made the Yankees a little harder to hate, especially when audiences saw O'Neill complain about having to hit two home runs in a game or Tartabull use a knife and fork to eat a candy bar. It was free, widely seen, widely loved publicity for a team on the cusp of creating a dynasty. The Mets, meanwhile, received no such acknowledgment. There were no Bonilla or Franco appearances. No episodes where Dallas Green talks to Costanza about what materials the Mets' uniforms are made out of. No scenes where a bereaved parent yells at Frank Cashen for trading Dykstra and McDowell for Samuel. None of it. After May 19, 1994, *Seinfeld* only further solidified the Yankees' recapturing of New York.

As June progressed, labor issues began to take hold over Major League Baseball. The issues were years in the making: the culmination of distrust between owners and players and of owners' dishonesty, which had been exposed in the late 1980s. The roots of baseball's impending work stoppage went back as far as the game itself.

For approximately the first hundred years of organized baseball, team owners held all the leverage; a players' association, or even the concept of one, was virtually nonexistent. If a player signed with a team, he usually signed a one-year contract; after the season, he signed another one. If he did not like the contract he was offered, he could refuse to play, but that was his only option if a club did not meet his salary demands. He could not offer his services to another team and was forever bound to play for that team unless ownership decided to trade or release him, a constraint known as the reserve clause. Holding out was rare, except among the game's greatest players.

In the early 1970s, under Marvin Miller, the new head of the Players Association, the players challenged the reserve clause. In the mid-'70s, an arbiter allowed two players, Andy Messersmith and Dave McNally, to offer their services to any major league team that wanted to pay for them. This ushered in free agency, completely changing baseball and the relationship between owners and players.

Free agency meant escalating player salaries, a trend that angered owners, especially those who could not afford the best players. The owners attempted to chip away at the players' bargaining position and overall power. As a result, there was a players' strike that lasted nearly two months in 1981 and another that lasted two days in 1985. There was also the lockout of 1990. Meanwhile, in the midst of these strikes and lockouts, in the late 1980s, owners colluded with one another to refuse to spend money on free agents. Players like Andre Dawson, Jack Morris, and Carlton Fisk, all future Hall of Famers, could not find teams willing to offer them contracts. Morris and Fisk were forced to re-sign with their current teams, while Dawson offered the Chicago Cubs the chance to pay him whatever they felt he was worth.

Collusion was a violation of the game's existing collective bargaining agreement (CBA). When the owners were exposed, not only did they have to pay hundreds of millions in restitution to the players, but the public exposure of their deeds created a permanent mistrust between players and ownership.

With this dynamic front and center, the owners and players now had to negotiate a new CBA in 1994. The owners made clear that any new agreement would have to include a salary cap. Many believed that small-market teams could no longer afford to keep pace with the Yankees, Mets, and Dodgers of the world, which could accumulate revenue from a far larger pool of resources than the Royals, Expos, or Brewers could. To the owners, the Pirates were a clear-cut example of this. Despite winning three consecutive division titles in the early '90s, Pittsburgh had been unable to re-sign any of its big-name players because it could not afford them. The average player salary had gone from just barely six figures at the start of the 1980s to $1.168 million in 1994.

The players were not buying it. They saw a cap as a clear attempt to keep salaries down. They were even more distrustful of the idea when owners refused to provide a clear accounting of team revenues. Players made clear throughout the first months of 1994 that a salary cap was a nonstarter. The owners proposed one in June anyway. It was a disheartening sign of things to come. The owners then did not make a required payment to the players' pension fund. Donald Fehr, the head of the Players Association, made clear that if these kinds of aggressive tactics continued, the players would have no choice but to go on strike. Negotiations through the summer yielded little progress; the specter of a work stoppage hung over everything in the game.

With George Costanza in their employ, even if only on TV, the Yankees moved along through June. Though they lost 8 of their first 9 games in the month, they never once fell out of first place, and balanced it out by winning 8 of their last 9 games to end the month. On June 17, after an 0-4 performance against the Brewers, O'Neill's average fell below .400 for the first time all season. The drop showed just how difficult hitting .400 over the course of a full season truly is: from June 3 to June 12, O'Neill went 16-40, including three separate three-hit games. But his average was lower when play ended the night of the twelfth than when it began on the third. Still, O'Neill's two-and-a-half-month run had been remarkable, and he retained the American League's highest batting average.

The Yankees headed into the All-Star break 50-35, a half-game ahead of second-place Baltimore. Three Yankees made the All-Star team, including O'Neill, despite his not being on the ballot. Joining him were Boggs and Key, the latter getting the start for the American League. The rest of the team took the three-day break to relax and look ahead to the start of the second half, which had the Yankees go through Seattle, Oakland, and Anaheim, places where they had faltered over the last few seasons. Moreover, the Yankees had a recent history of collapsing in the second half when they were near or at the top of the standings at the All-Star break. The 1988 Yankees led the East for all but three weeks of the first half of the season. They finished in fifth place after a 36-40 second half. The 1987 Yankees were in first place at the All-Star break, only to go 34-39 in the second half and finish fourth. Those second-half collapses had pressured Steinbrenner into making some notorious trades, the Phelps-for-Buhner deal among them. So far, The Boss had been largely quiet in 1994, letting his first-place team do the talking while he kept an eye out for a possible work stoppage. But, even with the strike looming, would a poor second half push The Boss to trade away Bernie or Hitchcock or Kamieniecki?

Turns out there was nothing to worry about. The Yankees began the second half with their most successful trip ever to the West Coast. The first night in Seattle, down two in the ninth, they combined four walks with four doubles to score seven runs for the win. The next night, a two-out, ninth-inning double by O'Neill scored two runs to tie the game and Tartabull won it in the eleventh with a single. Then they went out and hammered Randy Johnson for eight runs, with Mattingly becoming the first left-handed batter ever to achieve multiple three-hit games off The Big Unit. They swept the four-game series after scoring 46 total runs, 29 of which came in the seventh inning or later, and after three consecutive 13-hit games followed by a 14-hit game to end the series.

"I felt confident we'd have a good start in the second half," said Showalter, after his team completed its first four-game sweep ever in Seattle. "Of course, that's easy to say now."[23]

In Oakland, the Yankees took two of three, their only loss coming after Nokes struck out as the tying run to end the middle game of the series. In the first two games in Anaheim, they crushed the Angels by a combined score of 23–10. Tartabull, whose struggles earlier in the year resulted in Showalter's dropping him down in the lineup, was nearly unstoppable out west: a .432 average, six multi-hit games, a .512 on-base percentage, 3 home runs, and 12 RBIs in the first nine games.

The final two games of the trip, however, belonged to The Captain. In the second to last game, Mattingly recorded two singles, the last being his 2,000th career hit. Despite being three thousand miles away from Yankee Stadium, the home crowd in Anaheim stood and gave him a prolonged ovation, a measure of respect for a player many fans, even if he was a Yankee, had come to admire. Mattingly was just the sixth player ever to achieve 2,000 hits with the Yankees and the fourth to have all of those hits come solely with the Bronx Bombers. The Yankees won the game, but talk afterward was of Donnie's achievement. A shoo-in just five years earlier to reach the much vaunted mark of 3,000 hits, Mattingly instead reminded teammates and fans that his playing days were growing shorter and shorter. Perhaps shorter than some realized.

"I'd like to shoot for 3,000, but I don't think I'll play that long, to tell you the truth," said Mattingly, after the game. For months he'd been hinting that, once his contract was up after the '95 season, he might walk off into the sunset. "It seems I have to battle more and more just to be average. I don't complain about it because people don't want to hear it anyway. I'm playing major league baseball, and there's nothing wrong with that. I'm just enjoying the ride we're on."[24]

This notion of their captain playing on borrowed time only reinforced for many the dire need to remain in first place if a strike occurred. Mattingly's teammates adored him. They thought he was the ultimate professional and one of the few players who could handle the spotlight of New York, the meddling of Steinbrenner, and the media without creating controversy or ill will. Suzyn Waldman recalls seeing Pat Kelly watch Mattingly put on his socks so he could imitate him. Players referred to Mattingly as "Cap," even years after they had all retired.[25]

The fans, meanwhile, felt an adulation for Mattingly that perhaps no other New York sports athlete has ever enjoyed. His struggles, both with the bad teams of the '80s and '90s and with his back, were their struggles. He represented them on the field and their desire to get the Yankees back to the golden age of winning baseball.

The day after his 2,000th hit, on the trip's final day, Showalter gave Mattingly a rest against tough left-hander Mark Langston. The lineup couldn't figure out Langston; New York trailed 4–2 going into the top of the ninth. With one out, Stanley singled, Leyritz walked, and, when Langston was removed from the game, Showalter sent Mattingly to the plate. Despite all of his career success, Mattingly was a less-than-stellar pinch hitter and had never taken a pitcher deep in that role. But when reliever Joe Grahe tried to sneak a 3-2 fastball by him, Mattingly hit it over the right-field wall for a go-ahead, three-run home run. It was the kind of home run that had not been seen often from Mattingly in the '90s: a forceful, crushed ball that everyone immediately knew was gone. The Yankee bench exploded, as did the legions of fans that had taken over Angel Stadium.

Mattingly's 2,001st hit was the biggest of the Yankees' season and capped a historic 10-1 road trip, their best since 1953. They had started it up only a half-game in the East and ended it up five and a half. It was the largest division lead they had held at any point in fourteen years and, now, they had baseball's best record, too.

The mood in the clubhouse reflected a team looking to demolish opponents on its way to the postseason. There was giddiness and smiles at a level that had been almost nonexistent at the start of the '90s. There was even comic relief. Abbott, who had started the final game of the trip, said that, because of Mattingly's home run, he was thankful that now he would not be the only guy to lose on the road trip. But Abbott had actually gotten the only loss of the trip and, when told of that, he laughed at his mistake. "Well, I'm thankful for not losing a second time."[26]

Three days after the Yankees returned from their West Coast trip, players set a strike date of Friday, August 12. Negotiations had stalled, as neither side would budge. There was hope that setting an actual date might create a sense of urgency that would force both sides to the table to find a deal. But now the clock was ticking. In two weeks, players would walk off the job.

The Mets ended June with a victory, but the month had not gone well. Nine wins against eighteen defeats. They'd lost one starting pitcher to a drug suspension; another was livid at ownership over perceived lack of planning. They'd fallen to last in the division, the fourth-worst overall record in the league, and were nearly as many games out of the wild card as they were out of first place. Meanwhile, their crosstown rivals were mowing down opponents and only looking stronger by the day as they posted the American League's best record. The looming work stoppage made the situation even more dire. If the season had to be shortened because of a strike, it meant just that many fewer games the Mets would have to make a comeback. Things looked bleak. Then, unexpectedly, the team pulled it together.

Facing the California National League teams for 20 consecutive games to start the month, the Mets won 11 of those games, including a sweep of the Giants in San Francisco. They swept the Cardinals in St. Louis and took two of three in Pittsburgh. Everything was clicking for the Amazins. Bonilla was following up his solid '93 season with another strong performance. In July he racked up nine multi-hit games, including four in a row. By month's end he had 19 home runs and 61 RBIs for the year, on his way to his first 100 RBI season with the Mets.

One of the biggest and most pleasant surprises came from rookie first baseman Rico Brogna. Called up in late June after the Mets moved David Segui to the outfield, the lefty began his Mets career with three multi-hit games and a .727 slugging percentage in his first seven games. In July he collected a hit in 19 out of 23 games while amassing nine doubles and 13

RBIs in the process. In the midst of a 15-game hitting streak, on July 25 in St. Louis, he went 5-5. The next day, his eleventh inning, two-run home run gave the team a 10–9 victory. On August 1 Brogna was hitting .378 with a 1.106 OPS. Despite having only been up a little over a month, there was talk of him maybe being able to snag the National League Rookie of the Year trophy, assuming the season made it two more months.

In the pitching department, another rookie was making an impression. Bobby Jones began the month with a 7-7 record and a respectable 3.46 ERA. Then he went out and won four of his six starts in July, never going fewer than six innings in any appearance and pitching to a 2.87 ERA. The pitcher making the biggest impression, however, was the one who had spent two-and-a-half injury-filled years of misery in Queens. Now, healthy and looking to put his money where his mouth was, Bret Saberhagen became unbeatable. He started July with a dominating two-hit performance over the Giants and followed up by allowing a single earned run to the Dodgers in a 5–1 win. Against the Padres at Shea, he then threw 10 scoreless innings in a game the team lost in 14 innings. After beating the Dodgers again, he threw a complete-game seven-hitter against the Cardinals and ended the month with nine innings of two-run ball against the Pirates in a game the Mets again lost in extra innings. Saberhagen made six starts in July, won four of them, had two no-decisions in games in which he gave up a total of two runs, achieved a 1.43 ERA, pitched 50⅓ innings, struck out 41, and walked only 3 batters. In fact, Saberhagen had as many wins on the entire year (12), as he did walks the entire season. It was a masterful performance.

Despite the team's solid 16-10 record, they still lost ground in July. The Expos jumped ahead of the Braves and were competing with the Yankees for the game's best record, a scenario that would have seemed unthinkable just four years earlier. The Mets, however, had managed to jump from last to third place. The team began August 5-5, with Jones and Saberhagen continuing to provide solid performances. But the looming August 12 strike date cast a pall over everything. And it led to yet another instance of Bonilla having an on-camera confrontation with a reporter.

The Mets were in Philadelphia for what ended up being their last series of the year. During the postgame one night, WABC-NY reporter Art McFarland, who happened to be a Mets fan, was asking players their thoughts on the pending work stoppage. He got comments from player rep John Franco and then went to the locker of another player rep, Bonilla. Feeling that there was not much left to say about it, Bonilla offered no comment. McFarland, who was not a sports reporter, tried to keep the conversation going but was getting nowhere. Finally, he noted that Bonilla stood to lose the most money of any player in baseball should a strike happen. That set Bonilla off.

"Why are you being an asshole?" Bonilla asked McFarland, as multiple cameras rolled, yet again capturing Bonilla in the act of challenging a member of the media.

"Why do you have to use such language?" McFarland responded.

"Get the fuck out of my locker," said Bonilla, twice, before briefly walking away only to stop when McFarland asked if that was his normal vocabulary. Bonilla turned and came nearly nose to nose with him. Bonilla asked if they had a problem, and McFarland said they would if Bonilla touched him. Other players took notice. Hundley tried to get between the two. McReynolds came over and stood in front of one of the cameras in a valiant effort to protect his teammate, but it was too late. Multiple cameras had recorded the incident.

Had the season kept going, it might have created the kind of media war seen in 1992. But with the strike starting on August 12, it lived on only as just another time Bonilla faced off with the press in New York.

As if they did not want to face the potential end of the season, on August 11 in Philadelphia, the Mets played a fifteen-inning affair that did not end until 11:28 at night. Their lone run came on a home run from Jim Lindeman, a journeyman utility player. It was his last hit in the major leagues. Thirty-two minutes before midnight, Ricky Jordan singled home Billy Hatcher for a 2–1 Phillies win. The Mets, 55-58 on the season, packed up, headed back to New York, gathered their things, and then departed, as the players' strike began.

The Yankees kept rolling into August, winning eight games in a row, including another sweep of the Indians. On the morning of August 6 they held a ten-game lead in the division. The playoffs seemed inevitable. Even a minor slide that shrank the lead down couldn't ruin the team's mood. The only thing that could was the work stoppage.

On August 11, the Yankees played a day game against the Blue Jays. In what felt like a subliminal way for both teams to say they did not want the strike to start, it lasted thirteen innings. Down a run in the bottom of the thirteenth, Mattingly led off and drew a walk. Showalter replaced him with a pinch runner, earning Mattingly a standing ovation as he came off the field. Many were thinking it. Some even said it. But depending on how long the strike lasted, it was possible this was the last time anyone would see Don Mattingly in a major league uniform as a player. Three batters later, Nokes, one of the few remaining players from the dog days of 1990, flied out to end the game. The Yankees went back to the clubhouse, made some remarks to the press, packed their bags, and headed home as the strike began.

At 12:45 a.m. on Friday, August 12, 1994, after the last out of the Mariners-Athletics game, Major League players officially went on strike, the eighth work stoppage in a little over two decades. Strikes had happened before, the last one occurring in 1985. That one lasted all of two days, as both sides reached an agreement quickly. The strike amounted to a mere hiccup in the schedule, with missed games made up at some point during the season. But there was no indication that would happen this time. Players were adamantly against a cap. Owners were insistent the game could not survive without it. The two sides did not even bother to meet on the day the strike went into effect. Neither side would agree to a mediator. When President Clinton tried to get both sides to come together for a resolution, it went nowhere. There was simply no trust between the two and no chance a deal could be reached. Owners would not even sit at the bargaining table, delegating that task to MLB representatives and lawyers. That position angered the players. Steinbrenner, who had publicly indicated he did not love the idea of a salary cap, felt they had a point. The Boss would not break with the owners, but his public comments indicated that not all owners were on board with what was going on.

Days went by. Then weeks. No progress occurred. August turned into September. Rather than advance, things were going backward. The players became convinced that the owners' true goal was to declare an impasse in negotiations and simply force a salary cap system into the game. "I can't see the players ever playing under a salary cap they went on strike to resist," said Fehr. "I can't see the players accepting any system that restricts free agency or serves as a disincentive for the clubs to sign players."[27]

On September 14, acting Commissioner Selig canceled the rest of the season. While expected, the news was no less shocking. For the first time in ninety years, there would be no World Series.

"I know the short-term pain is intense, but I'll say what I've said all along, if this can serve as the impetus to constructing the long-range solution to the economic problems we have, then maybe there will be some good to come from that," said Selig. The players were not buying Selig's lipstick-on-a-pig approach. "[They'll] resist the salary cap until doomsday," said Players Association general counsel Gene Orza.[28]

The players lost $230 million in salary for the year, while the twenty-eight teams lost between $500 and $600 million. But more than the dollars, the cancellation closed the book on one of the most exciting seasons in baseball history. It meant no chance for Tony Gwynn, batting .394, to hit .400. It meant Ken Griffey Jr. and Matt Williams, both on pace to hit near or over 61 home runs, would not get a chance to break the single-season record. No triple-crown attempt by Frank Thomas, who led the American League in RBIs and was just behind Griffey for the home run lead and O'Neill for the batting crown. The Indians would not get back to the postseason for the first time since 1954. The Rangers, leading the American League West despite a record below .500, would not reach the playoffs for the first time ever. The Expos, with baseball's best record, would not bring Montreal back to the postseason for the first time since 1981. There would be no World Series north of the border and certainly no match-up with the Yankees, owner of the American League's best record.

Years later, countless former Yankees recalled and pondered the what-ifs of that season. "It was maybe the best team I ever played on," said Abbott. Much of the wonder centered around Mattingly; more than any other player on the team or perhaps even in baseball, the future seemed startlingly unclear for him. If the strike lasted long enough, would his career be over? If it lasted until well into the '95 season, would he seek another contract if the Yankees failed to win the World Series or even make the playoffs? Would the strike, however unfortunate, give his ailing back time to heal and perhaps afford an opportunity to be the player of old?

"I'm so sad for Don Mattingly," said Steinbrenner, after news of the cancellation. "I feel so badly for that kid."[29]

The Mets had not lost as much as the Yankees appeared to, at least on paper. But they had recovered remarkably well for a team that, just a year earlier, was among the worst of the expansion era. They had hovered around .500 for most of the season in a tough division and, while not completely free of incidents, had managed to keep the off-the-field drama to a minimum. Still, the cancellation of the 1994 season was heartbreaking. The team's record and player statistics, as they stood on the morning of August 12, were permanently frozen in time.

The Mets ended at 55-58, winning nearly as many games in a season that ended in early August as they did in all of 1993. Bonilla hit .290 with a team-leading 20 home runs. Kent was on pace to eclipse his home-run and RBI totals from the year before, showing signs of breaking out into the All-Star-caliber player the team felt he was. Brogna's .626 slugging gave hope for the future. Saberhagen went 14-4, winning more games than batters walked, and leading the league in fewest walks per nine innings and strikeouts-to-walk ratio. He finished third in the Cy Young voting. Bobby Jones's sophomore season of 12-7 meant the Mets had a stable one-two at the top of the rotation while they waited for more help from the minor leagues. Franco turned in one of his best seasons ever as a Met, leading the league in saves and placing seventh in Cy Young voting.

The Yankees ended at 70-43, six and a half games ahead in first. They finished second in runs scored and led the majors with a .374 on-base percentage. Six of their starters—Stanley, Mattingly, Boggs, Polonia, Williams, and O'Neill, finished with an OBP of .383 or better; five of those players, all but Williams, hit .300 or better. O'Neill had the greatest season of his career, finishing with a league-leading .359 average and a 1.064 OPS. Stanley batted .300 with 17 home runs. Mattingly hit over .300 for the first time since 1989 and won the last of his nine Gold Gloves at first base. Boggs finished at .342 with the second-highest single-season home run total of his career. Leyritz hit a career high in home runs. Kelly set a career high in batting average. Key, at 17-4, was on pace for his first 20-win season and finished second in the Cy Young voting. The starting rotation managed to stay healthy, with the same five guys making 94 percent of the team's starts. Howe rebounded from a rocky '93 season to lead the team with 15 saves and a 0.875 WHIP.

In the minor leagues, Stump Merrill had returned to manage AAA Columbus and was fostering the next generation of Yankees. Names like Pettitte, Rivera, Posada, and Jeter were making the rounds of both minor and major league baseball. Thanks to the work of scouts and organizational minds like Brian Sabean, Bill Livesay, Mark Newman, Kevin Elfering, and Mitch Lukevics, these players had been harvested and signed by the Yankees. Thanks to Gene Michael, all of them remained Yankees; none were used as Steinbrenner's bargaining chips like so many '80s prospects before them. They were all being groomed under "the Yankee Way," a literal system for how they were to conduct themselves and go about their business while representing the New York Yankees.

Buck Showalter, two years after inheriting a team filled with shortcomings and misery, took home American League Manager of the Year honors. He was the first Yankees skipper to win the award since its creation in 1983. But the awards, batting titles, and other accolades all felt hollow. "I know we were good enough to win the whole thing," said Michael, upset that his years of work to rebuild the team came to nothing in 1994. "We were in position. Selfishly, I wish we could have played. It just wasn't in the cards."[30]

At the end of the day, one could only ponder how things would have played out had the season continued until the last game of the World Series. And to ask just when there would be baseball again.

[9]

The Once Unfathomable Notion

The off-season is always grueling for diehard baseball fans. If their team fails to achieve success there are six long months of wondering what happened and when will it improve. If their team enjoys success there are six long months of desperately wanting them back on the field to achieve more winning. Baseball offers the promise that eventually the cold, dreary months of winter will end; that there will be a release from cabin fever for those who want a little bit of sunshine on their face and to leave their heavy coat at home. It's a cycle that repeats itself every fall and winter. But the 1994–95 off season offered no such promise, as fans, players, and owners were left to ponder the unfinished business of the '94 season and what might happen to their beloved game. With every passing day, fans became more embittered toward players and owners for failing to resolve their differences.

The fall months of 1994 produced no tangible results in negotiations. In December the owners did what the players felt they had intended to do all along: they declared an impasse in negotiations. Using that as an excuse, the owners unilaterally implemented a salary cap. When it became clear they would face an unfair practices complaint with the National Labor Relations Board, the owners relented, slightly. They agreed to reinstate the previous CBA but eliminated arbitration and designated their own Player Relations Committee as the only negotiating agent for free agent contracts. The players were outraged; in time, the National Labor Relations Board would get involved.

Meanwhile, even with the strike still going, teams were altering their rosters. Recognizing they would not be bringing Jim Abbott back, on December 14, the Yankees traded for Jack McDowell from the White Sox. McDowell was then informed by the Major League Baseball Players Association that the trade was null and void due to the strike. He sat around for months not knowing for whom, exactly, he was playing.

Also opting not to bring Mike Gallego back and with Randy Velarde about to become a free agent, the Yankees signed yet another former Met, Tony Fernandez. Coming off a successful season with the Reds after having helped the Blue Jays win the championship in '93, Fernandez sought to redeem his sluggish performance in Queens from the first half of that season. The team with the best record in the AL had just added one of the game's best pitchers and shortstops to its roster.

The Mets, meanwhile, sent Jeromy Burnitz to the Indians in exchange for four players, including young starting pitchers Paul Byrd and Dave Mlicki. Burnitz, after showing promise in his rookie season, had regressed in '94; the team wasn't confident that he could be counted on in the future. He went on to hit over 300 home runs in his career.

After these trades and signings, the market largely shut down, in part because, after the owners tried to implement a salary cap, Donald Fehr, the Players Association executive director, declared over eight hundred players to be free agents. The two sides refused to give in, each saying that the other's statements and edicts were null and void. President Clinton tried to force both sides back to the table, but to no avail. Tensions grew worse when, in January 1995, the owners agreed to use replacement players to start the season if necessary. "We are committed to playing the 1995 season and will do so with the best players willing to play," said Selig, in announcing the decision.[1]

Players were incensed, but they could not directly do anything to stop it. The situation was farcical, but when it came time to start spring training, the owners showed they were serious.

Replacement players flooded into camp, bringing with them the skills and physiques of a slow-pitch softball beer league. Marcus Lawton, the Mets' new center fielder, worked on a riverboat casino. Matt Stark, the

Yankees' newest version of Don Mattingly, collapsed a metal chair he tried to sit on due to his 6-foot-4, 275-pound frame.

Coaches and managers could hardly stomach what they were seeing. Detroit's Sparky Anderson refused to manage the replacement team and was placed on leave. Orioles owner Peter Angelos, afraid Cal Ripken's attempt to break Lou Gehrig's streak of all-time consecutive games played would go up in smoke, refused to field a team of replacement players and ignored Selig's threat of repercussions. The Orioles' spring training was canceled. The Blue Jays were told they would not be allowed to play home games with replacement players, as it would violate Canadian labor laws.

The whole situation was absurd, but the owners would not relent. Replacement players went through an entire spring training and were just a day away from starting the season when a breakthrough occurred. The National Labor Relations Board had filed a suit in late March, charging the owners with unfair labor practices for implementing the CBA with certain conditions. Judge Sonia Sotomayor, of the United States District Court for the Southern District of New York, ruled on the complaint and came down hard on the owners. They had no legal right to implement a new CBA. Days earlier the players had voted to end the strike if the courts ruled on their side. Sotomayor's injunction against the owners opened the door. With just hours to go before the season started, the strike ended after 232 days. A shortened, 144-game season, played under the old rules of the previous CBA, would start in late April, after an abbreviated spring training.

The Yankees got back to business. Days after the strike ended, they acquired premier closer John Wetteland from the Expos. Steve Howe had been exceptional in that role in 1994, but the Yankees couldn't turn down a chance from Montreal, a team which, having suffered substantially from the work stoppage after posting the best record in baseball, was now having a fire sale of its best players. Days later the Yankees brought back Velarde and then signed Dion James, the outfielder who had hit .332 for the team in 1993 but who had spent the next season playing in Japan.

The American League's best team in 1994, New York was going into Opening Day with an even better starting rotation, a better bullpen, and an offense that featured former, current, or future All-Stars at every position except left field and second base. The anticipation for the season was sky high, as just about every analyst and expert predicted the Yankees would not only make the postseason, but dominate the league on their way there. The prep work was already underway to write the perfect swan song for Don Mattingly. In the last year of his contract, and more certain now not to return once it was done, the captain was focused on getting to the postseason. In his time with New York, no team had presented him a better chance. If Mattingly was ever to get that World Series ring, 1995 was the year it was going to happen.

Opening Day did little to dispel the feeling of inevitability. Tartabull homered for the third consecutive Opening Day. Key pitched well into the sixth. Newcomer Fernandez had two hits and Wetteland pitched a perfect ninth for the save. Across the ballpark there was a feeling of relief mixed with sheer joy at the return of the game. But lingering anger over the strike was visible. The crowd of 50,425 was the smallest for the first home game of the year since 1990.

Whether fans forgave the players or not, the Yankees chugged on, leaving New York after Opening Day for Kansas City. McDowell made his team debut with a strong seven innings and a win. The Yankees took two of three, with the series being of note because of the appearance of a rookie left-handed pitcher in the middle game.

It was not hard to figure out from his accent that Andy Pettitte was from the South. Louisiana and then Texas, to be exact. The lefty had always been big but, as a teenager, he had had more of a football player's build than a baseball player's. It earned him a spot as the center at Deer Park High School. He also sported a good fastball, good enough to be drafted by the Yankees in June 1990. But he bypassed their offer to sign and instead went to San Jacinto Junior College, in part because the college's baseball coach, Wayne Graham, had told Pettitte he reminded him of a left-handed Roger Clemens. That just happened to be Pettitte's favorite baseball player. Under Graham's tutelage, Pettitte went on a strict exercise and diet regimen, losing fat while gaining muscle. The stronger he got, the higher his velocity got: two miles per hour faster, then four, then as much as seven or eight, until he was hitting 93 miles per hour. Graham also taught Andy a pick-off move, which morphed into one of the most deceptive and successful moves ever.

The Yankees kept tabs on Pettitte in college, knowing that, because he had gone to a junior college instead of a four-year college, they had one full year to sign him post-draft. If they did not, he would go back into the draft pool; with the team already eyeing several other candidates with their early-round picks, he would probably be scooped up by someone else. In what was yet another twist of fate that went the Yankees' way in the 1990s, that did not happen.

On the last day he was eligible to sign with New York, by coincidence Pettitte ended up running into the team scout that was trying to sign him. Andy had been resistant, believing the Yankees were not offering him enough. After several hours of haggling, in which the Yankees made a big show of increasing their offer, Pettitte finally just blurted out a price: $80,000. The Yankees agreed. Had they not done so, the next day Pettitte would no longer have been property of the Yankees and more than likely would have ended up on another big league team. Just like Derek Jeter could have. And Mariano Rivera.

"I should have asked for more money," said Pettitte, who would long resent taking an offer that was far below what he likely could have gotten had he reentered the draft.[2] Regardless, he was now a Yankee. Team scouts and brass loved the results immediately. Not only did Pettitte have a mid-nineties fastball, but it had sharp movement, especially on right-handed hitters. He added a curve to match. In his first six starts at rookie ball, Andy yielded only 16 total hits. The next year, at A ball, he went 10-4; by 1994 it was clear he would be a Yankee in the immediate future. Due to the shortened spring training in 1995, teams were allowed to carry twenty-eight players on their roster to start the year instead of the usual twenty-five. That gave Pettitte his opening. He made the club as a member of the bullpen. Despite making the team, he was angry at being passed over in the starting rotation in favor of Sterling Hitchcock.

In the third game of the season, he made his major league debut in the bottom of the seventh inning. It took seven pitches to record his first two outs. He did not get another, giving up three hits and two runs. It was not ideal, but the first of what would ultimately be known as the Core Four of Yankee players had now made his mark in the majors.

After Kansas City, New York came right back home for four against Boston. It was only the second week of the season, but it was still a big series: a chance for the Yankees to send an early message to their rivals that the division was theirs and theirs alone. They won three of four, with all three wins coming in dramatic fashion. In the final game of the series, down a run in the eighth, O'Neill homered, then Mattingly sent one just over the wall in right-center field for his first of the season. The Yankees held on to win. Mattingly, a notoriously slow starter, was on fire. Through eight games he was hitting .324 with 1 home run and 6 RBIs. Mattingly was hitting the ball hard, driving it in a way that had largely been absent the last few seasons. It looked as though the drive to get through the postseason would be enough to bring The Captain back to his earlier form.

The Yankees were 6-2 after the Red Sox left, a game up in first. The next night they beat Milwaukee to go two games up. New York was doing what they were supposed to do that year: running away with the division. But after that May 5 game, the Yankees would never have a lead that large again all season; just a week later, they would sit in first place for the last time in 1995.

The trouble started the night of the win against Milwaukee. Scott Kamieniecki began warming up during the top of the second inning when he felt a pain in his right elbow. He did not take the mound again until mid-July.

After beating the Brewers in the first game, the Yankees lost three in a row; they won three in a row to go a half-game up in the standings, then dropped four in a row. Amid that losing streak, the rotation took another blow. Key had gotten pummeled in two consecutive outings, the last a seven-run performance against the Indians. Something was wrong with the Yankees' ace. His left shoulder, which had been operated on after the end of the previous season, was in pain and he couldn't execute his pitches like normal. Fearing the worst but hoping for the best, the Yankees shut him down after his May 16 start. Pettitte, sent down after a few rough outings out of the bullpen so he could get more work in at Columbus, was called back up to take Key's spot in the rotation.

In late June Key attempted to throw during a workout session in the outfield at Yankee Stadium. He could not make it past ten pitches. Key's rotator cuff was torn, his season over.

"I can't do what I'm supposed to do," a dejected Key told a reporter, after the news was official. "I can't do what I'm paid to do. I want to be out there and I'm not. It's very frustrating to be in this situation."[3]

Sandwiched in between the Kamieniecki and Key injuries was more bad news. Mattingly not only had a left hamstring pull but also an infection in his right eye. He needed to wear sunglasses inside because light caused him irritation; the infection in his lead batting eye meant he could not adequately pick up the spin of the ball when a pitcher released it, preventing him from differentiating pitches. Though Showalter gave him a week off in the middle of the month to recover, the result of the infection was plain to see. Mattingly finished the month just 7 for his last 29 at bats. After his big home run against the Red Sox, he drove in only one more run the entire month. His struggles continued into June with no end in sight, slowly wilting away his hot start.

The Mets' expectations were not nearly as high as the Yankees'. They had been a pleasant surprise in 1994, largely because of how poorly the team had performed in 1993. While no one expected them to compete with the Braves, if they played well enough, they could vie for the wild card. A full season from phenom Rico Brogna and a still developing Todd Hundley could provide the pop the lineup needed. The team acquired former Yankees first-round pick Carl Everett from the Marlins that off-season; while he had not been overly impressive in his limited time in the Bigs, expectations were high for the outfielder's future. They'd also acquired pitcher Pete Harnisch to bolster the rotation and, with a bevy of free agents available after the work stoppage, signed outfielder Brett Butler. A small ball extraordinaire, Butler was a slap hitter with a great eye and among the active leaders in career stolen bases. He was, in many ways, Vince Coleman redux, but without any history of injuries and a track record of being a leader in the clubhouse. Butler filled the lead-off spot.

Franco, Bonilla, and Saberhagen, the core veterans among the club, returned, hoping to get the Mets back to respectability and the playoffs. While the Yankees began the year in the comfort of their home park, the Mets became a part of history for their Opening Day. In weather that hovered around the freezing point most of the evening, they faced the Colorado Rockies in the first official game ever at Coors Field.

"This year has a really special feeling to it because we came so close to not having it," said Mets radio announcer Bob Murphy. "And after going through the replacement-player thing for four weeks and suddenly have it come back really gives it a special feeling."[4]

The game would, in many ways, encapsulate the state of the team over the past several years. Down four in the sixth, the Mets tied the game on a Hundley grand slam. Falling behind, they tied it again in the seventh before taking the lead in the ninth. But Franco gave the lead up. The Mets took the lead again in the top of the thirteenth. Again, the bullpen blew it. Meanwhile, Bonilla got ejected in the eleventh for arguing a strike call, the first of many complaints lodged against the replacement umpires filling in for the regular umpires, who had also gone on strike. Green followed suit; he and Bonilla watched the rest of the game from the clubhouse. They gazed at the TV as the Mets took the lead again in the top of the fourteenth, only to watch Dante Bichette hit a three-run, game-winning home run in the bottom of the inning. Three separate blown leads by the bullpen and discontent from Bonilla and Green. It was as if the last two seasons had never ended.

The next day was a continuation of Opening Day's events. Staked to a 7–2 lead in the sixth, reliever Josías Manzanillo gave it all back. In the ninth, Kevin Lomon, in his major league debut, gave up a two-out single to hand Colorado the win. The loss was the only decision of Lomon's career. In two games, the offense scored 16 runs but the starting pitching allowed 8 and the bullpen 11.

Without a day's rest, the Mets headed back to New York for their home opener, a nighttime affair against the Cardinals. Like the opening series in Colorado, the game was a mix of positive and negative. Saberhagen, the Cy Young Award runner-up, gave up seven runs before exiting. Down

7–2, the offense staged a comeback, with home runs from Bonilla, Brogna, and Everett, leading to the team's first win of the year. The win, however, was marred by the discontentment of fans that had permeated other stadiums during opening week. Only 26,604 showed up at Shea, the smallest home-opener crowd since 1981. They made their post-strike unhappiness known. In five separate incidents, a dozen fans in total ran onto the field, each exhibiting their own unique form of protest.

In the fourth, three fans ran onto the field and began tossing dollar bills across the infield, scattering $150 total. Once the dollar bills ran out, the three, wearing T-shirts with the word "Greed" on them, stood at second base and raised their right fists in the air. They were taken off the field and charged with criminal trespassing, to them a small price to pay for making a point.

"We were trying to think of a good fan protest, and I remembered Abbie Hoffman throwing money on the floor of the New York Stock Exchange," said Vincent DeCrescenzo, a waiter who was one of the three protesters.[5]

While attendance picked up for the next two games, the fan backlash had to be particularly disconcerting for the Mets. A franchise that had not had a winning season in five years, that had suffered through numerous off-the-field distractions, and that had lost their host city to a crosstown rival now had to deal with fan anger like the game had never seen before. While the Mets were not at nearly the risk of other franchises like Montreal, there was certainly concern about attendance in the future if the team could not get past subpar performances.

Subpar performances, however, were in store for the next few months of Mets baseball. A 3–0 win at Cincinnati on May 5 brought them to 4-5 and within three games of first place. It was the closest to .500 or first place they would be the rest of the season. As the Yankees picked up right where they had left off before the strike, the Mets regressed. They took two of three from the Braves at Shea, with the one loss coming courtesy of Larry "Chipper" Jones's first major league home run, then lost three of four to the Expos. The seven-game home stand, played against the team's two biggest division rivals, drew an average crowd of only 14,800 a game. Yes, it was early in the season, with schools still in session, but attendance figures were matching those of the late 1970s and early '80s. Only the most diehard of fans were returning to see the Mets play.

As the Yankees' injuries mounted, the team headed west for a nine-game road trip. In the first game in Anaheim, the twenty-five-year-old kid from Panama who squeaked through the expansion draft made his major league debut for the Yankees. Mariano Rivera was given a chance to prove himself as a starting pitcher, to fill the gaps left by Kamieniecki and Key's injuries. But the Angels knocked Rivera around for 5 runs on 8 hits and 3 walks in his debut. New York lost 10–0. The next night McDowell took a no-hitter and a 1–0 lead into the eighth inning. He lost the no-hitter and the game after giving up three singles and a double. In the series' final game, Pérez could not get out of the second inning before giving up nine runs. The Angels swept the series. In Oakland the team lost two of three, the only win coming when Rivera held the A's to one run in 5⅓ innings, picking up the first of his eventual 82 career wins.

Moving on to Seattle, the team had a decision to make. Fernandez had suffered a rib-cage injury, joining a growing list of Yankees on the disabled list. It created an opportunity for former Met Kevin Elster, who had signed with the team the previous year and played in a handful of games in the strike-shortened season. Impressed years earlier by his steady defense, Michael had kept Elster on the roster; now Showalter put him in the lineup as the team's new shortstop when Fernandez went down. But while providing steady defense, Elster managed just two hits in seventeen at bats. Rivera's first major league win was also Elster's last game as a Yankee.

Needing a spark, the team called Derek Jeter up from Columbus. It had been a long, strange trip through three years of minor league baseball for Jeter. His gangly physique, matched with his aw-shucks manner, made teammates look askance. *This was the guy everyone was talking about?* Moreover, his fielding had caused concerns that the kid was not meant to be a shortstop. Better, some thought, to transition him to center field. It was hard to argue that point. In his first year of professional ball, Jeter made a staggering 21 errors in just 57 games. The following year at A ball, it was 57 errors in 126 games. These were goofy, *Bad News Bears*–type numbers for any player, let alone one as highly touted as Jeter. Coach Brian Butterfield took Derek under his wing and for hours on end ran drill after drill with him, focusing especially on turning double plays.

In 1994 it paid off. In the course of a single season, Jeter went from A to AA to AAA ball, a rare feat. He reduced his number of errors to 25 in 138 games and hit .344. He also added a .410 on-base percentage to the mix. Jeter won Minor League Player of the Year from *Baseball America*, *Baseball Weekly*, and the *Sporting News*. "Bring him up and see what happens," Merrill told the front office, when they wanted to know if Jeter was ready for the next step, adding that he was the best shortstop he had ever had.[6]

The strike prevented that from happening in 1994. But now, the soon-to-be twenty-one-year-old, who thought he had been traded to the Florida Marlins when he got the notice earlier that morning that something was up, was inserted into the ninth spot in the lineup as the Yankees began a three-game series at the Kingdome. Jeter went 0-5; the team blew a late three-run lead, their fifth blown save in twelve chances; and they lost in extra innings. They lost again the next night when, with two outs, the bullpen allowed five runs in the eighth inning, in a game noteworthy only because it included the first and second of Jeter's 3,465 career hits. Not only were they swept the next night, but a Randy Johnson fastball ricocheted off Leyritz's hand and hit him in the face, initiating a torrent of ill will between the two teams that would last several more seasons. Leyritz even claims he waited for Johnson outside the Yankees clubhouse after the game and had to be told to leave by Kingdome staff.

Nine games, eight losses, and a team full of injured players. The Yankees returned home 13-17; that's when controversy started to kick in. For the last two years the team had been almost completely free of the kinds of off-the-field distractions that had emanated from the clubhouse throughout the '80s and early '90s. Showalter had kept the team in check, managing the egos of guys like Tartabull and Leyritz, while Mattingly policed by his mere example. That, coupled with the unexpected winning in 1993 and the dominance of '94 had also kept The Boss largely at bay. But currently the team was spiraling, players were dramatically underperforming, and Steinbrenner was losing patience. When he finally did something, it reeked of the old George.

The Yankees had relaxed their facial hair policy in the spring to accommodate the newly acquired McDowell. Goatees were now allowed, along with mustaches. Suddenly, evil versions of the players sporting facial hair on their chins began popping up. Mattingly. Wetteland. Kelly. But as the horrific road trip came to an end, The Boss had had enough. Players would have to shave their goatees at the start of the next home stand, though they could keep their mustaches.

"It's like a slap on the wrist," said Mattingly, in comments that echoed those made by Goose Gossage and others in the early 1980s, when poor play resulted in petty acts from Steinbrenner. "They shouldn't have changed it in the first place if they were going to take it away."[7]

It made news across the country, if for no other reason than it was the first sign in some time of the old Steinbrenner. The new policy failed to do anything to motivate the team. The same day it was rescinded, the Yankees began a ten-game home stand against the same three teams that had just given them a beat-down on the West Coast. Down 3–2 with two outs in the ninth inning of the first game, Polonia tried to steal second and was thrown out to end it. He blamed the grounds crew for the caught steal, saying the area around first base was too wet for him to get a good running start. The Angels took two of three. The A's took two of three, giving Rivera a seven-run shellacking in his third major league start. The Mariners also took two of three. In ten home games, the Yankees had gone 3-7. Despite two of the three series taking place during the weekend, the entire home stand averaged only 19,000 a game. Fans were sticking by their pledge not to return to the game because of the strike.

Bruised and battered, the team went to Detroit in desperate need of something, anything, to get them going. Instead, in the first game, they were flummoxed by David Wells, down 5–0 before they got their first hit of the game. An error by Bernie Williams, in which he lost a ball in the lights, was the icing on the cake in a terrible, ugly loss. The Yankees were 16-25, nine and a half games out of first place and last in the division. Tartabull, their cleanup hitter, was batting .221 with just three home runs. He blamed his performance on injuries that many in the organization believed did not exist or were not nearly as serious as Tartabull claimed they were. His unhappiness became overwhelming, and he made clear he wanted out of New York. Bernie Williams appeared to be regressing, hitting only .227; despite his remarkable speed, he seemed incapable of stealing bases. Steinbrenner had tried to trade Bernie before, but never pulled the trigger. Now, he demanded Michael call every team until he found a willing partner to take the center fielder off the Yankees' hands. Ultimately, Michael claimed that he called every team, shot the breeze with the general manager, then reported back to Steinbrenner that no one had expressed interest in Williams, which was technically true.

Fernandez was hitting .182. Mattingly had not homered in a month. Kelly was on the disabled list. Outside of O'Neill and Stanley, hardly anyone in the lineup had presented any kind of offensive threat in the last three weeks. Things were so bad that rumors began swirling that Steinbrenner was thinking of signing Darryl Strawberry to add some flavor. It seemed preposterous. Strawberry was under house arrest. *He couldn't even legally play baseball right now!*

The starting rotation was patched together with duct tape, as three rookies—Rivera, Pettitte, and Brian Boehringer—were now fixtures. Rivera was pitching so poorly that he was about to earn a demotion to the minors and nearly be traded away. The bullpen was a disaster. Scott Bankhead, 5.48 ERA. Bob MacDonald, 6.08 ERA. Steve Howe, 6.57 ERA. Josías Manzanillo, 6.10 ERA. Bob Wickman, 5.04 ERA.

Showalter, the reigning American League Manager of the Year, nearly didn't make it to that year's All-Star game, where he was slated to lead the team. Steinbrenner was reestablishing himself as a force in baseball: reminding people that it was The Boss, and no one else, who was really the face of the Yankees. And The Boss made clear he would accept no excuses for what was going on with the team he was spending nearly $50 million on.

"It's more than just the injuries," Steinbrenner told reporters, while his team sat in last. "The Red Sox have had a lot of injuries, too."[8] No doubt it deeply annoyed the owner that Boston had emerged as the top team in the division and that they had done so largely without their best pitcher, Clemens, and power hitter, José Canseco, due to injuries.

It was time to make a statement, more than just having his players shave or demanding trades. Something that would make clear to everyone—

players, Showalter, Michael, the fans, the rest of baseball—that what was happening to the Yankees was not acceptable to their owner. The day after their embarrassing 6–1 loss to the Tigers, Steinbrenner decided to make that statement. And all he did was sit down to watch a baseball game.

Right around the time the Yankees began their nosedive on the West Coast, the Mets matched it with their own nosedive against West Coast teams at Shea. It started with a three-game sweep by the Dodgers that, at one point, saw the Mets go twenty-four consecutive innings without scoring a run. Against the Giants, they lost two of three with the first loss occurring after they blew a three-run lead. Reliever Doug Henry, acquired in the off-season from Milwaukee and on his way to actually having a solid season out of the pen, took the loss, his third in just the season's first twenty-eight games. A four-game split with the Padres provided some solace, but, overall, the home stand was a flop. They'd dropped three games in the standings and fell to seven games under .500.

As the hobbling Yankees headed back to New York, the stumbling Mets set out for ten games on the coast. They lost two of three to the Dodgers, split a series with the Giants, and were swept by the Padres. The final loss came after the team blew a two-run, two-out lead in the eighth, with Henry then allowing a walk-off home run in the ninth. At 16-27, the Mets were the second-worst team in baseball, eight and a half games out of the wild card spot that had seemed so possible on Opening Day. The starting pitchers had been solid, but they had gotten little support. Saberhagen had given up two runs or less in half of his eight starts, yet he had not won any of those games. Pete Harnisch had given up two runs or less in five of his nine starts and had a single win to show for it. Bobby Jones and Dave Mlicki were a combined 8-4. The one sour note had been Jason Jacome. The lefty, filling in for Gooden after his suspension, had thrilled in eight rookie starts the year before and came into spring training with a little swagger in his step. But in five starts, his ERA was 10.29 and he had allowed 49 base runners in 22 innings. Jacome was demoted back to Triple A and traded just after the All-Star break.

While players like Bonilla and Brogna were putting in All-Star perfor-mances, the lineup as a whole was largely punchless. Edgardo Alfonzo, a rookie who had so impressed in spring training that he earned the starting third base job and pushed Bonilla back to the outfield, was hitting just .232; over 25 games from mid-May to mid-June, he had just 2 extra-base hits. Hundley went 2-23 on the West Coast trip, driving in just two runs. After 39 games, Kent was hitting only .230 with just 9 extra-base hits. Butler was stable at lead-off but had noticeable difficulty tracking down fly balls, leading people to wonder if he was having vision or even vertigo issues.

Meanwhile, David Segui, one of the few players providing steady offensive output, now had no place to play. The outfield was full. Brogna, who had replaced the injured Segui a month before the strike, was following up his rookie performance with a bang, being among the team leaders in almost every offense category. That meant Segui had no spot at first base, either. The Mets traded him to Montreal during the West Coast trip for pitcher Reid Cornelius. Though they said it was for no reason other than that Segui simply did not have a spot to play, the trade also cleared $600,000 off the payroll, foreshadowing events to come. Cornelius pitched ten games for the Mets that year, was traded the following spring, and was out of baseball by 2001.

Returning home, the Mets were desperate. The season was slipping away and they had to decide whether to let it happen or make some last-ditch effort to save it. On June 17 they sent out an sos, launching what became the most anticipated period in team history since Dwight Gooden's rookie season. Taking the mound at Shea that afternoon was twenty one-year-old Bill Pulsipher. A lefty with remarkable stuff, Pulsipher was a standout high school baseball and basketball player in Fairfax, Virginia. During his senior year, the tall, strong left-handed pitcher who overpowered hitters drew interest from nearly every single major league team. He gave up a full scholarship at Old Dominion University to sign with the Mets. Once in the minor league system, Pulsipher became one of the highest-rated prospects in baseball.

His major league debut, however, was about more than just a highly touted prospect finally making it to the show. It was the first appearance of the triumvirate that eventually came to be known as Generation K. These were three young Mets pitchers—Pulsipher and righties Jason Isringhausen and Paul Wilson—who sported can't-miss stuff that, if they all stayed healthy, would carry the Mets to success throughout the decade.

Pulsipher and Wilson were high-end draft picks, the former having been selected in the second round of the 1991 amateur draft and the latter having been the first overall pick of the '94 draft. Isringhausen's forty-fourth-round selection made little difference: all three were viewed as big pitchers with blazing speed and devastating breaking balls. They had performed well in their early minor league careers; there was speculation that spring that, at a minimum, Pulsipher and Isringhausen would appear with the club in 1995. Wilson, the youngest of the three, needed another year or two of minor league seasoning. But 1996 or '97 would be the year where all three came together, dominated, and drove the Mets back to relevance. They were going to be Gooden-Darling-Ojeda or Seaver-Koosman-Gentry, only perhaps even better. It was a lot to expect from just one pitcher, let alone three, but at this point, all the Mets had was hope.

Not only were the Mets desperate for any kind of momentum that could save the season, but they were also trying to give fans a reason to keep watching and come back to Shea. Pulsipher was meant to be a reason. The first of the three to take the plunge, his scheduled debut had been the talk of the town in the days leading up. His appearance created a bump in attendance, drawing the largest crowd of the team's ten-game home stand. What that crowd saw at first was problematic.

It took Pulsipher twenty-two minutes and forty-four pitches to get through his first big league inning, as he allowed three walks, two singles, two doubles, two stolen bases, and five runs. All told, he gave up seven runs in seven innings, as the team lost 7–3. It was not the start Pulsipher, the fans, or the organization had hoped for; the comparisons to Gooden, Seaver, or Ryan were put on hold. Rather than focus on the negative, the team looked for a silver lining and found many. "He had movement like I've never seen before," said Hundley, of Pulsipher's fastball.[9]

Animated and jittery on the mound, Pulsipher tried not to get caught up in the hype, refusing to dwell on whether he was called up too soon and instead focusing on how to improve for his next start. Green, grasping at anything that could provide a modicum of joy or inspiration for the club, focused on Pulsipher's energy on the mound. "He's going to be that way. But there's nothing wrong with that. That's like [Montreal Expos pitcher] Carlos Pérez or Randy Johnson or any of the guys who have a little flair to them, a little charisma to them."[10]

Pulsipher's next start went nearly as poorly, with the Phillies knocking him around for 14 hits. But in his third start, he showed flashes of what everyone had been expecting, shutting out the Marlins into the eighth inning while striking out nine and winning his first big league game. It gave hope, but it could not overcome the avalanche of poor play that continued from the team. During the ten-game home stand where Pulsipher made his debut, the Mets lost 7 of 10, including a four-game sweep by Philadelphia that dropped them 16.5 games out of first. After losing three of the first four games of their next road trip, they fell to 20-37. The Mets were officially the worst club in the National League. Between them and the Yankees, New York was looking at some of its worst, most uninspired baseball in years.

The discontent that spreads through any clubhouse not meeting expectations began flaring up in Queens. Bonilla caused a minor stir during Pulsipher's debut when, in the eighth inning, his team trailing by five runs, he hit a fly ball to right field with a runner on third base. When the runner did not tag up and score, "Bonilla, apparently, upset about missing out on a run batted in, could be seen glaring at [third base coach Mike] Cubbage and then trashing two water coolers in the Mets' dugout."[11] Shortly thereafter, with the club drowning, McIlvaine announced that there would be a ten-game evaluation period of the team to determine if changes were needed.

The notion was laughable to fans and players, who did not need another ten games to see that something, anything, had to change. The review became even sillier because it happened just before the start of the four-game sweep by the Phillies and continued with two losses to the Braves. The Mets were 1-6 during the review. Bonilla had seen enough. He expressed the frustration of many fans by teeing off on the Mets' ownership.

"Why did they do that? It's stupid," said Bonilla, of the review period. "You don't say you're going to wait 10 days to make changes. If you're going to make changes, make them. Now we've got guys sitting around here waiting for the bomb to drop. Nobody knows what's going to happen."[12]

McIlvaine implied Bonilla was exaggerating the situation slightly, but the GM did not improve things when he said that, had the team simply done and said nothing, players might have grown apathetic given the Mets' record. Apathetic or not, the locker room was filled with players who had no idea if the club was going to try and improve or start shipping them off.

Once the review period ended, the team did nothing. No trades, no players signed or released or called up. Nothing happened except the Mets kept losing. They limped into the All-Star break at 25-44, the worst team in the National League and dangerously close to challenging the Brewers for the worst team in baseball. The idea of a wild-card berth was a laughable 14.5 games away. Perhaps their only saving grace was that the Yankees had faltered, leaving some space to reemerge as New York's top team in the near future if Generation K came to be. That was still a year or two away, though. As the team separated for the break, they still had another half-season of potential misery to get through. Something desperately needed to change. But what?

On June 13 a man wearing a light-blue button-down shirt with a blue-and-red-striped tie took a seat directly behind the visiting dugout at Tiger Stadium. Other than the shirt and tie, he did not stick out much more than any of the other 11,800 people in attendance. But everyone knew he was there. And that's just what George Steinbrenner wanted. Sheets of paper in his lap and pencil in his hand, the Yankees owner appeared to be taking notes as the Yankees faced off against the Tigers in the second game of the series. George's team was, at that moment, a last-place team; The Boss had had enough. He wanted the players, and Showalter in particular, to see him there in the front row, glowering at them. Maybe, Steinbrenner's thinking went, having The Boss around might spur these guys to right the ship.

Whether that is indeed what happened, no one will ever know. But, that night, the Yankees came out and scored 10, including 6 RBIs from Stanley. McDowell got his first win in nine starts. Meanwhile, MSG showed home viewers repeated shots of Steinbrenner, at one point slowly zooming in on him as he shuffled about in his seat. The next day newspapers were full of pictures of The Boss in attendance, with one image showing

Steinbrenner at the top left, watching the game and chewing on a pencil, while Showalter took up the bottom right, standing in front of the dugout, his arms folded.

The Yankees began to heat up. They returned home, swept the Blue Jays, and took two of three from the Tigers, going from last to third place. But even all of that was not without more distractions driven by Steinbrenner.

On June 19 Darryl Strawberry became a New York Yankee, signing a one-year deal with a team option for a second. "The once unfathomable notion that Strawberry could return to play baseball in New York, or return to play at all, was obliterated because the principal owner of the Yankees, George Steinbrenner, vigorously praised the former Met," wrote the *Times*'s Jack Curry.[13]

Steinbrenner was leery about the team's lack of power, with mostly just O'Neill and Stanley providing the occasional home run. He also wanted to make a splash, shake things up, and potentially mock the Mets in the process. What better way to do that than sign the greatest offensive threat his crosstown rival had ever had? The Boss loved the theatrics of it all. The former Met megastar donning pinstripes, hitting massive home runs into the upper deck as he carried the Yankees from the depths of despair to the postseason. And all while overcoming his personal troubles to shine once again in the Big Apple spotlight. It was like a Hollywood movie. So entranced with the idea of signing Strawberry was Steinbrenner that he had not consulted any of his baseball people on it. Not even his Tampa cabal. This was his decision and his alone.

"I appreciate and realize the opportunity Mr. Steinbrenner is giving me to return to baseball and particularly to New York," said Darryl, who later called The Boss an angel that helped rebuild his life. "I feel very fortunate."[14]

There were several problems, though. First, Strawberry was not yet eligible to play baseball. While the terms of his house arrest could change based on employment, after testing positive for cocaine use that winter, Selig had suspended him for the first sixty games of the season. Because of the delayed start, those sixty games weren't up yet. Even though they would be soon, Straw had not played since August 10, 1994; he had not played a full, uninjured, or unsuspended year since 1991. Would he even be in condition to get back on the field? And where was he going to play?

Polonia, Bernie Williams, Gerald Williams, Tartabull, and James were all already vying for the outfield and designated hitter spots. There was also the problem of Darryl himself. He had been a bad teammate with the Mets, brooding and confrontational. And for the last five years his off-the-field issues had far overshadowed anything he had done on the diamond.

"Darryl Strawberry is, of course, a bum," wrote the *Post-Standard*'s Bud Poliquin. "He's beaten his wife, he's neglected his children, he's indulged in cocaine, he's boozed to excess, he's cheated on his taxes, he's fought with teammates, he's currently suspended from baseball . . . . [His] return to New York . . . might be cause for some to consider lowering the flag to half-staff in the Bronx."[15]

"After two years of nothing but pure baseball—where nothing went on outside the lines—it feels like we are going back to the old days with a lot of distractions," noted Mattingly, who added that he was still looking forward to having Strawberry join the team.[16]

Meanwhile, the news had seeped its way into the Queens clubhouse of Darryl's former team. They had no desire to comment or even think about it. "Buck Showalter will answer all those questions," said Green. "I've got nothing to say."

"I've got more important things to worry about than what Darryl is doing," noted Hundley. Strawberry did get one ringing endorsement, though he may have been better off without it. "Hey, New York needs something like this right now . . . this city could use a dose of Darryl," said former teammate Len Dykstra, who happened to be in town to play the Mets when the news broke.[17]

Of all the quotes and statements made on the Strawberry signing, however, there was one that may have meant more to Steinbrenner than anything. Mets season ticket holder Bo Markocic said he he had gone to Shea all the time to watch Darryl play but had limited his games significantly since Strawberry had left for the Dodgers. "He's an exciting player," Markocic added. "Would I go to Yankee Stadium [to see him play]? Sure."[18]

Could Strawberry help the Yankees pick things up? Maybe. But if his signing resulted in even just one Mets season ticket holder attending more games at Yankee Stadium, then the deal was worth it to The Boss. Just how it would turn out, though, time would tell. Once his suspension was lifted, Strawberry had to rehab in the minor leagues first. That meant he would not join the team until late July or early August, assuming there were no setbacks.

A week after the Strawberry signing, more controversy engulfed the club. On June 27 fans awoke to a picture of Mattingly on the back page of the *Daily News*. Next to Mattingly, in big, bold, white type appeared the headline "Done Don." What followed on page 41 was a column from Bill Madden urging The Captain, hitting just .260 with only a single home run that he'd hit in the season's first week, to walk away from the game. The column itself had been spurred by Mattingly's insistence that he might want to keep playing after his contract ran out at year's end. To Madden, not only was that naive, but it would do a disservice to Mattingly's career if he forced the Yankees into choosing not to bring him back, versus simply retiring from the game.

Mattingly "will go down in history as one of the greatest defensive first basemen of all time, and that as much as anything is responsible for the respect he has in the Yankees' clubhouse," wrote Madden. "But as much as the Yankees have valued his presence, they shouldn't let it turn their backs on reality. The $4.4 million they are paying for Mattingly's courage this season should be spent on a middle-of-the-order hitter who is going to provide middle-of-the-order production. Hopefully, the agony of this season will bring Mattingly to that same conclusion."[19]

The column, while direct, was not mean-spirited. It took no cheap shots and acknowledged what had become obvious to many: Mattingly was not the same player he was five years earlier and the team should act accordingly. But the headline, which Madden did not write and regretted because he knew it would sting Mattingly personally, jumped out at people as especially cruel. Madden had struck an exposed nerve among fans, reporters, and sports talk media. What followed was a months-long war between what could be described as the pro-Mattingly side and the time-to-move-on side.

The pro-Mattingly side was led by those closest to the team on a daily basis. WABC team radio announcers Michael Kay and John Sterling, along with WFAN's Suyzn Waldman and many of the team's MSG television announcers, either staunchly defended Mattingly or did little to push the narrative that he was finished.

Kay in particular was incensed at the criticism, referring to those who questioned whether Mattingly should be playing or not as "classless."

"Once you get past the fact that he's not that [the mid-1980s Mattingly], and he's never going to be that anymore, he's really not a bad player," said Kay, in the midst of the war.[20]

The pro-Mattingly side also suspected that Steinbrenner had planted the story with Madden, in an effort to prevent The Boss from having to make an unpopular decision at year's end. If Mattingly simply walked away on his own, Steinbrenner would be spared public outrage.

Mike Lupica, long one of Steinbrenner's fiercest critics, wrote a counter-point to Madden's column three days later. "It is not the first slow start of [Mattingly's] career, although it suddenly is treated that way," said Lupica. "He is certainly better than his owner," Lupica continued, "Publicly George Steinbrenner talks about 'Donnie' Mattingly as if Mattingly were one of his children. And privately, Steinbrenner whispers that Mattingly cannot do the job anymore. It is typically gutless of him, predictably two-faced."[21]

WFAN's Mike Francesa and Chris "Mad Dog" Russo, cohosts of the most popular sports talk radio program in the country, felt Mattingly's defenders were closing their eyes to reality, while spouting the company line Showalter was feeding them. They could not understand the double standard being applied. Any other player in New York, with those numbers, would be run out of town. Waldman, despite working for the same station, did not hold back in response to comments like these, declaring, "You've got a lunatic fringe out there who are ready to hang Don Mattingly. It's so ludicrous. I just wish football season would hurry up and start so all these people, who know nothing about baseball, will go back to talking about football."

Francesa hit right back. "She's still wrong because she has absolutely no right to knock anybody, I don't care who she is talking about, for having an opinion that's an extremely valid opinion. As a matter of fact those people Suzyn and Kay and all the people who are taking these dives for Mattingly haven't a leg to stand on."[22]

Mattingly, who had relished the peace and tranquillity that had existed in the Yankees' clubhouse for two years, was now the center of an escalating controversy that would not abate so long as he took the field. He approached Showalter, believing it was in the team's best interest for Buck to remove him from the lineup. The Yankees' manager told him to shut up. Buck would make the lineup as he saw fit, not as Mike and the Mad Dog deemed appropriate. Not too long after, the Cleveland Indians were in town. Before the game Mattingly was warming up on the field when he heard a familiar voice.

"Donnie," called out his former teammate Dave Winfield, playing his final season. "Listen, don't let them get to you. You still got a lot to offer. You hang in there."

"Yep," replied Mattingly. "I'm going to just keep playing."[23]

The whole affair only further solidified the fans' love and appreciation for the first baseman. Nearly every time he came to bat at Yankee Stadium, Mattingly earned prolonged applause. Each base hit or run driven in drew a reaction louder and longer than it should have. Many recognized that this could be the swan song of a player who was the only good thing associated with the team for years. They were not going to drive him away just because he was not the Donnie Baseball of 1987. On July 20, when Mattingly hit his first home run in 107 days, a shot into empty right-field seats at Yankee Stadium, the 17,000 fans in attendance gave him a standing ovation. Three days later, on Cap Day, when Mattingly hit a ball deep over the right-field wall, perhaps his longest home run in years, fans tossed their free hats onto the field in a show of love and respect for The Captain that delayed the game several minutes. The media feud continued, creating long-lasting riffs between people like Kay and Francesa, but it was clear whose side the fans were on. All Mattingly wanted to do was focus on getting to the postseason. As July progressed, it looked like the Yankees might find a way to get there.

Generation K's second act began on July 17. Jason Isringhausen was the least likely of the three to be considered a cornerstone of the Mets' future pitching staff. From Brighton, Illinois, the son of an oil refinery machinist father and secretary mother, the tall righty was a catcher in high school before converting to the outfield in college. He was by no means a pitcher when the Mets chose him 1,156th overall in the 1991 draft. His lack of speed but amazing arm convinced the team to shift him from the outfield to the pitcher's mound. The results were immediate. In 28 starts at single and double A in 1994, he had a 2.61 ERA and a 1.05 WHIP. At triple A Norfolk in '95, he was nearly unhittable, going 9-1 and striking out 75 in 87 innings. It was a performance that mimicked that of one of his favorite players, Nolan Ryan, after whom Isringhausen had named his dog. That was enough for the Mets, who called him up just after the All-Star break to make his debut in Chicago, at the beginning of what was dubbed the "The Trip from Hell." Ten away games in ten days that, because of makeup games, meant six flights across three time zones and, in some instances, visiting the same city twice just days apart. It had the potential to break the back of the Mets' season.

It was, however, a perfect scenario for Isringhausen to debut at Wrigley Field. The reserved pitcher, whose personality on the mound was the polar opposite of the lively Pulsipher, made his debut just a few hours' drive north of where he grew up. His entire immediate family was there to cheer him on.

Isringhausen retired the first ten hitters he faced, including strikeouts to end each of his first three innings. While he gave up two runs in the fourth, he retired his last ten batters. Seven innings, six of them perfect. He left during a tie game that the Mets eventually won in the ninth. The win, however, was outshone by Isringhausen's performance. Pulsipher thought Isringhausen was going to throw a no-hitter, his stuff was so sharp early on. Mark Grace, the Cubs' first baseman, a career .303 hitter on his way to leading the league in doubles that season, offered praise: "The kid's real good. He had a great fastball and a good curve. He still has to develop a third pitch. But if he does, then he'll really be something."[24]

There was hope again in the clubhouse, especially after the Mets took the first three games of the road trip. Just as quickly, the team lost three straight before heading to St. Louis for two of the most devastating games of the season. In the first match-up, a two-out Carl Everett single tied the game in the ninth, but reliever Jerry Dipoto gave up two walks and a single in the eleventh to give the Cardinals the win. A frustrated Green kept the clubhouse closed off from reporters for nearly thirty minutes afterward. Once they were let in, the normally animated Green looked a beaten man, like someone watching a tragedy unfold that had no power to stop it.

The next day was even more torturous. After St. Louis tied the score at 1–1 in the second inning, neither team scored until the top of the eleventh, when Bogar singled in a run with two outs. The win felt so important. Even if it could not fully salvage the road trip, at least the team could head home on a high note. But Henry gave up a walk and a single, then put the tying run on third and the winning run on first. He managed to strike out Brian Jordan, but Green brought in lefty Eric Gunderson to face lefty Ray Lankford. Gunderson gave up back-to-back singles and, with them, the game was lost; the Mets limped back home after the 4-6 road trip.

Green again kept the clubhouse closed after the game and again looked like a man who had just seen a car accident. The Mets at 32-51 remained the National League's worst team, a mere seven games better than they had been at the same point in 1993.

"The long faces, the blank stares, the quiet acceptance of their hideous fate. We experienced it all in the first half of this ugly Met season. And after a brief and deceitful hiatus, the dreary atmosphere has returned with a vengeance," wrote the *Daily News*'s John Giannone, in his postgame wrap-up story.[25] For a few Mets, though, a reprieve from that hideous fate was days away.

Bret Saberhagen began packing his bags for Cincinnati. The Mets had just defeated the Pirates 4–1 to end an abbreviated home stand and were on their way to the Midwest. It was nearly 11:00 p.m. on July 31, meaning there was only an hour left before the nonwaiver trade deadline was up. It looked like Sabes was going to remain with the Mets. But, just as he began getting ready to leave the clubhouse, word came from management: he'd been traded to the Colorado Rockies. Saberhagen was shocked, not by the trade necessarily, but by the destination. Rumors had circled for some time that he was headed out. Saberhagen was due $4.3 million in 1996; his contract deferred some payments to 2004, when he would start receiving

$250,000 a year for twenty-five years. Only a few teams had the resources to take on that kind of deal. Boston was believed the obvious choice, with Cleveland and Baltimore also in the running. With just ninety minutes left, the Rockies snuck in and Saberhagen's time with the Mets ended.

"I wanted to finish something in New York," a disappointed Saberhagen said, just minutes after learning of the deal. "The reason I came here was to help this team win. But the time I was here, we didn't do much winning."[26]

His disappointment at being dealt may have seemed odd at first. Saberhagen's time in New York had been filled with injuries like bone spurs and knee surgery. Then there were incidents like the bleach spraying, the firecrackers, and the demolishing of his locker with a bat. There was also the lack of winning. But when healthy, Saberhagen put up impressive numbers. His 1994 walks-per-nine-innings ratio of 0.7 set a modern-day record; that same year he became just the fourth pitcher in history to record more wins than walks in a season of 150 innings pitched or more. But he'd been on the team at the wrong time.

Saberhagen was not the first big name to go that week. On July 28, as the Mets were about to begin their first home stand after "The Trip from Hell," they traded Bonilla to the Orioles just minutes before the team took the field against Pittsburgh. Though the Mets and Orioles had been in discussions for weeks about Bonilla, the Mets had refused to part with him unless Baltimore gave up top-prospect outfielder Alex Ochoa, who may have had the strongest throwing arm of anyone in organized baseball. The Orioles would not part with Ochoa though, holding on to him in the hopes he could help land a big-name starting pitcher. They offered prospect Damon Buford and pitcher Armando Benitez. The Mets did not budge. At 6:40 p.m. on July 28, after Baltimore owner Peter Angelos found out from a reporter that David Cone had been dealt to another team, the Orioles decided to make the best deal they could, acquiring Bonilla for Ochoa and Buford.

Bonilla, for all the off-the-field issues in his three years with the club, was also disappointed by the news. "I knew all along this could possibly happen," he told reporters. "I just didn't think that it would happen right now. I have to deal with it and get on."[27] For all the tumult, the fights, the confrontations, the anger, Bonilla's three and a half seasons in New

York had been highly productive. He'd twice been named an All-Star, set a personal single-season high for home runs, and was having the best year of his career in 1995, leading the National League in total bases and sporting a .325 average and .984 OPS at the time of the trade. His teammates were sorry to see him go. Green offered nothing but praise. "You don't replace a Bobby Bonilla or a guy like him in your lineup," said Dallas, when hearing the news.[28]

Despite all that, the fan reaction at Shea, when news of the deal flashed on the scoreboard, was a mix of cheers and boos. McIlvaine tried to put a positive spin on it, noting that Ochoa and Buford were going to contribute to the club, and sooner rather than later. "We're approaching where we were in the 1980s as far as player talent [in the system]," he said, after the deal.[29]

The words did not encourage fans or even some of the team's own players. Franco, especially, saw what was going on and was not enthused. "Another youth movement," he said, with a mix of reserve and dejection after Bonilla and Saberhagen were both jettisoned over a seventy-two-hour period. "Second youth movement in the six years I've been here." Franco was now, by far, the most senior member of the team, the last link to a period when a Mets dynasty was still a plausible idea. Franco talked about the disappointment of seeing all his friends get traded since he had joined the club in 1990, listing Bonilla, then Cone and Darling and Strawberry and Sid Fernandez and Viola. Franco's brother, who happened to be in the Mets clubhouse at the time, told him to stop. "Don't do the whole list," he said, "it's too many names."[30]

The clubhouse was now void of every single big-name acquisition made during the winter of '92. Without Bonilla or Saberhagen, the result was still the same. The Mets lost their next five games after the deadline, falling twenty-two games under .500. Then, out of nowhere, the 1995 Mets began to do something crazy: they began to win.

July brought the Yankees another series of on- and off-the-field developments that impacted that season and the trajectory of the team for years to come. The first was the most consequential. Mariano Rivera's Yankee career was nearing an end. After being rocked as a starter and suffering from a sore shoulder, he and Jeter were sent by the team back to the minors. At twenty-five years old, with his fastball fooling no one, Rivera, the Yankees decided, would be traded for a more certain commodity. Michael worked out a deal with the Tigers to send Mariano to Detroit in exchange for David Wells, a solid left-handed starter who often kept the Yankees at bay and in whom Steinbrenner had been interested for some time. The Tigers, however, had no desire to acquire someone with a bum shoulder. They wanted assurances Rivera was healthy enough to make a big league impact.

On June 26 Rivera started for the Columbus Clippers and threw five no-hit innings in a rain-shortened game. The next day Michael was reading a game report when something caught his eye. The radar gun had Rivera clocking in at 95 miles per hour. *Impossible*, thought Michael. Mariano had barely broken 90 in his time with the club, including the minors. The gun must have been broken. Not wanting to chance anything, Michael called the Clippers and verified the gun was working fine. He then called Jerry Walker, the Cardinals' director of player personnel. In the course of their conversation on a variety of topics, Walker confirmed that Rivera had been throwing that hard.

It was remarkable. Someway, somehow, Rivera's fastball had gained nearly five miles per hour overnight. The Yankees could not explain it. Rivera, a deeply religious man, called it "a gift from the Lord . . . What else could it be? It makes no sense."[31]

The Yankees did not care how it happened. All that mattered was that it did. It was another gift. The Marlins and Rockies had both passed on Rivera in the expansion draft. Now, miraculously, he was throwing the ball significantly harder than he had just weeks earlier.

Michael called the Tigers and canceled the deal. Then he phoned Showalter and informed him of what happened. In desperate need of starting pitching, the Yankees called Rivera up and gave him the ball in Chicago for a July 4 start against the White Sox. Mariano, starting the day with a 10.20 ERA and a near 1:1 walk-to-strikeout ratio, threw 8 scoreless innings while striking out 11, the most he would ever strike out in a single game. For those watching, however, the performance was about more than numbers. A radar gun was not needed to see that his fastball had significantly more zip on it than before. The ball looked like it was exploding out of his hand. The Sox weren't just going down one after another, they were overmatched, working off a scouting report that none of them knew was no longer relevant. While he never matched the dominance of that outing again the rest of the year, he also never again, for any period of time until his retirement, resembled the feeble, unable-to-record-outs pitcher who gave up 18 runs in his first 15 major league innings.

Two weeks later, at home against the White Sox, the Yankees suffered one of their most embarrassing days of the decade. In the first game of a doubleheader, former Yankee Jim Abbott threw a complete game and beat them, 9–4. In the second game McDowell gave up nine runs before the end of the fifth inning. Showalter removed him from the game; as McDowell walked toward the dugout, the 21,188 in attendance rained boos down on him. McDowell was frustrated and angry. He had come over to the team as their projected number one starter, no small task given how well Key had performed in New York. Then Key went down, followed by Kamieniecki. In late June Pérez suffered an elbow injury so severe he pitched only a single inning the rest of his career. In the absence of three of the team's five projected starters and a bullpen that could not keep opponents from scoring, McDowell tried to pick up the slack. He'd pitched into the seventh inning in 13 of his first 16 starts and nearly pitched a no-hitter in Anaheim. But, for all that, McDowell walked off the mound about to go 7-6 with a 4.87 ERA. He understood fan anger but did not appreciate their lack of appreciation for just how hard he was trying to carry this team. As McDowell approached the foul line, he raised his right arm and then just his right middle finger to the crowd. To ensure no one in the stadium missed out on his wrath, he swung his arm in a circular motion.

Hearing the boos get even louder and more vitriolic, Showalter asked Stanley what just happened. "You're not gonna like it," Stanley replied. "Jack just flipped off New York."

The condemnation of McDowell's single-fingered salute was immediate. Realizing what he'd done, the pitcher quickly owned up to it, calling the act stupid. As if that was not enough, the Yankees lost, 11–4, to Dave Righetti, who had started his first game in three years and his first in an American League ballpark in twelve. The doubleheader sweep dropped them to 33-40. The Royals and Rangers, teams the Yankees were competing with for the wild-card spot, came to town; New York swept both. After taking two of three in Kansas City, they were back at .500. In a week's time they shot up to second place and were just a game behind Texas for the wild card. On July 28, three days before the trade deadline, Michael pulled off two enormous deals in the span of an hour.

At 5:30 p.m. he traded three minor league players to the Blue Jays in exchange for another former Met. This time, it was David Cone. The reigning American League Cy Young Award winner became available once it was clear Toronto was out of contention. While the Yankees were still interested in Wells, reports from Jimmy Key, his former teammate, indicated he might not be the best fit for the clubhouse. With that, Michael outmaneuvered several other teams to land Cone.

When news reached the players, it was hard to find one who wasn't smiling. "I know Cone and, no knock on the guys we traded, but I have no idea who those guys are. We're getting a guy who has pitched in New York and in the postseason. I can't see anything that's not to like about it," said Mattingly.[32]

An hour after trading for Cone, Michael shipped Tartabull to Oakland in exchange for outfielder Rubén Sierra in a deal seen as one headache for another. Tartabull's presence on the team was no longer tenable. "I'm just glad it's all over," he said, sounding like a bank holdup hostage who had just been released.[33]

Sierra had his own issues in Oakland, repeatedly clashing with manager Tony La Russa. But he was a switch hitter with power, having driven in more runs over the last five years than any American League player except Cecil Fielder. The hope was that a change of scenery and a chance to win a World Series would motivate him to place ego aside.

The two deals put the Yankees' payroll at $47.8 million, the highest in the league. That meant that Steinbrenner would amplify the pressure on Showalter tenfold to get to the postseason. The trades had catapulted the Yankees, left for dead weeks earlier, into the team to beat in the American League. The acquisitions of Cone and Sierra, "coupled with the eventual arrival of Darryl Strawberry, leads many to expect the Yankees will sweep past the first-place Red Sox in the AL East," wrote Newsday's Jason

Molinet.[34] It was a remarkable statement, given that the Yankees were still several games out of first.

Cone won his first start. He won his second when Sierra hit a two-out, two-run, go-ahead double at the Stadium against the Brewers. The next night in Detroit Strawberry finally made his team debut. He said all the right things about not wanting to be a distraction and about just trying to help the team win. It was exactly what he did. In his first two games, Strawberry went 4-9 with a triple and two RBIs.

Meanwhile, even though he was brand new to the team, Cone began exhibiting the leadership qualities that would make him beloved in the clubhouse. Shortly after the trade, he realized that, while fans could not hear what Yankee broadcasters said between innings, their comments were broadcast into the team's clubhouse. Those comments were often more barbed and candid than what was said on live television, creating the opportunity for resentment among players who happened to hear them. He gave team broadcasters a heads-up to watch what they said, something they deeply appreciated, and which spared the team more drama.[35]

It was August 1995. David Cone and Darryl Strawberry were driving the Yankees toward the postseason while acting as model teammates. It was surreal, for Yankees and Mets fans alike.

After a slight stutter step against the Indians, the Yankees won the final two games of their last home stand before heading out on a grueling thirteen-game road trip. The final home game had been especially poignant, as team legend Mickey Mantle died earlier that morning. In commemoration, the Yankees wore a black armband with the number "7" above it on their left sleeve the rest of the season. Despite winning those final two games, the losses beforehand, coupled with a Red Sox team that would not stop winning, ended the American League East race. The Yankees were nine games out; when they lost two of the first three games of the trip in Boston, they dropped to ten out with forty-one games left to play. They were not going to catch up to the Red Sox, even if they offered the typical "it ain't over till it's over" platitudes.

The wild card, however, remained up for grabs. After leaving Boston, New York headed to Anaheim for the first of ten games on the West Coast.

The team had been embarrassed there earlier in the year, but McDowell held the Angels at bay, winning the first game and bringing the Yankees to within a half-game of Texas for the wild-card lead. It would be a sprint to the finish, but the Yankees were in a strong position for their first playoff appearance in fourteen years. What proceeded instead was the most disastrous series of games the team played in the entire 1990s, characterized by one brutal loss after another.

Following McDowell's win, the team trailed by two runs entering the ninth when Strawberry hit what appeared to be a game-tying home run. But Garret Anderson made a leaping catch for the out, preserving the lead and the win. Hitchcock got shelled for eight runs the next day. In Oakland, Pettitte failed to make it out of the first inning before giving up six runs en route to a 13–4 loss. Kamieniecki followed with another loss. Trying to avoid the sweep, McDowell held Oakland to just two runs, but the Yankees left twelve men on base and lost 2–1. They were in a free fall. Desperately needing a win, they turned to hired gun Cone, in the first of four games in Seattle. Despite giving up a first-inning grand slam, Cone held the Mariners in check long enough for New York to take a 7–6 lead into the ninth. Wetteland, who had blown two saves in the Indians series, retired the first two batters but walked former Met Vince Coleman, who had resurrected his career in the Pacific Northwest. Coleman promptly stole second and third. Still, when Joey Cora hit a soft liner to Tony Fernandez, the game appeared over. But Fernandez timed his jump poorly and, as he began his descent too soon, the ball went off his glove and into left field. Tie game. Before the team could process what happened, Mariners star outfielder Ken Griffey Jr., whose life's mission it was to destroy the Yankees due to their treatment of him as a kid when his father played for the team, put a Wetteland pitch deep into the right-field stands to end the game. It was the Yankees' most crushing defeat of the year. Cone, chewing on his fingernails, barely had the energy to stand and leave the dugout. Velarde and James sat on the bench, staring blankly out at the field.

In the clubhouse afterward, the atmosphere was bleak. "We got the first victory in Anaheim and we all felt it would be different this time," said Stanley. "Guess we were wrong."[36]

The heartbreaking loss and sense of desperation spurred no immediate turnaround. They lost the next two games by a combined score of 14–4. There was no way around it: the road trip had been an epic failure. The Yankees had left New York 51-48, nine games out of first and a half-game out of the wild card. They returned to New York 54-58, 15.5 games out of first, and 4.5 out of the wild card. Of 19 games on the West Coast that year, the Yankees won just 3, one in each city.

In the first game back at the Bronx, a makeup game against the Royals, they blew a 3–1 lead in the seventh, then failed to capitalize with runners on first and second and no out in the bottom half of the inning or with the bases loaded and one out in the ninth.

The season was over. No player, fan, coach, or owner thought that the Yankees were going to come back from this. The team was lifeless. A season of such hope was crashing down, with nothing to show for it. Mattingly would not make the postseason now, at least almost certainly not as a Yankee. And Showalter's fate was sealed. George was going to need someone to blame for all this and Buck's contract was up. At 54-59 the Yankees were barely better than the Mets, the team they were supposed to have stolen the city from, and with some of their best former players. The last thirty-one games of the year would be futile.

One of the great mysteries of baseball is how a team can look so bad one day and so great the next. It defies logic that the same group of players could perform miserably for a prolonged period of time, then suddenly become a perfect machine, incapable of doing wrong. But it happens. And after the Yankees' 4–3 loss to Kansas City, their miserable performance immediately turned into a do-no-wrong stretch of play that lasted until the end of the season. The Angels came to town and, in the beginnings of their own free fall, were swept by New York. O'Neill had his first career three homer game and, for the first time in a month, the Yankees had three consecutive starters win ballgames. Oakland arrived; not only did the Yankees take two of three, but they showed a fire that had been lacking for some time when McDowell stared down and even charged at Rickey Henderson after striking him out in a big moment. Seattle came next. Despite Seattle's surge up the American League West standings after Griffey's game-winning home run, New York took two of three from the Mariners, too. The only loss belonged to Rivera, marking the final start of his career.

Boston arrived. Even with the division race over, the Yankees made a statement with a three-game sweep, thanks in part to two big home runs from Strawberry. Having gone just 3-10 against those same four teams during the disastrous road trip, New York completely reversed the damage by going 10-2 against them at home. After a brief road trip, they returned to New York just a game out of the wild card with twelve left to play. They fought tooth and nail for every win; the urgency was that much greater as many realized this was probably the end of the road for Mattingly. Getting to the postseason itself became almost secondary to the notion of getting The Captain to the postseason just once in his career.

If Mattingly was their rallying cry, it worked. Beginning their last home stand of the regular season, Cone, Pettitte, and Hitchcock shut the Blue Jays down while the offense continued to shine. In the series' final game, an eighth-inning home run from Sierra brought them back from defeat, leading to a four-game sweep. Sierra, the problem child in Oakland, had been a revelation in the Bronx, on his way to driving in 42 runs in just 56 games with the team and providing the power and even swagger that Tartabull could not. While his defense was questionable at best, his outfits, garish and over the top, were a smash with teammates. His inability to remember names, referring to many simply as "guy," was funny in a Rickey-being-Rickey kind of way. And no one on the team, or even in baseball, had a home trot like Sierra. Famed sportswriter Roger Angell described it as a "two-step backward shimmy with a little pluck at his shirtfront . . . and only then the unsmiling, nothing-to-it, slow-and-then-slower tour of the bases."[37]

Sierra's continued big hits were a reason the team was back in it. The sweep of the Jays put them a half-game back of the wild-card lead. Winning their last home series of the year against the Tigers moved them to a half-game up, with five to play. In the final game of the series, not knowing if they would ever see him play again, Yankee fans gave Mattingly an ovation every time he came to the plate. In his last regular season at bat at Yankee Stadium, he lashed a double to the right-center field wall.

Two wins in Milwaukee built a one-game lead for the Yankees over the Angels in the wild card. But the Angels were also battling the Mariners for the American League West division lead, meaning three teams were fighting for two playoff spots going into the final weekend of the year. The Yankees were in Toronto, the Mariners in Texas, and the Angels were home against the A's. New York was in the driver's seat, needing only to win their games to be assured the wild card. That scenario was in deep trouble in the first game in Toronto. Down 3–0, the Yankees had to win doing something they had not done once the entire season: come from behind in the ninth inning. They caught a break when Toronto booted a sure double play ground ball, allowing a run to score and the tying runs to reach base. After another run, Pat Kelly came up. The second baseman had regressed in 1995 after a strong season the year before. Hitting just .238 and not having hit a home run since May, Kelly was coming to the plate in the season's biggest moment. Few could have been comfortable with that, but Showalter had already used up his bench, leaving him no choice. With Steinbrenner watching from a box above the SkyDome field, Kelly hit a shot just over the left-field fence, giving the Yankees a 4–3 lead. It was a Bucky Dent–esque home run, unthinkable in the moment and huge in its impact. A visibly relieved Steinbrenner exhaled, as Wetteland closed the game out. The win became all the more crucial when both Seattle and California won later that night.

The next day Kamieniecki pitched the game of his life, going the distance in a 6–1 win. At worst the Yankees would play a one game playoff that Monday to decide the wild card. At best, if they won on Sunday, the last regular season game, or the Angels lost, they, and Mattingly, were in the postseason. Circumstances put Showalter in a precarious situation, though. Cone was available to pitch, but it was Hitchcock's turn in the rotation. The Yankees had gotten Cone for situations just like this, which is almost certainly what was going through Steinbrenner's mind. But, to Buck, it was a no-brainer. Hitchcock had dominated in his last two starts, including a complete-game effort against these same Jays. Worst case, if the Yankees did not win and were forced into a one-game playoff, they'd have Cone on the mound. Best case, they'd have Cone pitching Game One of the Division Series at Yankee Stadium on Tuesday. Showalter went with

Hitchcock, a move that, should it not work out, would probably cost him his job after the season was over.

Any drama over the game disappeared in minutes. A first-inning double by Sierra put the Yankees up 2–0. They added two more in the second. Hitchcock pitched well enough to keep the Jays from scoring until the sixth. In the fifth, Mattingly hit a home run off the foul pole in right field. It was his 1,785th, and, as it would turn out, last regular season game, the largest number of games for any active player who had not yet made the postseason.

Mattingly's home run was the culmination of two different steps The Captain took in the season's final weeks to improve his game. Noticing that his teammates O'Neill and Sierra used a leg kick to drive the ball with power, Mattingly, ever changing his batting stance, began using one of his own. The other strategy was to endure his back pain, no matter the cost. For years Mattingly had undergone rigorous pregame rituals to keep him feeling good enough to play: stretching, sitting in the tub, having rub-downs, undergoing acupuncture, and so on. It was this grueling day-in, day-out routine that was, in part, one of the reasons he was considering retiring once his contract was up. But, when it looked like the Yankees might still have a chance of making the playoffs, he decided that he was going to ignore the aches and the pains, no matter how crippling. The injuries might permanently end his career, but, at this point, he was going to do whatever it took to play postseason baseball.

The result was a one-month stretch of play that had eluded Mattingly all year. From September 1 to October 1, playing a total of twenty-eight games, he hit .321, with eight doubles and a .453 slugging percentage. While he was not hitting more home runs, the leg kick allowed him to hit the ball with more velocity, driving it in a way he hadn't all season. His 222nd and last career regular-season home run gave the Yankees a 5–0 lead. Velarde homered in the eighth, meaning the team's two senior members contributed home runs in the first game in well over a decade that could send the Yankees to the playoffs. In the ninth, Mattingly sin-gled, his 2,153rd and last career regular season hit. In the bottom of the inning, Howe recorded the final out, giving the Yankees a 6–1 win and their first postseason berth since 1981. In that time they'd watched the Mets take over the city, win a World Series, win another division title, receive near legendary status, and constantly outdraw them. That was all behind them now. The years of lost no-hitters, bad trades, bad signings, clubhouse discontent, anger . . . that was done. All there was to think about in this moment was, at long last, the playoffs.

After the last out, attention immediately shifted to Mattingly, who got down on one knee and pounded the SkyDome turf. Hugs followed, the biggest reserved for Showalter. If Mattingly had gotten the monkey off his back, Showalter had alleviated some of the immense pressure that had built all season. The past year had been the most stressful of his managerial career. Steinbrenner had reverted to his manic, 1980s worst. The calls that had plagued every manager before Buck, calls filled with second-guessing and ultimatums, returned in full force in '95. The leaks about how Showalter better come through or how The Boss was unhappy had also returned. Even worse, the fans liked Buck. They liked the respectability and, of course, the winning he had brought back to the Bronx. That riled The Boss. Where was his adulation? Hadn't he been the one who put up the money to sign these players? Hadn't he given the green light to get Cone and Sierra? Why was Buck getting all this credit?

That tension was gone, at least in the moment Buck embraced Mattingly on the field. Typical of Showalter, he had first allowed his players their moment of glory before joining them in celebration. Watching from above, Steinbrenner allowed himself a moment of rejoicing. Being that it was the first-ever wild card, there was uncertainty about how far to take the celebration. Beers were opened, wild-card swag passed around. It was celebratory without being over the top. Reporters swarmed around Mattingly, gathering every last quote they could from the guy who was forty-eight hours away from his first playoff game. Once it was over, the team headed for the airport and got on a flight back home. "He moved everybody around," said Showalter of Steinbrenner. "Sat right next to me. Worst flight I ever took."[38]

At no point did Steinbrenner tell Showalter he made the right move pitching Hitchcock instead of Cone.

The Mets of August 6, 1995, were not, on paper, an impressive club. Their ace pitcher was Bobby Jones, a man with all of two-plus years in the bigs. Behind him were Pulsipher and Isringhausen, the first two members of Generation K; Dave Mlicki, who had yet to complete a full season in the majors; and Reid Cornelius, a rookie with eight games of experience who had joined the rotation in August after Pete Harnisch went down with a torn labrum.

Offensively, now that Bonilla was gone, the biggest threats were Brogna, the second-year first baseman, and Kent, putting up good numbers but not what many had expected of him. There was little reason to believe this team would finish much better than the '93 version that was supposed to represent the club's rock bottom. Yet from August 5 until the last day of the year, the Mets were among the best teams in baseball. It would have been impossible to imagine that, after the last game of the season, players and fans were desperate for the start of 1996; not because they wanted 1995 to end, but because they did not want it to stop.

It started with a six-game winning streak—the first of two during this stretch—that included a sweep of the Phillies. After a brief slip, they won five in a row. At month's end, when the West Coast teams came into Shea, there was no repeat of May's dreadful home stand. Instead, the Amazins won seven of ten games. They finished August with a 16-12 record, their first winning month of the season. The wins were more remarkable considering that, during the home stand, they had traded Butler to the Dodgers, the team they were playing. Butler, who had struggled in the season's first half, hit .438 after the All-Star break and provided leadership qualities that were largely absent in a team full of first-, second-, and third-year players. With the thirty-eight-year-old Butler gone, the average age of a Met was just shy of twenty-six and the payroll had fallen to $12.8 million, the lowest in baseball and nearly 75 percent less than that of the Yankees. And yet, the Bad News Mets kept winning.

In mid-September, another sweep of the Phillies boosted the team from last to third place in the division. There was no chance at a playoff spot by this point, but it was building hope for better things to come. Taking advantage of teams that had already clinched playoff berths, the Mets swept the last home stand of the series, winning all six games against the Reds and Braves. When the last game, an eleventh-inning walk-off win, was over, players and coaches stood outside the dugout and tossed their caps into the crowd. On the scoreboard, highlights from the season, almost all of them from the last two months, played; then, as the final image, an ad for Opening Day on April 1, 1996, at Shea appeared. The crowd loved it.

The clubhouse, so dour for most of the season, was alive after the exhilarating finish. Laughter could be heard, along with the sounds of Hootie & the Blowfish. Fred Wilpon appeared in the clubhouse. The last time he had done so, two years earlier, it was to inform players that Vince Coleman was finished as a New York Met and that their overall behavior was unacceptable. This time, the message was decidedly different. "I told them the future looks bright," said Wilpon. "I congratulated them. Not only for the way they've performed in the second half but for the way they've conducted themselves as professionals."[39]

"Make no mistake about it, I was just as guilty as the players. Trading Bonilla and Saberhagen brought us together as a unit. The freshness of the kids and the trades brought us together as a unit. This was a great learning experience and I hope it carries over into the spring," Green told reporters.[40]

The freshness of the kids. There was no better way to put it. On August 6 the Mets were 35-57 and in last place. They finished 69-75, in second place. Only one team in the last fifty-five years, the 1979 Dodgers, had made a greater first-to-second-half improvement. The kids had turned things around, starting with Generation K. Isringhausen was a revelation. In ten starts from August 9 to the last day of the year, he'd gone 8-1 and failed to pitch into the sixth inning only once. His wins in seven consecutive starts fell just one shy of the franchise record, held by Seaver and Cone. He ended the year 9-2 with a 2.81 ERA, earning him a fourth-place finish in Rookie of the Year voting. Pulsipher did not match Isringhausen but showed progress. In five August starts, he threw over 40 innings and had a 2.88 ERA, with the team winning four times. Soreness in his left elbow shut him down in mid-September but the hope was that the off-season would heal any injury and he would come back even stronger in '96. With Paul Wilson still on the horizon, the first grades were coming back for Generation K and the marks were high.

Alex Ochoa appeared in a handful of games in September and impressed with a .297 average. Brogna led the team in home runs and RBIS, not succumbing to any sophomore slump. Everett, initially struggling through his rookie year, caught fire in September, hitting .317 and driving in 23 runs. Alfonso recovered from his slow start in May to hit .278. Hundley set career highs in average on-base percentage and slugging. On the farm, the Mets had a defensive wizard waiting in the wings at shortstop in Rey Ordóñez. The twenty-four-year-old was a star Cuban player, inheriting his father's remarkable defensive abilities. In 1993, while in Buffalo for the World University Games, Ordóñez leapt a fence before his game against Team USA and snuck into a red Cadillac driven by a Cuban radio executive. They drove to the airport and flew to Miami, where Ordóñez stayed as a defector. He left behind his wife and child; they attempted numerous times to join him in the United States only to be denied by the Cuban government. Three months later the Mets won the right to sign Ordóñez in a special lottery for Cuban defectors. The '96 season was the time to see just what exactly he could do in New York.

The season had not played out as hoped. The Yankees, with several former Mets on board, were back in the postseason. Attendance dropped to just 1.2 million, the lowest since 1983, excluding the '94 shortened season. But still, the future looked bright at Shea. The hopes were big that, in the ten-year-anniversary season of the team's last championship, the Mets would again use a mixture of youth and veterans to win over New York City.

Seven hours after a Los Angeles jury found former NFL running back O. J. Simpson not guilty of double homicide, the first playoff game in the Bronx in fourteen years began. The Yankees were playing against the Seattle Mariners, who, after beating New York in the Griffey walk-off home-run game, overcame an eleven-and-a-half-game deficit to tie the Angels for the division lead and then beat them in a one-game playoff, which had taken place in Seattle the day before. The Yankees benefited not only from the Mariners' late, cross-country flight but also from Randy Johnson, about to win the AL Cy Young Award, having pitched all nine innings of the playoff game. Still, the match-up was no cakewalk for New York. Despite a David-versus-Goliath narrative that emerged years later—the small-market, can-do Mariners against the big-city, big-spending Yankees—the Mariners had won 9 of 13 regular season match-ups against the Yankees, including all but one of the seven games at the Kingdome. Going into the Division Series, the edge could have been given to either team. The Mariners' offense was better, featuring several power hitters that the Yankees could not match. But, apart from Johnson, the Mariners could not match the starting pitching of the Yankees. And the bullpens of both teams were highly suspect, as the series would show.

At the time, the team with home field advantage played the first two games away, then the last three games, if all were necessary, at home. That meant Seattle had home field and the first two games were in New York. Before the start of Game One, as players began taking the field to do their stretching and warm-up tossing, Mattingly emerged from the dugout and received a thunderous ovation. The atmosphere, even before first pitch, was electric; many who partook in that series would say it was unmatched in any other game or series they ever played in. After a season in which the average per-game attendance at The Stadium was just 23,684, over 57,000 crammed into the ballpark to watch playoff baseball. The anger over the strike that caused so many to stay away was gone, at least temporarily. All they cared about now was seeing the Yankees win a title, seeing Don Mattingly win it all. During pregame introductions, Mattingly received the loudest ovation. Second was Showalter, who stormed out of the dugout, waving his cap enthusiastically in the air. The moment further angered Steinbrenner, fueling his paranoia that Buck, not The Boss, was getting all the credit for the Yankees winning again.

The Yankees' playoff roster included three rookies. Andy Pettitte, coming off a strong finish that netted him third place in AL Rookie of the Year voting, would get the start in Game Two. Rivera, whose final numbers on the year did not inspire confidence, still showed enough for Showalter to have him in the bullpen for the series. Lastly, Jorge Posada, who had appeared in a single game that year as a defensive replacement in the ninth inning, was added as a third-string catcher. While not on the roster,

Showalter insisted that Jeter, along with up-and-coming prospect Rubén Rivera, be in uniform on the bench during the series. Buck expected big things from both players and wanted them to get a taste of postseason baseball in New York.

Adding to the pressure, many players, including Mattingly, Stanley, Velarde, Strawberry, McDowell, Cone, and Boggs, would be free agents after the season. Showalter's and Michael's contracts were up as well. The literal future of the team was riding on the outcome of this postseason. The result was a transformational series.

New York won the first two at The Stadium in games that featured all manner of drama. Fans, perhaps overanxious and overzealous after a decade and a half of missing the playoffs, threw objects at Mariner players and were especially vitriolic toward team personnel and players' families in the stands. Steinbrenner added to the circus-like atmosphere when he charged that one of the umpires, who grew up in Oregon, was deliberately trying to help the Mariners win; he also criticized the Mariners' ownership for spending money to improve their team while claiming baseball's financial system was out of whack. And this was just the off-the-field drama.

The games themselves were intense affairs. Two home runs by Griffey meant Game One was tied going into the seventh inning. New York then scored four runs, two of them on a Sierra home run that shook Yankee Stadium to its core. Despite a rocky ninth inning, Wetteland preserved the lead and the game. Game Two was one of the greatest games in postseason history. A fifteen-inning affair that saw the Mariners blow four separate leads, the game featured numerous arguments between Showalter and the umpires, spectacular defensive plays by both sides, and heroics that lived on for years in Yankee lore.

In the sixth inning, with the score tied at 2–2, Mattingly drilled a home run to right field, causing a mass cathartic celebration among the fans that lasted for several minutes; Mariners manager Lou Piniella ultimately pulled his team off the field for fear of their safety. It was Mattingly's last career home run. In the twelfth inning, down a run, Sierra hit a two-out double off the wall in left field that tied the game; however, Bernie Williams was thrown out at home trying to end it and the game moved to the thirteenth. Meanwhile, Rivera, on the roster almost as an afterthought, pitched 3⅓ scoreless innings of relief, striking out five Mariners. In the fifteenth, Leyritz's two-run home run ended the drama at 1:22 a.m., putting the Yankees a single win away from the ALCS. Few people, including the Mariners, thought there was much chance Seattle would come back.

The Kingdome, however, had long been a house of horrors for the Yankees. Outside of the '94 season, it felt like they never won there, even when facing Mariner teams that were among the worst in baseball. Still, all they needed was a single victory and they would move on to face Cleveland in the next round.

That victory never came. A series of seeing-eye singles put Game Three away for Randy Johnson and the Mariners in the sixth inning. In Game Four, the Yankees burst out to a 5–0 lead by the third, only to see it slowly whittled away until they trailed after six. With the game tied in the eighth, Wetteland entered and allowed three base runners before giving up a grand slam to Edgar Martínez. In that moment, Showalter permanently lost faith in Wetteland, whose ERA for the series was 14.54. The Yankees nearly came back in the ninth but fell five feet short of a game-tying home run. The series moved to a winner-take-all Game Five.

Cone, the hired gun, took the mound in Game Five. Tied at two in the sixth, Mattingly's base-loaded double, the last hit of his career, scored two runs, giving New York a 4–2 lead. Cone, who worked his way out of trouble at multiple points throughout the game, gave up a home run to Griffey in the eighth to make it a one-run game. After, with the bases loaded, two out, and Cone gassed from the effort, he threw his 147th pitch of the game, a splitter, for a ball, walking in the tying run. "It took me forever to get over that," said Cone. "I'd thrown a hundred and forty-six pitches in the game up to that point, and I had nothing left, but I was still sure that was the right call. I just didn't execute."[41]

Not trusting Wetteland, Showalter brought in Rivera. For just about anyone else, especially a rookie, this could have been a make-or-break moment in their career. The bases were loaded, the season was on the line, and 57,000 people were screaming for failure. A lesser pitcher might have succumbed to that pressure. For Rivera, though, this was just baseball. He had been through and seen far worse in his life. As a teenager working on his father's fishing boat, an accident caused a fatal injury to his uncle. Mariano had witnessed the whole thing. As a child, playing base-ball meant using a mound of wadded up tape and a broomstick handle. No one could afford a real ball, much less a bat, a glove, or cleats. Those experiences molded Rivera in a way where, in the most head-pounding, heart-thumping situations, his pulse barely accelerated at all.

Facing him was former Yankee Mike Blowers. A military brat who was introduced to baseball by his stepfather, Blowers read the scouting report on Mariano and expected much the same as the White Sox had back on July 4: "I remember taking a fastball and to this day it seemed like it wasn't his best fastball [but] it seemed like as the at bat went along his velocity started to jump."[42] Cool and collected on the mound, Rivera struck out Blowers on three pitches to end the inning. As Mariano walked off the mound, Michael, watching the game in a Kingdome box with Steinbrenner, turned to no one in particular and said, "I think we found something here."[43]

Game Five moved into the eleventh inning. Johnson, the Mariners' Game Three starter, was pitching in relief when Velarde singled home Kelly to give the Yankees the lead. McDowell, the Yankees' Game Three starter now also pitching in relief, could not hold it. He allowed a lead-off bunt single to Joey Cora, then a ground ball single to Griffey. Edgar Martínez, hitting over .500 for the series, doubled down the left field line, winning the game, the series, and changing the course of Yankees' history like few players have.

Watching from above, Steinbrenner said little. He had spent nearly all of Game Five making his fellow box occupants incredibly uncomfortable, questioning nearly every move and decision made by Showalter. He was especially irked that Buck, in a series that averaged over four home runs a game, had left Strawberry on the bench in Game Five. Why did Stein-brenner go out and get a power hitter if Showalter was going to bench him in favor of Dion James? The tension of the game itself was bad enough, but The Boss's continued barbs and second-guessing made sitting there unbearable. Eventually, after the loss, he went to the clubhouse, where he hugged Mattingly and thanked him for everything he had done for the organization. He approached the office of Showalter, prepared to say lord knows what. Buck sat at his desk, his head buried in his folded arms, tears streaming down his face. Even The Boss felt empathy. He could not say anything in that moment. To reporters afterward he played coy, saying they would have to wait and see if changes were coming.

Changes were coming. Big changes.

[10]

Full Circle

Bob Watson walked into his home just after noon on Monday, October 23, 1995, trying to get settled. The Houston Astros' general manager had just returned from Atlanta, where he'd watched the first two games of the World Series between the Indians and the Braves. He noticed there were a few messages on his answering machine. One of them took him by surprise. It was Yankees general partner Joe Molloy, asking Watson to reach out to him as soon as possible about a position with New York. Watson returned the call immediately. He was shocked when Molloy asked him if he'd like to be the Yankees' general manager.

It was a life-altering moment; Watson had little time to think it over. New York had a plethora of off-season issues clouding the future of the club and needed to secure a general manager pronto. Watson, however, was not going to make this important a decision without first consulting his wife, Carol, even if she was all the way over in Italy. They connected by phone and talked it through. Watson knew the pitfalls. He had played in New York. In fact, he was the last man to have batted in a World Series game at Yankee Stadium. He knew what life under George Steinbrenner was like. At the same time, he loved a challenge. He'd accepted the Astros job and inherited a team that had not made the postseason in nearly a decade. Some shrewd moves by the GM had gotten Houston within a game of the wild card in '95. But the future of the Astros was uncertain. Rumors abounded that the team would be sold off and relocated to Washington. Between that and the challenge of the Yankees, Watson was ready to move on. He accepted the job.

"Bob is a man who always has exuded class as a player, a baseball executive and a human being," said Steinbrenner, who would make Watson's life a living hell.[1]

Watson's hiring shocked many. When a press release announcing the news made the rounds during the Indians' World Series party at the Rock and Roll Hall of Fame, Joe McIlvaine and Cubs general manager Andy MacPhail thought someone was pulling a practical joke. There's no way, they thought, that Watson would leave Houston to work under the oppressive regime of Steinbrenner. But it was no joke. The Yankees were completely revamping their organization and structure. It started nearly the second the team landed at Newark airport after the funeral-like, six-hour plane ride back from Seattle.

The first to go was Gene Michael. In no other dimension in the plane of existence would the man who had rebuilt a decaying, once-proud franchise and got them back to the postseason be facing the wrath of his boss for doing so. But The Boss was embarrassed and humiliated by the loss to Seattle. People were going to pay a price, starting with Michael, to whom Steinbrenner had entrusted his franchise five years earlier when he faced banishment. A week after the ALDS loss, Steinbrenner offered to let Michael keep his job but at a reduced salary, from $600,000 down to $400,000. No way Steinbrenner was going to keep paying someone that much money for his team not to win championships. Michael saw the offer for what it was: an insult meant to push him out of the job. Sick and tired of the bullshit he had heard with intensifying frequency all year, on October 18, Michael announced his resignation as general manager to become the team's director of major league scouting. It was at a significantly reduced salary, but Michael preferred sitting in a stadium somewhere evaluating talent than in his office talking to Steinbrenner.

A frantic scramble ensued to find Michael's replacement. Several player contracts were up; Buck Showalter did not want to commit to any new deal without knowing who his partner in the front office would be. He'd developed a strong relationship with Michael and, if he could not trust the next guy, why bother coming back? In the proceeding days the team asked about or connected with several baseball lifers regarding the job. Cubs scouting director Al Goldis. Red Sox executive Mike Port. Cardinals scout Jerry Walker. Rangers executive Sandy Johnson. Former Cardinals manager Joe Torre. None of them were interested, largely because they felt the job would come with no authority so long as George was there. Some reportedly even laughed when offered the position. "George doesn't believe that nobody wants this job," Michael told assistant general manager Brian Cashman. "Right now, the first guy to say yes has got it."[2] Finally, Michael and Molloy recommended Watson, whom Steinbrenner signed off on.

Attention turned to Showalter. The consensus was that Buck wanted to return. It was unclear how much Steinbrenner wanted him back. With a general manager in place, George went back to Showalter and gave him an offer: two years at $1.05 million. The catch was that Buck had to drop coaches Brian Butterfield and Rick Down. No reason was given. Most likely it was about reminding Buck that, at the end of the day, no matter how popular he had gotten, George was still in charge.

As with his offer to Michael, Steinbrenner had to know that Buck would not accept those conditions. In fact, he did not. Steinbrenner said, fine, Butterfield could stay but Down had to go. "I don't know why," said Down, when asked to comment. "I don't think I've had more than 10 words with the man since I've been here."[3]

Showalter refused to part with Down and rejected the offer. Whether Steinbrenner legitimately thought Buck's rejection of that offer was his way of resigning from the Yankees or if he simply used it as an excuse for what happened next has been debated. Either way, three days after Watson became general manager and just as Game Five of the World Series was getting underway, Steinbrenner issued a statement: "We tried but were unable to dissuade Buck (from leaving). I have nothing but praise for Buck and the job he did for us and I told him I am very upset by his leaving. I wish Buck and his fine little family nothing but the best."[4]

Showalter was stunned. He thought they were still negotiating and had expected a counteroffer. Instead, as he came home from playing golf, his wife called to tell him that he was no longer an employee of the only organization he had ever worked for in baseball. The passage of time, coupled by how the remainder of the 1990s played out for the Yankees, has clouded the memory of events that followed Steinbrenner's announcement. But there was no mistaking it: not bringing Showalter back was, at that moment, one of the most unpopular personnel decisions any New York sports team had ever made. This wasn't one of George's manic firings of a sacrificial-lamb manager who oversaw a bad team. This was the guy who had brought playoff baseball back to the Bronx. Players were shocked. Fans were irate, flooding the Yankees' offices with angry faxes and filling the WFAN airwaves with angry rants about the decision.

What happened next only made the decision seem worse. A week later the team introduced their new manager: Joe Torre. A former MVP and batting champion who finished his career with over 2,300 hits, unlike Showalter, Merrill, or Dent, Torre had an established history as a big league manager, starting with the Mets in 1977. One of the last player-managers in baseball history, Torre's term in Queens was memorable for how awful it was. In five seasons, his teams finished last three times and second to last twice. His .405 winning percentage was the fourth worst of any full-time manager in team history. Mercifully let go after the '81 season, Torre took over the Atlanta Braves, led them to a division title, then watched as his former team, the Cardinals, swept them in the NLCS. Torre was fired after two more years and spent the remainder of the 1980s as a broadcaster. The Cardinals hired him in 1990 to help lead the team back to its glory days. But the closest they came was a second-place finish; after five years of mostly .500 ball, he was fired in the middle of the '95 season. Fifteen seasons as manager. No postseason wins. Three firings. An 894–1,003 record. This was the guy they wanted to lead the team?

Torre wasn't even the first choice. The brass had discussed several possibilities, including former Red Sox manager Butch Hobson, former White Sox manager Gene Lamont, former Tigers manager Sparky Anderson, and even Davey Johnson or Tony La Russa. La Russa instead went to St. Louis to lead the Cardinals, while Johnson was on his way to Baltimore to manage the Orioles. The other options, for one reason or another, were not viable. Meanwhile, Arthur Richman, a Steinbrenner confidant who knew Torre from his days with the Mets, put in a good word for the Brooklyn-born ex-manager. That was enough for The Boss.

"No way am I here to say, 'Hey, New York fans, forget about Buck Showalter,'" said Torre at his introductory press conference, at which Steinbrenner was noticeably absent. "I want them to remember Buck

Showalter. He is a fine manager and he accomplished an awful lot for this organization."[5]

The reaction to Torre's hiring was brutal. The criticism ran the gamut of Torre being too nice to withstand The Boss's ire to his lackluster win-loss record to comparisons to Showalter's performance. All Torre's press conference and hiring seemed to do was remind people of Buck Showalter. *The Daily News's* back page the following day had the infamous "Clueless Joe" headline, but the column itself, written by Ian O'Connor, was just as harsh: "He thinks he knows, but he has not a clue. Joe Torre described George Steinbrenner in rational terms yesterday, calling him an unyielding competitor and demanding boss. He just wants a winner on the field, and my job is to give it to him. New day, old song. Torre's smile belied the moment. It is always a sad occasion when man becomes muppet."

O'Connor laid out all the stats that, by this point, fans knew by heart. The number of games Torre lost as manager. The lack of any playoff success. The difference in win percentage between Buck and Joe. "Only Steinbrenner can't figure out why this is a bad trade," wrote O'Connor.[6]

Others piled on. "What's a nice fellow like Torre doing in a place like this?" asked George Vecsey of the *New York Times*.[7] "I wish he hadn't taken the job," added *Newsday's* Steve Jacobson. "I wish Bob Watson hadn't taken the general manager's job. They shouldn't be working for That Man."[8]

Sports talk radio lit up with angry callers wondering how this decision made any sense. Faxes poured into Yankee Stadium decrying both the decision to get rid of Buck and that to replace him with Torre. It became such a public relations mess that, one day soon thereafter, Showalter came back to his Pensacola, Florida, home to find a visitor in his living room eating cookies. Steinbrenner had come to all but beg Buck to take his old job back.

"You just hired Torre as your manager," said Buck.

"I'll find another job for Joe Torre," Steinbrenner replied.[9]

Showalter had already met with Jerry Colangelo, owner of the expansion Arizona Diamondbacks, about managing the club. They would begin play in 1998, meaning Buck had a chance to build a team from the ground up.

"You haven't changed your mind on the coaches," Buck pointed out.

"You're just being stubborn about that," Steinbrenner replied.

"But Colangelo is letting me bring all my coaches with me to Arizona."

"I don't know what to say. I tried but I guess you've got to take that job out there, Buck."[10]

Showalter signed with the Diamondbacks days later.

The Showalter drama was enough to make everyone forget about the questionable splash the Yankees had made a week after losing the Division Series. Based on workouts witnessed by team scouts, The Boss's love of giving and taking credit for second chances, and his infatuation with the Mets, the team signed Dwight Gooden to a multi-year contract. Doc had finished his yearlong suspension for substance abuse and by all accounts had cleaned up his life. But just what he could bring the Yankees was an enormous question mark. He had not thrown a major league pitch in sixteen months; even back then, his abilities had appeared to be diminishing. Steinbrenner, however, could not resist. If Gooden did not work out, it would be on Doc. But if he did, George could take all the credit for the resurrection of one of New York's most famous athletes. After a one-on-one meeting where they talked about life, not baseball, The Boss signed Doc just as Gooden was about to agree to a deal with the Marlins.

"Keith Hernandez would've killed me if he'd known ten years earlier that I'd end up in the Bronx," Gooden later wrote. "God, we hated the Yankees back then—their arrogance, their so-called tradition, the airs they put on that New York belonged to them, even though everyone knew the Mets were a better team."[11]

Weeks after Doc's signing and Torre's hiring, the team announced its coaching staff. In charge of the pitchers would be yet another person associated with the Mets' almost-dynasty years: Mel Stottlemyre. The team, meanwhile, continued to drop key personnel who had helped rebuild the club. Mitch Lukevics, Bill Livesay, Kevin Elfering, and other scouts and player developers who had recognized, groomed, and shaped the first generation of Yankee prospects to succeed in years, were all let go without reason.

On November 20, the Yankees traded two minor leaguers to the Colorado Rockies for catcher Joe Girardi. Influenced in part by his new bench coach, former manager Don Zimmer, Torre pushed for the team to acquire the more defensive-centered backstop. That meant that Mike Stanley, perhaps the second-most popular player on the team after Don Mattingly, was not coming back. Problem was, like Showalter before him, Stanley had no idea that was happening. He had made clear his desire to return to New York. The team, pushed by ex-pitching coach Billy Connors, part of Steinbrenner's unofficial Tampa group of advisers, never reached out with an offer. The two had butted heads during Connors's time in New York and even Stanley admitted that they "did not see eye to eye."[12] Still, he was saddened by the news.

"I'm disappointed that they didn't even talk to me," said Stanley, when called about the trade. "I love playing in front of those fans. I was really looking forward to getting the opportunity to go back. I wasn't given that opportunity."[13]

Stanley wasn't the only disappointed one. In a time before advanced analytics and metrics, fans fixated on two statistics: Stanley's 18 home runs in 1995 versus Girardi's 8 (while playing in the most hitter-friendly park in baseball), and Stanley's 83 RBIs in 1995 versus Girardi's 55. Stanley had never been classified as a defensive standout, with those offensive numbers making up the difference. Fans could not believe the team would make such a seemingly lopsided trade-off.

The next day, at 10:00 a.m., a carefully worded statement began printing out in fax machines across the tristate area. "Don Mattingly was unable to commit, at this time, to playing Major League Baseball next year," it read, in the first paragraph.[14] While the rest of the statement said little of actual substance, Mattingly gave the team his blessing to move on without him in 1996. He did not retire. He did not declare he would play somewhere else. He did not say he would return to New York at some point. The Captain left the door wide open for all possibilities but one: he was no longer the New York Yankees' starting first baseman. Steinbrenner had been prepared to offer him a one-year, $2.5 million contract to return. Mattingly, however, wanted to step away from baseball for a while and decide just what, exactly, he wanted to do with his life. The lack of detail, coupled with the fact that Mattingly disappeared with his family on a road trip somewhere in Florida, left plenty of speculation. Maybe he would sign with the Cardinals, the team closest to his hometown of

Evansville, Indiana. Maybe he would go to the Indians, not too far away either, who were looking for a new first baseman.

Even his leaving was not without controversy though. Those close to him said Mattingly was unhappy when, days before his announcement came out, newly crowned GM Watson publicly stated that Donnie would be making a decision within the next day. Mattingly had said no such thing to anyone; even Steinbrenner was mad that Watson had made it look like the Yankees were trying to force a beloved icon into a decision. It also appeared that Mattingly was unhappy that Showalter and now Stanley were not returning. Regardless, an era had ended. For the first time since early 1983, someone other than Donald Arthur Mattingly would be starting first baseman for the New York Yankees.

As reporters learned of The Captain's "retirement," another development took place. Randy Velarde, whose tenure with the Yankees went back to the days of Lou Piniella, signed with the Angels. Unhappy that the Yankees would not commit to playing him full time, Velarde headed west. In roughly forty-eight hours, the Yankees lost their three most popular players. The off-season was a full-blown disaster. Before the month ended, the team opted not to bring Strawberry back for 1996. "I don't understand, I didn't do anything wrong," said a floored Strawberry, who at that moment was playing winter ball in Puerto Rico for the Yankees' benefit. "I did everything they asked me to do."[15]

On December 7 the team pulled off its first big trade of the off-season. They acquired first baseman Tino Martinez, and relief pitchers Jeff Nelson and Jim Mecir from the Mariners in exchange for Sterling Hitchcock and Russ Davis. Martinez impressed the Yankees during the Division Series, so much so that they worked out a five-year, $20 million contract with him in advance of the trade. Tino hit for power, something they needed at first, and played excellent defense. Moreover, they felt the Tampa native had what it took to handle the pressure of replacing a legend at first base. Martinez grew up a Yankees fan, having always wanted to play for the team. Mattingly, who shared the same agent, offered his best wishes, providing a blessing that the deal sorely needed.

Nelson, the tall righty with the sweeping, nearly side-arm delivery, was death to right-handed batters and had also made an impression on the team during the five games in October. Meanwhile, the Yankees had held out trading Davis for some time. Originally a shortstop, he was viewed as a possible third baseman of the future, with a lightning-quick bat that drew comparisons to former Rookie of the Year Bob Horner. But Davis became expendable once the team brought Boggs back on a two-year deal. To complete the trade, they had to include either Pettitte or Hitchcock. They kept Pettitte, yet another fortunate break. They saw a brighter future for the Texan and were somewhat leery of Hitchcock's brashness and comments to the press.

Still, the trade began to expose the wear and tear that had already engulfed the new general manager. Word of the deal leaked out the day before it was announced. When contacted by a reporter, Watson claimed he knew nothing: "I'm not aware of that. I haven't spoken to Mr. Steinbrenner yet."[16] The comment put Watson in a lose-lose situation. He either truly did not know what was happening, which would be a damning indictment of his authority as GM, or he was outright lying to reporters, which, while understandable given Steinbrenner's known hatred for deals leaking before he could announce them, was a bad way to foster relationships with the fourth estate. It would happen again . . . and again . . . and again. In truth, Watson had largely not known about the trade. Steinbrenner had given the responsibility of making the deal to Gene Michael.

Left unresolved as the New Year approached was the team's starting pitching. Pettitte was a safe bet for 1996. But Key was coming off major surgery, as was Pérez. By the time spring training came around, Gooden would be nearly two years removed from an MLB mound. Kamieniecki had shone down the stretch but was injury-prone. If the Yankees did not retain either Jack McDowell or David Cone, they would be in grave danger going into the next season.

McDowell signed with the Indians on December 14, making it imperative to bring Cone back to the Bronx. It looked like that was going to happen two days later, when both sides agreed to a deal in principle. But Steinbrenner learned that the Orioles had offered Cone a smaller contract, which Cone had rejected. The Boss decided he was not going to negotiate against himself. He lowered his offer from $19 million over three years to $18.55 million, reneging on the deal. For approximately half a million dollars, Steinbrenner nearly changed the trajectory of the American League East. Cone, irate, opened up negotiations with the Orioles again. Baltimore was making a splash that off-season, adding All-Star second baseman Roberto Alomar, closer Randy Myers, reliever Roger McDowell, and the utility man B. J. Surhoff. Add in Jesse Orosco, Bobby Bonilla, and David Wells, and Cone had been teammates with nearly half the people on the team. Plus, Davey Johnson was now manager. It seemed a perfect fit. The Mets then came into play, tipped off by John Franco that there might be a chance to sign his old friend. They offered Cone a deal and a chance to come back to Shea and finish what he had started. The idea was enticing, but the Orioles' offer was better. Cone was just minutes away from signing with Baltimore. It was so close that Yankee players were told Cone was going to their American League East rival.

The thought of Cone signing with the Orioles over a mistake he would have to own made Steinbrenner queasy. In a Tampa hospital recovering from eye surgery, George found a payphone and called Cone. He apologized for what had happened and made it clear he wanted Cone back: "David, what do we have to do to get this done?"

They discussed the money, but Cone added one more thing. He was tired of the hired gun label. He wanted a baseball home. A team he could live out his career and retire with. What better place than New York? He asked for a no-trade clause, which Steinbrenner accepted. As abruptly as it had nearly fallen apart, it came back together. Cone signed for three years at $19.5 million, the highest contract ever given a pitcher. The Yankees had their ace, saving the off-season from potential disaster. Even in his best moments, though, Steinbrenner could not help being Steinbrenner. The team's public relations director, Rob Butcher, had traveled back to Ohio for a long-planned family reunion as the Cone deal became final. Despite Butcher's having told and reminded various people several times that he would not be in New York, Steinbrenner was livid that his PR director was not there to announce the signing. When Butcher called to explain what happened and that he was heading back to New York as soon as possible, The Boss fired him, just days before Christmas. Word got out. Steinbrenner was again castigated by the press, enough that he called Butcher to offer him his job back. Butcher did not take it.

Butcher missed out on the team's final two big moves of the off-season. Largely thanks to his friendship with his agent, Steinbrenner traded for White Sox outfielder Tim Raines. Second to Rickey Henderson on the active stolen bases list, Raines was a future Hall of Famer who had played well in Montreal and Chicago. But his full-time playing days were behind him and just where exactly he fit in the team's outfield picture was a mystery. Looking to solidify the rotation, Steinbrenner also signed Rangers' lefty Kenny Rogers to a four-year, $20 million deal. The size of the contract raised eyebrows, but Rogers was coming off several good seasons in Texas. He was fond of clubhouse pranks, which meant he might bring some needed levity to a locker room that usually carried about in a highly corporate, stuffy manner. It also meant that, going into spring training, the Yankees had seven pitchers competing for five starting slots: Cone, Pettitte, Key, Rogers, Pérez, Gooden, and Kamieniecki. If no injuries occurred, two pitchers were going to be unhappy come Opening Day.

The off-season soon came to a close. The team had been completely reassembled, changed to a degree and manner that no Yankee team had ever been changed before. A new general manager. A new manager. Except for Willie Randolph, an entirely new coaching staff. Nearly an entirely new scouting department. A new first baseman. A new second baseman. A new catcher. New starters. New relievers. And no team captain.

Just as U.S. history is divided into eras by certain watershed moments, such as the Kennedy assassination or the Great Depression, so the history of the New York Yankees is divided into eras as well. There was everything that happened before 1995, and there was everything that happened after. The New York Yankees and New York City baseball would never be the same again.

John Franco strolled through the team clubhouse at Thomas J. White Stadium in Port St. Lucie. It was a late February day in the Sunshine State and the Mets had just completed an early spring workout. The team's seniority leader—the man who had witnessed nearly every twist a franchise could go through in just six seasons with the club—was desperate for the team to get back to relevancy. He had watched for years now as player after player left New York only to make significant contributions elsewhere. Franco would turn thirty-six that season, an age when most players start to wonder just how much time they have left in the game.

Franco pointed to three players across the room who sat at adjacent lockers.

"There's my ring," he said.

"You got that right," replied Bill Pulsipher, with Paul Wilson and Jason Isringhausen beside him.[17]

Generation K was all the talk of the Mets' spring training. The future was here. The team had played impeccable ball the last two months of 1995, with just two of the three rising stars. While Isringhausen and Pulsipher showed an ability to pitch at the big league level, Wilson shone at Double and Triple A ball, striking out 194 in 186⅔ innings. Combining the minors and majors, Generation K went 42-41 with a 2.80 ERA in 1995. *Baseball America* ranked Wilson as the number one, Isringhausen as the number two, and Pulsipher as the number four prospects in baseball.

The Mets now had all three ready to go for a full season. Expectations were through the roof.

"The only pitcher with more potential I've ever brought up is Dwight Gooden," noted McIlvaine. "He was the best prospect I've ever seen, and these guys might go two, three, four."

"These are guys you're going to hear about for a long time. In this league there hasn't been a pitching staff this intimidating in a long time," said Expos outfielder Moisés Alou, after facing all three.[18]

Green predicted they might each win fifteen games, something that no three pitchers this young had done in a single season since 1886. The only National League team in the last forty-five years to have even two pitchers twenty-three or younger win fifteen or more games was the 1986 Mets, with Gooden and Fernandez.

The organization and its fans could not help but be giddy. The chance to have three amazing, high-quality arms of this caliber in one rotation at the same time was like something out of a cheesy Hollywood movie. Still, the Mets were cognizant of an echo chamber being created around all three; they wanted to make sure the pitchers did not succumb to the pressures of New York or believe the hype before producing. The memories of Gooden and Strawberry were still fresh. "The big leagues are something that can bite you in the ass in a hurry," Green warned them in spring training.[19]

Still, not only were the three immensely talented, but they were also fun to watch. So similar on the mound, so different in personality. They bantered and joked with one another.

"I hope we're not alike," said Isringhausen said one day, while staring at Pulsipher.

"Don't worry. No one's like you," replied Pulsipher.[20]

Pulsipher was the eccentric of the group. The guy who wore his emotions on his sleeve, not shy to express himself in the clubhouse. Isringhausen was reserved, but willing to engage in the chatter that creates chemistry. Wilson, whose pregame ritual included a half-hour nap before each start, was the guy who smiled without adding a word, observing everything but keeping his thoughts, if he had any, to himself.

Newsday's Marty Noble described the three differing personalities in terms of how each approached the standard pitchers' fielding practice drill that happens every spring training. "Generally speaking," he wrote, "Wilson does it right, whatever it is. Izzy does it right most of the time. And Pulse, well, he doesn't do it wrong, he does it differently."[21]

The mood in Port St. Lucie was one of renewed optimism. The Mets had had a productive yet largely quiet off-season, a sharp contrast to their crosstown rivals. There would be no spending spree on top free agents. No eleventh-hour call to pluck players away from rival teams. No firing of staff or demoting of personnel because they went home for the holidays or because the team lost a series to one of their former managers.

They were content with their starting pitching, which featured Generation K plus the return of Pete Harnisch and Bobby Jones. It was enough to give the Mets a chance at the wild card. Offensively, the team was also going to rely on the kids. Brogna, Everett, and Alfonzo were expected to contribute, while at shortstop the Mets were finally going to give Rey Ordóñez a chance. Recognizing the lack of power and of a lead-off hitter, the team made two acquisitions that ultimately paid off handsomely. Lance Johnson, the reigning American League hits leader and a four-time leader in triples, signed in December to bat leadoff and play center field. They also traded for outfielder Bernard Gilkey, who had power potential, from the Cardinals. Johnson, Gilkey, and Everett made for potentially one of the best outfields in the league. Brogna and Kent at the corners also had potential to be one of the best corner infields in the game.

Potential. Hope. Youth. That was the name of the game in Mets spring training. Only four players on the team's roster had at least five years' major league experience; nearly three-fourths of the roster had less than three years' experience.

When the Mets began to roll over teams in March, fans could not help but think that, after five years—years that felt like decades—their beloved Amazins were back on track and charting a course for October. There were, however, warning signs, like Pulsipher leaving a game on March 18 because of elbow soreness. And Isringhausen, after pitching scoreless ball all spring, got pummeled in his last few starts. They were mere blips on the screen, though, as the team traveled north to open the season at home against the Cardinals.

Hope quickly turned to despair in the first three and a half innings of Opening Day. It was a miserable afternoon, cold and overcast with occasional drizzle. In many ways, it resembled Opening Day from eleven years earlier. Fans withstood the elements to see Jones give up six runs before being yanked in the fourth inning. But then, once again, hope.

Hundley's home run in the fourth made it 6–2. Gilkey's first home run on the team made it a 6–3 game into the seventh. Then came the play. The one that would be shown again and again throughout the season, the decade, and seemingly all defensive highlight reels for years to come.

Royce Clayton was on first with two outs when Ray Lankford slashed a ball down the left-field line. Gilkey cut it off before it reached the corner and, as Clayton rounded third and headed for home, threw a short, one-hop throw right down the line, almost spiking the ball into the ground. Ordóñez, the cutoff man, sunk down to his knees and, in one motion, cradled the ball, turned, and fired toward home plate. The one-hop toss, thrown like a laser while Ordóñez was on both knees, reached Hundley just in time to nab Clayton and end the inning. No one could believe what had happened.

"A marvelously instinctive play by a rookie who's never seen that baserunner," said McIlvaine afterward, also predicting that Ordóñez would lead the league in standing ovations.[22]

"Never, ever, ever seen anything like it," said Lance Johnson. "I'm still not sure what I saw. I can't wait to go home and see that on the highlights."[23]

Had the game remained 6–3, Ordóñez's play would have been a mere footnote. But, in the bottom of the inning, five straight singles led to four runs; Franco closed it out for a 7–6 Opening Day win. It was the first Mets comeback from a six-run deficit since 1980. After, the clubhouse felt like the second half of '95 had not ended. Hootie & the Blowfish again blasted through the room. Green even smiled, overjoyed that his team had stolen the game away. It was enough to start making people think this team could do some real damage.

"Everyone says we have a chance at the wild-card, but why not go for the whole thing?" asked Brogna.[24]

"If opening day is any indication of what the Mets have in store for themselves and their fans, then those woeful seasons of the early 1990's will quickly be forgotten, replaced by the kind of excitement that has not been seen here in nearly a decade," wrote George Willis of the *New York Times*.[25]

The good times continued three days later, when Paul Wilson made his major league debut in the rubber match-up of the Cardinals series. With his parents in the stands, having flown all the way up from Orlando, Florida, Wilson looked sharp. He yielded just a single run until the fifth inning, when he mistakenly threw an 0-2 fastball that led to two more runs. He left the game after six innings with a 7–3 lead, on track for his first big league win. In the seventh, though, the Mets tied a club record by committing four errors in the inning, eliminating Wilson's win and giving the Cardinals the lead. Rather than sulk, as might have been the case in years past, the Mets fought back in the ninth off Dennis Eckersley and won the game on a two-out single.

"My team came back to win. It was kind of ugly at the end, but as long as we came out on top," said Wilson, who wisely didn't lament his lost win but rather focused on his team's victory.[26]

The next day the *Washington Post* ran a story with an opening paragraph few would have thought possible in July 1995: "The most intriguing team in baseball is not the Atlanta Braves . . . It is not the imposing Cleveland Indians. And it is not the Baltimore Orioles, the New York Yankees, the St. Louis Cardinals or the Florida Marlins, the sport's biggest offseason spenders. Meet the New York Mets, who may be overflowing with more possibilities than any other major league club this year."[27]

No less an authority on the topic than Davey Johnson was quoted as saying that this Mets team could be as good as the one he had led to a championship ten years earlier.

The morning that story appeared, the Mets were 2-2 and a single game out of first place.

Second baseman Tony Fernandez dove to his right, trying to snare a ground ball hit up the middle. It was an inconsequential spring training game against the Astros just a week before the season began, but Fernandez went all out. As he dove, he crashed to the ground, landing on his right elbow. The pain was immediate. He rose to grab the ball, which he'd managed to stop, but quickly found he could not close his hand and pick it up. Fernandez had fractured his right ulna, ending his season and his Yankees career on the spot.

The injury, unfortunate as it was, became just another serendipitous moment in the team's path to a dynasty. It created a ripple effect that nearly resulted in a catastrophic trade by the club while ultimately securing the path of the two men who received the largest percentage of votes in the history of the Baseball Hall of Fame.

It began weeks earlier, when the new and vastly different Yankees assembled for the first time in 1996 at Legends Field in Tampa, Florida. The name said it all. If you were a Yankee fan, it spoke to the impressive history of the franchise. If you were a Yankee hater, it reeked of the self-indulgent nonsense that had grown stale from a team that had not won a championship for nearly two decades. Built with $30 million of taxpayer money, along with $17 million from Steinbrenner, there was no denying the facility was impressive. It was yet another indication of the change that had come to the Bronx Bombers. After three decades in Fort Lauderdale,

Steinbrenner fulfilled his dream of moving the team's spring operations to his backyard in Tampa.

It was an eventful spring. Torre began by assembling the team and telling them, "All of my coaches have been to the World Series. That's what I want. But I don't want to win just one. I want to win three of them in a row. I want to establish something that's special."[28]

Such a claim might ordinarily put a lot of pressure on a team. Here, it had the opposite effect. It created a sense of calm, backed by the notion that this guy believed in everyone in that clubhouse. That belief was shown when Torre anointed twenty-one-year-old Derek Jeter as the team's shortstop from the get-go. Torre, along with several members of the team hierarchy, felt it was time for the 1994 minor league Player of the Year to start shining. That meant Fernandez lost his starting job. That is, until Pat Kelly went down with a right shoulder injury. Fernandez agreed to move to second base. It gave the Yankees a veteran at the position who, when healthy, could still hit. It also gave them an insurance policy, should the rookie shortstop from Michigan not work out.

As spring went on, it looked like that insurance policy might get cashed in. Jeter appeared uncomfortable in the field, tossing errant throws and booting grounders. At the plate he was overmatched, a bad indicator in spring when pitchers are still loosening up and the talent is largely Single and Double A level.

Steinbrenner grew more nervous with each passing day. But at least they had Fernandez in reserve, if Jeter could not get his act together come April. Then Fernandez broke his elbow. There was now no one else to play shortstop for the New York Yankees but the struggling kid. The Boss would not have it. He was not putting a $52 million team on the field just so the Yankees could start a bumbling, no-hit shortstop.

Desperately seeking another shortstop, the Yankees reached out to the Mariners about veteran Félix Fermín. He was no big bopper, but Fermín would be a steady presence on the field and in the lineup. Seattle, with Alex Rodriguez now ensconced at short, was willing to make a trade. They wanted Mariano Rivera. In hindsight, the deal sounds like sheer lunacy, the kind of thing an irate caller might propose on WFAN at one in the morning. At the time, however, it was not so far-fetched. Rivera shone in the Division Series, but he was still the guy who got rocked in nearly all of his starts in '95. He had yet to develop the cut fastball that would make him the most famous closer in history. In March 1996 Mariano Rivera was just a middle reliever with potential—nothing more, nothing less.

Pushing the deal was Clyde King, a former team manager and general manager who was one of Steinbrenner's Tampa Kitchen Cabinet. The proposed trade drew intense controversy within the organization, so much so that a meeting was called in Joe Torre's office with the team hierarchy, including Steinbrenner. People took turns explaining where they stood; King said he felt Jeter was just not ready yet and the team needed a backup plan. After much back and forth, Michael stood up and made clear he thought the idea was insane. "You promised you wouldn't do this," Michael near screamed at The Boss, referring to a deal that had been made in the off-season to give Jeter at least half a season without interference or trades.[29] Stick had personally worked hard to ensure that none of the team's blue-chip prospects were traded during his time as general manager. Even if that was not his job anymore, he would be damned if someone was going to undo all his work before things had even got off the ground.

Michael won out. The deal was not made. Jeter remained the shortstop and Rivera remained a Yankee. Fermin had sixteen more at bats in his career before it was over. The team had avoided making perhaps the worst trade in baseball history, while setting Jeter on the path of a storied career.

Even with the shortstop situation settled, the starting pitching created another headache for Torre. Days before breaking for the regular season, Cone, Pettitte, and Key were etched into the rotation. Gooden also secured a spot, despite having had a train wreck of a spring where he went 0-3 with an 8.88 ERA.

Doc was not fooling hitters with his curve nor overpowering them with his fastball. Steinbrenner, however, was not going to let go of his human-interest story that easily. Gooden was in the rotation. That left Rogers, Pérez, and Kamieniecki fighting for the last spot. The idea that he was fighting for that spot was news to Rogers, who could not fathom that the Yankees had invested that much money in him to sit in the bullpen. But his spring numbers were just as bad as Gooden's, leaving Torre what he felt was no choice. Two days before the season started, he named Pérez as the fifth starter. Rogers, irate, told people he would tear up his contract if he began the year in the bullpen. The next day, in his last start of the spring, Pérez's fastball dropped ten miles an hour in velocity. The Yankees were horrified. The balky right elbow that had doomed Pérez in '95 had doomed him once more. He required season-ending surgery and never pitched in the majors again. With that news, Rogers was back in the rotation, but still felt bitter over the perceived slight. The episode did not reflect positively on Torre, who seemed to have needlessly bungled the decision. The Yankees did not exactly appear a team to reckon with as they left Florida and headed to Cleveland for Opening Day.

The concerns about Derek Jeter playing shortstop lasted until the third pitch of the season's fifth inning. Batting ninth for the Yankees on Opening Day in Cleveland, Jeter drilled a Dennis Martínez fastball deep into the left-field stands at Jacobs Field. The home run, his first in the majors, was a statement to all those who doubted him. No Yankee rookie had homered on Opening Day in twenty-seven years. Two innings later, with the Yankees clinging to a 2–0 lead, Jeter sprinted into short left field to make an over-the-shoulder catch, à la Willie Mays in the 1954 World Series, to end the inning. The Yankees won 7–1 and Jeter was the star.

"Lucky," was how he described his home run. And his catch in short left? That was "a lucky play," too.[30] The first rookie to start at shortstop on Opening Day for the Yankees since 1962 was a hit. His defensive play drew comparisons to Ordóñez, though Jeter was having none of it.

"Rey and I are good friends and I saw his play on 'SportsCenter,'" remarked Derek, who had come to know Ordóñez during their days in the minor leagues. "But I didn't say, 'OK, Rey had a good game so I have to have a good game.'"[31]

Try as he might, though, Jeter could not stop the brewing fan battle that harked back to the days when people would argue over who was better, Keith Hernandez or Don Mattingly. The two were polar opposites away from the field. Jeter said everything and nothing to the press, giving them access and quotes for the next day's paper without ever raising eyebrows, a trait he learned from Mattingly. Ordóñez's Cuban upbringing made him distrustful of authority. He was especially private. On the field, the first few months of their career drew such frequent comparisons that, throughout the spring and summer, Yankee and Mets fans argued passionately over who was the better defensive shortstop, the better offensive shortstop, and the better overall shortstop. After a single month, when Jeter's average dipped below .300 and Ordóñez was hitting .342, Mets fans claimed they had the better guy in every aspect.

It created renewed interest in the rivalry after ten years in which, largely, one team was good while the other slogged through the season. Jeter kept hitting through the team's first five games, sporting a .333 average as the Yankees hosted their home opener against the Royals on a frigid afternoon. At noon snow began falling, then a full-on storm engulfed the field. Temperatures were just high enough to keep the snow from accumulating; the game went on as planned. The customary pregame player introductions were scrapped, ostensibly because of the weather but perhaps also out of concern over how the fans would react to certain names. When the lineups were announced, boos could be heard for both Girardi and Martinez. "You sense in the stands, when you introduce Tino, when you introduce Girardi, some grumbling because there are a couple of favorites who aren't here any more," said Torre. "But I'm sure when they get a chance to see them play, they'll be pleased with what we have."[32]

Meanwhile, a group of local politicians and some fans staged a protest outside the stadium against a recently announced plan to move the team to a new stadium located near Penn Station in Manhattan. For years, Steinbrenner had grumbled about fans not coming to the park; he blamed the surrounding area for making people too afraid to attend a game. A new stadium, he argued, would boost attendance, while allowing the Yankees to create a modern park with an abundance of luxury boxes that would also fill team coffers. The protesters disagreed, highlighting crime statistics that disproved the security-related issues The Boss kept touting. "George wants to move to the West Side? How about he leaves the ballclub and moves himself to the West Side of Kansas," said fan Charlie Gordon.[33]

Even with the snow, the booing, and the protests, the Yankees pulled out a 7–3 win. Over the next two and a half weeks, they stayed above water but never found a groove. A few wins here. A few losses there. Jeter continued to impress. Others not so much. Martinez, desperate to show fans what he was capable of and pressing too hard, went 3 for his first 34. He failed to drive in a run until the tenth game of the season and did not hit his first Yankee home run until his eighteenth game of the year. Fans were all over him. Girardi hit .234 with 3 runs driven in while Mike Stanley was in Boston hitting over .300 again. Gooden's first three starts were abysmal: 20 hits, 11 walks, 17 runs allowed, 3 losses. Hitters teed off on anything Doc threw; the team could not keep putting him out on the mound, feel-good story or not. He was one more bad start from being sent down or released.

Heading into Baltimore on April 30 for two games, the Yankees were 12-10, not overly impressive but just a half-game behind the Orioles. It was only April, but these games were important. The team needed to win or risk falling out of the division race just a month into the season. What proceeded was ten hours' worth of baseball and two grueling victories for New York.

In the first game, the Yankees fell behind 9–4 when Pettitte failed to record an out after the first inning. A five-run rally in the fifth tied it. Then Martinez, in the biggest moment yet of his short Yankees career, hit a three-run home run in the seventh to give his team the lead. Ultimately, New York pulled out a 13–10 win in the longest nine-inning game in history, to that point. There were 400 pitches thrown, 96 different baseballs used, eight pitching changes, two ejections, and four lead changes. And it wasn't even the most interesting game of the series.

That honor went to the second game, which extended into the fifteenth inning when Martinez came to the plate with one out and the bases loaded. Both sides were exhausted. The Orioles squandered multiple chances to win the game, including in the tenth, when Brady Anderson batted with the bases loaded, two outs, and worked the count to 3-0. Jim Mecir, acquired in the Martinez-Nelson deal with Seattle, was on the mound. A native of Smithtown, Long Island, Mecir grew up liking both New York teams but became a full-time Yankees fan in the 1980s, when he felt too many bandwagon fans had joined the Mets' cause. One of his favorite players was Mattingly. Staring 3-0 to Anderson and pitching his first inning of the season, Mecir did not back down. "You can't walk him, that's worse than giving up a hit," he recalled, of the moment.[34] Mecir came back at Anderson and struck him out.

By the fifteenth, both sides had collectively used thirteen pitchers and twenty-three position players and tied an American League record with seven intentional walks. Pettitte, crushed the night before, entered in relief in the thirteenth. An American League curfew of 1:00 a.m. meant that, if neither team scored this inning, the game would be suspended.

Martinez came through, hitting an outside pitch just over the wall in left-center field for a grand slam. It was a signature moment for the first baseman, one that jumpstarted his season and helped silence The Stadium's boos. The Yankees won 11–6 and, by taking both games, created a one-and-a-half game lead in the division. At no point through the remainder of 1996 did they leave first place.

"I don't think after these two games that anybody can question the character, class and ruggedness of this team," said a spent but ecstatic Torre afterward.[35]

Returning home, the Yankees took six of their next seven games, increasing their lead in the division and creating excitement in the city. The anger and bitterness of the off-season faded. Just as the team was feeling great about itself, an unexpected jolt left some wondering if the Yankees would be able to hang on the rest of the summer.

The Mets' troubles started the day after Opening Day, when the team learned that Pulsipher's injury was far more serious than they'd thought. He had torn a ligament in his pitching elbow. The tear was an extension of the same injury that had caused Pulsipher to miss the final weeks of 1995. Devastated and shocked by the news, Pulsipher told reporters, "I just need a day to collect my thoughts." He then left Shea Stadium.[36]

The injury brought about the end of Generation K. At no point did Pulsipher, Isringhausen, and Wilson ever pitch together on the Mets, much less make it through a single turn in the rotation. On April 17 Pulsipher underwent season-ending surgery. He did not pitch in the majors again until June 22, 1998.

Green tried to put the best face on all of it. "Had this happened in 1994, we'd be scrambling like hell. We'll miss him. No question. But I don't think we'll miss him as much as we should if this were 1994."[37] Green was not technically wrong. The Mets had, days earlier, acquired starter Mark Clark from Cleveland, a capable pitcher who had his best overall season that year. The loss was more than that, though. For a franchise for which nothing had seemed to go right since 1988, it felt like Pulsipher's loss, in the midst of such grand hope and expectations, might merely be the first domino to topple.

After taking two of three from the Cardinals, the Mets lost their next five series. Wilson, so close to winning his first game, gave up 12 runs over 6 innings in his next two starts. While he turned in a strong performance on April 22 against Cincinnati, finally earning his first win, he ended the month with a 6.92 ERA, having allowed 45 base runners in 26 innings. The season was still young, but the next Generation K domino was falling.

The sluggish start made little sense just looking at the numbers. Gilkey began his Mets career with a banner month, hitting 7 home runs and driving in 23, while slugging .596. In a decade where few team acquisitions seemed to be paying off, Gilkey gave the Mets even more than they could have hoped for. Brogna began the year strong, with seven multi-hit games in April. Hundley and Johnson had solid months; Ordóñez, against expectations, was hitting like Rod Carew, poking and slashing his way to a .354 average and .820 OPS.

While most of the offense clicked, Harnisch, Clark, and Isringhausen sandwiched bad starts with good ones. The good starts, however, never seemed to mesh with the Mets' offense production, while the bad ones always seemed to come when the team was putting crooked numbers on the scoreboard. They scored 6 against Cincinnati on April 8 and lost 7–6, then 7 two days later to lose 9–7. They got 6 against the Astros on April 16 and lost 9–6, then 5 the next day to lose 7–5. Six against Pittsburgh on April 26 to lose 10–6. In Florida in early May, a potent Marlins offense was held to 13 runs in three games. The Mets were held to 6, losing all three.

Returning home, they showed some fire on May 11. Against the Cubs, the two teams exchanged early beanballs with one another. In the fifth, Cubs pitcher Terry Adams threw behind Harnisch. As warnings were issued, Harnisch began arguing with the Cubs catcher, his former teammate and good friend Scott Servais. Harnisch snuck a right hand into Servais's jaw, igniting an all-out brawl that lasted sixteen minutes. Everywhere you looked, players could be seen pushing and shoving one another, with bodies strewn across the infield and backstop, reminiscent of the on-field fight scene in the movie *The Naked Gun*. Just when it looked like order had been restored, it ignited all over again, with players moving in a human wave toward the front row seats just to the right of the Cubs' dugout. So many players were meshed together it was hard to tell who was tussling with whom, though at one point it was clear that Mets pitcher Blas Minor was going directly after Mark Grace.

Eight players were ejected, none with greater irony than Franco. Before the game, the Mets had held a ceremony honoring the pitcher for recently notching his 300th save, declaring that day "John Franco Day" at Shea Stadium. Getting thrown out of the game at which you were honored was a move straight out of the Scum Bunch.

Order was restored but, with Franco out of the game and unable to close, the Cubs tied it up in the ninth. In the bottom of the inning, Brogna sent one just over the wall in right to win it. The victory was more than just a win. It was vengeance. This team was tired of getting beaten and pushed around. It felt like one of those signature moments that can trigger a turnaround.

The intensity of it all lasted less than twenty-four hours. The next day they were two-hit by Jim Bullinger, who came into the game with an 8.02 ERA. "We must have left our emotions on the field yesterday," said Green. "We didn't have much today."[38]

At 15-20 the Mets were barely ahead of the Rockies for baseball's worst record. Two days later came the indignity of watching the second-greatest pitcher the franchise had ever had throwing his first career no-hitter in navy-blue pinstripes then being carried off the field at Yankee Stadium.

While play improved slightly, for the next two months, the Mets were, at best, a near .500 team and, at worst, the worst team in the division. The tepid play might not have felt so painful if not for the first-place performance of their crosstown rivals, or the fact that several Mets players were in the midst of fantastic seasons. On July 7, the final game before the All-Star break, Hundley hit his twenty-second home run of the year. Not only had he already established a career high just halfway through the season, but Hundley was on pace to break Strawberry's single-season franchise home run record and also challenge Roy Campanella's single-season home run record for catchers. His performance earned Hundley his first-ever spot at the All-Star game. Hundley and Gilkey were both on pace to drive in over one hundred runs; both had a chance to break the club record for RBIs in a season.

Johnson had been a godsend at the lead-off spot, hitting .322 and earning his first and only All-Star game nod. Alex Ochoa, after a cup of coffee with the team in '95, returned in late June and slugged .621 in his first fifteen games. On July 3 in Philadelphia, he went 5-5, becoming just the sixth Met in history to hit for the cycle. Even having missed the first two and a half months of the season, Ochoa was in contention for Rookie of the Year.

In a year, however, when home runs flew out of the park at a record pace, no one on the Mets, outside of Hundley and Gilkey, was driving anyone in or hitting with much power. José Vizcaíno hit above .300 but had driven in just 15 runs since May 1. He hit one home run. In 56 games played at the break, Alfonzo had no home runs and 8 RBIs. From May 5 to June 12, Kent hit only one home run. Butch Huskey, who had won an outfield job away from Everett by hitting .385 with 9 home runs in spring training, hit just 6 in the first half, only two of which happened with a runner on base. Brogna got off to another hot start, then went through 2-29 and 4-21 stretches as his play was hampered by a string of injuries. Finally, a torn labrum in his right shoulder put him out for the season in mid-June. The man who, at certain points, had been one of the few reasons fans tuned in for games over the last three seasons never played again for the Mets.

With 41-46 at the break, the Mets came back and played strong baseball for the first week. A home sweep of the Phillies put them just two games under .500 and four and a half behind the Expos for the wild card, with Montreal coming to town for four games. For all they been through so far, New York had a chance to put themselves in the postseason race by winning at least three of these games. Though the crowd was small, just under twenty thousand, there was real anticipation in the air as fans settled in for Game One. It lasted 14 pitches. Henry Rodríguez crushed a Harnisch pitch over the right-field fence, giving the Expos a 3–0 lead in the first inning. While the Mets attempted several comebacks throughout the night, they fell 7–3. Montreal won again the next night, when Isringhausen couldn't hold a 4–1 lead with two outs in the fifth. The teams split the next two games, but with the Mets now six and a half back and trailing four other teams for the wild-card lead, the season felt over.

A six-game losing streak clinched it; with that, the clubhouse discord returned. Players began brooding about another lost season in Queens and the commitment of some fell into question. Sensing that, yet again, the team was going to fall into an awful pattern of angst and self-pity, Franco and Hundley began publicly expressing concern about the state of the team. Where was the Mets' heart? Where was their desire? It did little. Instead, management stepped in to send a message that, if you were not happy here, you could play somewhere else.

David Cone could not understand it. Shortly after his Opening Day win in Cleveland, his right ring finger started to feel funny. In fact, it did not have feeling at all. The numbness was a mystery, even more so because there was not any pain that went with it. Not only could he still grip and throw the baseball, but he was throwing it better than perhaps at any other time in his career. After Cleveland, in back-to-back starts against Texas, he allowed only a single run while striking out 16 over 14 innings. Coney was proving to be everything The Boss had hoped for when he made that payphone plea in December. Even a clunker against Milwaukee was erased when he held down the Royals for his third win of the year.

Still, that finger was not right, and he needed answers. Cone checked into Columbia Presbyterian Hospital, missing a scheduled start so they could run a series of tests. The results showed no discernible issue; while doctors were cautious, he was cleared to get back on the mound but remained under constant observation. Even though his finger turned purple, he made his next start, going nine innings and allowing only two hits to Chicago, in a game that barely lasted over two hours. Cone had the lowest ERA in the American League.

After that start, though, it was not just his ring finger. Cone's palm and middle and index fingers had gone numb. Something was seriously wrong. On Monday, May 6, he returned to the hospital for more tests.

This time they found an aneurysm in his right shoulder. Not only was this a potentially career-threatening injury but a life-threatening one as well. Because they caught it early, doctors felt both of those dire consequences were avoidable. Cone was not certain, but he always wondered if his throwing 147 pitches in ALDS Game Five, an effort that had left his arm hurting for days after, led to the aneurysm.

When Cone might pitch again was anyone's guess. Some thought a late-season return was fully possible. Others thought that was wishful thinking. Regardless, he would be out for months, leaving the team without its ace starter.

Informed of the news after a 12–5 win over Detroit, Cone's teammates were stunned. "I didn't envision being in the rotation this way," said Kamieniecki, who was moved from reliever back to starter, to fill in for Cone. "I'm not gonna try to replace him. Hopefully, we can tread water while he's gone."[39]

"When I signed with the Yankees, I thought I'd be here with Darryl and Coney. Then Darryl was gone and now Coney. I'm just hoping he's OK," said Gooden.[40]

Doc's remarks highlighted a simple fact: Cone was gone and someone had to step up in his absence. Few thought that someone would be Gooden. Just ten days earlier Doc was near done as a New York Yankee. Needing something to change, he turned to an old and trusted friend for support. Mel Stottlemyre had seen nearly every single game Dwight had pitched. He knew this was not the same Gooden of 1985, yet Gooden was still using the same windup and delivery as if he were a twenty-year-old. Stottlemyre recommended that Gooden remove the ball from his glove more quickly, shortening his delivery to the plate. He also "taught him to use the sinking, two-seam fastball that I always thought he should have developed as a complement to his high-riser," noted Stottlemyre.[41]

Even with a new delivery, Torre had seen enough. After three starts, Gooden went to the bullpen. Before he could make his first relief appearance, Cone missed his start against the Twins to undergo his first series of tests. In his place, Torre gave Doc the ball. The result was one run in six innings, earning Gooden another start. The next outing was even better, as he kept the White Sox scoreless for six innings. The day after Cone's aneurysm was revealed, Doc took the mound at Yankee Stadium. As if willing himself to stand up and replace his fallen teammate, Gooden whipped the crowd into a frenzy by going eight innings, yielding only two hits, striking out eight, retiring the last twenty-two hitters he faced, and winning his first game since June 19, 1994.

The change was miraculous. The adjustment in Gooden's pitching motion had unleashed movement and velocity that had not been present in spring training or early April. He was not blowing hitters away or buckling their knees like it was the '80s, but adding just enough finesse to his fastball and curveball to keep hitters off balance.

Then came May 14. The Mariners were at The Stadium, the two teams playing each other for the first time since Seattle walked off the Kingdome field in Game Five. The Yankees were a vastly different team from that one, but there was still a feeling that New York wanted some measure of retribution.

Gooden got the ball. He was not especially sharp early, walking four in the first three innings. But he retired the side in order in the fourth and fifth, and got out of a mini-jam in the sixth by striking out Griffey. In the seventh, he retired the side in order and noticed that, with each passing out, the crowd was getting louder and louder. Gooden realized he had yet to allow a hit.

The eighth inning came and went—three up, three down. The Yankees had built a two-run lead against a familiar face, Sterling Hitchcock. In the ninth, with the entirety of the crowd on its feet on every pitch, Gooden sandwiched an out between two walks. A wild pitch moved both runners into scoring position. Doc responded by putting everything he had into a fastball that blew past Jay Buhner for the second out. Gooden later admitted that, by this point, he had almost nothing left. Pitching on a mix of fumes and adrenaline, sweat pouring across his face, Gooden got Paul Sorrento to swing under a curveball and pop out to Jeter at short.

A surreal scene followed. Teammates surrounded Gooden, lifted him on their shoulders, and carried him off the field as Tina Turner's "Simply the Best" blared from the sound system. Making the moment even more poignant, Gooden's father, Dan, was scheduled to undergo open-heart surgery the following day.

"Thinking of where I was a year and a half ago, I never even thought I would pitch again," said a still-beaming Gooden to reporters after the game. "And then to throw a no-hitter, I wouldn't have thought it was possible in my wildest dreams."[42]

The incredible had happened. Dwight Gooden, who missed a season and a half of baseball because of drug suspensions, who once sat in his bedroom with a loaded gun contemplating taking his own life, who had once been the most promising phenom in the history of New York Mets baseball, had just thrown a no-hitter as a member of the New York Yankees.

"I couldn't be happier," said McIlvaine, upon hearing the news. "The last few performances have really been Doc. I guess he's all the way back. It's ironic, with all the great years he had with the Mets, he never pitched a no-hitter."[43]

No matter how happy Mets fans might have been for Doc, that last point hurt. No Met had ever thrown a no-hitter. Now, their beloved Gooden had done it in just his seventh start with the Yankees. It was a bitter pill to swallow from their crosstown rivals.

Gooden's performance was no anomaly. He won eight of his next ten decisions through July and gave the team exactly what it needed as they waited for word on Cone's recovery. The Yankees continued to play steady ball through May and into June, winning just enough games to keep themselves ahead of the always-in-pursuit Orioles. Their style of play, heavily influenced by Zimmer and Torre's days as managers in the National League, was different from that of nearly every successful Yankees squad of the past. Whereas Buck Showalter's teams averaged 48 stolen bases a year from 1993 to 1995, Torre's Yankees stole 96; everyone got in on it. Five players had double-digit steals, including the catcher, Girardi, who finished third on the team in that category. They double stole. They hit and run. They caused chaos for teams in the field. On May 12, after falling behind 8–0 in Chicago, they chipped away enough to make it a four-run game in the sixth. Leading off the inning, utility infielder Andy Fox, who spent most of his time that season as a pinch runner, hit a weak ground ball up the line to first baseman Frank Thomas. Fox hustled as hard as he could out of the box, causing Thomas, who fielded the ball cleanly, to panic momentarily and miss stepping on first base. Fox's determination led to a five-run inning and a 9–8 win. It was exciting baseball, even if Steinbrenner did not think so because of the lack of home runs.

Maybe the most exciting element of the team, though, was the twenty-six-year-old Panamanian out of the bullpen. Mariano Rivera was not just getting people out. He was making them look overmatched. Not sure what to expect, Torre used him out of the pen in no particular pattern to start the season. But, in those first few appearances, it became clear that Mo's Division Series performance was for real. Hitters could not touch him. On April 19 in Minnesota, he pitched three scoreless innings of relief, striking out five. In his last inning of work, he gave up a one-out single. He did not yield another hit for fourteen innings. After Rivera pitched six total innings of scoreless, hitless relief against the Twins at home, Minnesota manager Tom Kelly had seen enough.

"This Rivera guy, we don't want to face him anymore," said Kelly. "He needs to go a higher league. I don't know where that league is. He should be banned from baseball. He should be illegal."[44]

Recognizing what he had, Torre inserted Rivera into the setup role, asking him to maintain leads largely in the seventh and eighth innings so that John Wetteland could close them out in the ninth. In May Rivera made nine appearances, giving up only a single run in 15 innings while striking out 14 and walking just 3. His performances became almost comical in how easily he dispatched hitters. When Rivera blew a save opportunity in Detroit on June 7, people wondered if he was injured. But Mariano continued to dominate and pile up numbers few Yankee relievers had ever touched.

Through June 20, the Yankees maintained a lead over the Orioles. Heading into Cleveland for a four-game series with the Indians, however, they were in trouble. Injuries forced Key to the DL and Pettitte to miss a start. That, coupled with a doubleheader to begin the series, meant New York was desperate for starters. Torre had no choice but to use Brian Boehringer in the first game and Ramiro Mendoza in the second. Boehringer had made a fleeting appearance with the team in 1995 and was pitching in the minors until the injuries forced the Yankees to call him up in June. In his first start, the week before the at-home against Cleveland, he gave up six runs in five innings. Mendoza, so shy he was practically mute, was a sinkerballer from Panama scooped up by the team years earlier as an amateur free agent. Expectations were not high, but he had good downward movement, enough to force hitters to pound the ball into the dirt for easy ground-ball outs. Pressed into service, like Boehringer, because of injuries, he won his debut start only to give up 19 runs in his next 17 innings of work.

Steinbrenner anticipated a fiasco. The day before the series began, he called an emergency meeting in New York to discuss what the hell they were going to do to get past this. Since the team wasn't in New York, he called Torre on his cell phone and put him on speaker, with the rest of the staff assembled in the room. Torre was in the midst of a golf game with several of his coaches.

"Where are you?" Steinbrenner barked.

"I'm playing golf," replied Torre.

"Well, while you're out in the goddamn woods having fun, we're trying to figure this damn thing out for tomorrow."

"How the hell did you know my ball is in the woods?"[45]

The line drew a laugh from those listening and exemplified Torre's cool demeanor under pressure. Having been fired three times before, the idea of having it happen a fourth time did not concern Torre in the least. He did not take George's behavior personally or let it wear on him; he often used humor to deflect tense situations. It was a path no manager had taken before with The Boss and it worked.

The Yankees climbed back from a 5–1 deficit in the first game, tying it with two runs in the ninth, then winning it with two more in the tenth. It was their first win of the year when trailing after the sixth inning. In the doubleheader's nightcap, they exploded for seven runs in the first three innings, while Mendoza pitched his best game of the year. It was the first time New York swept a road doubleheader since July 1990. The next day Rubén Sierra, struggling all year to drive in runs and gradually alienating Torre and his teammates with his mood, became the sixth Yankee to homer from both sides of the plate in the same game, helping the team prevail after trailing 5–0. In the final game, with Gooden on the mound, they completed the four-game sweep of the series, the first in Cleveland since 1964, and a season sweep of games at Jacobs Field.

"The fiasco considered so probable never developed," said Jack Curry of the *New York Times*.[46] The sweep was an incredible morale booster for the club, coming as it did against the best team in the American League and with a roster full of injured players. Unfortunately, between the first and second games of the doubleheader, Torre found out that his older brother Rocco, who had been watching the game on TV, died. Additionally, Torre's other brother, former major league player Frank, was in failing health, desperately in need of a new heart. These struggles—grappling with the loss of a loved one, waiting for news about the health of a family member—humanized Torre and, in turn, the Yankees, in a way that had largely not happened in some time. This, combined with their new style of play and the emergence of youthful talent like Jeter, Pettitte, and Rivera even made the team likeable. It was a crazy thought, especially for the faithful supporters of the Mets. "Likeable Yankees" felt like an oxymoron and, yet, it had happened.

At full capacity, just over six thousand could squeeze themselves into Midway Stadium. Located roughly equidistant from the downtowns of Minneapolis and St. Paul, in 1996 the ballpark was home to the Independent League's St. Paul Saints. Owned by the son of the eccentric Bill Veeck, the team drew crowds through an array of nontraditional events and promotional nights. They were interesting enough to have a television show follow them throughout the course of the season. It was there, at Midway Stadium, in June 1996 that a former big league star—a man who stuck out among his teammates and opponents for his sheer size and ability—was wowing the crowds with every swing of the bat and crushing titanic home runs.

St. Paul, Minnesota, was the best Darryl Strawberry could do. After the Yankees refused to pick up his option, despite his being a model teammate and staying out of trouble, Strawberry sat around waiting for other offers. None came. He started to wonder if he was being blackballed from the game, designated a nuisance whose powerful swing wasn't worth the inevitable headache. Soon thereafter, over a six-week span that winter, his agent Bill Goldstein, whom Strawberry loved, died unexpectedly and Strawberry's mother died of breast cancer. Heartbroken over the losses and disappointed but not deterred by his perceived blackballing, Darryl searched around for any place where he could keep playing the game. He found it in Minnesota.

Watching Strawberry play in the Independent League was like watching the 1992 U.S. Olympics men's basketball "Dream Team" take on Cuba. In 29 games, Strawberry hit .435, with 18 home runs and 39 RBIs. Extrapolated out over a full season, that was 101 home runs and 218 RBIs. And he did it all for $2,000 a month.

People began to take notice of what was going on in the Land of 10,000 Lakes, especially George Steinbrenner. The Yankees were now wildly successful, leading the division for weeks and taking down top team after top team. But The Boss could not get past how few home runs they hit. These were supposed to be the Bronx Bombers, and yet here they sat in June, ahead of only the Royals and Twins for lowest AL home run totals. That would not do. George wanted Darryl back.

Bob Watson did not. In mid-June he told reporters Darryl just "didn't fit" with the club and that he was 99 percent certain the team would not sign him.[47] Then word got to The Boss that the Orioles were interested in the guy leading the Independent League in home runs. There was no way George was going to let that happen. On July 4, Steinbrenner's sixty-sixth birthday, the team announced they were bringing Strawberry back to New York. The announcement embarrassed Watson, who had to play it like he was fine with what happened and that he had been a part of the decision, which he almost certainly was not. "I stand by that statement," he told reporters, referring to his comments weeks earlier, "but I can change my mind."[48]

George now had a second chance to give Darryl a second chance. "What sometimes gets lost was that he really believed that people deserved second chances, and sometimes third and fourth ones," said Willie Randolph, then serving as the team's third base coach. "Sure, he liked the headline attention, the gate receipts they might generate [and did], and all the rest that went with the great story, but he also wanted to give these guys [Doc and Darryl] another opportunity to do what they did best—hit and pitch."[49]

As if to prove Randolph's point, as part of Darryl's contract, Steinbrenner agreed to pay child support payments Strawberry owed to his ex-wife. The Boss wanted that slate wiped clean so Darryl could start over with a sole focus on baseball. Strawberry reported to Columbus to begin prepping for big league pitching and immediately hit two home runs. Three days later he was at Yankee Stadium. "Just hearing the news, I got chills again," said Doc, when told his former teammate was joining the club.[50] After six years apart, Darryl Strawberry and Dwight Gooden were back on the same New York baseball team, one that played in the Bronx and not Queens.

Strawberry's impact was immediate. Coming back from the All-Star break with four games against Baltimore, the Yankees picked up another sweep, giving them all six games at Camden Yards for the season. During the second game of a Saturday doubleheader, with Gooden on the mound, Strawberry hit his first two home runs of the season, the second a moon-shot that nearly left the stadium in right center. The sweep put New York ten games ahead of the Orioles.

Two weeks later, in another game started by Gooden, Strawberry hit a dramatic two-run home run, the 300th of his career, in the bottom of the ninth to win the game. This was exactly what Steinbrenner had in mind when he signed Darryl. Wins were great, but wins with home runs were even better.

That philosophy led The Boss to make his next big move. On July 31, still not satisfied that the team had enough power and fearful of facing a string of left-handed starters in the postseason, he approved the acqui-sition of Cecil Fielder from Detroit. The deal was a shocker for the rest of the league. New York was ten games up and, while Fielder was widely known to be on the trading block, the Yankees were not viewed as seek-ing his services. But just before the deadline expired, they sent Sierra and minor league pitching prospect Matt Drews to the Tigers.

Drews never made it to the majors, and Sierra's time with the Yankees had run out. After not playing on May 31 in Oakland, he called Torre a liar, saying he'd been promised more outfield playing time. Torre was not thrilled about the comments, but, as was his style, he tried privately to talk things through and explain why Sierra was not in the field. It did not work. Moreover, while Sierra's struggles all year frustrated Steinbrenner, his unwillingness to take any sort of advice rankled the coaching staff.

By June the team had had enough. "We told him if he didn't make the adjustments, then he wouldn't play," Watson told the press during the Cleveland series.[51] Despite the tension between him and the club, he was devastated by news of the trade. "I've been in this league for 10 years, so none of this surprises me," said Sierra, as he began packing his things. "But this is hard, man. This team could go to the World Series. This is hard."[52]

If Sierra was heartbroken, Fielder was over the moon. Joining the team in Arlington in the middle of a road trip, the smile on Big Daddy's face as he walked into the visitor's clubhouse could be seen all the way from Jerome Avenue. The first Tiger to hit 25 home runs in seven straight seasons and only the second player to lead the league in RBIs for three straight seasons, Fielder was now the designated hitter on a ballclub seemingly two months away from the playoffs. In his first 11 games with the team, he hit 4 home runs and drove in 11 runs.

While Fielder's presence should have meant less playing time for Strawberry, Torre continued to find ways to get him in the lineup. Over a three-game series in early August against the White Sox, Darryl hit five home runs, including three in one game. Everything was working for New York. They had ridden out the Cone injury through the resurgence of Gooden and the steady pitching of Pettitte, on his way to a twenty-win season in just his second year. The offense had shifted from small ball to the "wait around for a three-run home run" kind of play. It was all working. The clubhouse atmosphere was peaceful, the chemistry visible in shirts sporting the team motto crafted by team second baseman Mariano Duncan: "We play today, we win today. Das' it."

On August 9 the Yankees were nine games up and sporting the second-best record in baseball. They were on top of the world. For now.

On July 29 the Mets traded Kent and Vizcaíno to the Indians for Carlos Baerga and former Yankee shortstop Álvaro Espinoza. Kent was never at ease in New York; his perceived inability to lighten up irked a clubhouse that for years had been known for pranks and roasts. It started as early as his first month with the team, when in Montreal players left some crazy clothes in his locker to wear as a prank. He did not go along with it. When talking to reporters after the trade, he remarked how the deal that brought him to New York had in fact helped the Mets head in the right direction. It was an obtuse remark that only highlighted what teammates felt about him. Few thought the team was better off trading away Cone in 1992; now, the Mets had almost nothing to show for it.

Despite all that, as so many had before him, Kent expressed sadness at leaving New York. "If Cleveland and New York play in the World Series this year, I'd rather be playing for the Mets," he said, in a comment sure to make his new teammates unhappy.[53]

Kent never blossomed the way they had hoped; his defense left questions about whether he could play third base (which, after 1996, he never did again), but he had still put up decent numbers. Baerga had been an All-Star second baseman with Cleveland in the early '90s, but as the team improved his numbers slowly began to fall until by 1996 he was having the worst year of his career. The Mets chanced that a change of scenery might spark his level of play. They even talked about how Baerga's well-known after-hours activities could be an added benefit. "The '86 Mets were a hard-partying team and a little loose at times," said McIlvaine. "Carlos brings that."[54] The idea that the Mets were embracing the extracurricular activities of the 1980s was enough to make Frank Cashen's bowtie spin.

As bad as April through July had been, August was worse. The Mets tied one series against the Marlins and lost the other seven series in the month. Only once did they win back-to-back games. The kicker was a West Coast trip in which the team won only two of nine games, including a loss in San Francisco, despite scoring 11 runs, and a sweep in Los Angeles, despite scoring five runs in each game. The team was a mess. It was time for yet another change. Much the same way Showalter's hiring in 1991 altered the course of Yankees history, the team's next move ushered in a whole new era of Mets baseball.

As with the previous year, a series of games against the West Coast teams in August potentially destroyed the Yankees' season. It began with losing three of four against Seattle at home, including a heartbreaking twelfth-inning loss after the team came back from an 8–0 deficit. California then took two of three. Heading out to the coast, they lost all three at the

Kingdome, a brutal reminder of what had occurred last October. While all this losing was going on, the Orioles kept gaining ground. Baltimore had made their own trade before the deadline, bringing Eddie Murray back to Charm City to bolster a lineup that was on its way to breaking the single-season home run record for a team. By the start of September, the Yankees' twelve-game lead was down to just four.

Meanwhile, the Yankees made a series of seemingly low-key acquisitions. First, they claimed infielder Luis Sojo off waivers from the Mariners to serve as a backup infielder. They traded Wickman and Gerald Williams to the Brewers for reliever Graeme Lloyd and infielder Pat Listach. A week later they brought Charlie Hayes back to the Bronx in a deal with the Pirates. Hayes would give Boggs a break at third during the last month of the season and serve as a right-handed bat off the bench. All three of these deals would impact the team, in some fashion, for years to come.

The Brewers trade, however, quickly became noteworthy for how seemingly bad it was. Lloyd, acquired for the sole purpose of getting left-handed batters out, couldn't retire anyone. In five appearances during his first week with the club, he allowed ten runs in less than two innings. "Graeme Lloyd, perhaps the most popular Yankee since Ed Whitson right about now," remarked ESPN's Rich Eisen, after Lloyd gave up four runs without recording an out to the Angels.

Listach had hurt his foot days before the trade but thought it was a minor injury. It turned out to be a broken bone. He never played a game for New York. The Brewers sent pitcher Ricky Bones as compensation, who gave up seven runs in his eleven innings as a Yankee. Then it was discovered that Lloyd was pitching with bone chips in his left arm, a likely reason for his continued pummeling on the mound. The Yankees accused the Brewers of conducting the trade in bad faith, knowing Lloyd was hurt. Eventually, they even sent Listach back to Milwaukee.

More than the Brewers, however, Steinbrenner was mad at Watson. He wanted to know how on earth his general manager could make such a bad deal, getting two injured players for two healthy, fully functioning players. The move sapped what little faith Steinbrenner had left in Watson. Shortly thereafter, a "source in the Yankee organization" said that Watson "is already out of here."

The source was almost certainly Steinbrenner. This was a tried and true tactic of his, going back twenty years. He had avoided doing this kind of thing all season, directing most of his comments about specific individuals to either Watson or Torre. But Watson had gotten the worst of it; now he'd had enough. If the Boss was going to take these things public, then the general manager was going to respond in kind. "It doesn't surprise me that he would do this, but it surprises me that he would it leak it without telling me," he told a reporter about the story. "I hope he would be enough of a man about it to come and tell me."[55] Watson began informing team personnel and some reporters that there was no way he would return in 1997.

The one shining moment amidst all this was that, on Labor Day, Cone returned to the mound. He'd undergone an amazing recovery from the surgery to remove the aneurysm, making it back sooner than many thought possible. Cone picked up right where he left off, taking the ball in Oakland and no-hitting the A's through seven innings. Concerned more with preserving his ace pitcher than with history, Torre took him out of the game after that. The Yankees lost the no-hitter in the ninth but won the game.

On September 9 the Yankees' lead fell to just two and a half games. There was panic in the air, even if Torre was playing it cool. Steinbrenner was losing patience. The idea of blowing a twelve-game lead to the Orioles, the team he had stolen Cone and Strawberry from, was inconceivable to him. The Yankees embarked on a seven-game road trip through Detroit and Toronto. Aided at one point by a dropped fly ball by their former teammate Sierra, they swept the Tigers and took three of four from Toronto. The Orioles matched them game for game and came to town just three games out.

The situation reached DEFCON 1 status when the Yankees entered the ninth inning of the first game trailing by one, but it was defused by Bernie Williams's game-tying single, leading to a win in the tenth. A split of the next two games gave New York a four-game lead. A week later, after Baltimore failed to make up any additional ground and 148 days after they had taken over possession of first place, the Yankees clinched the American League East title.

After the last out of the clinching game, Torre had tears in his eyes. "I got very choked up," he said. "At this stage of my career, that I thought was over last year, to know that we have a lot of veterans going for this thing, this could be the start of my greatest experience in baseball."[56] Fans threw confetti and toilet paper into the air and began chants of "We want Texas," the Yankees' most likely opponent in the Division Series.

"It's something good for New York," said Strawberry, just three months removed from playing ball in front of a few hundred people in Minnesota. "I remember winning on the other side with the Mets. Now I have a chance to win on this side."[57]

Four days later the team ended the regular season with a 92-70 record. The concerns and panic of spring training were so far away at that moment. The kids—the young players that Steinbrenner had for so long traded out of New York for spare parts—had been allowed to play and flourish. Jeter hit .314, becoming the first Yankee shortstop to win the American League Rookie of the Year Award since 1962. What stood out most, however, were his demeanor, calm presence, and maturity. In an August game at Chicago, Jeter tried to steal third with two outs and Fielder at the plate. He was thrown out. The normally reserved Torre displayed his anger in the dugout over a rookie making the last out of the inning at third base with a 50 home-run player at bat. Torre decided to wait until after the game to let Jeter have it. Derek stayed in the field for the bottom of the inning then, after the third out, headed to the dugout and sat right down next to his manager, as if to offer up his own head for the chopping block. "I hit him in the back of the head and said, 'Get out of here,'" remembered Torre, who could not believe a rookie would have the guts to bear such responsibility.[58]

Jeter also established a rapport with the team, perfecting a pregame ritual that saw him shake hands or touch fists with everyone in the dugout, followed by a rub of Zimmer's bald head. Then he would approach Torre and say, "This is the biggest game of the year."[59]

Even at twenty-one and just a rookie, Jeter was on his way to becoming a clubhouse leader.

Pettitte won twenty-one games and finished second in the AL Cy Young Award voting. Rivera finished right behind him after going 8-3 in relief while striking out 130 hitters in 107 innings, a 10.9 strikeout-per-nine innings ratio that was remarkable in a time when hitters still largely made contact. Bernie Williams, the shy, guitar-playing kid mocked just five years earlier by the Mel Halls of the world, broke through with career highs in home runs and RBIS while playing Gold Glove–caliber defense in center field.

Martinez overcame his early-season slump to lead the team in RBIS. Girardi hit .294 and drew fan support through his all-out hustle on the bases and game-calling behind the plate. Wetteland recovered from his disastrous 1995 ALDS performance to lead the league in saves.

George's contingent of ex-Mets had all come through. Gooden stepped up in Cone's absence, finishing the year 11-7 and giving the team innings at a time where the bullpen was seriously depleted. Toward the end of the year, his arm gave out from fatigue, likely a result of not having pitched in nearly two years, distorting some of his final season numbers. He was unavailable for the postseason, but the team would never have made it that far without his performance. Strawberry put up eleven home runs in less than half a season, providing the pop Steinbrenner was looking for. Cone came back to win three games down the stretch, reestablishing himself as the team's ace, heading into the playoffs.

No matter the success, though, every single player, every single coach, and Joe Torre was fully aware of one thing: it would mean nothing to George Steinbrenner if the Yankees did not get to the World Series.

Bleary-eyed players filed out of the Mets' chartered plane shortly after two-thirty in the morning on Monday, August 26. The team came back from its West Coast trip 12 games out of the wild-card spot, with just 31 games left in the season. Since July, only one team in baseball had played worse. The previous day, in Los Angeles, Franco had blown a 5–4 lead with two outs in the eighth inning. Three singles and a walk later, it was 6–5 Dodgers. That's how the game ended, the 478th and final loss of Dallas Green's managerial career. "I think we've hit rock bottom. We may have passed rock bottom," said Franco, after the loss.[60]

As Green and coaches Greg Pavlick and Bobby Wine left the plane, Mets vice president Dave Howard informed all three that McIlvaine wanted to see them at eleven that morning at Shea. The purpose of the meeting was clear, even more so because it was an off day. Green had been on thin ice for some time now. The year before, when the Mets were having their resurgent second half, Green was just what the young players needed. Now, with the team set to play meaningless baseball the entire month of September, Green was the opposite of what the young players needed. His abrasive manner no longer got through to anyone; in fact, it might have hurt the growth of some.

The two remaining members of Generation K had, like the team, struggled through the season. Isringhausen displayed flashes of brilliance through the first two months. Then in June he gave up six runs in back-to-back starts and eight runs in his last appearance of the month. His July was no better. Worse, people began to question his heart. While he didn't see it this way, there were whispers in the clubhouse that he was not as motivated as he had been the year before. Green certainly thought so. He publicly complained that the pitcher was relying just on his talent alone and had not educated himself about aspects of the game. In mid-August, after an appearance that saw his ERA climb to 4.85, the team placed him on the disabled list, ostensibly because of a pulled rib-cage muscle. Really, it was more meant to give him time to clear his head.

Isringhausen's struggles paled next to Wilson's. After his promising debut, the righty went 1-5 with a 7.13 ERA in his first 10 starts. His control was off and, when it wasn't, he was getting battered left and right. In June an MRI revealed a tear in the cartilage lining his pitching shoulder. The hope was that the injury had caused the poor results and that, with some time off on the disabled list, Wilson could come back and pitch to his expectations. After six weeks, Wilson returned and it looked fully healed. At the end of July, he one-hit the Pirates for eight innings, though he still got a no-decision. But, in August, he gave up 22 earned runs in his first four starts of the month, losing all four games. Wilson was 4-10 with a 6.55 ERA.

The combined performances were too much for Green, who, after Wilson was hit for six runs in a game against San Diego, remarked that Isringhausen and Wilson "don't belong in the major leagues. That might sound harsh and negative, but what have they done to get here?"[61] It was exactly the kind of comment Green had been hired to make three years earlier because Jeff Torborg would never have said such a thing publicly. Now, it was exactly the kind of comment that would get Green fired, because the Mets no longer wanted a manager who said such things publicly. The remark was not only a smack at the two young pitchers, but a shot at the front office, which decided Dallas was finished. Green knew it. This was the man who had directly challenged Steinbrenner to fire him in 1989. He recognized the signs. So when Howard asked him to be at Shea later that morning, Green could see the end of the line.

After getting a few hours' sleep, Green and his two coaches headed to Shea for their meeting. Shortly thereafter, they were all fired. Dallas ended his managerial career with the Amazins at 229-283. He had the distinction of being Mets manager for four years without having managed a full season. The Mets had now fired four managers during the decade. It was just one more than the Yankees had canned, but it felt like fifty more. Still, Green's firing, while not provoking nearly the level of anger seen over Showalter the previous fall, was not a popular decision in the way that Harrelson's or Torborg's was. There were several players who enjoyed his style and thought he was doing the best with what he had. Hundley, as catchers often do with aggressive managers, bore the brunt of many of Green's criticisms. But he felt Green had been good for him, molding him into a better player.

Fans were not happy either. "What's the matter with them? I like Dallas Green," remarked Diana Mercado, as she bought tickets at Shea for the following day's game. "They should can the front office, not the manager."[62]

Any feelings of empathy or sadness for Green evaded Dwight Gooden. Doc had never gotten along with Dallas, particularly after an incident early in his tenure. In a game against the Marlins in Florida, Gooden put in seven innings of work under a blistering sun. With the Mets down 4–3, he told Stottlemyre he had nothing left in the tank. When informed, Green yelled for everyone to hear, "These goddamn guys, they just want to pitch their seven innings and get their ass out of there. They don't know how to pitch late in games. They don't know how to suck it up and finish the job."[63] It was an unfair criticism of Gooden, who hardly fit that profile. Doc went back out in the eighth and gave up three runs, putting the game out of reach.

Three years later, Gooden now ripped into his former manager after hearing the news. "Dallas' problems came from alcohol," Doc told the Associated Press, reflecting an anger that had built since Green harshly criticized Gooden's drug suspension two years earlier. "I have no respect for him, as a person or as a manager. The way he was with his players—he was your friend if you were going good, but if you went bad, he didn't want to talk to you anymore. It was 'we' if the team was winning, but as soon as it started losing, it was 'you.' It was never his fault. Nothing was ever his fault."[64]

Green eventually returned to the Phillies in various capacities, but his days as a big league manager were over. Replacing him in the dugout in Queens was forty-six-year-old former player, former manager, and former Mets coach Robert John Valentine.

"This is about utilizing a kinder, gentler approach to getting the most of those young players," wrote the *Bergen Record*'s Steve Adamek. "That is an approach Valentine is supposed to possess and Green . . . didn't."[65]

Bobby Valentine had been in baseball for decades and never, at least publicly, given off the image of a father-figure kind of manager. He was not a Joe Torre type. But Valentine was funny and outspoken, sometimes to his detriment. Above all, he was smart. Bobby Valentine knew baseball. He knew what could work; if he didn't know if it could work, he was not afraid to try it anyway. He was a mix of Casey Stengel's wit, Gil Hodges's baseball know how, and Davey Johnson's inventiveness. None of that seemed apparent when he became Mets manager in 1996. In fact, the idea that Valentine was the kinder, gentler alternative for Mets manager was laughable to some.

Born in Stamford, Connecticut, Valentine was a multi-sport athlete as a teenager, excelling in both football and baseball. He became the only football player in the history of the state to be voted All-American three years in row. Recruited to play football out of Rippowam High School by USC in 1967, Valentine played baseball that summer in the Cape Cod Baseball League in Massachusetts.

"I told them that I would treat Bobby like a son, that they had nothing to worry about," said NHL Hall of Famer Lou Lamoriello, who, as manager of the league's Yarmouth Indians, met with Valentine's parents to ask that their son join his team. "I guess it worked because they agreed to let him come to the Cape, where he played extremely well against some of the best college ballplayers in the country."[66]

A year later, the Dodgers selected Valentine fifth overall in the draft; he chose them over USC. He made his debut a year later, appearing in five games, all as a pinch runner. Playing nearly every infield position and the outfield, Bobby became a permanent part of the team in 1971. Injuries soon took their toll, in no small part because Valentine did everything full bore. He fractured a cheekbone, broke his nose, separated his shoulder, and suffered from bone spurs. In May 1973, after being traded to the Angels, he fractured his leg running into the wall at Anaheim Stadium, missing the rest of the season. The bone was set incorrectly, and he never truly regained the speed for which he was known. Over the next several seasons, Valentine was limited to part-time playing duty, going from the Angels to the Padres to the Mets. In a season and a half with the Mets, he hit just .222, with a higher on-base than slugging percentage. Before he turned thirty, his playing career was over.

Valentine joined the Mets organization in 1982 as a minor league baserunning instructor. In little time, he impressed many with his instincts and coaching ability. It was enough that, in just one season, he joined the big league club as third base coach, staying in the position despite the managerial changes from George Bamberger to Frank Howard to Davey Johnson.

Five weeks into the 1985 season, the Texas Rangers gave Valentine his first managerial job. It was a rocky experience over the seven and a half seasons he was there. A strong, second-place finish in 1986 was followed by two losing seasons and two seasons just above .500. As the Rangers struggled year after year, Valentine began being "perceived as headstrong and egotistical," alienating players and personnel.[67] When Rangers pitchers suffered through a string of arm injuries, the blame fell on Bobby, with claims that he overused his staff. The fact that Valentine's pitching coach, Tom House, advocated unconventional methods such as having pitchers train by throwing a football also came under scrutiny, though House would eventually be hailed as a pioneer for his science-based training methods. Valentine's habit of baiting opposing players from the dugout was seen as both attention-grabbing and overly annoying.

Valentine pushed back on all this. He was not the reason pitchers broke down. Nor was he the reason the team did not win: the talent just wasn't there. As for his on-the-field habits, well that was just part of the game. The pushback only added to the notion that Valentine always thought he knew better. After seven years, the Rangers decided to move on, letting him go in the middle of the '92 season. After he had spent some time with the Reds, the Mets hired him to manage AAA Norfolk in 1994. He left after a year to manage the Chiba Lotte Marines of the Japanese league. The club performed surprisingly well under a manager who had no experience in the league and a barely passing understanding of the language. The Marines finished in second place, a rarity for them, but Valentine clashed with upper management often. His methods, fairly common in the United States, were anathema to Japanese traditionalists. He engaged with fans, cut down on batting practice, and refused to allow starting pitchers to blow their arms out by completing every game. His popularity became too much for team executives, who made clear he would not be welcomed back for a second season. Valentine became so popular in his one season that Marines fans petitioned the team to bring him back, without success.

Valentine returned to Norfolk and led the Mets' AAA affiliate to a post-season appearance. He seemed like a different guy from the one who was constantly alienating people in Texas. His experiences had matured him, made him more patient.

"I think he's a great manager," remarked Norfolk's twenty-three-year-old outfielder Jay Payton. "He has us in second place and in the playoffs. That says a lot. He also has helped me personally stay focused because I've been in and out with injuries."[68]

That was exactly the kind of feedback the Mets wanted to hear as it became clear the team could not move forward under Green. By the penultimate day of the West Coast trip, McIlvaine had already made up his mind that Dallas was going. He and assistant general manager Steve

Phillips met with Valentine and Bob Apodaca, Norfolk's AAA pitching coach, that day to discuss taking over the Mets. Not everyone was enthused. Privately, co-owner Nelson Doubleday had doubts Bobby V was the right choice; he thought that he had been ruled out. McIlvaine himself was believed not to have wanted him on board, perhaps fearful that the outspoken Valentine would undermine him in the press. Fred Wilpon, however, was a Valentine fan. He'd wanted to drop Green and bring in Bobby before the season started. Now, he was leaving nothing to chance, putting his foot down and asserting who the new manager would be.

"I think you're looking at a different person than the man who went out and managed the Texas Rangers," said McIlvaine to reporters, an attempt to quell the notion that Valentine's persona could lead to the same problems the team was currently trying to dig out of.[69]

No one expected Valentine to come in and immediately turn the team around. Managing the AAA affiliate all year meant he hardly ever had a chance to watch a Mets game, much less witness one in person.

"I don't even know this team," said Valentine. "The important thing right now is for me to sit back and maybe listen more than I talk."[70]

Instead, he would do what Billy Martin had done when he took over as Yankees manager late in 1975. He would review the talent he had, weed out those who did not fit into a winning mentality, and recommend improvements where needed, all with the goal of success in the following season.

What he saw he could not have been thrilled with. In his first series as manager, the team was swept, continuing a losing streak that reached eight games. After his first two wins as Mets manager, they lost four out of five. The lone remaining highlight of the season came on Saturday 14 at home against Atlanta. Hundley had already broken the franchise record for home runs in a season by hitting 40. That number also tied him with Roy Campanella for the most by a catcher in a single season. Down 5–2 in the seventh, Hundley took an outside pitch from Greg McMichael and drove it just over the wall in left field for a game-tying, history-making home run. No catcher had ever hit more in a season. It was also the fourth-highest single-season total for a switch hitter, ever. The ball had bounded back into the field of play; Braves outfielder Jermaine Dye, not realizing he held history in his hands, flipped it into the crowd. Hundley eventually got the ball back.

It was the last joyful moment of the season. The Mets ended the year by losing 10 of their last 14 games after the Hundley home run. On September 26, one day after the Yankees clinched the American League East title, Wilson took the mound in a nearly empty Astrodome. He went five innings, giving up only two unearned runs. It was his last appearance in a Mets uniform. A series of injuries throughout the rest of the decade limited Wilson to minor league appearances or the disabled list. He did not step on a major league mound again until the next millennium. In his single year as a Met, Wilson went 5-12 with a 5.38 ERA and a 1.53 WHIP. Isringhausen finished 6-14 with a 4.77 ERA and a near identical WHIP.

A loss on the season's final day left the club 71-91 and in fourth place. There were some success stories that year. Lance Johnson put together one of the strongest and most forgotten seasons in Mets history, leading the league in hits and triples, while finishing second in stolen bases and sixth in runs scored. Gilkey put in what, to that time, was one of the best offensive seasons ever by a Met, setting the club record for doubles and tying the club record for RBIs while hitting .317, with 30 home runs. Hundley and Gilkey became the tenth and eleventh players respectively in franchise history to drive in 100 runs and the first pair of Mets teammates to drive in over 100 runs in the same season.

Overall, though, the season was a failure. Only 1.58 million had come to Shea, the lowest full season attendance in thirteen years and 670,000 fewer than had gone to Yankee Stadium. Even though the season was over, the Yankees' imminent postseason performance would make things worse. Still, while they did not know it yet, the pieces to bring the Mets back to prominence were already in place. They just needed a little more time.

Will Clark balled up his right fist, turned, and delivered a haymaker to the Rangers' dugout wall. The Texas first baseman then reared back and delivered another. Clark had just flied out in the bottom of the ninth inning in Game Four of the ALDS, with the tying runs on base and his team on the brink of elimination. His frustration was about more than just that one out. It was also about how Texas could possibly have found itself in this situation. They'd silenced the Yankee Stadium crowd in Game One, when home runs by Juan González and Dean Palmer gave them a 5–1 lead in the fourth inning that they never relinquished. In Game Two, González hit two more home runs before the end of the third inning, giving Texas a 4–1 lead.

Things looked glum for New York. But Fielder homered to get the crowd back into the action and, in the eighth, his single tied the game, sending it to extra innings. In the twelfth, an error on a sacrifice bunt handed the game to the Yankees. With the series tied at 1-1, events shifted to Arlington, a place that had, for years, been brutal to the Yankees. In Game Three, Bernie Williams homered in the top of the first and robbed a home run in the bottom of the inning. Still, the Rangers took a 2–1 lead into the ninth inning. Singles by Jeter and Raines led to a game-tying sac fly. Duncan then lashed a two-out single into center to give the Yankees the lead. Wetteland held it down in the ninth, putting his team one win away from the ALCS.

That win looked like it might never happen. Kenny Rogers did not make it past the second and the Yankees were down 4–0 after three innings. Sparked by Williams, New York cut the lead to 4–3. Bernie then homered in the fourth to tie it; a two-out single by Fielder in the seventh gave them the lead. "I don't care how you get it done," said Fielder. "I just wanted to get it done. In that situation, with two outs, with us with a chance to go ahead, I've just got to try to get that runner home."[71]

An insurance run in the ninth, Bernie's third home run of the series, made it 6–4. In came Wetteland. The Yankees closer had caused cardiac issues all year among players and fans. He allowed at least one runner in 42 of his 62 appearances, often putting the tying or go-ahead runs on base before getting out of trouble. The playoffs had been no different. In Game Two he allowed three runners in two innings. In Game Three, he put the tying run on base before saving the game. Now, three outs away from the next round, he walked the lead-off hitter, recorded an out, then walked González, setting up Clark to be a hero. One could not help but have flashbacks to Wetteland's last Game Four performance, where he recorded no outs before giving up a grand slam to Edgar Martínez. Here, though, he got Clark to fly out, sparking the punches that followed when Clark returned to the dugout.

The frustration was understandable. The Rangers had led in 18 of the series' 39 innings. The Yankees had led in only 9, 3 of them in their Game One loss. At no point did they lead in Game Two until the game-winning run scored. Both teams scored 16 runs and Texas had out-homered the Yankees. The difference had been the bullpens. David Weathers of the 9.35 regular season ERA, Graeme Lloyd of the 17.47 regular season ERA, and Jeff Nelson of the 4.36 ERA all erased their difficult regular seasons by combining for nearly ten innings' worth of scoreless ball. Rivera allowed only a single base runner in 4⅔ innings. In total, Yankee relievers pitched 19⅔ innings, giving up just a single earned run and only six hits. "We knew that if we could just get a couple of runs, our bullpen would shut them down and we would have a chance," said Williams.[72]

The bullpen—the component of the team that had created the most headaches in the season's final month—was now its saving grace. Wetteland, having disposed of Clark, delivered a wicked curveball to strike out Palmer and end the series. There would be no repeat of last year's performance. New York, despite trailing in the eighth and ninth innings of Games Two and Three respectively, and despite being behind 4–0 in Game Four, was moving on to play the Orioles in the ALCS. "It's disappointing" said Palmer, "because every one of the games was so close, and every one could have gone either way."[73]

Champagne and beer flowed throughout the clubhouse, so much so that players could not keep their celebratory cigars lit. The team enjoyed the moment before heading back to New York to prepare for the Championship Series. That it would be against Baltimore was apt. The Orioles had been chasing New York since May 1. Having dispatched the Indians in their ALDS match-up, Baltimore came to Yankee Stadium steeped in controversy. Second baseman Roberto Alomar had gotten into a late-season altercation with umpire John Hirschbeck, spitting in the umpire's face over what Alomar claimed was a derogatory comment. The public overwhelmingly turned on Alomar. The commissioner's handling of the situation nearly caused the umpiring crew of the Yankees-Rangers Game One match-up to refuse to take the field.

Alomar was suspended, but not for the postseason; he near single-handedly beat the Indians in the series-clinching game of the ALDS. Coming to New York, however, would be different. Fans had already engaged in dangerous behavior during the '95 series against the Mariners. Alomar was now a prime target. Moreover, after an incident in Game Two against Texas, where a fan reached across the foul pole to snare a González home run, a meeting was held with both teams before Game One of the ALCS. The Yankees were going to provide extra security in the outfield to prevent fans from leaning over railings or trying in any way to interfere with a ball in play. It was, said Davey Johnson, something they promised.

It all created a supercharged atmosphere for Game One. Pettitte struck Alomar out on a questionable call in the first inning, creating a frenzy. After the lead changed hands early on, the Orioles were up 4–3 with one out in the eighth when Jeter came to bat. Out in right field, in Section 31, Box 325, Row A, Seat 2, sat twelve-year-old Jeffrey Maier of Old Tappan, New Jersey. Maier, a Yankee fan and pretty good ballplayer himself, was not supposed to be at Game One. He was there with a friend whose family had originally asked someone else to attend. But Game One was rained out and moved to the afternoon time slot that had originally been scheduled for Game Two. That time change created a conflict for the original holder of Maier's ticket. Asked to attend instead, Maier grabbed his black Mizuno mitt and headed to the ballpark.

Maier watched as Jeter swung at the first pitch he saw and sent a high fly ball to right field. As the ball traveled closer and closer to the fence, several fans, Jeffrey Maier among them, began creeping toward the top of the right-field wall, hoping to snag a souvenir. As they did so, the security guard placed there, as part of the team's effort to prevent fans from doing exactly what they were now doing, stood and watched the play unfold. He made no effort to stop any fan from approaching the wall.

Orioles right fielder Tony Tarasco, a defensive replacement who had entered the game that inning, stepped further and further back until his body was pressed up against the wall. Facing home plate, he reached up and appeared about to make the catch. The ball then disappeared over the fence. Maier had stuck his glove out past the top of the wall and deflected the ball from the playing field into the crowd. Right field umpire Richie Garcia immediately ruled the play a home run.

"I pointed up," said Tarasco. "It was so obvious, which is what made my teakettle pop. I turned and looked right at Richie Garcia. Richie just looked at me and said, 'No, no, I thought that ball was going out.' I'll keep what I said between Richie and I but every single thing that came out of my mouth gave him reason to eject me from that ballgame."[74]

As Tarasco argued, the crowd went crazy. Maier, not fully realizing what he had just done, was immediately lifted onto the shoulders of a man he did not know as reporters rushed from the press box to track him down. Johnson argued with Garcia and was ejected. Baltimore filed an official protest, but there was nothing they or the league could do. It had been a judgment call by Garcia in a time when instant replay did not exist. Maier became a household name, returning home that night to find invitations to appear on *Good Morning America* and *The Late Show with David Letterman*.

"I didn't mean to do anything wrong," said the twelve-year-old. "It just happened. I thought it was going over."[75]

Years later, Maier and Tarasco ended up both taking part in a baseball clinic sponsored by the Mets. "We actually sat down and had lunch together. I learned a lot about the kid and what he actually endured when it first happened," said Tarasco.[76]

In the bottom of the eleventh, Williams homered into the left-field stands to end it. The Yankees and their fans had stolen Game One. "I usually say one play doesn't beat you in a ballgame," said Johnson, after the game. "But this is about as close as it comes to one play beating you."[77]

Baltimore managed to win Game Two, but they were still outraged over the Maier incident. Returning to Camden Yards for Game Three, fans sold gloves on foot-long sticks outside the gates. The Orioles maintained a 2–1 lead with two outs into the eighth, when Williams singled in Jeter to tie the game. The next batter, Tino Martinez, lined a double down the left-field line; when Baltimore third baseman Todd Zeile tried to pump fake Williams, he accidentally spiked the ball into the ground, allowing Bernie to scramble home with the eventual game-winning run. In Game Four, Rogers could not protect leads of 3–1 and 5–2, failing to get out of the fourth. Four home runs, including two from Strawberry, gave New York an 8–4 win. Game Five saw Pettitte hold the Orioles to just three hits over eight innings as the Yankees exploded for six runs in the third, thanks largely to home runs by Fielder and Strawberry. When Cal Ripken Jr. grounded out to end the game, the Yankees were back in the World Series after fifteen years. For the first time in his career, after a major league record 4,280 games as a player and manager without making it, Joe Torre was going to the World Series. After the final out, cameras panned to the dugout, capturing the Yankees' teary-eyed manager. "God, it was a long time coming," said Torre, after the game.[78]

"This time it is a lot sweeter," replied Strawberry, who hit three home runs in the series and established an ALCS record 1.167 slugging percentage, when asked how this team compared to the '86 Mets. "Eighty-six was a great team. But this is a very great team. This team has a lot of pride."[79]

The Yankees hit ten home runs, a record for a five-game ALCS. The bullpen, again, threw up zero after zero, with Rivera, Lloyd, and Weathers throwing nearly nine innings of scoreless ball. Williams, a year after Steinbrenner wanted so badly to trade him, won ALCS MVP. New York was 5-0 on the road in the postseason; five of their seven wins had come after trailing. After celebrating in the clubhouse, the team boarded a bus and headed back to New York. When they arrived just after midnight, more than four thousand fans were at Yankee Stadium, waiting both to greet their heroes and grab World Series tickets as soon as they went on sale. Boggs ran out into the crowd, high-fiving anyone in sight. Shortly thereafter, Torre, Jeter, Leyritz, and others made their way to the Official All Star Café in the city, where the celebration continued. The Yankees were the toast of New York. All they needed to do now was bring home the championship against the Atlanta Braves.

Jim Leyritz sat on the bench at Fulton County Stadium, reconciled to the Yankees' inevitable loss in the World Series. It was the bottom of the fifth inning of Game Four in the 1996 World Series and New York was down 6-0. They were on the cusp of falling behind 3-1 in the series.

After a week of celebrating the ALCS victory and prepping for the Fall Classic, the first two games in New York had gone poorly. In Game One, the Yankees had suffered "perhaps their most humiliating moment in their proud history," as nineteen-year-old Braves rookie Andruw Jones hit two home runs and Atlanta amassed 13 hits in a 12–1 win.[80] Pettitte allowed 7 runs before leaving in the third inning; the offense could barely touch the soon-to-be National League Cy Young Award winner John Smoltz.

"That was an old-fashioned butt-kicking," said Strawberry, of the worst loss in team playoff history to that time.[81]

"It was kind of like the Super Bowl," said O'Neill. "You wait a week, and then there's a blowout."[82]

Game Two was no better for New York. Fred McGriff knocked in three runs and the offense again could not put up any support, this time against Greg Maddux. The future Hall of Famer limited the Yankees to six hits and snuffed out their only potential rally when he induced Boggs to hit into a double play with first and second and no outs in the sixth. The final score was 4–0. The Braves, the reigning champions who had represented the National League in four of the decade's six World Series, had outscored their opponents 48–2 in their last five postseason games. They appeared well on their way to retaining their title.

In the Yankees clubhouse after, the mood was funereal. The idea of going to Atlanta and having to win, at a minimum, two games felt like a near impossibility. Perhaps the only person who believed it would happen was Joe Torre. Prior to Game Two, Torre informed Steinbrenner that he wasn't sure the team was focused enough to win the game but that they would go down to Atlanta (a town Torre knew well), sweep the Braves there, then return home the coming Saturday and win the whole thing at Yankee Stadium.

Steinbrenner looked at Torre like he was insane. The Atlanta papers surely would have scoffed at such an idea had they been aware of Torre's comments. When the Yankees arrived in Atlanta before Game Three, they were greeted by a flurry of stories and columns saying they had no business competing against the hometown team. One Atlanta columnist remarked that the Braves were good enough to beat the 1927 Yankees, considered among the greatest teams of all time. Another wrote about "stopping the World Series after the first two games because the Yankees had no chance of beating Atlanta's starting pitching."[83]

Three RBIs by Williams and an ulcer-inducing, tightrope-walk performance by Cone gave New York the victory in Game Three. Rogers got the
start in Game Four, having been told after Game Two by Steinbrenner,
as The Boss jabbed him in the chest, that he was "tired of talk. I want to
see something." Rogers told him he would.[84] But after giving up a home
run to McGriff to start the second, Rogers fell apart, allowing two walks,
a single, a double, and three more runs to score. He faced two more batters in the third, allowing both to reach base, before Torre pulled him.
By the bottom of the fifth, the Braves had a 6–0 lead. The Yankees had
never come back from a six-run deficit in postseason play.

Leyritz, reflecting the mood that many felt in the moment, turned to
Pat Kelly. The two were the longest-serving members of the team, the only
ones to have been a part of the Stump Merrill era. "At least we didn't get
swept," Leyritz told Kelly.[85]

In the top of the sixth inning, however, things began to shift. Since
that July day in 1990, when Steinbrenner was banished, events had con-
spired to bring the Yankees to this moment. Pettitte signed just before
reentering the draft. Rivera not being selected in the expansion draft.
Jeter passed over by five teams. Cone getting the payphone call from The
Boss. Gooden changing his delivery. Darryl going unsigned in St. Paul.
Hayes being selected by the Rockies, forcing the Yankees to sign Boggs.
Williams not being traded for Wells.

Everything had fallen just right to get the Yankees here. Then, like all
championship teams, they needed breaks on the field to go their way.
They had gotten that in pieces so far, with the Maier interference being
the largest. But starting in the sixth inning of Game Four, every single
break went New York's way. It started when Braves' right fielder Jermaine
Dye, while chasing a Jeter pop-up in foul territory, ran into the umpire,
and failed to make the play (though replays showed Dye taking the wrong
track to the ball, meaning he probably would not have caught it anyway).
Given a second chance, Jeter singled. Williams walked. Fielder then lined
a single into right that Dye misplayed, allowing two runs to score. It was
6–3 before the Braves bullpen struck out the side to prevent more damage.

In the eighth, Hayes led off with a swinging bunt, a ball that rolled
down the third base line and that, by all logic, should have gone foul but

did not. A single brought Duncan up as the tying run, but Mariano, in a terrible postseason slump, lined a double play ground ball to shortstop Rafael Belliard. Brought into the game specifically for his defense, Belliard misplayed the ball, absorbing it off his chest, and recording only one out instead of two. That allowed Leyritz, a defensive replacement an inning earlier, to bat as the tying run. Leyritz had become Pettitte's personal catcher; with Andy starting in Game Five, this meant The King would be in the starting lineup the next day.

"I remember looking at Darryl Strawberry and saying, 'Straw, I only have two bats tomorrow to face Smoltz. Can I borrow one of yours?' He had a brand new box of Mizunos so he said, 'Yeah, take one of those.'"[86]

Using one of Strawberry's bats, Leyritz stepped into the box against Braves closer Mark Wohlers, who, with a fastball reaching nearly 100 miles per hour, was one of the hardest throwers in baseball. Leyritz was a dead fastball hitter; after he timed a few of Wohlers's heaters, the pitcher opted instead to throw sliders. On the sixth pitch of the at bat, Wohlers hung a slider that Leyritz hit over the left-field wall, tying the game. An ecstatic Yankee bench could be heard screaming, as the Braves' home park fell silent.

It can never be known with certainty, but if Jeter's pop-up hadn't been dropped, or if Dye had not misplayed Fielder's hit, or if Hayes's dribble had gone foul, or it Belliard had handled Duncan's shot cleanly, or if Wohlers had not hung a slider, the course of Game Four, the World Series, and the 1990s might have been drastically different. But everything went the Yankees' way, a pattern that continued when the game entered the tenth inning. After Braves pitcher Steve Avery recorded the first two outs, the Yankees loaded the bases, in part because manager Bobby Cox opted to walk Williams intentionally, with runners on first and second.

"Smart move," said Cox, of the walk. "Why not? He is the best hitter on their team. He has knocked the living hell out of us."[87]

Torre sent up the last position player he had on his bench, Boggs, who nearly struck out looking twice before drawing a walk to give the Yankees the lead. On the next pitch, first baseman Ryan Klesko dropped a Hayes pop-up, allowing another run to score. In the bottom of the inning, Wetteland nearly gave up a game-tying home run to Dye. With two out,

Terry Pendleton hit a deep fly ball to left, which Raines caught as he fell down on the warning track. Lloyd, yet to give up a run in the postseason, earned the win, becoming the first Australian to pick up a victory in a World Series game. It was redemption for both Lloyd and Bob Watson.

"My GM is pretty smart, isn't he?" Torre told reporters after the game, in a not-so-subtle shot at Steinbrenner. "He made a hell of a deal."[88]

Despite entering Game Five with their starters having the highest ERA of any World Series team since the 1989 Giants, who were swept in four games, the Yankees had evened the series. Game Five, the last game ever played at Fulton County Stadium, was another tense affair that again featured a series of breaks that all went the Yankees' way. In the fourth inning, the game still scoreless, Hayes hit a fly ball to medium right-center field. Braves center fielder Marquis Grissom and right fielder Dye miscommunicated, resulting in Grissom's dropping the ball. Fielder doubled Hayes in for a 1–0 lead. Pettitte, devastated by his Game One start, held the Braves scoreless through five. In the sixth, he allowed two singles to start the inning. When Mark Lemke dropped down a bunt, Pettitte fielded the ball on a hop, turned, and fired to third, just barely getting the force out. Any hesitation or bobbling of the ball would have resulted in the bases loaded. Instead, it was now first and second with one out. Chipper Jones then hit one back to Pettitte for a 1-4-3 double play.

Torre allowed Pettitte to start the ninth inning so he could face lefty McGriff. But Chipper Jones doubled before that could happen and moved to third, when McGriff grounded out. Torre brought in Wetteland; Pettitte spent the rest of the inning on the bench with a towel draped around his head, unable to watch as Wetteland tried to preserve the win. Wetteland's first pitch was hammered directly to Hayes at third; Hayes smothered it, prevented Jones from scoring, and got the out at first. Had the ball been hit nearly anywhere else on the field, Jones likely would have scored to tie the game. After an intentional walk, Wetteland faced former teammate Luis Polonia. The Yankees decided to throw him nothing but fastballs, believing the slap-hitting Polonia would be unable to catch up. There was just one problem. The Yankees' defense was not aligned to match the pitch selection.

"The way Luis was swinging the bat I could see he was struggling to get around. There was no way he would get around on John's fastball," said first base coach José Cardenal. Polonia fouled off pitch after pitch without pulling the ball. Looking into the outfield, Cardenal saw that O'Neill was too close to the line. There was no way Polonia was going to pull the ball to right. Cardenal began frantically motioning for O'Neill to move closer to right-center field, which, after another pitch, he did. Wetteland delivered another fastball, but left it over the plate. Polonia turned on it and drilled it to right-center. O'Neill, running with a limp because he was playing with a bad left hamstring, turned and sprinted toward the gap.

"I thought I had a good chance to catch it when he hit it, but once I started running it took off," said O'Neill.[89]

Polonia's drive would end the game if O'Neill did not catch it. With two out, the runner on first was off with contact, leaving the Yankees no chance to throw him out if the ball went over O'Neill's head. After sprinting several yards, O'Neill, bad hamstring and all, stretched out his right arm and snagged the ball just before the warning track. His momentum took him to the wall, where he slapped it with both his hands before screaming, "YEAH!"

"If Paul doesn't move those eight feet, I don't think he gets the ball," said Cardenal.[90] It was the difference between the Yankees returning to New York up 3-2 instead of down 3-2 in the series. Here they were, just as Torre had promised, heading back home just a win away from the title.

The makeup of the team and the playoff path to Game Six— the constant comebacks and memorable moments—made the Yankees likable in a way they had almost never been. "C'mon, admit it," wrote Ken Rosenthal, of the Baltimore Sun. "If you like baseball, you like the Yankees."[91]

Even the team's most virulent haters had to feel some sense of compassion when Torre's brother Frank, in the hospital for three months with a failing heart, received his long-needed heart transplant the day before Game Six. It was the feel-good moment of the season; Torre secured six tickets to the game for the medical staff that helped save his brother's life.

In Game Six, after all that had gone their way in the postseason, the Yankees did not need breaks or lucky bounces to secure the title. In the third inning, propelled by an O'Neill lead-off double, they scored three runs off Maddux. Key, the consolation prize after New York had failed to sign Maddux four years earlier, allowed only one run before leaving in the sixth. Up 3–1 in the ninth, Wetteland again made things interesting, allowing a run and putting the tying and go-ahead runs on base with two outs. With 56,000 people on edge, and fans from Waterbury, Connecticut, to Pompton Lakes, New Jersey, glued to their TVs, Wetteland induced Lemke to pop out to Hayes, sparking a cathartic celebration eighteen years in the making. Up in the owner's box, even Steinbrenner cracked a smile as he hugged and kissed his assembled guests. Watson, the first African American general manager in baseball history to win a title, could not help but take a jab at his employer.

"All the moves I made, and Joe Torre made, have worked out. I know my business. I know talent. I know people," said Watson.[92]

The Yankees hit just .216 in the World Series and their team ERA was a run and a half higher than the Braves'. Yet, through timely hits, a strong bullpen, and a series of fortunate breaks, they persevered. They won all eight postseason games on the road; for the season, they went 18-0 at Baltimore, Cleveland, and Atlanta. Moreover, New York had fallen in love with these Yankees in a way that matched the feeling for the '86 Mets, even if the reasons for the love affair could not have been more different. "They are not the best Yankee team we will ever see," wrote Mike Lupica, "But no Yankee team in history ever gave us a better month."[93]

One day short of the ten-year anniversary of Jesse Orosco's hurling his glove in the air at Shea Stadium, Joe Torre, Mel Stottlemyre, Willie Randolph, Don Zimmer, José Cardenal, David Cone, Dwight Gooden, and Darryl Strawberry—all of whom had worn a Mets uniform at one time—celebrated a New York Yankees championship at Yankee Stadium.

Sitting in the left-field stands that night was a familiar face to many Yankee fans. He wore a burgundy-colored suit that easily stuck out amidst the sea of dark-toned fall apparel in the crowd. Even if his suit did not stick out, his 6-foot-6 frame did. Dave Winfield was providing pregame analysis for Fox as the network broadcast its first-ever World Series. He sat there and watched as the New York Yankees celebrated a championship that he had helped set in motion. And all because of compound interest.

Notes

1. COMPOUND INTEREST

1. Winfield and Parker, *Winfield*, 160–61.
2. Murray Chass, "Yanks Sign Winfield," *New York Times*, December 16, 1980.
3. Golenbock, *George*, 214.
4. Winfield and Parker, *Winfield*, 237.
5. Madden, *Steinbrenner*, 289.
6. Robert McG. Thomas Jr., "Winfield Approves Trade to the Angels," *New York Times*, May 17, 1990.
7. Thomas, "Winfield Approves Trade to the Angels."
8. Tom Verducci, "Yes, and It Counts; Winny Agrees to Trade after Gaining Huge Pact," *Newsday*, May 17, 1990.

2. OUT OF PLACE

1. Golenbock, *Amazin'*, 536.
2. Paul Hoynes, "Hernandez Is Hobbling Again," *Cleveland Plain Dealer*, July 27, 1990.

3. BORDERS ON THE BIZARRE

1. John Sterling, interview with author, February 2008.
2. Malcolm Moran, "No Joy for Yanks, despite a Victory," *New York Times*, July 31, 1990.
3. Fay Vincent, interview with author, April 16, 2020.
4. Pennington, *Chumps to Champs*, 15.
5. Fay Vincent, interview with author, April 16, 2020.
6. Madden, *Steinbrenner*, 312.
7. Fay Vincent, interview with author, April 16, 2020.
8. Fay Vincent, interview with author, April 16, 2020.

9. Golenbock, *George*, 257.

10. Maryann Hudson, "The Steinbrenner Decision; Owner Must Give Up Control," *Los Angeles Times*, July 31, 1990.

11. Dave Anderson, "Steinbrenner Whine Fails 'Smell Test,'" *New York Times*, July 31, 1990.

12. "Decision on Steinbrenner; a Finding Based on 2 Key Premises," *New York Times*, July 31, 1990.

13. Jon Heyman and Bob Glauber, "George Is Out as Yanks' Boss; Yankees Players in Shock," *Newsday*, July 31, 1990.

14. Malcolm Moran, "No Joy for Yanks, despite a Victory," *New York Times*, July 31, 1990.

15. Greg Boeck, "Steinbrenner Benched; Bronx Cheers; Fans' 'Mission Accomplished,'" *USA Today*, July 31, 1990.

16. "Decision on Steinbrenner; a Finding Based on 2 Key Premises," *New York Times*, July 31, 1990.

17. Joe Gergen, "George Is Out as Yanks' Boss; It's Freedom at Last for Suffering Fans," *Newsday*, July 31, 1990.

18. C. W. Nevius, "Now Steinbrenner Knows What It's Like to Be Fired," *San Francisco Chronicle*, July 31, 1990.

19. Madden, *Steinbrenner*, 259.

20. Bill Madden, "Hank Steinbrenner's Ascension to the Yankees' Reluctant One," *New York Daily News*, April 14, 2020.

21. Rick Hummel, "Reds, Mets Swap Ace Relievers," *St. Louis Post-Dispatch*, December 7, 1989.

22. Greg Boeck, "Steinbrenner Benched; Bronx Cheers; Fans' 'Mission Accomplished,'" *USA Today*, July 31, 1990.

23. "Wealthier Winfield oks Trade Contract Extension Totals $9.2 Million," *Associated Press*, May 17, 1990.

24. Jon Heyman, "Dent Is Dumped Boss Breaks Word; Stump Takes Over," *Newsday*, June 7, 1990.

25. Dan Shaughnessy, "His Back against the Wall," *Boston Globe*, June 7, 1990.

26. "Steinbrenner to Bucky Dent: Goodbye; Yankees' Turnover: Two Coaches Also Get Walking Papers. Owner Calls up 'Stump' Merrill from Farm Club," *Los Angeles Times*, June 6, 1990.

27. Jon Heyman, "Dent Is Dumped Boss Breaks Word; Stump Take Over," *Newsday*, June 7, 1990.

28. Tom Pedulla and Rachel Shuster, "Players Blame Themselves, Fans Point to Steinbrenner," *USA Today*, June 7, 1990.

29. Michael Martinez, "18 Years, 18 Times: Yanks Once Again Replace a Manager," *New York Times*, June 7, 1990.

30. Chapin Wright and Rose Marie Arce, "As Bucky Goes, Fans Find Plenty to Blame," *Newsday*, June 7, 1990.

31. Tom Pedulla and Rachel Shuster, "Players Blame Themselves, Fans Point to Steinbrenner," *USA Today*, June 7, 1990.

32. Dan Shaughnessy, "His Back against the Wall," *Boston Globe*, June 7, 1990.

33. Marc Topkin, "Don't Expect Merrill to Right the Yankee Clipper," *St. Petersburg Times*, June 7, 1990.

34. Stump Merrill, interview with author, February 1, 2020.

35. Jon Heyman, "Dent Is Dumped Boss Breaks Word; Stump Take Over," *Newsday*, June 7, 1990.

36. "Steinbrenner to Bucky Dent: Goodbye; Yankees' Turnover: Two Coaches Also Get Walking Papers. Owner Calls up 'Stump' Merrill from Farm Club," *Los Angeles Times*, June 6, 1990.

37. Jim Leyritz, interview with author, March 10, 2020.

38. Mel Antonen, "Yankee's No-Hitter Is No Winner," *USA Today*, July 2, 1990.

39. Chuck Cary, interview with author, March 31, 2020.

40. Andy Hawkins, interview with author, January 14, 2020.

41. Michael Martinez, "Mattingly Sidelined, but Yanks Roll On," *New York Times*, May 28, 1988.

42. "Mattingly Rips George after Loss," *Associated Press*, August 22, 1988.

43. Joe Giglio, "Blast from the Past: Yankees Nearly Traded Don Mattingly in His Prime for NL Slugger," NJ.com, March 25, 2020.

44. Jon Heyman, "Back Pain Puts Donnie on DL," *Newsday*, July 26, 1990.

45. "Mattingly May Retire If Back Gets No Better," *Toronto Star*, July 30, 1990.

46. Heyman, "Back Pain Puts Donnie on DL," *Newsday*, July 26, 1990.

47. John Kass, "When It Comes to Hear, Truth Hurts Sanders," *Chicago Tribune*, January 30, 2011.

48. Jon Heyman, "Deion Flees to Falcons; Walks Out after Yankees Refuse $1-Million Contract," *Newsday*, July 31, 1990.

49. Jon Heyman, "Deion Flees to Falcons; Walks Out after Yankees Refuse $1-Million Contract," *Newsday*, July 31, 1990.

4. PUT OUT OF HIS MISERY

1. Joseph Durso, "Knight, an Oriole, Takes a Cut," *New York Times*, February 12, 1987.

2. Golenbock, *Amazin'*, 497.

3. Joseph Durso, "Aguilera Sidelined 3 Weeks," *New York Times*, May 29, 1987.

4. Joseph Durso, "Aguilera Sidelined 3 Weeks," *New York Times*, May 29, 1987.

5. Mike Geffner, *Associated Press*, October 10, 1985.

6. "Amazin'," 533.

7. Joe Donnelly, "Through the Years with Darryl," *Newsday*, November 9, 1990.

8. "The Davey Chronicles," *Newsday*, May 30, 1990.

9. Golenbock, *Amazin'*, 517.

10. Gooden and Klapisch, *Heat*, 81.

11. Klapisch, *High and Tight*, 72.

12. Marty Noble, "Davey Saw It Coming," *Newsday*, May 30, 1990.

13. Johnson and Sherman, *Davey Johnson*, 255–56.

14. "The Davey Chronicles," *Newsday*, May 30, 1990.

15. Marty Noble, "Davey Saw It Coming," *Newsday*, May 30, 1990.

16. Marty Noble and Joseph W. Queen, "Strawberry Signs into Rehab for Alcohol Problem, Mets Say," *Newsday*, February 4, 1990.

17. Marty Noble and Joseph W. Queen, "Strawberry Signs into Rehab for Alcohol Problem, Mets Say," *Newsday*, February 4, 1990.

18. Klapisch, *High and Tight*, 26.

19. Marty Noble, "Cone Bent Out of Shape; Lets Two Runners Waltz Home While Disputing Call," *Newsday*, May 1, 1990.

20. Ed Christine, "Mets Fire Johnson; Harrelson Moves up to Manager," *USA Today*, May 30, 1990.

21. Marty Noble, "Mets Dump Davey; Harrelson Gets Job through '91 Season," *Newsday*, May 30, 1990.

22. "Irked at Firing, McReynolds, Strawberry Apt to Quit Mets," *Associated Press*, May 30, 1990.

23. Bernie Miklasz, "Mets' Bosses Failed Johnson, Not Vice Versa," *St. Louis Post-Dispatch*, May 30, 1990.

24. Steve Jacobson, "Sizzle Became Fizzle," *Newsday*, October 1, 1990.

25. Steve Jacobson, "Sizzle Became Fizzle," *Newsday*, October 1, 1990.

5. LONG HAIR, SHORT TEMPERS

1. Jack Curry, "Tigers' Fielder Makes History with 2 Homers to End with 51," *New York Times*, October 4, 1990.

2. Strawberry and Strausbaugh, *Straw*, 117.

3. Wendy Lane, *Associated Press*, November 9, 1990.

4. Marty Noble, "Former Teammates Can't Believe the Mets Let Strawberry Slip Away," *Newsday*, November 9, 1990.

5. Rick Hummel, "Mets Catch Coleman . . . Cardinals Fall Short by $1.45 Million," *St. Louis Post-Dispatch*, December 6, 1990.

6. Joseph Durso, "Coleman Signed by Mets for Nearly $12 Million," *New York Times*, December 6, 1990.

7. Richard Justice, "Gooden Gets $15.45 Million in 3-Year Deal with Mets," *New York Times*, April 2, 1991.

8. Joe Sexton, "Viola and Mets Strike Out," *New York Times*, April 7, 1991.

9. Jon Heyman, "Yankees Notes & Quotes," *Newsday*, February 24, 1991.

10. Michael Martinez, "Mattingly Is Named Captain; Will He Go down with the Ship?" *New York Times*, March 1, 1991.

11. Michael Martinez, "Mattingly Is Named Captain; Will He Go down with the Ship?" *New York Times*, March 1, 1991.

12. S. L. Price, "Just like Old Times: Brooks' Blast Lifts Mets," *Miami Herald*, April 10, 1991.

13. Harvey Araton, "Hubie the Hero Blushes at Success," *New York Times*, April 10, 1991.

14. Jon Heyman, "Gone with the Wind; Sanderson No-Hitter Is 'Blown' in Ninth," *Newsweek*, April 11, 1991.

15. Jon Heyman, "Gone with the Wind; Sanderson No-Hitter Is 'Blown' in Ninth," *Newsweek*, April 11, 1991.

16. Michael Martinez, "Yankees Drop Hawkins and Recall Howe," *New York Times*, May 10, 1991.

17. Alan Drooz, "Strawberry Can't Homer Again," *Los Angeles Times*, May 8, 1991.

18. Jon Heyman, "A Mel of a Game for the Yankees; Hall's Blast in 9th Caps Comeback," *Newsday*, May 28, 1991.

19. Tom Verducci, "A Taylor-Made Victory; Young Arms like Wade's Valued Now," *Newsday*, June 3, 1991.

20. Michael Martinez, "Taylor Adds Touch to Yanks' New-Found Magic," *New York Times*, June 3, 1991.

21. Jon Heyman, "A Taylor-Made Victory; Rookie Helps Yanks Move 4 Games Out," *Newsday*, June 3, 1991.

22. Pennington, *Chumps to Champs*, 94.

23. "Signing of Taylor Irks Steinbrenner," *Associated Press*, August 29, 1991.

24. Pennington, *Chumps to Champs*, 95.

25. Marty Noble, "Teufel Traded for Templeton," *Newsday*, June 1, 1991.

26. Rick Hummel, "Mets Are Making a Run, Even without Coleman," *St. Louis Post-Dispatch*, July 14, 1991.

27. Marty Noble, "Bye, Darling; Ron Traded to Expos for Burke," *Newsday*, July 16, 1991.

28. Tom Verducci, "Bud Just Hasn't Got a Clue," *Newsday*, July 31, 1991.

29. Marty Noble, "Managing to Stay Aloof," *Newsday*, July 31, 1991.

30. Joe Donnelly, "Finally, Bud Gets Nipped," *Newsday*, September 30, 1991.

31. Jack Curry, "Heartfelt Plea? Vintage Whine? Jeffries Writes Fans," *New York Times*, May 25, 1991.

32. Joe Donnelly, "Finally, Bud Gets Nipped," *Newsday*, September 30, 1991.

33. Tom Verducci, "Future Road Dim for Mets," *Newsday*, September 30, 1991.

34. Verducci, "Bud Just Hasn't Got a Clue," *Newsday*, July 31, 1991.

35. Michael Martinez, "Forward to the Future and Yankees Love It," *New York Times*, July 21, 1991.

36. Stump Merrill, interview with author, February 1, 2020.

37. Stump Merrill, interview with author, February 1, 2020.

38. Murray Chass, "Mattingly Flap; Hair Today, Gone Tomorrow?" *New York Times*, August 16, 1991.

39. Jon Heyman, "Hairy Don to Yanks: 'Stick It,'" *Newsday*, August 16, 1991.

40. Jack Curry, "Mattingly Chooses Seat on Yank Bench over Barber's Chair," *New York Times*, August 16, 1991.

41. Jon Heyman, "Hairy Don to Yanks: 'Stick It,'" *Newsday*, August 16, 1991.

42. Stump Merrill, interview with author, February 1, 2020.

43. Joe Sexton, "Mets Gain Split on Shutout to End Slide," *New York Times*, August 22, 1991.

44. Stottlemyre and Harper, *Pride and Pinstripes*, 115.

45. Tom Verducci, "Future Road Dim for Mets," *Newsday*, September 30, 1991.

46. Ira Berkow, "The Short, Unhappy Reign of Harrelson," *New York Times*, September 30, 1991.

47. George Jordan and Beth Holland, "No Fans of Buddy," *Newsday*, September 30, 1991.

48. Charlie O'Brien, interview with author, January 15, 2022.

49. Neil Best, "Cone Enjoys 19-K Finale," *Newsday*, October 7, 1991.

50. Jon Heyman, "Tradition Goes On: Stump Goes; No Fingers Are Pointed by Merrill," *Newsday*, October 8, 1991.

51. Jack Curry, "The Ex-Man: Yanks Usher Merrill Out The Door," *New York Times*, October 8, 1991.

52. "Stump Ill-Equipped for the Managers Job," *Newsday*, October 8, 1991.

53. "Stump Ill-Equipped for the Managers Job," *Newsday*, October 8, 1991.

54. Jack Curry, "The Ex-Man: Yanks Usher Merrill Out The Door," *New York Times*, October 8, 1991.

6. NOW TRADE THE REST OF THEM

1. Joe Sexton, "Mets Make a Good Catch: Torborg as Manager," *New York Times*, October 11, 1991.

2. Tom Verducci, "Exit Upsets Coach, Players," *Newsday*, October 11, 1991.

3. Marty Noble, "Big Mets Pact for Torborg," *Newsday*, October 11, 1991.

4. Pennington, *Chumps to Champs*, 22.

5. Matt Nokes, interview with author, February 24, 2020.

6. Tom Verducci. "Mets Get Murray," *Newsday*, November 28, 1991.

7. Bob Klapisch, "$29-Million Man," *New York Daily News*, December 3, 1991.

8. Tom Verducci, "Harazin Makes His Mark," *Newsday*, December 12, 1991.

9. Marty Noble, "Musical Chairs," *Newsday*, December 12, 1991.

10. Jon Heyman, "Tartabull Fighting Bad Image," *Newsday*, January 7, 1992.

11. Dave Anderson, "Tartabull: Headlines or Headaches?" *New York Times*, January 7, 1992.

12. Kevin Maas, interview with author, March 4, 2020.

13. Dave George, "For This N.Y. Money, Tartabull Will Need Pocketful of Miracles," *Palm Beach Post*, January 7, 1992.

14. "Yanks Sign Stanley," *New York Times*, January 22, 1992.

15. Jim Leyritz, interview with author, March 10, 2020.

16. Jon Heyman, "Perez Is Banned until March '93," *Newsday*, March 7, 1992.

17. Michael Farber, "Best Day of Baseball's Year Spoiled by the One and Only's Problems," *Montreal Gazette*, March 7, 1992.

18. Bruce Jenkins, "A.L. East Preview," *San Francisco Chronicle*, April 6, 1992.

19. Claire Smith, "A Stadium Charged with Shared History," *New York Times*, April 8, 1992.

20. Claire Smith, "A Stadium Charged with Shared History," *New York Times*, April 8, 1992.

21. Jack O'Connell, "For Yankees, as Great a Place to Start as Any," *Hartford Courant*, April 8, 1992.

22. Mel Antonen, "Fast Start Has Yankee Fans Talking," *USA Today*, April 14, 1992.

23. Jon Heyman, "Just Another 'W'," *Newsweek*, April 14, 1992.

24. Jack Curry, "Amazin' Yankees (6–0) Win Battle of Unbeatens," *New York Times*, April 14, 1992.

25. Shirley Perlman, "No Charges; Rape Evidence Too Thin against Mets," *Newsday*, April 10, 1992.

26. Bob Glauber and Marty Noble, "3 Women Sue Cone And Mets," *Newsday*, March 27, 1992.

27. Tom Verducci, "Straw Is Hog-Wild," *Newsday*, March 30, 1992.

28. Bob Klapisch, interview with author, January 29, 2022.

29. Joe Donnelly, "Cone's Image Tainted," *Newsday*, April 11, 1992.

30. Klapisch and Harper, *The Worst Team Money Could Buy*, 57–58.

31. Joe Sexton, "Now It Can Be Told, by Mets," *New York Times*, April 6, 1992.

32. Klapisch and Harper, *The Worst Team Money Could Buy*, 121.

33. Joe Sexton, "Boos Bounce off Bonilla's Back," *New York Times*, May 31, 1992.

34. Joe Sexton, "Hold the Phone! Mets Try to Explain," *New York Times*, June 27, 1992.

35. O'Connor, *The Captain*, 32.

36. O'Connor, *The Captain*, 41.

37. Jack O'Connell, "Yankees Pick Shortstop with Offensive Talent," *Hartford Courant*, June 2, 1992.

38. Joe Donnelly, "Leary: What'd He Do?" *Newsday*, June 22, 1992.

39. Jack Curry, "Mmmmm, Good! Leary Dines," *New York Times*, June 22, 1992.

40. Bill Madden and Jeff Bradley, "Vincent Threatens Yankees," *New York Daily News*, July 2, 1992.

41. Bill Madden, "Fay Vincent Cutting Own Throat with Recent Actions," *New York Daily News*, July 5, 1992.

42. Fay Vincent, interview with author, April 16, 2020.

43. Fay Vincent, interview with author, April 16, 2020.

44. Pessah, *The Game*, 50.

45. Michael Martinez, "For Yanks, It's the Calm before Steinbrenner," *New York Times*, July 25, 1992.

46. Jack O'Connell, "George Returns March 1," *Hartford Courant*, July 25, 1992.

47. Joe Sexton, "Cone's Parting Shot: Mets Want Yes Boys," *New York Times*, August 28, 1992.

48. Marty Noble, "Mets Decide His 'Demands' Can't Be Met," *Newsday*, August 28, 1992.

49. Klapisch and Harper, *The Worst Team Money Could Buy*, 170.

50. Marty Noble, "Mets Decide His 'Demands' Can't Be Met," *Newsday*, August 28, 1992.

51. Klapisch and Harper, *The Worst Team Money Could Buy*, 244.

52. Marty Noble, "Mets Decide His 'Demands' Can't Be Met," *Newsday*, August 28, 1992.

53. George Vecsey, "Cone Deal: Too Much, Too Soon," *New York Times*, August 28, 1992.

54. Steve Jacobson, "Move All of 'Em Out?" *Newsday*, August 28, 1992.

55. Golenbock, *Amazin'*, 553.

56. Jennifer Frey, "M Stands for Masterful, or a Rookie Named Militello," *New York Times*, August 10, 1992.

7. MOST PLAYERS DETEST THE PLACE

1. Pepe, *Core Four*, 2.

2. Rivera and Coffey, *The Closer*, 31.

3. Rivera and Coffey, *The Closer*, 4.

4. Rivera and Coffey, *The Closer*, 45.

5. Greg Hanlon, "The Many Crimes of Mel Hall," *SB Nation*, July 2014, chapter 1.

6. Jon Heyman, "Spike Clouds the Infield Picture," *Newsday*, December 5, 1992.

7. Jim Dwyer, "Gentleman Champ," *Newsday*, September 5, 1993.

8. Jon Heyman, "Abbott a Yankee," *Newsday*, December 7, 1992.

9. Jon Heyman, "Locking Up Key," *Newsday*, December 11, 1992.

10. Randy Miller, "How a Heart Attack Led to Hall of Famer Greg Maddux Spurning Yankees for Braves," NJ.com, https://www.nj.com/yankees/2022/01/how-a -heart-attack-led-to-greg-maddux-spurring-yankees-for-braves.html, January 29, 2022.

11. Jack O'Connell, "Michael Gets Key to New York," *Hartford Courant*, December 11, 1992.

12. Olney, *The Last Night of the Yankee Dynasty*, 59.

13. Dan Shaughnessy, "Changing His Stripes," *Boston Globe*, December 16, 1992.

14. Jack O'Connell, "Boggs Gets Deal with Yankees," *Hartford Courant*, December 16, 1992.

15. Joe Molloy, "He Wades In," *Newsday*, December 12, 1992.

16. "The Yankees and Mets, in Their Own Words," *Newsday*, October 4, 1993.

17. Pessah, *The Game*, 54.

18. Bill Center, "Meet the New Boss, Same as the Old Boss," *San Diego Union-Tribune*, March 2, 1993.

19. Jack Curry, "Just like That, It's Monday in Park with George," *New York Times*, March 2, 1993.

20. "The Yankees and Mets, in Their Own Words," *Newsday*, October 4, 1993.

21. Marty Noble, "Doc Steals Spotlight," *Newsday*, April 6, 1993.

22. Joe Gergen, "Doc Steals Spotlight," *Newsday*, April 6, 1993.

23. Bob Klapisch, "War Stories," Baseball Analysts, http://baseballanalysts.com /archives/2006/06/war_stories.php.

24. Steve Serby, "Bobby Explains Run-in with Book Author," *Baltimore Sun*, April 13, 1993.

25. Chris Baldwin, "Cardinals Steal Man Vince Coleman Brings His Swagger to Golf," *Bad Golfer*, http.//www.badgolfer.com/departments/features/cardinals -steal-man-vince-coleman-golf-4993.htm , March 23, 2007.

26. Jennifer Frey, "Gooden's Frustration Is Brought to Boiling Point," *New York Times*, April 28, 1993.

27. Jessie Mangaliman, "The Fans Go Batty in Bronx," *Newsday*, April 13, 1993.

28. Jack Curry, "For One Day, It's the House That Abbott Owns," *New York Times*, April 13, 1993.

29. George Vecsey, "A New Yank Appreciates the Stadium," *New York Times*, April 13, 1993.

30. Jennifer Frey, "Like Old Times," *New York Times*, May 22, 1993.

31. Mike Stanley, interview with author, April 7, 2020.

32. Jim Donaghy, *Associated Press*, May 20, 1993.

33. Jim Donaghy, *Associated Press*, May 20, 1993.

34. Joe Donnelly, "Tony First to Go," *Newsday*, June 12, 1993.

35. Dave Anderson, "What Will Mets Rebuild With?" *New York Times*, June 23, 1993.
36. Joe Sexton, "Forget Fine-Tuning; Mets Seek Overhaul," *New York Times*, June 23, 1993.
37. Steve Jacobson, "Turmoil at Shea/The Harazin Resignation," *Newsday*, June 23, 1993.
38. Rory Costello, "Anthony Young," Society for American Baseball Research, https://sabr.org/bioproj/person/anthony-young/#sdendnote13sym.
39. Chuck Johnson, "Loss Leaves Young Alone with History," *USA Today*, June 28, 1993.
40. Chuck Johnson, "Loss Leaves Young Alone with History," *USA Today*, June 28, 1993.
41. Charlie O'Brien, interview with author, January 15, 2022.
42. Jennifer Frey, "The Scariest Number: Young Drops 24th," *New York Times*, June 28, 1993.
43. "The Yankees and Mets, in Their Own Words," *Newsday*, October 4, 1993.
44. Rory Costello, "Anthony Young," Society for American Baseball Research, https://sabr.org/bioproj/person/anthony-young/#sdendnote13sym.
45. George Vecsey, "Poor George: Yet Another Huge Crowd," *New York Times*, August 6, 1993.
46. Mel Antonen, "Yankees Edge Jays 5–4 to Salvage Split," *USA Today*, August 6, 1993.
47. "The Yankees and Mets, in Their Own Words," *Newsday*, October 4, 1993.
48. "Saberhagen Admits to 'Joke,'" *New York Times*, July 28, 1993.
49. Wallace Matthews, "Excuses Are Weak," *Newsday*, July 29, 1993.
50. Dave Anderson, "Light a Fuse on Coleman's Departure," *New York Times*, July 27, 1993.
51. Marty Noble, "Coleman's a Cancer, So Cut Him Out," *Newsday*, July 27, 1993.
52. Marty Noble, "Vince Speaks," *Newsday*, July 30, 1993.
53. Marty Noble, "Coleman's a Cancer, So Cut Him Out," *Newsday*, July 27, 1993.
54. Art Thiel, "Coleman Stunt Shows Athletes' Disdain for Fans," *Seattle Post-Intelligencer*, July 28, 1993.
55. Jennifer Frey, "Saberhagen Belatedly Admits to Bleach Squirt," *New York Times*, August 11, 1993.
56. Marty Noble, "Saberhagen Comes Clean," *Newsday*, August 11, 1993.
57. Bob Klapisch, interview with author, January 29, 2022.
58. Matt Nokes, interview with author, February 24, 2020.
59. Joe Donnelly, "No-No? It's Yes-Yes!" *Newsday*, September 5, 1993.
60. "The Yankees and Mets, in Their Own Words," *Newsday*, October 4, 1993.

61. Jack O'Connell and Sean Horgan, "Tanana Goes Crosstown and Uptown Just like That," *Hartford Courant*, September 18, 1993.

62. Mike Stanley, interview with author, April 7, 2020.

63. Jon Heyman, "9th Life for Yankees," *Newsday*, September 19, 1993.

64. Jack Curry, "Save by the Fan: Yanks Win It In 9th," *New York Times* September 19, 1993.

65. Jack Curry, "Yankees Now Have the Time off for Regret or Rejoicing," *New York Times*, October 4, 1993.

66. Tom Friend, "Kile No-Hits Incredible Shrinking Mets," *New York Times*, September 9, 1993.

67. Tom Friend, "Kile No-Hits Incredible Shrinking Mets," *New York Times*, September 9, 1993.

68. Marty Noble, "Mets Bid Mel Adieu," *Newsday*, October 4, 1993.

69. Marty Noble, "Everything Went Wrong Mets Were Simply Wretched," *Newsday*, October 4, 1993.

70. Jim Donaghy, *Associated Press*, October 4, 1993.

71. Steve Zipay, "It's a New Era," *Newsday*, September 10, 1993.

8. THE BEST TEAM I EVER PLAYED ON

1. Marty Noble, "Left Turnover," *Newsday*, January 6, 1994.

2. Jack Curry, "For Yankees, a Familiar Yet Surprising Face," *New York Times*, December 21, 1993.

3. "The Arm That Changed the Major League Draft," Yahoo Sports, https://sports.yahoo.com/jp-taylor060506.html, June 5, 2006.

4. Pennington, *Chumps to Champs*, 177.

5. Matt Michael, "Yankees Keeping Rookies down on the Farm," *Post-Standard*, May 13, 1994.

6. Jim Leyritz, interview with author, March 10, 2020.

7. Steve Jacobson, "Doctor K Blowin' in the Wind," *Newsday*, April 5, 1994.

8. Marty Noble, "Hey, That's One," *Newsday*, April 5, 1994.

9. Murray Chass, "Ode to Joy," *New York Times*, April 18, 1994.

10. George Willis, "A Rising Star," *Newsday*, April 18, 1994.

11. Gerald Eskenazi, "Let's Go, Sweep!" *New York Times*, May 30, 1994.

12. "Yanks Sweep up in Homer Derby," *Newsday*, May 9, 1994.

13. Jack Curry, "Yankees Are Perched in Highest Spot Around," *New York Times*, May 10, 1994.

14. Jon Heyman, "Yankees Stand Alone in First," *Newsday*, May 10, 1994.

15. Mike Stanley, interview with author, April 7, 2020.

16. Jennifer Frey, "From Frustration and Isolation, a Costly Choice," *New York Times*, June 30, 1994.

17. Klapisch, *High and Tight*, 147.

18. Mark Hermann, "Doc's Time May Be Up," *Newsday*, June 29, 1994.

19. Jennifer Frey, "From Frustration and Isolation, a Costly Choice," *New York Times*, June 30, 1994.

20. "Gooden Violates Drug Program," *Hartford Courant*, June 29, 1994.

21. Marty Noble, "Doc Pays Price," *Newsday*, November 5, 1994.

22. "Gooden Discloses Near Suicide Attempt," *Associated Press*, June 21, 1996.

23. Jack O'Connell, "A September Mood for Yankees," *Hartford Courant*, July 18, 1994.

24. Jack O'Connell, "Milestone Night Is Pure Mattingly," *Hartford Courant*, July 25, 1994.

25. Anthony McCarron, "The Season That Wasn't," *New York Daily News*, August 9, 2014.

26. Jack Curry, "Mattingly Pounds Out the Exclamation Point," *New York Times*, July 25, 1994.

27. Ross Newhan, "Baseball Season, Series Cancelled," *Los Angeles Times*, September 15, 1994.

28. Jack O'Connell, "It's Official," *Hartford Courant*, September 15, 1994.

29. Anthony McCarron, "The Season That Wasn't," *New York Daily News*, August 9, 2014.

30. Jon Heyman, "Yanks Mourn Season," September 15, 1994.

9. THE ONCE UNFATHOMABLE NOTION

1. Craig Calcaterra, "Baseball Strike in 1994–95 Began 25 Years Ago," NBC Sports, https://mlb.nbcsports.com/2019/08/12/baseball-strike-in-1994-95-began-25 -years-ago/, August 12, 2019.

2. Pepe, *Core Four*, 11.

3. Jack Curry, "Key Is Out for the Season, and Possibly Longer," *New York Times*, July 4, 1995.

4. Rob Parker, "There's Nothing like It," *Newsday*, April 27, 1995.

5. "Mets Trip Cardinals before Angry Fans," *Times Union*, April 29, 1995.

6. Pennington, *Chumps to Champs*, 195.

7. George Willis, "The Hair Goes, and So Does Offense, for Slumping Yank," *New York Times*, June 3, 1995.

8. Peter Schmuck, "Yankees Lose '94 Magic, Are Up to Old Tricks," *Baltimore Sun*, June 19, 1995.

9. Joe Donnelly, "A Shaking Debut," *Newsday*, June 18, 1995.

10. Claire Smith, "Rough Go on Diamond for Diamond in Rough," *New York Times*, June 18, 1995.

11. Jason Diamos, "The Mets' Fans Get a Chance to Glimpse the Future, and It Blinks," June 18, 1995.

12. George Willis, "The Cellar Is Getting Dingier For Mets," *New York Times*, June 27, 1995.

13. Jack Curry, "Please Check All Baggage," *New York Times*, June 20, 1995.

14. Mel Antonen, "Start Spreadin' the News," *Baltimore Sun*, June 20, 1995.

15. Bud Poliquin, "Even Worse, He's an Ex-Met," *Post-Standard*, June 20, 1995.

16. Mel Antonen, "Start Spreadin' the News," *Baltimore Sun*, June 20, 1995.

17. John Giannone, "City Needs Dose of Darryl," *Daily News*, June 20, 1995.

18. Jason Diamos, "New York, New York, It's Strawberry's Town," *New York Times*, June 20, 1995.

19. Bill Madden, "Done Don," *New York Daily News*, June 27, 1995.

20. Bob Raissman, "On Air, Mattingly Is Still a Holy Cow," *Daily News*, June 27, 1995.

21. Mike Lupica, "Mattingly Just Getting Started," *Newsday*, June 30, 1995.

22. Bob Raissman, "Mattingly Stirs Media War," *Daily News*, July 21, 1995.

23. Harvey Araton, "Mattingly Should Play Elsewhere," *New York Times*, November 22, 1995.

24. John Giannone, "Mets Amazed as Izzy Does It," *New York Daily News*, July 18, 1995.

25. John Giannone, "Road To Ruin!," *New York Daily News*, July 27, 1995.

26. George Willis, "Saberhagen Dealt (No Surprise) to Rockies (Surprise)," *New York Times*, August 1, 1995.

27. Jason Diamos, "The Mets Get Their Man for Bonilla," *New York Times*, July 29, 1995.

28. Jason Diamos, "The Mets Get Their Man for Bonilla," *New York Times*, July 29, 1995.

29. Joe Gergen, "Mets Rebuild, Shed the Past," *Newsday*, July 29, 1995.

30. Mike Lupica, "Sabes Is Out, Youth Is In," *Newsday*, August 1, 1995.

31. Rivera and Coffey, *The Closer*, 73.

32. Tom Yantz, "Start With Cone," *Hartford Courant*, July 29, 1995.

33. Jon Heyman, "Double Dealers," *Newsday*, July 29, 1995.

34. Jason Molinet, "Mets Say Bye-Bye Bo," *Newsday*, July 29, 1995.

35. George Vecsey, "Cone Faces Unfinished Business," *New York Times*, December 22, 1995.

36. John Giannone, "Starting over Yanks Can Forget Poundings They Took in Regular Season," *New York Daily News*, October 3, 1995.

37. John Feinstein, *The Best American Sports Writing 1996*, 169.

38. George Vecsey, "George Used Buck's Pride to Ditch Him," *New York Times*, October 27, 1995.

39. Frank Isola, "Mets Close Book on Year, Turn Page to Next Spring," *New York Daily News*, October 2, 1995.

40. Chris Sheridan, *Associated Press*, October 2, 1995.

41. Angell, *A Pitcher's Story: Innings with David Cone*, 12.

42. Mike Blowers, interview with author, April 20, 2020.

43. David Sussman, interview with author, September 5, 2007.

10. FULL CIRCLE

1. Terry Blount, "Watson Leaves Astros for Yankees," *Houston Chronicle*, October 24, 1995.

2. Madden, *Steinbrenner*, 359.

3. Jeff Bradley, "Boss to Toss Odd Bouquet Buck to End, One of the Guys," *New York Daily News*, October 28, 1995.

4. Murray Chass, "No Yankee Jacket Required: Is Showalter In or Out?" *New York Times*, October 27, 1995.

5. John Giannone, "Joe Is in Eye of Storm," *Daily News*, October 3, 1995.

6. Ian O'Connor, "Taking Job a Torre-Ble Mistake," *Daily News*, November 3, 1995.

7. George Vecsey, "Joe Torre as Manager? So Be It," *New York Times*, November 3, 1995.

8. Steve Jacobson, "As the Yankees Turn," *Newsday*, November 3, 1995.

9. Golenbock, *George*, 288.

10. Madden, *Steinbrenner*, 362–63.

11. Gooden and Klapisch, *Heat*, 2.

12. Mike Stanley, interview with author, April 7, 2020.

13. Jon Heyman, "Girardi's In, Stanley Out," *Newsday*, November 21, 1995.

14. Bill Madden, "If at First, Yanks May Try Captain Again," *Daily News*, November 22, 1995.

15. John Giannone, "A Confused Straw Axed," *New York Daily News*, December 1, 1995.

16. Jon Heyman, "With Tino, It's Love at 1st Sight," *Newsday*, December 8, 1995.

17. Jeff Green, "Generation K," *The Stuart News*, February 29, 1996.

18. Marc Topkin, "Generation K Troika Hopes to Power Mets to Pennant," *St. Petersburg Times*, March 18, 1996.

19. Jeff Green, "Generation K," *The Stuart News*, February 29, 1996.

20. Marty Noble, "Kind, but Mets Young Pitchers Share Talent, Vision and Zest," *Newsweek*, March 31, 1996.

21. Marty Noble, "Kind, but Mets Young Pitchers Share Talent, Vision and Zest," *Newsweek*, March 31, 1996.

22. Marty Noble, "Marvelous Mix," *Newsday*, April 2, 1996.

23. John Harper, "A Rey Gun That Stuns Even Mets," *Daily News*, April 2, 1996.

24. Roger Farrell, "Young Mets Dealt Some Tough Cards," *Newark Star-Ledger*, April 2, 1996.

25. George Willis, "Determined Mets Climb Out of 6–0 Hole to Top Cards," *New York Times*, April 2, 1996.

26. Rob Parker, "Overshadowed, He Still Shines," *Newsday*, April 5, 1996.

27. Mark Maske, "Looking like New York's Next Big Hit," *Washington Post*, April 6, 1996.

28. Torre and Verducci, *The Yankee Years*, 8.

29. Pennington, *Chumps to Champs*, 289.

30. Don Burke, "Hey Mets! Yankees' ss Not Bad Either," *Newark Star-Ledger*, April 3, 1996.

31. Mike Vaccaro, "Jeter, Rey Ordonez, Nomar: How One Reigned Supreme," *New York Post*, September 6, 2014.

32. Murray Chass, "Yankees Hope Fans Warm to New Cast," *New York Times*, April 10, 1996.

33. Mike Lupica, "It's a Yankee Wonderland," *Daily News*, April 10, 1996.

34. Jim Mecir, interview with author, April 13, 2021.

35. John Giannone, "Tino, Yankees Go Deep Again," *Daily News*, May 2, 1996.

36. George Willis, "Injury Will Likely Keep Mets' Pulsipher Out for Season," *New York Times*, April 3, 1996.

37. Marty Noble, "Out for Season," *Newsday*, April 3, 1996.

38. Mark Herrmann, "Mets Throw No Punches," *Newsday*, May 13, 1996.

39. John Giannone, *Daily News*, May 8, 1996.

40. John Harper, "Yankee Players in Game of Life," *Daily News*, May 8, 1996.

41. Stottlemyre and Harper, *Pride and Pinstripes*, 96.

42. *Associated Press*, May 15, 1996.

43. Jack Curry, "Dr. No: A Revived Gooden No-Hits Mariners," *New York Times*, May 15, 1996.

44. Joel Sherman, "The Worst of Mariano Rivera Revealed His Absolute Greatness," *New York Post*, January 22, 2019.

45. Stottlemyre and Harper, *Pride and Pinstripes*, 156–57.

46. Jack Curry, "Yankees' Finest Day Is Also One of Torre's Saddest," *New York Times*, June 22, 1996.

47. David Lennon, "Darryl's Back Again," *Newsday*, July 5, 1996.

48. David Lennon, "Darryl's Back Again," *Newsday*, July 5, 1996.

49. Randolph, *The Yankee Way*, 147.

50. John Harper, "Darryl's Return Will Be Just What Doc Prescribes," *Daily News*, July 5, 1996.

51. Jack Curry, "Yankees Finish Off Indians for a Perfect Weekend," *New York Times*, June 24, 1996.

52. Jack Curry, "Right-Handed Pop in Pinstripes," *New York Times*, August 1, 1996.

53. Marty Noble, "Infield Hit," *Newsday*, July 30, 1996.

54. Rafael Hermoso, "Mets Add Some Star Quality," *Bergen Record*, July 30, 1996.

55. Pessah, *The Game*, 182.

56. Jack Curry, "Yankees Clinch and Paint Town in Pinstripes," *New York Times*, September 26, 1996.

57. Rafael Hermoso, "Yankees Clinch AL East Tittle," *Bergen Record*, September 26, 1996.

58. Pepe, *Core Four*, 58.

59. Jack Wilkinson, "Zimmer Is Reborn as a Yankee," *Atlanta Journal-Constitution*, October 25, 1996.

60. George Willis, "Green's Message Didn't Get Through," *New York Times*, August 27, 1996.

61. Murray Chass, "Mets, in Move to Serve Their Youth, Dismiss Green," *New York Times*, August 27, 1996.

62. K. C. Baker and Donald Bertrand, "Dallas Exits to Love & Hisses," *Daily News*, August 27, 1996.

63. Stottlemyre and Harper, *Pride and Pinstripes*, 117.

64. "Doc Gooden Says Dallas Green Has Alcohol Problems," *Associated Press*, August 27, 1996.

65. Steve Adamek, "Mets Fire Green," *Bergen Record*, August 27, 1996.

66. "Former Cape Leaguer Valentine Named Red Sox Manager," Cape Cod Baseball League, https://capecodbaseball.org/news/league-news/index.html?article_id=21, December 2, 2011.

67. Marty Noble, "Valentine's Day," *Newsday*, August 27, 1996.

68. Murray Chass, "Mets, in Move to Serve Their Youth, Dismiss Green," *New York Times*, August 27, 1996.

69. Murray Chass, "Mets, in Move to Serve Their Youth, Dismiss Green," *New York Times*, August 27, 1996.

70. D. L. Cummings, "A Valentine for Dallas," *Daily News*, August 27, 1996.

71. Claire Smith, "Fielder Became Yankees' Significant Other," *New York Times*, October 6, 1996.

72. Ronald Blum, *Associated Press*, October 6, 1996.

73. Susan Slusser, *Dallas Morning News*, October 6, 1996.

74. Tony Tarasco, interview with author, April 15, 2020.

75. Peter Schmuck, "Orioles Fall in 11th Inning," *Baltimore Sun*, October 10, 1996.

76. Tony Tarasco, interview with author, April 15, 2020.

77. Mark Maske, "Fan Runs Interference for Yankees in Game 1," *Washington Post*, October 10, 1996.

78. Steve Jacobson, "Yankees Win the Pennant," *Newsday*, October 14, 1996.

79. Jon Heyman, "Yankees Win the Pennant," *Newsday*, October 14, 1996.

80. Bob Nightengale, "New York, with All Its Fabled History, Suffers Its Greatest Humiliation in Postseason Competition," *Los Angeles Times*, October 21, 1996.

81. Bob Nightengale, "New York, with All Its Fabled History, Suffers Its Greatest Humiliation in Postseason Competition," *Los Angeles Times*, October 21, 1996.

82. Jon Heyman, "Blown Away/Jones Duo Rips Yanks with 8 RBI," *Newsday*, October 21, 1996.

83. Rob Parker, *Newsday*, October 25, 1996.

84. Joe Strauss, "Given Another Chance, Rogers Puts Team in Hole," *Atlanta Journal-Constitution*, October 24, 1996.

85. Jim Leyritz, interview with author, March 10, 2020.

86. Jim Leyritz, interview with author, March 10, 2020.

87. I. J. Rosenberg, "Heartbreaker; Braves Blow 6–0 Lead, Assure Return to N.Y.," *Atlanta Journal-Constitution*, October 24, 1996.

88. David Lennon, "Believe It or Not, Lloyd Has Earned a Little Trust," *Newsday*, October 24, 1996.

89. Jon Heyman, "Yanks a Win Away as Andy Makes Run Stand Up," *Newsday*, October 25, 1996.

90. John Giannone, "Yankee Doodle Andy Pettitte Puts Bombers 1 from Ring," *Daily News*, October 25, 1996.

91. Ken Rosenthal, "Those 'Darn Yankees' Played, Won with One Heartbeat," *Baltimore Sun*, October 27, 1996.

92. Joe Strauss, "Watson Has Thoughts of His Own, by George," *Atlanta Journal-Constitution*, October 27, 1996.

93. Mike Lupica, "'96 Yankee Fable Is Forever," *Daily News*, October 27, 1996.

Bibliography

Materials and quotes gathered from interviews with the following people were used for this book: Jim Abbott, Wally Backman, Steve Balboni, Jesse Barfield, Mike Blowers, Wade Boggs, Homer Bush, Brian Butterfield, Greg Cadaret, Frank Cashen, Gary Carter, Chuck Cary, Rick Cerrone, Russ Davis, Rick Down, Dave Eiland, Steve Farr, Sid Fernandez, Tony Fernandez, Dave Gallagher, Lee Guetterman, Al Harazin, Bud Harrelson, Andy Hawkins, Jeff Idelson, Jeff Innis, Dion James, Moss Klein, Ray Knight, Jim Leyritz, Kevin Maas, Bill Madden, Dave Magadan, Don Mattingly, Jack McDowell, Jim Mecir, Stump Merrill, Sam Militello, Alan Mills, Rich Monteleone, Matt Nokes, Charlie O'Brien, Paul O'Neill, Jesse Orosco, Dave Pavlas, Ken Phelps, Lou Piniella, Eric Plunk, Scott Sanderson, Steve Sax, Glen Sherlock, Buck Showalter, Mike Silva, Luis Sojo, Andy Stankiewicz, Mike Stanley, John Sterling, Mel Stottlemyre, David Sussman, Tony Tarasco, Wade Taylor, Randy Velarde, Fay Vincent, Wally Whitchurst, Mookie Wilson.

Angell, Roger. *A Pitcher's Story: Innings with David Cone.* New York: Warner Books, 2001.

Carter, Gary, and Phil Pepe. *Still a Kid at Heart: My Life in Baseball and Beyond.* Chicago: Triumph Books, 2008.

Darling, Ron, with Daniel Paisner. *108 Stitches.* New York: St. Martin's Press, 2019.

Feinstein, John. *Best American Sports Writing 1996.* Boston: Houghton Mifflin Harcourt, 1996.

Golenbock, Peter. *Amazin': The Miraculous History of New York's Most Beloved Baseball Team.* New York: St. Martin's Griffin, 2002.

———. *George: The Poor Little Rich Boy Who Built the Yankee Empire.* Hoboken: John Wiley & Sons, 2009.

Gooden, Dwight, and Bob Klapisch. *Heat: My Life On and Off the Diamond.* New York: William Morrow And Company, 1999.

Johnson, Davey, with Erik Sherman. *Davey Johnson: My Wild Ride in Baseball and Beyond*. Chicago: Triumph Books, 2018.

Klapisch, Bob. *High and Tight: The Rise and Fall of Dwight Gooden and Darryl Strawberry*. New York: Villard Books, 1996.

Klapisch, Bob, and John Harper. *The Worst Team Money Could Buy: The Collapse of the New York Mets*. Lincoln: University of Nebraska Press, 1993.

Klapisch, Bob, and Pail Solotaroff. *Inside the Empire: The True Power behind the New York Yankees*. New York: Houghton Mifflin Harcourt, 2019.

Madden, Bill, and Moss Klein. *Damned Yankees*. New York: Warner Books, 1990.

Madden, Bill. *Steinbrenner: The Last Lion of Baseball*. New York: HarperCollins Publishers, 2010.

O'Connor, Ian. *The Captain: The Journey of Derek Jeter*. New York, Houghton Mifflin Harcourt, 2011.

Olney, Buster. *The Last Night of the Yankee Dynasty: The Game, The Team, and the Cost of Greatness*. New York: Echo, 2004.

Pearlman, Jeff. *The Bad Guys Won!* New York: HarperCollins, 2004.

Pennington, Bill. *Chumps to Champs: How the Worst Teams in Yankees History Led to the '90s Dynasty*. New York, Houghton Mifflin Harcourt, 2019.

Pepe, Phil. *Core Four: The Heart and Soul of the Yankees Dynasty*. Chicago: Triumph Books, 2013.

Pessah, Jon. *The Game: Inside The Secret World of Major League Baseball's Power Brokers*. New York: Back Bay Books, 2015.

Randolph, Willie. *The Yankee Way: Playing, Coaching, and My Life in Baseball*. New York: It Books, 2014.

Rivera, Mariano, with Wayne Coffey. *The Closer*. New York: Little, Brown and Company, 2014.

Sherman, Joel. *Birth of a Dynasty*. Emmaus PA: Rodale, 2006.

Stottlemyre, Mel, with John Harper. *Pride and Pinstripes: The Yankees, Mets and Surviving Life's Challenges*. New York: Harper Entertainment, 2007.

Strawberry, Darryl, and John Strausbaugh. *Straw: Finding My Way*. New York: HarperCollins, 2009.

Torre, Joe, and Tom Verducci. *The Yankee Years*. New York: Doubleday, 2009.

Winfield, Dave, and Tom Parker. *Winfield: A Player's Life*. New York: W.W. Norton & Company, 1988.

Index

60 Minutes, 208
1994 MLB Strike, 219–25
1995 AL Division Series, 262–67
1996 ALCS, 317–20
1996 ALDS, 315–17
1996 World Series, 320–26

Abbott, Jim, 137–39, 152–54, 172, 177–
    79, 181, 184, 195, 202–3, 215–16, 220,
    224, 251
Adamek, Steve, 311
Adams, Margo, 141
Adams, Terry, 291
Adkins, Steve, 57
Aguilera, Rick, 40
Alfonzo, Edgardo, 236, 281, 293
Alomar, Roberto, 64, 278, 317–18
Alou, Moises, 280
Anderson, Brady, 289–90
Anderson, Dave, 9, 104
Anderson, Garrett, 254
Anderson, Sparky, 183, 225, 272
Angell, Roger, 256
Angelos, Peter, 225, 248
Arizona Diamondbacks, 273–74
Associated Press, 80, 186, 194, 311
Atlanta Braves, 11, 36, 42, 50, 60, 114, 128,
    138, 143, 161, 187, 217, 229, 231, 239, 261,
    269, 272, 284, 314, 320–26
Atlanta Falcons, 34–35

Ausmus, Brad, 133
Avery, Steve, 323
Azocar, Oscar, 33, 65

Backman, Wally, 44–45, 55, 58, 160
Baerga, Carlos, 153, 178, 201, 303–4
Balboni, Steve, 68, 99
Baltimore Orioles, 24, 39, 90, 114, 119,
    120–121, 172, 178, 191, 213, 225, 248,
    272, 277–78, 284, 289, 297, 301–2, 305–
    6, 317–20, 326
Baltimore Sun, 325
Bamberger, George, 312
Bankhead, Scott, 235
Banks, Ernie, 191
Barfield, Jesse, 29, 33, 57, 69–70, 74, 103,
    109, 119–20, 141
Belle, Albert, 201
Belliard, Rafael, 323
Benes, Andy, 167, 194
Benitez, Armando, 248
Berkow, Ira, 93
Bichette, Dante, 230
Blowers, Mike, 28–29, 68, 73, 105, 266
Blyleven, Bert, 9–10
Boehringer, Brian, 235, 298–99
Bogar, Tim, 159, 191, 247
Boggs, Wade, 133, 140–41, 145, 152–55,
    169–70, 181–82, 193–99, 203, 213, 221,
    264, 277, 305, 320–23

Bonds, Barry, 138–39, 142
Bones, Ricky, 305
Bonilla, Bobby, 81, 101–4, 111–12, 115–17, 128, 139, 142, 147–50, 157–58, 165, 167, 173–74, 184–85, 191, 197–99, 207, 211, 216–18, 221, 230–31, 236–37, 239–40, 248–49, 260–61, 278
Boras, Scott, 79–80, 194
Boston, Daryl, 59, 102, 109–10, 194, 202
Boston Globe, 140
Boston Red Sox, 24–25, 27, 62, 72, 74–76, 130, 137, 154, 168, 180, 187, 201, 228, 235, 248, 253, 256, 272, 289
Boyer, Clete, 146
Bradley, George, 24, 27–28
Brogna, Rico, 191, 216–17, 221, 229, 231, 236–37, 260, 262, 281–83, 291–93
Brokaw, Tom, 153
Brookens, Tom, 105
Brooks, Hubie, 61, 67, 72, 85, 102
Brown, Kevin, 33
Buechele, Steve, 105–6
Buhner, Jay, 20–21, 23, 210, 213, 296
Burke, Tim, 82, 129
Burnitz, Jeremy, 224
Burns, Britt, 19
Butcher, Rob, 278–79
Butler, Brett, 229, 237, 260
Butterfield, Brian, 233, 271
Butterfield, Jack, 26
Byrd, Paul, 224

Cadaret, Greg, 20, 87, 94, 108, 141
Calderon, Ivan, 29
California Angels, 1, 5, 7, 9, 72, 86, 99, 101–2, 137, 169–70, 192, 201, 203, 214, 232, 234, 254–55, 257, 262, 276, 305, 312
Caminiti, Ken, 184
Campanella, Roy, 293, 314
Canseco, Jose, 235
Cardenal, José, 325–26
Carew, Rod, 291
Carreon, Mark, 83

Carter, Gary, 7–10, 43–46, 55, 61, 67, 73, 102, 126, 197
Carter, Joe, 21, 64, 171
Cary, Chuck, 30, 68, 76
Cashen, Frank, 38–42, 44, 48–49, 51, 53, 58–60, 63, 92–93, 99
Cashman, Brian, 179, 271
Cedeño, Andújar, 184
Cerone, Rick, 25, 61, 67, 85
Chass, Murray, 3
Chiba Lotte Marines, 313
Chicago Cubs, 45, 47, 91, 116, 138, 142, 162–65, 168, 183, 191, 196, 204, 212, 246, 270, 291–92
Chicago White Sox, 16, 19, 28–30, 34, 97–98, 101, 104, 145, 178, 192, 224, 250–51, 266, 279, 295, 303
Cianfrocco, Archi, 167
Cincinnati Reds, 20, 22–23, 36, 39, 51–52, 72, 118–19, 135–36, 141, 198–99, 224, 260, 313
Clark, Jack, 11, 20–23, 64
Clark, Mark, 291
Clark, Will, 32, 315–17
Clayton, Royce, 282
Clemens, Roger, 62, 78–79, 107, 154, 226, 235
Clements, Pat, 21
Cleveland Indians, 9–10, 21, 97, 152–53, 172, 178–79, 187, 194, 201, 218, 220, 224, 228, 245, 253–54, 269–70, 276–77, 284, 298, 303, 312, 317–18
Clinton, Bill, 219, 224
Colangelo, Jerry, 273–74
Coleman, Vince, 60–61, 67, 80–81, 83, 85, 91, 101–102, 109–10, 113, 116, 128, 142, 150–51, 156, 173–75, 177, 190–91, 205, 229, 254, 261
Colorado Rockies, 133, 135, 146–47, 185, 230, 247–48, 250, 274, 292, 322
Cone, David, 40, 42–43, 50, 62–63, 80–82, 85, 93, 98, 102, 109–12, 125–27, 138–40, 152–53, 190, 197, 248–49, 252–54, 256–

57, 259, 261, 264–65, 277–79, 286, 294–95, 297, 303–4, 306, 308, 322, 326
Connor, Mark, 77
Connors, Billy, 275
Cora, Joey, 254, 266
Cornelius, Reid, 237, 260
Costanza, George, 209–11, 213
Costello, Robert, 122
Craft, Terry, 120
Crews, Tim, 152
Cubbage, Mike, 46–47, 83, 92, 128, 157–58, 239
Curry, Jack, 181, 202, 241, 300
Curtis, Clifton, 162–65

D'Alessandro, Dave, 173
Darling, Gary, 128
Darling, Ron, 41–42, 55, 61, 81–84, 238, 249
David, Larry, 209–10
Davis, Eric, 39, 173–74
Davis, Russ, 276–77
Dawson, Andre, 212
Deer, Rob, 64
Dell'Isola, John, 17
Dent, Bucky, 5, 23–28, 51, 100, 171, 257, 272
Detroit Tigers, 18, 57, 64, 68–70, 86, 107, 120, 130, 169, 183, 191, 200, 225, 234, 236, 240–41, 250, 256, 272, 295, 298, 302, 306
Dewey, Mark, 129
Díaz, Mario, 54
Dillard, Harrison, 18
DiMaggio, Joe, 1
Dinkins, David, 153
Dipoto, Jerry, 246
Disarcina, Gary, 171
Donaghy, Jim, 186
Doubleday, Nelson, 49, 52, 159–61, 314
Dowd, John, 13–14, 123
Down, Rick, 156, 203, 271
Drabek, Doug, 19–21, 23, 77, 138, 142
Drews, Matt, 302
Duncan, Mariano, 303, 316, 323

Dye, Jermaine, 314, 322–24
Dykstra, Lenny, 39, 45–46, 54–55, 125, 127, 160, 211, 242

Eckersley, Dennis, 283
Edwards, Doc, 85
Eisen, Rich, 305
Elfering, Kevin, 119, 222, 274
Ellis, Sammy, 98
Elster, Kevin, 61, 83, 113, 142, 232
Espinoza, Álvaro, 105, 303
ESPN, 120, 151, 305
Esquire Magazine, 45
Everett, Carl, 133, 229, 231, 246, 262, 281–82, 293

Farr, Steve, 64–65, 68, 86, 88, 104, 179, 192
Fehr, Donald, 212, 220, 224
Feller, Bob, 165
Fermín, Félix, 177–78, 285–86
Fernandez, Sid, 40, 42, 82–83, 110, 185, 190, 249, 280
Fernandéz, Tony, 64, 143, 156, 159, 224, 226, 232, 236, 254, 284–85
Fielder, Cecil, 11–12, 57, 191, 302–3, 307, 316, 320, 322–24
Fisk, Carlton, 34–35, 101, 212
Fletcher, Scott, 98
Florida Marlins, 133, 142, 167, 233, 284, 291, 310
Foster, George, 57
Francesa, Mike, 244–45
Franco, John, 54–55, 82, 93, 111, 113, 115–16, 129, 158, 163, 179, 185, 198–99, 211, 218, 221, 230, 249, 278–80, 283, 292, 294, 308
Friend, Tom, 184

Gallego, Mike, 104, 106, 109, 139, 171–72, 180, 192, 224
Garcia, Richie, 319
Gardner, Jeff, 167

Gehrig, Lou, 225
Geren, Bob, 68
Gergen, Joe, 17
Giamatti, Bart, 12
Giannone, John, 247
Gibson, Kirk, 44
Gibson, Paul, 129
Gilkey, Bernard, 282, 291, 293, 315
Girardi, Joe, 274–75, 288–89, 297, 308
Giuliani, Rudy, 153, 208
Glavine, Tom, 143
Gleason, Paul, 209
Goldis, Al, 270
Goldstein, Bill, 300
Golenbock, Peter, 18, 46
González, Juan, 316, 318
Gooden, Dwight, 37–38, 40–43, 45–46,
    50, 54, 59, 61–63, 67, 79–83, 98, 102,
    109–11, 113, 142–43, 147, 149–51, 156,
    158, 163, 165, 173, 183–85, 190, 195–96,
    205–8, 236–38, 274, 277, 279–80, 286,
    289, 295–97, 299, 302–3, 308, 310–11,
    322, 326
Gordon, Charlie, 288
Gossage, Rich "Goose," 234
Grace, Mark, 246, 292
Graham, Wayne, 226–27
Grahe, Joe, 215
Gray, Ken, 25
Green, Dallas, 22–23, 28, 52, 158, 165, 167–
    68, 175–77, 185, 197–98, 205, 211, 230,
    238, 242, 247, 249, 261, 280–81, 283,
    290–92, 308–11, 313–14
Griffey, Ken, Jr., 77, 220, 254, 256, 262,
    264–66, 296
Grissom, Marquis, 324
Guetterman, Lee, 129
Gunderson, Eric, 247
Guzmán, José, 138
Gwynn, Tony, 220

Hall, Mel, 68, 74–76, 87, 94, 108, 136,
    141, 308

Harazin, Al, 44, 48, 51, 60–62, 92, 101–2,
    125–26, 142–43, 150, 157–61
Harnisch, Pete, 194, 229, 236, 260, 281,
    291, 293
Harper, John, 114, 116, 147–48
Harrelson, Bud, 52–55, 61, 67, 83–86, 91–
    93, 97, 116, 128, 158, 310
Harrington, John, 187
Harris, Greg, 180–81
Harvey, Bryan, 167
Hatcher, Billy, 218
Hawkins, Andy, 28–31, 68, 71, 86, 177
Hayes, Charlie, 105–6, 109, 133, 305, 322–
    24, 326
Henderson, Rickey, 11, 20–21, 23–24, 60,
    70–71, 192, 255, 279
Henry, Doug, 236, 247
Hernandez, Keith, 9–10, 44–46, 55, 58, 85,
    148, 208, 274, 287
Hernandez, Xavier, 192, 200, 202
Herr, Tom, 84
Hershiser, Orel, 44
Herzog, Whitey, 137, 175
Heyman, Jon, 75, 141, 182
Hibbard, Greg, 29
Hirschbeck, John, 317
Hitchcock, Sterling, 130, 195, 213, 227, 254,
    256–59, 276–77, 296
Hobson, Butch, 181, 272
Hodges, Gil, 311
Hohn, Bill, 151
Home Improvement, 208
Horner, Bob, 277
Horwitz, Jay, 116–17, 149–51, 175
Howard, Dave, 308, 310
Howard, Frank, 94, 312
Howe, Steve, 71, 74–75, 121, 179, 203, 207,
    222, 225, 235, 258
Howell, Jay, 43
Humphreys, Mike, 105
Hundley, Todd, 8, 183, 190, 198, 218, 230,
    237–38, 242, 262, 282, 291–94, 310,
    314–15

Huskey, Butch, 293

Indiana Pacers, 198
Innis, Jeff, 112
Isringhausen, Jason, 238, 245–46, 260–61, 280–82, 290–91, 309, 315

Jackson, Bo, 30–31, 34
Jackson, Darrin, 159
Jackson, Reggie, 2–4, 18, 153
Jacobson, Steve, 127, 273
James, Dion, 156, 194, 225, 242, 254, 266
Jean, Domingo, 104, 192
Jefferies, Gregg, 44, 46–47, 50, 59, 67, 84–85, 102
Jeter, Charles, 118
Jeter, Derek, 118–19, 210, 222, 227, 232–33, 250, 264, 285–88, 296, 300, 307, 316, 318–20, 322–23
Jeter, Dorothy, 118
Jobe, Frank, 194
John, Tommy, 22, 194
Johnson, Davey, 8, 43, 46–53, 58, 92, 99, 185, 272, 278, 284, 312, 318–19
Johnson, Howard, 41, 59, 83, 85, 93, 102, 113, 157, 191,
Johnson, Jeff, 76–77, 86, 129
Johnson, Lance, 281–83, 291, 293, 315
Johnson, Randy, 79, 193, 214, 235, 239, 262–63, 265–66
Johnson, Sandy, 271
Jones, Andruw, 321
Jones, Barry, 129
Jones, Bobby, 217, 221, 236, 260, 281–82
Jones, Larry "Chipper," 231, 324
Jordan, Brian, 247
Jordan, Ricky, 218

Kamieniecki, Scott, 76, 78, 86, 125, 168, 179, 195, 203, 213, 229, 232, 254, 257, 277, 279, 286, 295
Kansas City Royals, 28, 30, 32, 39, 40, 64–65, 70, 88, 102–3, 138, 153–54, 178–80, 190, 197, 202, 212, 226, 228, 252, 255, 288, 294, 301
Kay, Michael, 33, 145, 243–45
Kelly, Pat, 74, 77, 105, 120, 130, 139, 171, 192, 215, 222–23, 234–35, 257, 266, 285, 322
Kelly, Roberto, 77–78, 87, 103, 107, 109, 130, 135–36, 152
Kelly, Tom, 298
Kent, Jeff, 127, 142–43, 156, 167, 190, 196–98, 205, 221, 237, 260, 282, 293, 303–4
Key, Jimmy, 139, 152, 154, 156, 169, 183, 195, 200–201, 203, 213, 222, 226, 228–29, 232, 251–52, 277, 279, 286, 298, 325
Kiefer, Steve, 15
Kile, Daryl, 183–84
King, Clyde, 286
Klapisch, Bob, 43, 102, 110, 114, 116, 147–50, 177
Kleinman, Leonard, 122
Klesko, Ryan, 323
Knight, Ray, 39, 55
Kranepool, Ed, 52

Lamont, Gene, 272
Lamoriello, Lou, 312
Langston, Mark, 215
Lanier, Hal, 98–99
Lankford, Ray, 247, 282
Lans, Allan, 49
LaPoint, Dave, 12, 17, 57–58, 65–66, 195
Larkin, Barry, 118–19
La Russa, Tony, 252, 272
Lasorda, Tommy, 73
Lawton, Marcus, 224
Leach, Terry, 42,
Leary, Tim, 20, 68, 76, 120–21
Lemke, Mark, 50, 324, 326
Letterman, David, 160, 181, 319
Levine, Randy, 124
Leyritz, Jim, 29, 68, 105–6, 155, 169, 182, 195, 203, 215, 221, 233, 265, 320, 322–23
Livesay, Bill, 79, 222, 274
Lloyd, Graeme, 305, 317, 320, 324
Lofton, Kenny, 201

Lomon, Kevin, 230
Los Angeles Dodgers, 1, 3, 9, 17, 42–45,
    58–61, 72–73, 82, 91, 114, 140, 150,
    162–63, 167, 206, 212, 216–17, 236, 242,
    260–61, 304, 308, 312
Lovullo, Torey, 68, 105
Lukevics, Mitch, 222, 274
Lupica, Mike, 127, 157, 244, 326
Lyle, Sparky, 18

Maas, Kevin, 33, 68, 71, 89, 103–4, 107, 156
MacDonald, Bob, 235
MacPhail, Andy, 270
Madden, Bill, 243–44
Maddux, Greg, 116, 138–39, 143, 152,
    321, 325
Maddux, Kathy, 138
Magadan, Dave, 47, 59, 85, 101, 112–13,
    127, 133
Magrane, Joe, 165
Maier, Jeffrey, 318–19, 322
Major League Baseball Players Associa-
    tion, 112, 211, 220, 224
Mantle, Mickey, 31, 253
Manzanillo, Josías, 230, 235
Maris, Roger, 31
Markocic, Bo, 242
Marshall, Mike, 50
Martin, Billy, 21–22, 24, 100, 314
Martínez, Dennis, 202, 287
Martínez, Edgar, 265–66, 316
Martinez, Tino, 276, 288–90, 308, 319
Mattingly, Don, 1, 24, 26, 31–33, 66, 68,
    70–72, 74, 77, 87–90, 94, 99, 109, 114,
    141, 145–46, 169–72, 178, 181–82, 193,
    200–203, 214–15, 219–21, 225–26,
    228–29, 233–35, 242–45, 252, 256–59,
    263–66, 275–76, 287, 289
Mays, Willie, 287
Mazzilli, Lee, 45, 58
McDowell, Jack, 203, 224, 226, 232, 234,
    240, 251, 254–55, 264, 266, 277
McDowell, Roger, 40–42, 45, 47, 55, 67,
    125, 127, 211, 278

McFarland, Art, 218
McGee, Willie, 23, 41, 60
McGraw, Tom, 127
McGriff, Fred, 64, 321–22, 324
McIlvaine, Joe, 44, 48, 60, 143, 161, 166,
    185, 196, 208, 239–40, 249, 270, 280,
    283, 297, 304, 308, 313–14
McKnight, Jeff, 129
McMichael, Greg, 314
McNally, Dave, 211
McRae, Hal, 190
McReynolds, Kevin, 42, 44, 47, 51, 67, 102,
    190–91, 197, 218
Mecir, Jim, 276, 289–90
Mediate, Frank, 94
Mendoza, Ramiro, 298–99
Mercado, Diana, 310
Merrill, Carl "Stump," 26–27, 29, 32–33,
    66–67, 69, 71, 75, 86–88, 90, 94, 99–
    100, 124, 171, 222, 233, 272, 322
Messersmith, Andy, 211
Meulens, Hensley, 68, 105
Michael, Gene, 3, 58, 64–66, 71, 73–74,
    77–78, 80, 87–90, 94, 98–99, 101, 105,
    121, 124–25, 131, 133, 135–42, 145–46,
    152, 178, 180, 182, 192, 194–95, 202–3,
    222, 232, 235–36, 250, 252, 264, 266,
    270–71, 277, 286
Miklasz, Bernie, 51
Militello, Sam, 130–31, 195
Miller, Keith, 59, 102
Miller, Marvin, 211
Minnesota Twins, 1, 7, 30–31, 44, 89, 108,
    109, 145, 154, 295, 298, 301
Mitchell, Kevin, 38–39, 42, 48, 55
Mlicki, Dave, 224, 236, 260
Mobley, Randy, 27
Mock, Julian, 119
Mohorcic, Dale, 53
Molloy, Joe, 133, 140–41, 269, 271
Monteleone, Rich, 24
Montreal Expos, 23, 40, 53, 67, 69, 81–82,
    102, 113, 115, 119, 126, 142, 157, 163, 165,

198, 205, 212, 217, 220, 225, 231, 237, 239, 279–80, 293–94

Morgan, Mike, 183

Morris, Hal, 20–21, 23

Morris, Jack, 212

Mottola, Chad, 119

MSG Network, 36, 145, 171, 240, 243

Mulholland, Terry, 195, 200, 202

Munson, Thurman, 170

Murphy, Bob, 54, 230

Murphy, Dale, 93

Murray, Eddie, 101–2, 111–14, 116, 142–43, 148–49, 151, 158, 165, 167–68, 184, 190–91, 201, 305

Myers, Randy, 42, 46–47, 278

Nagy, Charles, 202

National Labor Relations Board, 223, 225

The Natural, 169

Nederlander, Robert, 64, 99, 123

Nelson, Jeff, 276, 289, 317

Nevin, Phil, 119

Nevius, C. W., 17

Newhouser, Hal, 119

New Jersey Devils, 198

Newman, Mark, 222

Newsday, 17, 65, 75, 86, 127, 141, 175, 182, 186, 252, 273, 281

New York Daily News, 4, 12, 33, 43, 102, 127, 147, 149, 243, 247, 273

New York Knicks, 199

New York Mets, 2, 5, 7–10, 19–20, 37–55, 58–63, 67–68, 72, 77, 80–86, 91–95, 97–98, 101–4, 109–17, 125–29, 142–44, 146–51, 156–61, 163–69, 171–77, 180, 182–87, 189–91, 194–200, 204–8, 210–12, 216–18, 221, 224, 229–32, 236–42, 245–49, 253, 255, 259–62, 272, 274, 278–84, 288–94, 297, 300, 303–4, 307–15, 319–20, 326

New York Rangers, 198

New York Times, 3, 93, 104–5, 107, 127, 161, 172, 181, 184, 202, 207

New York Yankees, 1–6, 11–12, 14–15, 17–37, 48, 57–58, 60. 63–72, 74–82, 86–91, 94–95, 97–109, 113, 118–22, 125, 129–32, 133–42, 144–46, 152–56, 158–60, 168–72, 176–83, 186–87, 189, 191–95, 199–204, 209–22, 224–36, 239–45, 249–60, 262–67, 269–79, 284–90, 295–310, 314–26

Niekro, Phil, 21

Nielsen, Jerry, 138

Nisson, Mike, 17

Noble, Marty, 175, 186, 281

Nokes, Matt, 68, 71, 88, 100, 105, 152, 156, 178, 214, 219

Oakland Athletics, 1, 20, 57, 64, 68–72, 79, 86, 104, 170, 193, 200–201, 213–14, 219, 232, 252, 254–56, 302, 306

Oates, Johnny, 120

O'Brien, Charlie, 61, 93, 166

Ochoa, Alex, 248–49, 262, 293

O'Connell, Jack, 139

O'Connor, Ian, 273

Ojeda, Bob, 40, 42, 56, 61, 152, 194–95, 200, 202–3, 238

Olin, Steve, 152

O'Malley, Tom, 53

O'Neill, Paul, 135–36, 141, 152–54, 156, 168–71, 181–82, 195, 203–4, 210–11, 213, 220–21, 228, 235, 241, 255, 258, 321, 325

Ordóñez, Rey, 262, 281–83, 287–88, 291

Orosco, Jesse, 37, 42, 44, 55, 278, 326

Orsulak, Joe, 184

Orza, Gene, 220

Owen, Spike, 137, 139, 152–53, 182, 192

Pagliarulo, Mike, 105

Pall, Donn, 192

Palmer, Dean, 316–17

Pavlick, Greg, 308

Payton, Jay, 313

Pecota, Bill, 102

Pendleton, Terry, 41–42, 60, 324

Pérez, Carlos, 239

Pérez, Mélido, 30, 104–6, 107–9, 129, 232, 251, 277, 279, 286–87
Pérez, Pascual, 23, 68, 76, 88, 105–6
Pettitte, Andy, 222, 226-28, 235, 254, 256, 263, 277, 279, 286, 298–90, 298, 300, 303, 307, 318, 320–24
Phelps, Ken, 20, 210, 213
Philadelphia Phillies, 22, 26, 45, 47, 52, 54, 63, 67, 81, 92–93, 98, 105, 142, 162–63, 165, 192, 195, 205, 217–18, 239, 260, 293, 311
Philbin, Regis, 153
Phillips, Dave, 120
Phillips, Steve, 314
Phillips, Tony, 69
Piniella, Lou, 4, 14, 21–23, 31, 48, 135–36, 264, 276
Pittsburgh Pirates, 19, 37–38, 50, 54–55, 67, 81–82, 91, 106, 114–15, 128, 138, 142, 157, 162, 165, 191, 198, 205–6, 212, 216–17, 247–48, 291, 305, 309
Plunk, Eric, 20, 24
Poliquin, Bud, 242
Polonia, Luis, 20, 24, 193, 199, 203–4, 221, 234, 242, 324–25
Port, Mike, 270
Posada, Jorge, 222, 263
Puckett, Kirby, 31
Pulsipher, Bill, 237–39, 246, 260–61, 280–82, 290–91

Rader, Doug, 99
Raines, Tim, 98, 279, 316, 324
Ramírez, Manny, 201
Randolph, Willie, 102–3, 111–13, 128, 279, 301, 326
Reardon, Jeff, 74, 194, 200, 202
Reinsdorf, Jerry, 16, 97, 145
Rhoden, Rick, 22
Rhodes, Karl "Tuffy," 196
Richman, Arthur, 272
Righetti, Dave, 25, 64–65, 68, 251
Rijo, José, 23
Ripken, Cal, Jr., 119, 225, 320

Rivera, Mariano, 134–35, 222, 227, 232, 234–35, 249–50, 256, 263–66, 285–86, 298, 300, 307, 317, 320, 322
Rivera, Rubén, 264
Rizzuto, Phil, 109
Robinson, Bill, 47
Rodriguez, Alex, 285
Rodríguez, Henry, 293
Rogers, Kenny, 279, 286–87, 316, 319, 322
Rose, Pete, 13, 52
Rosenberg, Bob, 29
Rosenthal, Ken, 325
Russo, Chris "Mad Dog," 244
Ryan, Nolan, 33, 101, 238, 246

Sabean, Brian, 222
Saberhagen, Bret, 102, 113, 129, 142–43, 147, 156, 165, 172–73, 176–77, 185, 206, 217, 221, 230, 236, 247–49, 261
Salmon, Tim, 169
Samuel, Juan, 45, 125, 127, 211
Sanders, Deion, 30, 33–36
Sanderson, Scott, 64, 68–70, 76, 106–7, 129
San Diego Padres, 2, 7, 20–21, 28, 38, 60, 64–65, 81–83, 143, 150, 157, 161, 167, 172, 184, 217, 236, 309, 312
San Francisco Chronicle, 18, 107
San Francisco Giants, 7–8, 10, 32, 38–40, 65, 82–83, 97, 107, 114, 138, 142, 156, 207, 217, 236, 304, 324
Santos, Amanda, 174
Sasser, Mackey, 61
Sax, Steve, 17, 68, 74, 89, 104–5
Schofield, Dick, 142
Schourek, Pete, 143
Schueler, Ron, 97
Schuman, Fred, 153
Scioscia, Mike, 43–44
Seattle Post-Intelligencer, 175
Seaver, Tom, 52, 238, 261
Segui, David, 191, 216, 237
Seinfeld, 208–11
Seinfeld, Jerry, 171